Hopeful Pedagogies in Higher Education

Bloomsbury Critical Education

Books in this series explore the relationship between education and power in society and offer insights into ways of confronting inequalities and social exclusions in different learning settings and in society at large. The series will comprise books wherein authors contend forthrightly with the inextricability of power/knowledge relations.

Series Editor: Peter Mayo

Advisory Board:

Antonia Darder (Loyola Maramount University, USA), Samira Dlimi (École Normale Supérieure, Rabat, Morocco), Luiz Armando Gandin (Federal University of Rio Grande do Sul, Mexico), Jose Ramon Flecha Garcia (University of Barcelona, Spain), Ravi Kumar (South Asian University, India), Antonia Kupfer (University of Dresden, Germany), Peter McLaren (Chapman University, USA), Maria Mendel (University of Gdansk, Poland), Maria NIkolakaki (University of Peloponnese, Greece) and Juha Suoranta (University of Tampere, Finland)

Also available in the series:

Pedagogy, Politics and Philosophy of Peace: Interrogating Peace and Peacemaking
edited by Carmel Borg and Michael Grech

Critical Human Rights, Citizenship, and Democracy Education: Entanglements and Regenerations
edited by Michalinos Zembylas and André Keet

Course Syllabi in Faculties of Education: Bodies of Knowledge and their Discontents, International and Comparative Perspectives
edited by André Elias Mazawi and Michelle Stack

Education, Individualization and Neoliberalism: Youth in Southern Europe
by Valerie Visanich

Ecopedagogy: Critical Environmental Teaching for Planetary Justice and Global Sustainable Development
by Greg William Misiaszek

Hopeful Pedagogies in Higher Education

Edited by Mike Seal

BLOOMSBURY ACADEMIC
LONDON • NEW YORK • OXFORD • NEW DELHI • SYDNEY

BLOOMSBURY ACADEMIC
Bloomsbury Publishing Plc
50 Bedford Square, London, WC1B 3DP, UK
1385 Broadway, New York, NY 10018, USA
29 Earlsfort Terrace, Dublin 2, Ireland

BLOOMSBURY, BLOOMSBURY ACADEMIC and the Diana logo are trademarks of
Bloomsbury Publishing Plc

First published in Great Britain 2021
This paperback edition published 2023

Copyright © Mike Seal and Bloomsbury, 2021

Mike Seal and Bloomsbury have asserted their right under the Copyright, Designs and
Patents Act, 1988, to be identified as editor of this work.

For legal purposes the Acknowledgements on p. xix constitute an extension
of this copyright page.

Series design: Catherine Wood
Cover image © Studiojumpee/Shutterstock

All rights reserved. No part of this publication may be reproduced or transmitted
in any form or by any means, electronic or mechanical, including photocopying,
recording, or any information storage or retrieval system, without prior
permission in writing from the publishers.

Bloomsbury Publishing Plc does not have any control over, or responsibility for, any
third-party websites referred to or in this book. All internet addresses given in this
book were correct at the time of going to press. The author and publisher regret any
inconvenience caused if addresses have changed or sites have ceased to exist,
but can accept no responsibility for any such changes.

A catalogue record for this book is available from the British Library.

Library of Congress Cataloging-in-Publication Data
Names: Seal, Mike, editor.
Title: Hopeful pedagogies in higher education / Edited by Mike Seal.
Description: London; New York: Bloomsbury Academic, 2021. | Series: Bloomsbury
critical education | Includes bibliographical references and index.
Identifiers: LCCN 2020049411 (print) | LCCN 2020049412 (ebook) |
ISBN 9781350116535 (hardback) | ISBN 9781350116542 (ebook) |
ISBN 9781350116559 (epub)
Subjects: LCSH: Critical pedagogy. | Universities and colleges--Research. |
Educational change. | Education, Higher--Aims and objectives.
Classification: LCC LC196 .H68 2021 (print) | LCC LC196 (ebook) | DDC 370.11/5--dc23
LC record available at https://lccn.loc.gov/2020049411
LC ebook record available at https://lccn.loc.gov/2020049412

ISBN: HB: 978-1-3501-1653-5
PB: 978-1-3502-1679-2
ePDF: 978-1-3501-1654-2
eBook: 978-1-3501-1655-9

Series: Bloomsbury Critical Education

Typeset by Deanta Global Publishing Services, Chennai, India

To find out more about our authors and books visit www.bloomsbury.com and
sign up for our newsletters.

Contents

List of Figures	vii
Notes on Contributors	viii
Series Editor's Foreword	xvi
Acknowledgements	xix

Introduction: Are Hopeful Pedagogies Possible in Higher Education?	1
Part I Key Ideas and the Conceptual and Policy Terrain	15

1. Key Concepts in Critical Pedagogy: How We Teach *Mike Seal, Response from Alan Smith* — 17
2. Critiques of Critical Pedagogy: The Post-critical *Leoarna Mathias and Mike Gilsenan, Response from Joris Vlieghe* — 28
3. Perspectives on the Possibility of Hopeful Critical Pedagogies within Higher Education *Mike Seal, Response from Stephen Cowden* — 37
4. The Policy Context of Higher Education: Resistance Is Possible *Sarah Parkes and Jane Beniston, Response from Neil M. Speirs* — 48
5. The Pedagogy of Partnership *John Peters and Leoarna Mathias, Response from Mike Neary* — 59

Part II Hopeful Pedagogies in Higher Education	75
Part II A Hopeful Pedagogy within Courses	76

6. Early Years to Higher Education: Legacy and the Creation and Connection of Hopeful Spaces *Julie Boardman and Jane Beniston, Response from Carol Aubrey* — 77
7. Widening the Cracks: Co-constructing Learning within Dialogical Spaces *Jane Beniston and Debbie Harris, Response from Dr László Varga* — 86
8. Preparing for an Unexpected Journey: Exploring the Experience of Teaching Critical Pedagogy through Critical Pedagogy *Helen Bardy and Mike Gilsenan, Response from Christine Smith* — 97
9. Academic Identities: Conversations across the Cracks *Roger Willoughby and Parminder Assi, Response from Marina Tornero Tarragó* — 108

Contents

Part II B Hopeful Pedagogies within Structures — 117

10 The 'Rehearsal Space': Viewing Induction and Transition Work as a Critical Pedagogy Practice *Leoarna Matthias and Sarah Parkes, Response from Liz Thomas* — 118
11 'Very Much a Democratic Thing': Enacting the Pedagogy of Partnership *Leoarna Mathias and John Peters, Response from Gill Gilbert* — 128
12 Foundation Years: Undoing Discourses of Deficit *Pheobe Hall, Kace McGowan, Leoarna Mathias, Samantha Snelleksz, Sarah Parkes and Mike Seal, Response from Sarah Hale* — 137

Part II C Becoming the Hopeful Pedagogue — 149

13 A Mindful Journey: Person-centred and Contemplative Critical Approaches to Higher Education *Ruth Roberts, Response from Luca Tateo* — 150
14 Rethinking Critical Pedagogy in Higher Education through a Psychosocial Lens *Pete Harris, Response from Jo Trelfa* — 161
15 It's Been Emotional: Exploring the Emotional Impact of Critical Pedagogy Practice with Non-traditional Students *Pauline Grace, Lorna Morgan and Adellah Snape, Response from Fin Cullen* — 171

Part II D Hopeful Pedagogies in the Spaces In-between — 179

16 Sit Down Next to Me: Reflections on Academic Advising and Pedagogical Love *Peter Sharpe, Response from Stephen Cowden* — 180
17 Pushing at an Open Door *Tina McLoughlin* — 188
18 Quality Assurance or Assured Silence? *Lorraine Loveland-Armour, Response from Seán Bracken* — 194

Part II E Hopeful Pedagogies beyond the Institution — 207

19 University as Community: Breaking the Circle of Certainty *Tina McLoughlin, Lea Randolf and Mike Seal, Response from Simone Helleren* — 208
20 College-Based Higher Education: A New Hope *John Keenan and Karima Kadi-Hanifi, Response from Paula McElearney* — 220
Conclusion: Hopeful Pedagogies Are Possible in Higher Education — 228

References — 241
Index — 276

Figures

18.1 Initial stages of dyslexia identification journey for university students   196
18.2 Additional access stages required for university students recently identified with dyslexia   197

Contributors

Parminder Assi taught in primary and secondary schools, worked as an LEA advisor, managed a team of peripatetic language support teachers and was a member on the Ofsted inspectorate before moving into higher education. Parminder has taught extensively on the BA degrees in Education Studies, Studies in Primary Education and various postgraduate, Initial Teacher Training and masters programmes in education. Specializing in equality issues and diversity with specific attention to learners for whom English is an additional language and in widening participation in higher education, Parminder's research interests include pupil attainment and assessment, participation and educational equity, baseline assessment in reception classrooms.

Helen Bardy is the programme leader for the postgraduate certificate in chaplaincy at Newman University, UK and teaches on the foundation year in social sciences. Previous to this she was a programme leader in the BA in Youth and Community Work, where she was lead for a module on critical pedagogy. She was previously a youth and community worker for local authority and voluntary sector organizations, including being Director of Catholic Youth Services in England and Wales. She is currently involved in governance of voluntary youth service provision and undertaking research into school chaplaincy.

Jane Beniston is a Senior Lecturer in Early Education and care at Newman University, UK. She is a Senior Fellow (HEA) and also acts as a reviewer for an international journal. Jane has been involved in many student partnership projects since 2014, winning an award for best student partnership project. These projects have led collaborative journal articles and numerous conference presentations. Jane was also the lead researcher on the two-year-funded REACT project, investigating student engagement, definitions of engagement and visibility of engagement opportunities. She has also developed new innovative student-led modules. Her current doctoral research focuses on transformative learning and student experience.

Julie Boardman is a Senior Lecturer in Early Childhood Education and Care. She is a Fellow of the Higher Education Academy (FHEA). She is currently working on an Education Doctorate with a focus on the 'datafication' of young children and how that impacts on practitioners working in early years. The research aims to offer practitioners a 'voice'. She is responsible for the Staff Student Consultative Committee and supporting Erasmus students. She has collaborated with colleagues internationally as part of Erasmus teaching exchanges to Italy, Norway and Hungary.

Seán Bracken is a Principal Fellow of the Higher Education Academy. He has a distinguished international career in teaching, as a teacher educator, lecturing and as an educational project manager. Seán's dedication to inclusive education has taken him to live, work and teach in Samoa, Vanuatu, the United States of America, Ireland, Tonga and, for the past ten years, the United Kingdom. He is currently based at the University of Worcester, UK, where he is a Principal Lecturer and a learning and teaching co-ordinator. He is also the course co-ordinator for the National Award SENCO, which involves professional development of teachers who have responsibility for special educational needs (SEN) and disabilities within state-maintained schools and within further education colleges in England.

Stephen Cowden is a Senior Lecturer in social work and course director for the MA Social Work at Coventry University, UK. Alongside his work on critical pedagogy and social work ethics, he has also developed research on the sociology of religious fundamentalism and he is a member of the Feminist Dissent Editorial Collective, where he has also published a range of material on this subject. He is also a commissioning editor for the Peter Lang series 'Critical Perspectives in Education', with Dr Jones Irwin.

Fin Cullen is a feminist activist, scholar, youth worker and parent. She is based at St Mary's University, Twickenham, UK, where her teaching and research focuses on social justice issues in education, youth cultures, girlhoods and youth policy and practice.

Gill Gilbert first became involved in student–staff partnership projects during the last year of her BA degree in early childhood education and care. Engagement in the programme has continued during her postgraduate studies for an MA in education (specializing in safeguarding) and includes projects such as reviewing the student induction process, capturing students' access to mentoring services and understanding what students do to protect their well-being.

Mike A. S. Gilsenan is Senior Lecturer and joint programme leader for the BA Hons Youth and Community Work at Newman University, UK. Currently studying for a Doctor of Education (EdD) at Liverpool Hope University, UK his thesis is a collaborative exploration of the unplanned, incidental and spontaneous learning that occurs outside of any formal or planned 'learning activity'. He has collaborated on two chapters in Mike Seal's *Teaching Youth Work in Higher Education* (2019), and writes on the subject of ordinary adventures.

Pauline Grace is a Senior Lecturer and MA programme leader of Youth and Community Work at Newman University, UK and has over thirty years of youth-work experience. Pauline is Co-founder and Vice-President of Professional Open Youth Work in Europe (POYWE), a pan-European group. She is the chief editor of the *International Journal of Open Youth Work* and the director of International Projects, Youth Work Europe. Her overtly feminist standpoint is also informed by her commitment to social justice and emancipatory practice which leads her into dynamic co-produced projects.

Sarah Hale is Programme Director for Foundation Years at the University of Sheffield, UK. Prior to joining the Department for Lifelong Learning in September 2012, Sarah spent five years in the Faculty of Lifelong Learning at Birkbeck, University of London, UK, and previously held posts at the University of Huddersfield, UK and the University of Portsmouth, UK. She has undertaken consultancy work for the Institute for Public Policy Research and the Higher Education Academy. She has been a local authority councillor, and a founding member and company secretary of a large community development association, actively involved in local regeneration partnerships.

Phoebe Hall is a second-year psychology and counselling student at Newman University, UK. She is also Vice-Chair of the LGBTQ+ Society at Newman University, UK. She has a passion for equality and diversity and promoting positive well-being. In her spare time, she finds joy in writing poetry and attending month poetry jams and performing. Emotional expression is a key part of her identity and she loves finding new ways to express thoughts and feelings.

Deborah Harris is a Senior Lecturer for the BA (Hons) Early Childhood Education and care programme at Newman University, UK. She is a senior fellow of the Higher Education Academy (SFHEA) and acts as a reviewer for international journals and academic texts. She has co-authored peer-reviewed journal articles and research reports, presenting at both international and national conferences. Deborah has been involved in the REACT Project 'Realising Engagement through Active Culture Transformation' and has also been actively engaged with students working on staff–student partnership projects. Deborah's research interests include student engagement and developing the early years graduate workforce.

Pete Harris worked for eighteen years as a youth worker and then as a senior manager of a children's charity before moving into higher education in 2010. He has published research that focuses on youth work, pedagogy in higher education and youth crime.

Simone Helleren is a doctoral researcher at the University of Birmingham, UK in the Department of Social Policy, Sociology, Criminology. Her PhD is an exploration of what enables and constrains effective engagement with help, through a longitudinal case study with young people on pathways out of homelessness. Previously, Simone worked with Groundswell, UK, for over eight years, overseeing their peer and participatory research programme. Before Groundswell, she worked across the voluntary and statutory sectors with diverse groups focusing on 'involvement and participation', frequently using theatre methods. She is an experienced facilitator of Open Space Technology events.

Karima Kadi-Hanifi is a Senior Lecturer in education at Newman University, UK. A Doctor of Linguistics, she specialised in English language, linguistics and English as a second language in her earlier career in the post-compulsory sector, including adult and community education, further education and higher education, before moving into the subject of teacher education and education studies more recently. Her research and publications have centred on critical pedagogy, race, EAL, decolonization, postgraduate study skills and college-based higher education.

John Keenan is a Senior Lecturer and teaching fellow at Newman University, UK and University of Leicester, UK. His current teaching subject is education but he has previously taught English and media in schools and further education and among his many roles was co-ordinator of the advertising and media degree at Coventry University, UK. He has published work on the subjects of teaching through autoethnography, epistemology and college-based higher education.

Lorraine Loveland-Armour, a Doctor of Education and Fellow of the Higher Education Academy, has taught at secondary schools, colleges and universities in both California and Washington, in the USA. Her professional roles have ranged from further education college programme manager, specialist clinician to residential counsellor. She was employed as Dyslexia Support Services Team Leader at Newman University, UK for over sixteen years. She is committed to reducing barriers to learning and empowering adult students to better understand their dyslexia. Her particular research interests and publications include: the experiences of adult university students with dyslexia, phenomenology, andragogy, disability theories, visual methods and student voice.

Paula McElearney is a lecturer and full-time PhD student at Worcester University, UK researching critical pedagogy in the lifelong learning sector. Prior to this she spent thirteen years in a large further education college, where she was firstly a programme co-ordinator and lecturer on adult and community courses and then a course leader and lecturer for community-based courses for adults with special educational needs. She was head teacher at a small, rural residential special school. She also worked with higher education students with specific learning difficulties.

Kaece McGowan is a lived-experience psychology and counselling undergraduate. Her current achievements include contributing to this book, leasing with practitioners in the NHS on a new personality and complex trauma pathway, and she attends the University of Oxford, UK every two years to inform postgraduates about personality disorder.

Tina McLoughlin was the International Co-ordinator at Newman University, UK and previously the Aimhigher Manager, working with schools and colleges across the west midlands. She has a long held interest in widening participation reflecting her own education journey as a mature student and previous posts in higher education. Her research interests include widening participation, class, staff development and identity, intercultural communication and transitions. She is a member of Erasmus+ Sector Consultative Group for Higher Education and a member of Critical Pedagogy Group at Newman University, UK and Associate Fellow of the Higher Education Academy.

Leoarna Mathias is Senior Lecturer for student engagement at Newman University, UK, and her scholarship is focused on how students experience modern higher education contexts, and the nature of academic labour in the twenty-first century.

She has delivered papers, including at EFYE, SEDA and the UCLAN International Paolo Freire Conference, and published two peer- reviewed papers in 2018. She has also recently become a TedX Speaker, having presented in June 2019 at an event hosted by Aston University, UK, in which she spoke about repurposing degree-level studies beyond their economic worth. She is a Senior Fellow of the Higher Education Academy.

Lorna Naomi Morgan is a youth-work practitioner from Birmingham and a third-year undergraduate student of youth and community work at Newman University, UK. Lorna is the youth worker heading up a transgender-focused youth group with Birmingham LGBT called Emerge, which evidences her commitment to supporting emancipatory informal educatory practice with queer young people. Lorna is transgender and has, through the experience of coming out and coming to terms with her queerness, gained a great appreciation of the structural inequalities evident within all of society and especially within the field of education, leading her to have a great love of critical pedagogy.

Mike Neary is Emeritus Professor of Sociology in the School of Social and Political Sciences at the University of Lincoln, UK. He was previously the dean of Teaching and Learning, 2007–2014, the head of the Centre for Educational Research and Development, 2007–2012 and the director of the Graduate School 2011–2014. He was also the director of Research in the School for Social and Political Sciences, 2017–2019. Prior to taking up his appointment at the University of Lincoln, UK, he taught political sociology at the University of Warwick, UK, 1993–2007.

Sarah Parkes is a 2020 National Teaching Fellow, 2019 Collaborative Award for Teaching Excellence winner and Senior Fellow of the Higher Education Academy. Working with staff and students across Newman University, UK, she leads activities aimed at supporting student retention. This has included establishing a suite of pre-entry and transition programmes, the Newman Foundation Year and promoting ethical use of student engagement data to foster student success. While a founding member of the University's Romero Freire Institute and the Critical Pedagogy group, she teaches across a range of undergraduate and postgraduate courses including the Post Graduate Certificate in Higher Education practice.

John Peters is Professor of higher education practice, Director of Learning, Teaching and Scholarship, and convenor of the Romero Freire Institute at Newman University, UK. A National Teaching Fellow (2001), he is on the Executive of the Staff and Educational Development Association, chairs its Scholarship and Research Committee and sits on the editorial board of *Innovations in Education and Teaching International*. His current research interests include student partnership, critical pedagogy in higher education, appreciative inquiry, collaborative educational development and personal tutoring. An experienced research supervisor, he regularly publishes and presents in partnership with undergraduate and graduate student researchers.

Paul Prinsloo is a Research Professor in Open and Distance Learning (ODL) in the College of Economic and Management Sciences, University of South Africa, South Africa. His academic background includes theology, art history, business management, online learning and religious studies. Paul is an established researcher and has published numerous articles in the fields of teaching and learning, student success in distance education contexts, learning analytics and curriculum development. His current research focuses on the collection, analysis and use of student data in learning analytics, graduate supervision and digital identity.

Ruth Roberts is a Lecturer in counselling and psychotherapy. Ruth's emergent research interests are in critical approaches to higher education and the psychological contract between students and universities. Ruth has practised as a counsellor since 2004 and worked as educational counsellor at the University of East Anglia, UK for nine years. Her counselling practice is strongly influenced by the person-centred and experiential approaches as well as mindfulness-based approaches. Ruth co-edited a book, *Counselling and Psychotherapy in Organisational Settings for Learning Matters* and is a student on the PhD Higher Education: Research, Evaluation and Enhancement programme at Lancaster University, UK.

Mike Seal is Professor of Education and Social Mobility at the University of Suffolk, UK. He was previously a Reader in Critical Pedagogy at Newman University, UK and chair of the Romero Freire Institute. He has also taught at the YMCA George Williams College, the Open University, UK and the University of Oxford, UK. He is a National Teaching Fellow, a Principal Fellow of the Higher Education Academy and a Fellow of the Royal Society of the Arts. He has written fourteen books, twenty book chapters, fourteen journal articles and over twenty-five other publications. He has presented at over eighty conferences and seminars worldwide.

Peter Sharpe works as a student well-being advisor at University Centre Shrewsbury, at satellite campus of Chester University, UK. Prior to this, he has worked as an academic support advisor at Newman University Birmingham, learning development officer in the Department of Information Studies at Aberystwyth University, UK, and as PA to research directors in psychology and political science at Birmingham University.

Alan Smith is Principal Lecturer and Head of Youth and Community Work at Leeds Beckett University, UK. He has been teaching for over twenty-five years,. Alan is the past chair of the Professional Association for Lecturers in Youth and Community Work/Community and Youth Work Training Agencies Group (TAG) and is Vice-Chair of the National Youth Agency Education and Training Standards (ETS) Committee (England) and Co-Chair of Education and Training Standards for England, Scotland, Wales and all-Ireland.

Christine Smith has worked in higher education since 2007 where she worked in the South West of England as programme lead for the MA in youth and community work and more recently as a lecturer in youth and community work education at Hull University, UK. Beyond her teaching role, Christine is a committed trade unionist and including roles such as Branch casework co-ordinator and Chair of UCU trade union, Social Policy Lead for a local Citizens Advice Bureau and UK-based Chair of the Professional Association for Lecturers in Youth and Community Work.

Adellah Snape is a third-year youth and community work student at Newman University, UK. She is a community activist in her local community. She has organized and co-created local community events, which were direct actions stemming from a participatory action research project. She is a youth worker at Youth Work Europe and she lends her expertise in a weekly youth café.

Sammie Snelleksz is currently part way through year one of a foundation degree in psychology and counselling.

Neil M. Speirs from The University of Edinburgh, works as a manger, practitioner and researcher in areas concerning access & participation and related policy – across primary, secondary and tertiary education. He has strategic oversight and management of a number of self-generated community based projects and teaches on matters concerning social reproduction, critical pedagogy, education as the practice of freedom and peer related pedagogies.

Marina Tornero Tarragó graduated in English philology from the University of Seville, Spain and obtained her Doctor of Education degree from the University of Seville, Spain with a cum laude thesis on media literacy. Marina taught at Columbia University, USA and elsewhere in New York City from 2007 to 2010 before returning to Spain where she currently works at CES Don Bosco in Madrid. A member of the University of La Rioja Picture Books research group and the ALEC network, Marina has written and given conference papers on media literacy, language teaching in multicultural contexts and the study of popular culture and the media.

Luca Tateo is an associate professor in the Department of Special Needs Education, University of Oslo (Norway). He is also a visiting associate professor, Federal University of Bahia (Brazil), and associate professor, Research Centre for Cultural Psychology, Aalborg University (Denmark). His research interests are general areas of social psychology; cultural psychology of education; art and affect; the study of imagination as higher psychological process; affective logic and the aesthetic dimension of psychic life; the cultural mediation of grief; and the epistemology and history of psychological science.

Liz Thomas is an independent researcher and consultant for higher education and Professor of Higher Education at Edge Hill University, UK. Liz has twenty years' experience of undertaking and managing research about widening participation, student retention and success and institutional approaches to improving the student experience and outcomes. She is committed to using research to inform national and institutional policy, practice and evaluation, and has developed and led change programmes to facilitate this.

Jo Trelfa is Head of Academic Professional Development at Winchester University, UK and Assistant Director of the Winchester Institute for Contemplative Education and Practice, leading on its introduction into the university. Previously she lectured in youth and community work at Majrjon University, UK. Her areas of specialism are teaching about the theories and practice of individual work and group facilitation; individual and group communication; conflict management, resolution and transformation; supervision; management of people and classrooms; informal and formal education with large and small groups; and professional practice. She was Chair of TAG, 2008–2011.

László Varga currently works at the Benedek Elek Faculty of Pedagogy, University of Sopron, Sopron, Hungary. László does research in pedagogic theory, educational theory, early childhood education and early childhood neuropedagogy.

Joris Vlieghe is an Assistant Professor at the Laboratory for Education and Society, KU Leuven, Belgium, where he teaches philosophy of education. With Piotr Zamojski, he recently published *Towards an Ontology of Teaching. Thing-centered pedagogy, Affirmation and Love for the World*. His research focuses on the impact of digitization on the future of the school, study practices and post-critical ways of thinking about and researching education. With Naomi Hodgson and Piotr Zamojski, he has written *Manifesto for a Post-Critical Pedagogy*.

Roger Willoughby, originally from New York, is qualified in philosophy, clinical psychology and psychoanalytic studies. Having practised in the British NHS, he currently works at Newman University, UK, directing the MA Education programme. His writing spans several fields, including psychology, psychoanalysis, education studies and genocide studies. He has published in various journals, including the *International Journal of Psychoanalysis*, and his book *Masud Khan: The Myth and the Reality* (2005) and the edited volume *Education Studies: The Key Concepts* (2018) have proved popular texts. Roger is currently editing the collected works of Esther Bick, and writing on the history of psychoanalysis in Britain.

Series Editor's Foreword

This new book series was introduced against an international background that comprised, and continues to comprise, situations that are disturbing and intriguing. The onset of Covid-19 has thrown into sharp relief arguably the major casualty of this pandemic, an unprepared, failed state. We have been left with a state shorn of the facilities and provisions one would expect of a purportedly 'democratic' entity that dances only to the tune of capital accumulation and not to that reflecting the concerns of all people under its jurisdiction; with regard to the provision of social safeguards, the state has, in many places, been rendered almost threadbare by its accommodation of nefarious neoliberal policies which leave everything outside the demands of capital to the market and voluntary organizations. While wealth is concentrated, as a result, in the hands of a few, there are those who are left to struggle for survival in a Darwinian contest that rewards the 'winners' and renders others disposable. Questionable wealth is concentrated in the hands of a few, who take advantage of their network of spin-doctors and 'fake news' soothsayers, to play the victim with regard to the pandemic. They, and the many policymakers who accommodate them, deflect their responsibility onto ordinary citizens and further justify curtailing the state's social spending, to the detriment of the many, 'the multitudes', as referred to by Michael Hart and Toni Negri.

The series was launched at a time when the 'social contract', ideally one which transcends the capitalist framework (as Henry Giroux astutely remarks), is continuously being shredded as several people are removed from the index of human concerns. Many are led to live in a precarious state. Contract work has become the norm, a situation that renders one's life less secure. There is also criticism targeted at the very nature of production and consumption with their effects on people and their relationship to other social beings and the rest of the planet, hence 'questionable wealth'.

These are also difficult times because the initial enthusiasm for the popular quest for democracy in various parts of the world has been tempered by eventual realism based on the fact that strategically entrenched forces are not removed simply by overthrowing a dictator. Far from ushering in a 'spring', the uprisings in certain countries have left political vacuums – fertile terrain for religiously motivated terrorism that presents a real global security threat. This threat, though having to be controlled in many ways, not least tackling the relevant social issues at their root, presents many with a carte blanche to trample on hard-earned democratic freedoms and rights. The situation is said to further spread the 'culture of militarization' that engulfs youth, about which much has been written in critical education. Terrorist attacks or aborted coups allow scope for analyses on these grounds, including analyses that draw out the implications for education.

The security issue, part of the 'global war on terror', is availed of by those who seek curtailment of human beings' right to asylum seeking and who render impoverished migrants as scapegoats for the host country's economic ills. The issue of migration would be an important contemporary theme in the large domain of critical education. This phenomenon and that of Covid-19, as with any other pretext, are availed of by powers acting exclusively in the interest of capital. This leads to a further siege mentality marked by increasing otherizing, scapegoating, surveillance and incarceration. Security extends beyond the culture of fear generated through terrorism to include health issues such as the pandemic, the latter said to be spread by those who, in reality, are the least equipped to work and live safely in their homes, including rejected asylum seekers and other migrants denied citizenship, those who live in restricted and overcrowded spaces or who do not have a home at all. They face a stark choice: exposure or starvation. Barbarism, in Rosa Luxemburg's sense of the term, is a key feature of this choice and the society in which many live.

The series was introduced at a time when an attempt was made for politics to be rescued from the exclusive clutches of politicians and bankers. A more grassroots kind of politics has been constantly played out in globalized public arenas such as the squares and streets of Athens, Madrid, Istanbul (Gezi Park), Cairo, Tunis and New York City. A groundswell of dissent, indignation and tenacity was manifest and projected throughout all corners of the globe, albeit, as just indicated, not always leading to developments hoped for by those involved. Yet hope springs eternal. Some of these manifestations have provided pockets for social action alternative to the mainstream, including educational action. Authors writing on critical education have found, in these pockets, seeds for a truly and genuinely democratic pedagogy that will, hopefully, be explored and developed, theoretically and empirically, in this series.

It is in these contexts, and partly as a response to the challenges they pose, that this new series on critical education was conceived and brought into being. Education, though not to be attributed powers it does not have (it cannot change things on its own), surely has a role to play in this scenario: from exposing and redressing class politics to confronting the cultures of militarization, consumerism, individualism and ethnic supremacy. The call among critical educators is for a pedagogy of social solidarity that emphasizes the collective and communal in addition to the ecologically sustainable.

Critical educators have for years been exploring, advocating and organizing ways of seeing, learning and living that constitute alternatives to the mainstream. They have been striving to make their contribution to changing the situation for the better, governed by a vision or visions of systems that are socially more just. The ranks of the oppressed are swelling. Hopefully, it is the concerns of these people that are foremost in the minds and hearts of those committed to a social-justice-orientated critical education. I would be the first to admit that even a professed commitment to a critical education can degenerate into another form of radical chic or academic sterility. We need to be ever so vigilant towards not only others but also ourselves, coming to terms with our own contradictions, therefore seeking, in Paulo Freire's words, to become less incoherent.

This series offers a platform for genuinely socially committed critical educators to express their ideas in a systematic manner. It seeks to offer signposts for an alternative approach to education and cultural work, constantly bearing in mind the

United Nations Sustainable Development Goals that, albeit difficult to realize, serve as important points of reference when critiquing current policies in different sectors, including education. The series' focus on critical education, comprising the movement known as critical pedagogy, is intended to contribute to maintaining the steady flow of ideas that can inspire and allow for an education that eschews the 'taken for granted'.

This particular volume targets an important institution constantly reshaped by neoliberalism and many of the issues touched upon throughout this foreword: higher education. This major institution is often said to be caught in the struggle between a 'system world' and the 'lifeworlds' of people working inside or in relation to it. The system world renders higher education as increasingly governed by neoliberalism and its market policies. The dominant discourse is no longer of a community of people engaging in scholarly endeavour and facing the democratic challenge of opening to and engaging with communities hitherto at the furthest remove from the institution. On the other hand, we have the lifeworlds of people working within or in connection with it. Some go with the flow and actually embrace its 'new managerial' approaches, often furthering their careers around them. Others struggle against all this. More correctly, they struggle 'in and against' the system. They remain steadfast in the sense that they cling to higher education's one-time declared mission of being a public good where pride of place is accorded to criticality and seeing things in their broader complexity; knowledge, in Freire's words, evolves through epistemological curiosity and co-investigation. These people resist and seek, in various ways, to overcome the hegemonic idea of higher education being a consumption good where they are meant to be either service providers (faculty members) or clients/consumers (students). There emerges, from this struggle, often within the system's interstices, a pedagogy of hope and possibility, as this book reveals. There are pockets of this found within established higher education institutions and others mushrooming outside them, among social movements (e.g. Escola Nacional Florestan Fernandes in Brazil or UNITIERRA in Chiapas, Mexico) and other networks of people demonstrating that 'another world is possible'. Happily, the higher education field, like most of the education field, is a site of contestation. This specific volume provides ample proof of this.

Peter Mayo
Series Editor
University of Malta
Msida, Malta

Acknowledgements

Mike would like to acknowledge that while he is the named author, all members of Newman staff who made a contribution to the book functioned as an editorial board. The book is dedicated to all self-identifying critical pedagogues in higher education. Our ambition is that the book serves as a source for you in difficult times.

Introduction

Are Hopeful Pedagogies Possible in Higher Education?

With notable exceptions, such as the work of Henry Giroux, many accounts of critical pedagogy, particularly accounts of trying to enact it within higher education (HE), express a deep cynicism about being able to counter the ever-creeping hegemony of neoliberalism, neo-conservatism and new managerialism within higher education (Cowden and Singh, 2013; Van Heertum, 2006). Yet as Freire himself says, the 'global tendency to accept the crucial implications of the New World Order as natural and inevitable' (2000, p. 23) transforms these forces from modes of repression to commonsensical norms, re-inscribing their inescapability. Freire (2000) believed that while we are conditioned by these forces, we are not determined by them, and are thus free to revolt.

Post-critical pedagogies (Hodgson, Vlieghe and Zamojski, 2018) critique critical pedagogy for its utopianism and its often-exclusive focus on liberation and achieving structural, social and economic change. Cynicism emerges from the often-failed attempt to actualize these changes, something post-critical pedagogues call 'cruel optimism' with a disdain for present action that does not measure up to an unattainable utopian ideal. Post-critical pedagogues instead call for a celebration of the present, seeing acts of progressive education as liberatory ends in themselves rather than merely tools for planning future social action and change.

This volume acknowledges some of these criticisms, but attempts to rescue critical pedagogy, locating some of its associated pessimism as a misreading of Freire. These misreadings are also located in our experiences of the present, in that unless change comes within the lifetime of the project, critical pedagogy has somehow failed. Instead, this book argues that a positive utopianism is possible (Levitas, 2013). Present actions need to be celebrated, and cultivated as symbols of hope, possibility and generativity for the future – which the concept of hope implies. This book therefore makes the case for celebrating pedagogies of HE that operate in liminal spaces. We dance both in the spaces between the present (the world as it is) and the future (the world as it could be); and also, in the cracks that are beginning to show in neoliberalism, neo-conservatism and new managerialism, hoping to widen and penetrate them further.

The seed for this book was nurtured within a critical pedagogy group at Newman. It meets weekly and uniquely brings together academic, professional and support staff and students. Both academic and practical concerns are combined, exploring issues such as divisions between academic and professional staff, the nature of partnerships, developing staff weeks and how the university presents and represents itself to the community. This book is one of the outcomes of that group, and as such, it features contributions from all stakeholders mentioned, who also constitute our intended audience: students, third-space professionals, academics and experts alike. While this book presents the experience of trying to enact hopeful pedagogies in a single, small university we intend for this to be an example that has resonance with other institutions, who we invite to consider these ideas within the contexts of their own higher education institutions (HEIs). Indeed, the book is structured to convey this.

We think this book will be of interest to the international academic field of critical pedagogy and to the wider field of education studies. More specifically, it will be of use to anyone within higher education that has an interest in pedagogic issues. The audience reflects the authors, in that we wish to appeal to academics, but equally to support third-space staff and students. Critical pedagogy work is also a growing field in Europe and beyond, and we have links and a reputation across Europe on the topic having had a strong presence at last year's International Freire Conference in Cyprus. Critical pedagogy is growing in Europe, particularly in Eastern Europe and the Nordic countries, where it is relatively new. There is an existing tradition of social pedagogy, but critical pedagogy is a different angle, with a different emphasis on working with power. Critical pedagogy more broadly is a truly worldwide field, particularly in Europe and North and South America, South Africa and Australasia. However, we want the readership to extend beyond the academic community and to reach both educators and practitioners of critical pedagogy, educating others being an essential part of the role of being a HE practitioner.

There are a number of publications that are close in territory to this intended publication, but we would not consider any to be competition; rather they are complementary, and our publication offers something different. The two closest are Groenke and Hatch (2009) and Cowden and Singh (2013). Both share with this intended volume a focus on finding openings and spaces in higher education where critical pedagogy can be enacted. Groenke and Hatch concentrate on teacher education as a context. Cowden and Singh do examine wider classroom context, and also, as their title suggests, against and beyond the university, including student activism and making links with wider social movements, as well as giving a number of theoretical explorations, such as chapters on indigenous pedagogy and Bourdieu.

Both volumes explore and analyse the neoliberal context of HE. What this intended volume does differently is consider other contexts within HE, particularly third spaces such as international placements, student support, constructions of disability, structural attempts at enacting student partnership such as student–staff partnerships, issues around retention and recruitment, and foundation years. It also explores different approaches within courses, such as running a module specifically on critical pedagogy, as well as complementary practices such as emotional work and contemplative work. Also, Groene's volume is over ten years old and by the time our volume is published, Cowden and Singh's will likely be seven years old.

Other volumes such as Davies and Barnett (2016) do cover aspects of critical pedagogy but have a much wider reach examining critical theory and a more theoretical and conceptual, rather than pedagogic, orientation. Other volumes examine pedagogies of hope, such as Hammond (2017) and the forthcoming *The Transformative Power of Hope in Education,* again for Bloomsbury, but both have a wider theoretical base and reach than critical pedagogy and are thus complementary rather than competition. We believe this publication is unique and has benefits for the reader in a number of ways:

- While others have seen the relevance of hope in pedagogic approaches, this book reframes and reorientates critical pedagogy into the idea of hopeful pedagogies.
- It represents a collective approach to developing hopeful pedagogies, beyond bringing in different authors for an edited collection. As an example, it presents the chapters as a series of ongoing dialogues between Newman authors and others within the field.
- It uniquely has contributions, and thus relevance for, the whole community of higher education institutions, including students, professional support and third-space staff, and academics.

As a very broad structure, the book has two parts; a first that outlines the issues, theory base and praxis of critical pedagogy, particularly within a higher education institution, and a second part that gives specific examples from across Newman of attempts to enact it. In Part I we invited a number of critical collaborators to engage with the chapters and write responses or vignettes commenting on the themes that have arisen. This included other academics and experts in the field, as well as students and practitioners, as appropriate. Some had already been identified and others were named as chapters developed. The book has three aims:

- To re-examine the conceptual terrain for critical pedagogy, assessing its potential to be actualized within HE through hopeful pedagogies.
- To showcase examples of attempts to dance in the cracks and enact critical pedagogy within a higher education institution, across all arenas from student support, through student partnerships, to curriculum design.
- To engage with wider debates and relate to examples of praxis from other higher education institutions and countries.

Part I: Key Ideas and the Conceptual and Policy Terrain

In the first chapter Mike Seal explores the key concepts in critical and hopeful pedagogies as they are introduced to students on youth and community work programmes and foundation year routes at Newman via the document 'How we teach'. This document attempts to articulate how the teams' approach to teaching is fundamentally different to the more traditional 'Banking' approach to education criticized by Freire. Using this document as a basis, this chapter explores some of the key themes of critical pedagogy, including its epistemological basis, 'conscientization' and developing critical thinking, creating democratic learning environments, developing generative moments, finding teachable moments, using authentic materials and developing praxis.

In doing this it explores critical pedagogy's development from Paulo Freire through other key authors such as Henry Giroux, Ira Shor, Michael Apple, Joe L. Kincheloe, Shirley R. Steinberg and Peter Maclaren. It also considers critics of critical pedagogy on grounds of ignoring power (Elias and Merriam, 1980; Illich, 1978; Zachariah, 1986), for absence of analysis of colour (Ellsworth, 1989) and for failure to address gender (Brady, 1994; hooks, 1994). In particular it looks at the contribution of Rancière (1992), who accuses Freire's idea of 'conscientization' as having Freire's authoritarian tendencies and condemning the masses as unknowing and in need of liberation. Instead, akin to Zachariah (1986), Rancière views the working class as inherently capable of learning and developing intellect. However, they have been led to believe that they are not intelligent by a hegemonic system that deliberately undermines their self-belief, thus the role of the educator work on people's will and self-belief.

In the second chapter, Leoarna and Mike Gilsenan explore the relevance of post-critical critiques of critical pedagogy. Their starting point is a shared understanding between the authors of the meaning of the work they do with students here at Newman. It also draws upon a shared interest in the growing body of post-critical literature that reconsiders the purposes of education in neoliberal societies. They have recognized that they work in similar ways with their students; they are transparent, wanting to challenge their students to address their assumptions about what a higher education lecturer is, and they want to work outside the curriculum to engage more fully in the individual and collective transformation that education can bring. They have an idea to move beyond the cynicism and despair, as well as the ideological utopianism that can sometimes characterize critical pedagogy: instead, they wish to do good work without needing to see it 'direct' our students to particular ends. In this way they 'meet' the ideas that surface within the post-critical literature. This chapter takes the form of an 'informed' conversation between the authors. Their approach collates a reading list that they both become familiar with, and then record our conversation as we respond to the readings and consider their meaning for our work. Through dialogue, they hope to demonstrate the impact that both critical pedagogy and the post-critical literature can have in shaping teaching and learning in higher education that can, and does, resist instrumentality.

In Chapter 3, Sarah and Jane explore the social policy context of higher education, arguing that 'resistance' is possible. They begin by exploring how neoliberalism as a worldview and process pervades the very 'ontology of our everyday lives' (Martin in Downs, 2017, p. 61) through a process called 'biofinancialization' (Lilley and Papadopoulos, 2014, pp. 972–4). This creates tensions between experiencing HE as a collusion with and a resistance to capitalist notions of 'value'. This chapter uses Stephen Ball's 'policy sociology' (2008, 2012, 2017) to argue that the current UK HE policy context fundamentally repositions the relationships between and within education in relation to the needs of the state and the global 'knowledge economy'. Through this exploration, it argues for the intrinsic value and worth of HE to the individual, organization and society via the ways in which it develops a criticality towards knowledge claims: a way of being, knowing and acting (Lea, 2016, pp. 114–8). This positioning necessitates pedagogy and approaches that resist enacting a 'prescribed set of procedures or rules' (Green, 2011, p. 120) legitimized by both internal and external systems: what Paulo Freire calls *conscientização* or conscientization (Giannakaki et al., 2018) that promotes democratic engagement, meaningful dialogue and co-operative working with and between staff, students and external organizations.

In the fourth chapter, Mike Seal asks under what conditions critical pedagogy is possible within higher education, exploring the literature on accounts of trying to enact critical pedagogy in this context. Many such accounts express a deep cynicism about being able to counter the ever-creeping hegemony of neoliberalism, neo-conservatism and new managerialism within higher education (Cowden and Singh, 2013; Van Heertum, 2006) and as such there are calls to abandon the attempt (Belton, 2014), or that an authentic attempt lies outside the academy (Neary, 2011). The chapter explores how, in many ways, higher education, which is hierarchical, centrally driven and reinscribes elitism, is inherently a problematic site to try and enact critical pedagogy. Compounding this has been the penetration and domination of neoliberalist, neo-conservatist and new public managerialist thinking. The chapter then assesses whether critical pedagogy has a place in the changing vision at a structural level and explores whether self-identifying critical pedagogues (SICPs) can have an influence at a local level. It explores Mottas's (2013) work which outlines the characteristics of critical pedagogy in the classroom. The chapter advocates that critical pedagogy cannot be meaningfully enacted by lone SICPs, and that to be meaningful there needs to be a collective approach. It builds on Mahon's (2014) work on practice architectures examining cultural-discursive, material-economic and social-political dimensions that critical pedagogy needs to operate within higher education. It concludes that this is possible.

In the final chapter of Part I John and Leoarna explore the 'pedagogy of partnership'. The idea of student partnership in higher education was proposed most forcefully in the UK by the National Union of Students (NUS) as just such an 'alternative work model'. The NUS 'Manifesto for partnership' took aim both at the neoliberal concept of student as customer and the traditional liberal concept of student as apprentice (NUS, 2012). It set out a vision of partnership as a commitment to student co-creation of knowledge, learning and the HE institution itself. Fundamentally the NUS 'Manifesto for partnership' called for 'a meaningful dispersal of power' (NUS, 2012, 8) and provided 'a statement of the folly of trying to sell HE to students when we can unleash the power of working *with* students to transform HE' (Peters and Mathias, 2018). Newman University is a small university in the UK committed to social justice and values-based HE. From 2014 we set out to enact student partnership as a means of promoting democratic engagement, meaningful dialogue and co-operative working (Peters, 2014b, 2016). One key way in which we did this was though articulating and sharing six principles of a 'pedagogy of partnership' based on the work of Paulo Freire. This chapter sets out these principles of shared hope, shared dream, respectful dialogue, co-investigation, co-construction and continuing transformation.

Part II: Hopeful Pedagogies in Higher Education

Hopeful Pedagogy within Courses

In the first chapter in Part I Julie and Jane reflect on influences throughout the journey from early year's settings to spaces supporting students in higher education. Working within an institution of mainly female Muslim students as part of the widening participation agenda, they explore the concept of hopeful pedagogic spaces, to include relationships, approaches, values and democratic working. Using Ball's (2012) ideas around power and education they investigate the links between the Reggio Emilia early years approach in Italy (Rinaldi, 2006); thus, social and critical pedagogy is central (Freire, 1996) to this investigation. Students working as early years practitioners lend their voice to spaces in HE that make the difference (Morgan, 2000). A positive utopianism (Moss, 2007; Levitas, 2013) is possible where young children are imbued with a sense of strength and competence to shape their future. The authors explore whether this thread can be possible within an HE context.

Following on from this in the second chapter, two Senior Lecturers (Jane and Debbie) critically reflect on how pedagogical approaches have been adopted to develop co-constructed learning (Freire, 200), providing a space for 'transformative pedagogy'. Drawing on theoretical perspectives from Giroux (2006, 2011), and Freire (2000), two student-led modules at levels five and six were developed within an Early Childhood Education and Care degree programme. Students studying on this programme are predominantly female, Muslim, 'commuters' (Jacoby, 1989) from disadvantaged backgrounds. Such students have been 'problematized' in discourse of late (Thomas, 2012; Donnelly and Gamsu, 2018). This chapter explores how practice aligned to a 'generative' curriculum (Massey, 2008) enabled students to 'have a voice' to be able to engage in collaborative dialogue to plan, deliver and support the assessment process of the modules. The importance of relational pedagogy (Brownlee and Berthlesen, 2005) focusing on the role of the tutor and the concept of 'spaces to belong' are explored. Reflections of this pedagogical approach from both students and tutors around challenges to this way of working, and ways in which this pedagogical approach can enhance the learning experience for both students and tutors, form an integral part of the chapter.

Similarly, but different, in the next chapter in this subpart 'Preparing for an unexpected journey!', Helen and Mike explore their module on critical pedagogy, which has been run for the last four years, with four separate cohorts of students. Run over a twelve-week period, the aim has been to co-create a process that captures elements of critical pedagogy while exploring the tensions, paradoxes and liberating aspects not only of understanding the underpinning theoretical concepts within critical pedagogy but also of attempting to break down teacher–student power imbalance by offering the whole teaching, learning and assessment process over to the group as a collective, critical endeavour. This chapter draws on staff and student reflections of the overall experience, including the content, process and whether the experience has influence twelve months later. This process (or journey as they like to envisage it) is not something that can be planned or fits neatly into a modular structure, and can be a rollercoaster. As with any journey, the traveller has to be prepared for any terrain they think they will come across, in any weather. How to prepare for the journey requires consideration of a number of factors that are pertinent to the experiences of all the travellers.

Finally in this subpart, Roger and Parminder, with the academy as a site of both contest and hope in late modernity, consider multiple dilemmas of togetherness. They argue that we live in an interconnected, globalized world, yet one that is profoundly fractured along lines of culture, ethnicity, gender and economic inequality. Such lines of fracture pervade our student bodies, potentially segregating them into various ghettos. The students are not alone in this; these fissures also pervade our own sense of selves as academics and as human beings. One pedagogic and academic challenge is to articulate, and where possible address, these structures leading to an active process of reflection and recognition of our habitus and potential spaces for transformation. We discuss one particular instantiation of this in our experience of an innovative International Education module using colonialism and gender studies as theoretical framings to explore experiences of disconnection, mistrust and resistance.

Hopeful Pedagogies within Structures

In the first structural chapter, Sarah and Leoarna explore viewing induction and transition work as a critical pedagogy practice. Newman University appointed its first Tutor for Transition and Widening Participation Officer, latterly Tutor for Transition and Retention, in 2008. Within the remit of this post, a suite of programmes has been developed across the last decade, all aimed at aiding students both new to the institution and moving between academic years, to become socially and academically integrated (Thomas, 2002; Tinto, 2006; Yorke and Longden, 2008). The programmes draw upon a particular understanding of the challenges students face in feeling both that they belong to their higher education institutions community and prepared for challenges of completing their studies (Thomas, 2012; Thomas and Jones, 2017; Jones, 2008). This heartfelt attempt to understand 'who the student is' when they arrive resonates with a critical pedagogic approach, in that those delivering induction, transition and retention programmes at Newman recognize the starting points of our students (Ausabel, 1968) and fully acknowledge that retention forms part of a complex cultural and social picture (Walker, 2004; Quinn, 2004, 2010). They also recognize the value of forming genuine relationships with students, and creating democratic spaces for them, so that every student can explore the meaning of their decision to study, and can flourish on their own terms, throughout their time as part of the Newman community. This chapter explores the challenges of delivering induction and transition work through an enactment of critical pedagogy that values the hopes, fears and humanity of every student that enrols at the institution.

Next John and Leoarna explore putting into practice the principles of the pedagogy of partnership outlined in Chapter 5. Newman University's Student Partnership Project programme draws upon a Freirean model that seeks to challenge hierarchical structures and promote democratic practice. Projects are proposed by students, and they are paid for their participation by the university. This chapter explores the joys and challenges of the partnership projects across a four-year period, during which time more than seventy projects have been completed. The projects are organized across the following three strands: student experience, students as research partners and community engagement. Those that centre on the student experience strand prove the most popular and have often resulted in projects that tell the institution something about itself. Elsewhere, students as research project partners have led to students writing for peer review, and those focused on community engagement have enabled students to, for example, gain funding for youth work projects or establish a Children's University programme at Newman. The evaluation that forms the basis of this chapter was conducted through focus groups with students and staff and analysed against the six principles for Freirean partnership working outlined in Part I. While participants experienced some of the common limitations of project work that arise when it sits outside the curriculum, students and staff nevertheless felt their participation in the projects was 'hope-full', and that they had entered a space in which collaborative pedagogies can and do flourish.

In the final chapter of this subpart, Sarah, Mike and a number of students build on the previous chapter on foundation years and explore whether they truly undo discourses of deficit. Newman University Birmingham had its first intake of students onto the foundation year programme in Autumn 2017, very much a 'widening participation' cohort. The foundation year(s) have adopted a particular approach to the delivery of the programme through a commitment to the principles of critical pedagogy. This approach, unlike many traditional approaches to 'study skills' or deficit models of student development, seeks to develop an awareness of the subtle injustices legitimized by the current education system: what Paulo Freire calls 'conscientization' (Giannakaki et al., 2018) to promote democratic engagement, meaningful dialogue and co-operative working. Given this context, the staff working at Newman, in particular those of us involved in the foundation year, are privileged to witness the nature of our students' experiences; their emergent academic identities that bring together with it, an appreciation of the complex trajectories towards degree completion. This chapter shares their learning around working with the 'Newman student' while exploring the ways in which they embed the foundation year alongside our other strategic work in relation to student transition, retention and success. In particular, current foundation year students share their experience of making the transition into higher education, providing commentary on our particular pedagogical approach.

Becoming the Hopeful Pedagogue

In this subpart, colleagues explore how staff and students transform themselves in trying to be hopeful pedagogues. In the first chapter Ruth explores 'Person-centred and contemplative critical approaches to higher education'. The chapter argues that the use of the term 'potential' in higher education policy and in institutional advertising contributes to drawing students into an ill-defined contractual relationship with their institution prior to entry. In the context of a marketized higher education sector, this 'rhetoric of potential' implies that engagement with education as a consumer will lead to individual success. However, the intangible goal of 'reaching one's potential' can lead to disengagement and disillusionment on the part of students. As an antidote to this, Ruth suggests that embedded contemplative practices and opportunities for dialogic encounter with students can help develop an awareness of internal motivations for study and encourage questioning of assumptions about the purpose of being in higher education. In short, this is about encouraging focus on the experience and process of learning rather than on future outcomes. Similarly, the mindful use of language and clear contracting can serve to lessen the messiness of unclear expectations and boundaries of the academic contract. For staff, an awareness of institutional reactivity to student dissatisfaction and distress can highlight practices that favour technical means to 'student satisfaction' over the transformational practices that encourage learning as an intrinsically motivated process of personal growth and challenge.

In the next chapter Pete explores the ideas of the 'pedagogical self' as a way that students construct and transform themselves in late modernity. It explores student experiences of higher education on their youth and community work course at Newman University. It illustrates how the critical pedagogy they encountered there made available an alternative representational space, enabling them to develop a major transformation of their sense of identity. It foregrounds their naming of pedagogy as central, in their terms, to this self-transformation, coining the term 'pedagogical self'. First, the author suggests that the students' experiences need to be read through the theoretical lens of late modern subjectivity which places demands on students to build skills of reflexivity. He then outlines a number of features of the pedagogic approach that seem to underpin this process of self-reinvention and reflexive awareness. These include orthodox Freirean praxis such as the use of generative themes, along with more experimental methods such as the assessment of improvisational dispositions in students and the creation of opportunities for building psychic recognition of the 'other' in the classroom. The chapter concludes by outlining the potential for these innovative approaches to be mirrored elsewhere as a way of actualizing critical pedagogy within the constraints of neoliberal forces in the higher education sector.

Again, exploring youth and community work student experiences, but from a very different angle, in the next chapter Pauline and a group of students explore the emotional impact of critical pedagogy practice on non-traditional students. It examines the impact that using a critical pedagogy philosophy, approach and practice has on the students' higher education experience, with a focus on the emotional state that this approach inevitably brings about. In particular, it explores and shares from direct experience, from both the student and the lecturer, the nature of this emotional response. It is posited that this emotional response comprises two complimentary components: partly based on a student's recognition of inequality; but also, on the use of non-formal learning methodologies within classroom.

The following chapter contributes to the discussion about critical pedagogy, Giroux (2011) transformative learning and what Freire (1968) describes as 'conscientization'; the latter concerns the experiences of non-traditional students, and the role and responsibilities of the lecturer. This two-way, collaborative, responsibility for the 'education' journey is also explored. Drawing on co-operative enquiry Heron (1996) methodology, and narrative interviews (Clandinin and Connelly, 2004) with 'non-traditional' students, the chapter explores the contemporary nature of inequality and how the various forms of inequality intersect (Crenshaw, 1989) and overlap in higher education and society. An overtly critical feminist standpoint is explored, as well as critiquing the notion that emotion has no place within the academic realm. Utilizing a dialogic, participatory and experiential approach to teaching and learning (Chow et al., 2003), this chapter seeks to speak, capture and value this complex process as well as to privilege the student's narrative.

Hopeful Pedagogies in the Spaces In-between

This subpart explores a number of experiences of 'third-space' professional staff who operate in-between educational spaces, starting with Peter's experience of academic advising. In the first chapter, Peter discuss issues arising from reflection on twelve years of HE academic advising and student support including two years working with Newman University's students, a majority of whom come from 'widening participation' contexts. It is important to understand the impacts of neoliberal policy on the lived experience of students and on the HE system. Adoption of neoliberal values in a marketized HE system can lead to 'industrial' approaches that objectify and instrumentalize students and undermine our ability to work from a genuinely student-centred perspective. Such values can enhance experiences of alienation and discourage integration of students' lived experiences into their studies. He sees the advisory encounter as one important space in the contested HE environment wherein this can be countered. Peter discusses 'pedagogical love' as a framework which should lead us to genuinely know and value our students; he considers what it means to love our students. He suggests that this should include our evaluation of how well our institutional processes and structures acknowledge and accommodate the reality of our students' lives. We have a responsibility to practise and cultivate the values of pedagogical love throughout the institution. We should also be actively prepared to challenge, expose and disrupt practices and values that are contrary to them

In the second chapter of this subpart, Tina explores how, as the International Co-ordinator, she feels she is in a privileged position for two reasons. She has a legitimate reason to work across the institution and second, she is allowed to work autonomously. The words 'legitimate' and 'allowed' are important as in the main she has not actually asked permission but looked for the open doors. This chapter discusses the benefits of collaborative work with academics, professional staff and students in co-constructing outcomes that enables us to be student-centred. This sometimes means resisting the structural constraints that are assumed to be immoveable within a HE environment. The benefits of working across departmental and subject areas mean sometimes unlikely collaborations and ideas arise and the more this is done, the more it models possibilities for further work. Tina feels it is important to admit that she is able to work this way, which is, in part, due to her personal propensity to disregard boundaries, being what Whitchurch calls an 'unbounded professional' (2013, p. 8). Where she does see boundaries, it is natural to find alternative paths. However, working in a hierarchical and bounded institution is not without problems and raises interesting questions about why working differently can be troublesome for some. Therefore, this chapter is about exploring these tensions and offering solutions through practical examples. The more we work together the more we find we are pushing at an open door.

In the third chapter of this subpart 'Quality assurance or assured silence?', Lorraine begins by acknowledging that students with dyslexia are known to be the largest volume of students with disabilities within UK higher education institutions (Rodgers et al., 2015; HESA, 2015). Increasingly, monitoring and restricting Disabled Students Allowance (DSA) funding for students with dyslexia in higher education contributes to delays in accessing expert support. This issue has become a progressive obstacle for students as, despite being identified with dyslexia, they are not able to access dyslexia support until funding is confirmed by Student Finance England (SFE), which presents particular difficulties for smaller higher education institutions who seek to attract students from non-traditional backgrounds, such as Newman. In this chapter, Lorraine presents an overview and discussion of access issues that arise in practice. She argues that, without guidance to aid navigation through forms and agencies, higher education students with dyslexia can become lost in bureaucratic processes that in effect prioritize procedure over access. More specifically, drawing upon the works of Giroux (2014, [2011] 2017, 2001) and Freire (1996), Lorraine use the concept of critical pedagogy as a base from which to interrogate the impact of audit culture (Shore and Wright, 1999, 2015) and the role that power plays (Foucault, [1975] 1995; Morley, 2003) in the negotiation and navigation of DSA support. This chapter argues that the combination of increased monitoring through DSA audits, and the different demands and requirements of needs assessors, SFE, higher education institutions/service providers, dyslexia tutors and students, contributes to a cumbersome and confusing system that, whether intentionally or not, results in systemic discrimination against higher education students with dyslexia. The chapter is addressed to tutors of students with dyslexia and professionals in higher education.

Hopeful Pedagogies Beyond the Institution

In the first chapter of this subpart, Tina and Mike explore how John Henry Newman's vision of a university was of a community of thinkers, with all staff and students coming together for a common cause. To these ends, in 2019 Newman a staff week bringing together academics, support and professional staff and students from across Europe to assess the relevance of the idea of a university as a community for modern higher education institutions and to explore together actions and ideas that can help make it a reality. In keeping with a Freirean approach, they encouraged all parties to think differently, be open to mutual learning and committed to working collectively across traditional boundaries. Building on the Freire concept of generative themes, the themes worked through were developed over the course of the week, rather than being decided beforehand. People had to be prepared to take responsibility for, first, bringing ideas, second, for going through a democratic process to share those ideas and come up with common themes and, third, taking collective responsibility for developing a vision for these themes to become realities. This chapter is a write up of the process of the week and of developing critical and hopeful pedagogy in a higher education institution and serves as an example of developing generative themes, something which is acknowledged as being sadly lacking in the literature.

In the final chapter, Karima and John, having worked first-hand as teachers in the further education (FE) sector followed by managing a successful partnership and community of practice between HE and FE, came to realize the strengths that the FE sector has, in particular its student-centred, action-meaning and action-taking pedagogy. The FE sector's history as a second chance (and for some, second-rate) sector has given it a sense that it is a Cinderella sector – underfunded, under-appreciated.

Consequently, college-based higher education (CBHE) may not be considered to constitute a worthwhile model for the development of academic as well as agentic adults. CBHE, however, the authors believe, is ripe for growth in an over-expensive and increasingly marketized model of HE education (which may mean high-price-low-value). It is a good time to review the way the ideas of Freire (1996), Goodson (2008) and others who herald a pedagogy of and for 'the oppressed' can be realized in CBHE. This is not to suggest that FE colleges have not also adapted to the needs of a marketized, outcomes-based education but that CBHE lecturers have strong beliefs in inclusive pedagogy, outreach to all, learner-centred teaching, local provision and the diversity of their own profiles and experiences (see Kadi-Hanifi and Keenan, 2015, 2016). Often, the lecturers had experiences of being failed by schools, alienated by a hierarchical class system and 'rescued' by the FE sector.

As FE colleges have to adapt to the expansion of their HE provision they seem to be reinventing themselves, but to what extent can they keep the strengths that managed to 'save' many youngsters from failure or falling out of the education system altogether? This chapter calls for a greater confidence in CBHE, starting with a sense of identity and unity among providers. It also calls for a greater research profile among the lecturers and a promotion of the transformational learning that the sector has provided at its best. The obstacles to this are outlined and critically examined in this chapter. These include the business-model approach adopted by some FE providers, the restricted curriculum brought on by national funding priorities (such as for apprenticeships and key skills) as well as other more subtle, but potentially detrimental, barriers to the success of a CBHE, such as the hierarchy that seems to prevail in the wider HE sector, making CBHE seem inferior, less rigorous and less prestigious than universities. The chapter uses the voices of those teaching and managing in the sector alongside a range of critical sources to make a case that CBHE could be not only a site of resistance to the marketization of HE, but also a new hope.

Conclusion: Taking Forward Hopeful Pedagogies in Higher Education

Overall, we have a simple conclusion: critical hopeful pedagogies are possible in higher education, but there are permanent tensions to be ameliorated in trying to enact them. A number of themes that have emerged and criss-cross across the chapters are then outlined. These are that:

1. Self-identifying critical pedagogues need to cultivate hope and articulate its importance.
2. As SICPs we need to both loosen, and be sure of, our boundaries and develop explicit contracts with students including expectations of each other.
3. SICPs should have a collective approach and need the right practice architectures to be effective.
4. Critical pedagogic spaces should be authentic, visceral, pedagogic and in the moment, but not necessarily safe.

5. SICPs should not forget our indigenous knowledges once we enter HE.
6. SICPs have more in common than we do difference, across subjects and staff divides – our differences enrich us.
7. Students are pedagogues, producers and partners, not consumers and customers.
8. Being student- and staff-centred have been colonized terms. Do not invest in internal conflicts and let them become part of your identity terms – we need to move towards being human.
9. We can work within higher education's structures, but continually need to push them and highlight their absurdity.
10. SICPs need to help rearticulate what a university is and could be.

Part I

Key Ideas and the Conceptual and Policy Terrain

Chapter One

Key Concepts in Critical Pedagogy

How We Teach

Mike Seal, Response from Alan Smith

Introduction

Many students in higher education will have gone through at least twelve years of indoctrination into what education is and, even if their experiences have often been negative, it is nonetheless the model they have internalized and expect when they go into a classroom. To counter this, the first thing I give to students on the courses I teach is a document called 'How we teach', which tries to pull apart and reconstruct any expectations of education. I will refer to it several times in this chapter as it tries to put the idea of critical pedagogy in 'lay' terms. The opening lines of the document are as follows:

> You might have thought university would consist of a teacher, who 'knows' the 'subject', at the front of a classroom giving a 'lecture' i.e. giving you information which you are to write down. At some point you will be required to regurgitate this information back in the form or an essay or exam to show that you understood. You then promptly forget this information to make room for the next bit of knowledge you are meant to 'learn'. For us this is not education, this is temporary rote learning of uncontested information. In this day and age, you can quickly access what we could give you in terms of information via the internet in seconds – so what is the point of that? For us education is something else, it is helping you become critical thinkers to discover, or uncover, knowledge and assess its worth.

This implies that we also need to challenge associated structures of education, such as exams, assignments and 'learning outcomes', and I think we should. Fundamental for educators is to give students, and people in general, the tools to undo, rethink and challenge their received wisdoms about what constitutes knowledge and education. This goes against a tradition of teacher-dominated education where the learner and teachers operate what Freire (1972) calls a 'banking' approach whereby the student receives a fixed curriculum that they accept unquestioningly. I think the undoing and reforming of educational expectations needs to be an active process. Ira Shor, a critical pedagogue, says we are trying to cultivate in learners:

> Habits of thought, reading, writing, and speaking which go beneath surface meaning, first impressions, dominant myths, official pronouncements, traditional cliches, received wisdom, and mere opinions, to understand the deep meaning, root causes, social context, ideology, and personal consequences of any action, event, object, process, organization, experience, text, subject matter, policy, mass media, or discourse. (Shor, 2012, p. 129)

This is the starting point for the tradition of critical pedagogy. This chapter will explore the key concepts of critical pedagogy and assess whether the approach has potential resonance with educationalists looking for 'another way', who wish to make education vital and relevant again. It will look at critical pedagogy's background and its views on the nature of knowledge and learning. It will examine some key principles of its educational approach and some of its characteristics and techniques.

Background on Critical Pedagogy

Critical pedagogy has existed as an approach to education for over forty years. The ideas behind critical pedagogy were first described by Paulo Freire (1972) and have since been developed by authors such as Henry Giroux, Ira Shor, Michael Apple, Joe L. Kincheloe, Shirley R. Steinberg and Peter Maclaren. It is a broad school that combines critical theory, a neo-Marxist approach and educational theory. It grew out a concern among educationalists with how education was being used as a method to reinscribe power relations in society.

Critical pedagogy seeks to illuminate the oppressed about their situation in which the state and the education system create a 'common sense' that reinscribes dominant elites' social positions as 'natural and inevitable'. It seeks to interrogate received wisdoms and 'go beneath surface meaning, first impressions, dominant myths, official pronouncements, traditional clichés, received wisdom, and mere opinions' (Shor, 2012, p. 125). As well as Marxism, critical pedagogy draws on other influences including humanism, existentialism and post-colonialism (Seal, 2014; Davies, 2012). Giroux (2020) describes it as an

> educational movement, guided by passion and principle, to help students develop consciousness of freedom, recognize authoritarian tendencies, and connect knowledge to power and the ability to take constructive action. (Giroux, 2020, p. 1)

Knowledge and Education: What Are They and Who Creates Them?

What is Education?

In understanding critical pedagogy, it is important to outline and undo our preconceptions about what education is and what it is not, what knowledge is and is not and to de-neutralize education and acknowledge its inherently political nature. Critical pedagogy seeks to challenge traditional concepts of both knowledge and education. A common association with knowledge, and particularly theory, is that it is something created or discovered by 'objective', 'neutral' 'experts', often under scientific conditions. Knowledge and theory are therefore abstracted from most people's everyday lived experience. Education is then traditionally seen as the process whereby this 'knowledge', often via a teacher who 'knows' it, is given to students who do not.

The process of students absorbing this knowledge is called 'learning'. When a student applies this 'learning' to their experiences, it should make sense of them. However, if it does not apply, they have either not understood the knowledge properly, or applied it properly, or their experiences are 'not representative'. Critical pedagogy challenges these views on knowledge and education on many levels

What is Knowledge?

Aristotle makes a claim for three types of knowledge. The first is 'episteme', which is scientific knowledge that largely does not change (although this idea is itself heavily contested). Second is 'techne', which is the technical knowledge and skills a person needs to put this science to use. His third type of knowledge is 'phronesis'. 'Phronesis' says we need to ask *why* we are applying this knowledge – what our aim for doing this is and what moral values we are operating to when we do. The person is making a judgement about what knowledge we apply in *particular* situations. We should not try and find universal truths that apply to people, as the variables are so great and in flux.

Aristotle saw this as particularly important when taking about people and society rather than about objects. However, phronesis has fallen from favour as a concept, because it necessitates judgement, and also recognizes that social situations and phenomena are contextual and there are rarely fixed truths.

Everyone has a view on society and what is valuable, therefore this knowledge is not neutral and we should all be a part of creating it. Much of what is presented by ruling elites and educational systems as episteme, i.e. as facts that are objective, neutral and natural, are, in actuality, 'phronesis', knowledge that is a result of, and underpinned by, a particular moral view, a choice, and, as such, could be different. Much in society, including the idea of education itself, is not neutral, but stems from a particular ideology. Indeed, attempts to say education should be neutral, again re-enforces a view of society that favours existing power structures and hinders change.

Who Gets to Create Knowledge: Praxis

A part of not being neutral, and having values and morals behind the application of knowledge, is that knowledge, for critical pedagogues, needs to relate to the lived experiences of people, and where necessary, seek to change it for the better. One word for this is praxis and critical pedagogy has consistently described itself as a praxis (Batsleer, 2012; Smith, 1994; Ord, 2000). Praxis is often interpreted as the synthesis of theory and action. However, it is more complex, subtle and radical than this. Critical pedagogy has a dynamic, dialectical view of how knowledge is created (Aristotle, 1976). It sees knowledge as an evolving thing (Carr and Kemmis, 1989):

> knowledge is not static, it is dynamic. It is created through dialogue. In a very real sense I cannot tell you what is right, for there is rarely a 'right'. Common sense is rarely common, as in everyone agrees, or makes sense in that it is logical. Facts that were 'known' 100 years ago, are now discredited. Those in power might tell you that it is 'common sense' that things stay as they are. Knowledge is power and rarely neutral. ('How we teach')

Principles of Critical Pedagogy: Democracy, Consciousness-raising and Developing Critical Thinkers

Democracy and Equality in Learning Environments

Critical pedagogues also view knowledge as something we create through dialogue with each other. Cho (2010) describes knowledge as 'democratic, context-dependent, and appreciative of the value of learners' cultural heritage' (Cho, 2010, p. 315). The creation of this evolving knowledge is an active democratic process that entails interrogation of the world by all parties. However, this means not simply acknowledging the diversity and multiculturalism in the room, accepting people's views of their cultures as monolithic. Critical pedagogy may well entail challenging and changing cultural norms (Freire, 1972, p. 12), as being oppressed does not make us less subject to dominant hegemonies. However, learners have their own theories and ideas about the world, and this needs to be our starting place (Bolton, 2010). We try and capture the spirit of this in 'How we teach', declaring:

> We try, in what we teach and how we teach, to create these dialogical spaces. We want to create a debate about a topic which will inspire you to go and find out more about it. We will try and make these spaces democratic – that you can challenge us, and each other, and even change what we are learning.

This can be difficult for some educators as it means, as Foley notes (2007), that they need to challenge the structure they operate within including their own teaching approaches and, fundamentally, the 'power which is given to them through their titles' (Foley, 2007). As we say in 'How we teach', we need to be explicitly humble and challenging of our own privilege. 'Sometimes you will know more than we do, and we should acknowledge this and let you educate us.'

To be a critical educator can mean challenging the power the 'teacher' has in the educational spaces they inhabit. Years of experience of education in its narrow school form means that the 'teacher' gets a certain level of deference. They are assumed to be 'in charge', of both the educational experience and the classroom itself, and learners are passive receivers of information. As Joldersma (1999) notes, there is a certain familiar complacency in this for learners; they can sit back and receive, not taking responsibility for their learning, or the learning environment. Some learners passively resist, as they may have done at school, taking small chances to undermine the authority of the teacher. However, this can be in a non-constructive way that can in turn be infantilized by the teacher. Resistance can also happen when encountering new ideas, as well as ways of conveying them, As Kopelson notes:

> Resistance is often, at the least, understandably protective: As anyone who can remember her or his own first uneasy encounters with particularly challenging new theories or theorists can attest, resistance serves to shield us from uncomfortable shifts or all-out upheavals in perception and understanding-shifts in perception which, if honored, force us to inhabit the world in fundamentally new and different ways. (Kopelson, 2003, p. 120)

For the learning to be real, this 'play' of accepted roles again needs to be challenged.

> To be democratic means that we all have responsibility for these spaces. We have heard students say that it is the tutor's 'job' to 'control' the class. Where is the democracy in that? – there are 30 of you and only one of us. Also, if we control the class though our perceived power, either of our personality or status, haven't we all fallen into the same old traps again?

Teachers have to admit their vulnerabilities in an educational environment, that they are not all-knowing and their 'power' is an illusion which students can, and should, challenge. I have had colleagues who have found this difficult. However, at the same time, critical pedagogues challenge constructions of democracy in education as consumerism. In this view, students pay for a product that they consume, often embodied in comments about 'what do I pay my fees for?'. Under this construction, education needs to be delivered in a way that they like and say things that they like – this is not critical pedagogy, which can be very challenging. As we say in 'How we teach':

> while we are trying to provide stimulus, we are not entertainers. It is not our job to perfectly match your 'learning style' – how many learning styles are in one room? It is all too easy to fall back into being a consumer of knowledge, 'give me what I want in the way I say I want it'. Remember we are creating knowledge together, and at times there will be clashes, conflict and worst of all apathy and boredom – it is the responsibility of all of us to work these things through.

Developing Critical Thinkers

The most important thing we are doing as educators is enabling people to become critical thinkers: knowledge creators, able to apply and synthesize new ideas and information into new ways of thinking as situations change and evolve. The break between experience, practice and theory needs to be challenged and students need to see how they have a right and a duty to create new knowledge. As we say in 'How we teach':

> We hear a lot of students say that they are not academic, they are practical, they learn by doing. There is a lot of truth in this statement, but for all of us. Much learning is experiential and all knowledge creation is – we try things out and discover them for ourselves how they work. You do not learn to ride a bike through a book, you do it by trying it out – and sometimes the instructions are wrong and need to be challenged – by you.

However, this is not an easy process. Learning to be critical is, and should be, challenging, particularly as the first thing we need to do is challenge our own assumptions about learning and re-evaluate our previous experiences of it. Capitalism is clever in that it distances people from their natural critical thinking skills and at the same time encourages people to think individualistically about their views, as though they are commodities to which they have a right. Both sides of this need to be challenged, as we say in 'How we teach'.

> Some say the essentials of education are reading, writing and arithmetic. This comes from Arabic education and was originally reading, writing and logic. Logic being how to reason and argue and for us this is crucial. Schooling has forgotten this. Often students say, after asserting something, 'well that's what I think', quickly followed by 'I am entitled to my opinion', as if your views are a commodity. Sorry, but in our spaces, this isn't good enough – you have to defend your opinions, be open to change, and sometimes have the bravery to stand alone.

Consciousness-raising

Critical Pedagogy challenges any form of domination, oppression and subordination with the goal of emancipating oppressed or marginalized people.
(Aliakbari and Faraji, 2011, p. 77)

More fundamentally, as Aliakbari and Faraji (2011) go on to state, critical pedagogy aims to 'transform oppressed people and to save them from being objects of education to subjects of their own autonomy and emancipation'. Fundamental here is the idea of developing critical consciousness, the process of which Freire calls 'conscientization'. Drawing on Gramsci, it is the aforementioned idea that people need to unlearn the received wisdoms that society wishes them to believe, particularly about the naturalness and inevitability of their oppression. Critical pedagogues work to encourage students to 'develop a critical consciousness of who they are and what their language represents by examining questions of language, culture, and history through the lens of power' (Brito, Lima and Auerbach, 2004, p. 23).

Freire (1972) names three levels of consciousness: intransitive, semi-transitive and critical consciousness. Those with an intransitive consciousness accept their lives as they are and take the view that any changes are either for reasons beyond their control or are seen as fate. Those with a semi-transitive consciousness are aware of their problems and still think of them as inevitable, but they may think they can change things on a local level. Actions are therefore often localized and short-term.

It is only when people have a critical consciousness that they see the structural dimensions of their problems, making connections between their problems and the social context in which these problems are embedded, both in terms of analysis and actions that will challenge their structural oppressions as well as addressing some of their immediate concerns.

There are issues with the idea of conscientization, particularly the idea of 'false consciousness', in that it presents those who are oppressed as not having agency and awareness, needing an outsider to enlighten them. However, this underestimates people, as Zachariah says:

> Do ordinary men and women need to be conscientized before they recognize that they lead desperate, oppressed lives marked by hunger, disease, and the denial of dignity? They know the score and do not need middle class do-gooders to tell them. They acquiesce in their oppression because they have no other choice. (Zachariah, 1986, p. 123)

Nevertheless, consciousness-raising remains pivotal. However, its focus and who takes responsibility for it may need to shift. Rancière (1992) critiqued Bourdieu for privileging the role of the intellectual and condemning the masses as unknowing and in need of liberation. Instead. Rancière views the working class as inherently capable of learning and developing intellect. However, they have been led to believe that they are not intelligent by a hegemonic system that deliberately undermines their self-belief. In addition, they may have lost the will to use their analytic abilities, in the face of seemingly monolithic social forces where they have been forced to prioritize short-term survival.

For Rancière, the pedagogue should act under the assumption that we are all intelligent enough to understand the world, and that, given access to resources, we can discern the knowledge that will facilitate this understanding. He invites the pedagogue to become 'ignorant', not to deny their knowledge, or hide it, but to privilege it – we should 'uncouple our mastery from our knowledge'. The role of the educator is two-fold. First, to act on the students' will, self-belief and efficacy, the will to engage and challenge themselves and others, and to desire to learn. As we echo in 'How we teach'

> We have heard some students groan when we don't give 'answers', and ask us why we are making it hard for them, can we not just tell them what is right. This is not us being awkward. In a very real sense I cannot tell you what is right, for there is rarely a 'right'. We have to create and contest knowledge together.

Second, an educator's role is to attend to the content of what argument people are creating – but only in terms of ensuring people's arguments have logic and internal consistency – and that they attend to, understand and deconstruct the language behind those arguments and the concepts behind the language. This entails gaining access to resources – often intellectual resources – but it does not mean we determine the content of those resources. This is not always an easy process, or unchallenging, as we say to students:

> The language we use, for this is our major medium, is laden with concepts, ideas and assumptions, and it needs to continually be unpacked and re-packed. Avoid the trap of asking for things in 'plain English' as it does not exist. We do not try and be obscure, but it is equally not our job to translate everything for you. Some ideas are hard to sometimes understand because they are trying to look at difficult things – they are not obvious because they are trying to get beyond the obvious. However, sometimes ideas are deliberately made hard - those with power trying to keep power by using long words to silence you – the onus is on you to not let this happen.

Characteristics and Techniques of Critical Pedagogy

Some of the fundamental techniques within critical pedagogy that flow from these principles are as follows: having a flexible curriculum with authentic materials, finding teachable moments and discovering generative themes.

Flexible Curriculum and Using Authentic Materials

A fundamental within critical and emancipatory education is that no one methodology can work for all cultures, populations and situations (Degener, 2001). All decisions related to curricula, including the material to be studied, should be based on the needs, interests, experiences and situations of students (Giroux, 202020; Shor, 1992). Furthermore, students, as Giroux (2020) puts it, should be active participants in designing and correcting the curricula. Most fundamentally, the curriculum needs to relate to the lived social and economic lives of the learner, and help them move from the 'micro' of their situations and crises to see the wider socio-economic forces behind them, and their contradictions (Degener, 2001).

Furthermore, the materials used for education should come from and have resonance with people's everyday lives and include books poems, films, adverts etc. (Ohara, Saft and Crookes, 2000; Kessing-Styles, 2003; Kincheloe, 2005). They can be brought to the table by tutors and students equally, and especially students as their consciousness develops. It is in linking people's everyday experiences and crises to wider socio-economic forces that people start to see 'both the reproductive nature and the possibility of resistance to problematic content' (Aliakbari and Faraji, 2011, p. 80).

Generative Themes

Taking this further is the idea of generative themes (Aliakbari and Faraji, 2011). This is where the group, in deciding the curriculum and theme to be explored, is seeking themes with certain characteristics. Themes should, first, be a galvanizing force for the community, something about which there is passion and feelings. Second, the theme must have tensions and contradictions within it, things that do not add up that need to be worked through and have a potential to create something new that resolves these tensions. These tensions should not be allowed to become negative, but their energy turned into a positive incentive to change. Generative themes should also open up discussion about, and relate to, wider social issues. In doing so they can lead to the opening up of other generative themes (i.e. a generative theme has the seed of other generative themes within it). Finally, generative themes must have the potential for action: that something concrete can be done about them.

Within the foundation year, we get students to explore their own educational experiences, and not to see themselves as in deficit. They then explore higher education and look at who it is for and how it is structured. A field trip is organized to Oxford – both the university and the town – and many students experience a visceral sense of contradictions and unease, aware of their own lack of social capital, coterminous with a belief that they have a right to higher education. This is then unpacked back at the university and has meant that a number of students have become engaged in challenging the Augar Report, which is a direct threat to foundation years and widening participation.

Teachable Moments

One of the characteristics of critical pedagogy is the ability to think in the moment and to improvise (Seal and Harris, 2014; Smith, 1994). This can mean recognizing that a particular session plan is not working or having resonance, and adjusting it accordingly. On another level it can mean spotting and seizing an opportunity to relate a discussion to wider issues. However, the responsibility for this should not lie with the pedagogue alone. Key features of my own foundation year include three hours a week of a curriculum-free, student-led, small-group tutorial. This is cited by students as one of the transformative elements of the course.

Conclusion: The Need for Hope and Symbolic Resistance.

We talked in the introduction about the danger of critical pedagogy: it is good at critique but leaves us with little hope. We will look at this further in the next chapter when we explore how critical pedagogues can leave students in higher education with a sense of 'learned hopelessness'. Freire always came back to hope and talked about the need for hope as a fundamental part of being human:

Hope is an ontological need . . . I am hopeful, not out of mere stubbornness, but out of an existential concrete imperative. (2004a, p. 2)

Crucially, as a part of the human condition, the role of education is not conceived as instilling hope but rather evoking it (Webb, 2010). However, Webb did not see it as faith, or a naive belief in fate that leads to utopianism over action. He also recognized that it takes time, and action rather than reflection can be a false road. Another statement by Freire on hope is that 'the impatiently patient wait' (Freire, 2004a, p. 81). This is an interesting way of putting it. He wants to dissociate true authentic hope from the 'naïve rebelliousness born of willful impatience' (2004a, p. 64). Freire equates hope with love, trust, serenity, humility, courage and perseverance (2004a, pp. 82–3). Freire warns that the hope of the progressive educator cannot be that of 'an irresponsible adventurer' (2004a, p. 77). Several times in his writings Freire equates hope with 'waiting' – not the passive waiting of one who folds their arms in resignation but the 'active waiting' of one who persistently seeks and struggles (Freire, 1972). I have commented on this elsewhere, in looking at youth and community workers, who see critical pedagogy as their driving force, with regard to the balance between hope and realism and the dangers of the rhetorical radical.

> We should not fall into traps of thinking that if the rebellion does not take power, the revolution does not succeed, we have failed. Foucault taught us that power plays out at lots of levels, so by definition it can be contested at those levels – and will eventually start to falter at them. There is power in symbolic resistance, just as there is reality in the symbolic violence of the state. Symbolic resistance becomes part of a mythology that others take up and carry as expressions of hope. Only the deluded or selfish think the revolution will happen in their lifetime, it is a greater project we are all a part of. (Seal and Frost 2014)

Response from Alan Smith

As I sit enjoying Mike's latest chapter on critical pedagogies, I am struck by the irony of my situation. Like Mike and his colleagues, I lead and manage a youth and community work programme, underpinned by a similar ideological foundation, informed by models of empowerment education and Freirean values. However, unlike Mike's utopian ideals, and the practices his team have embraced, I am just about to 'mark' my fourteenth rather bland response to a predetermined essay question, using a predetermined marking schema and pro forma to judge the 'learning' of yet another youth and community work student. I will decide what mark it deserves, and whether it meets the required standards as defined by the university.

This nexus – as opposed to the praxis presented by Mike – marks the conundrum at the heart of our work. While I can teach in a way that reflects the values and ethics of our shared belief in critical pedagogy, I can embrace the sharing of knowledge and power, the journeying together such that my praxis is informed by democratic principles. Yet ultimately, the demands of the academy are such that the power dynamic returns at the point of assessment; in fact, it is present throughout the course design and the curriculum model which shape and guides it. In presenting his principles of critical pedagogy, Mike acknowledges the significance of knowledge, learning, dialogue and challenging dominant hegemonies through the way we teach, but he completely ignores the missing part of the equation – the power dynamics at play within the combined bureaucracies of higher education funding regimes, Quality assurance systems and procedures and the requirements of a professional body which may espouse innovation, empowerment and advocacy but which operates, as do other professional, statutory and regulatory bodies, to perpetuate the safety of an existing model. Youth and community work courses represent a failed testimony to Freire's work, the development and design of a course, underpinned by values and ethics and benchmarked against both occupational standards and benchmark statements which encompass empowerment, but which require adherence, having been constrained by these validation requirements, further constraints are applied to meet the funding criteria and institutional quality requirements.

By the time we actually teach a student, the course (or topic) has been sanitized and disempowered by a range of bureaucratic castration such that the only 'space' in the student experience of learning happens when the 'teacher' *chooses* (power-laden in itself, as it implies privilege) to apply critical pedagogy to the teaching – it does not remove any of the dominant practices of higher education: submission deadlines, Harvard Referencing and marking criteria. In acknowledging this, I can apologetically shrug my shoulders and say I share responsibility for the aspects of university life I have some control over, but all that does is reinforce that which is not open for negotiation or sharing. Maybe this mirrors Freire's commitment to empowering impoverished workers by giving them access to the language of their oppressors, and helping them see the nature of their oppression – but if the closest I can offer is to tell students that life is tough and they must 'learn to play the game of higher education', I am offering neither a critical nor an emancipatory education.

Chapter Two

Critiques of Critical Pedagogy

The Post-critical

Leoarna Mathias and Mike Gilsenan, Response from Joris Vlieghe

Introduction

Leoarna: While he was working on his doctorate, Mike encountered post-critical literature, and shared it with colleagues while presenting a paper at our university's learning and teaching conference. I was in the audience, and went away to read the key sources Mike had shared. A little while later, the idea for this book emerged, and we saw this as an opportunity to bring this scholarship, and the ways in which it both informed and reflected our teaching practice, together. To construct the chapter we wrote a series of reflections, with the loose aim of 'conversing' with each other and introducing each other to the post-critical texts that had inspired each of us. We noticed a difference in our voices, and points of debate between our perspectives, but also shared connections, and understandings of what it is we do in the teaching space. The initial abstract for the chapter stated:

> We have an idea to move beyond the cynicism and despair, as well as the ideological utopianism that can sometimes characterise critical pedagogy: instead, we wish to do good work without needing to see it 'direct' our students to particular ends. In this way we 'meet' the ideas that surface within the post-critical literature.

What follows is our written conversation, in which we hope to demonstrate the impact that both critical pedagogy and the post-critical literature can have in shaping teaching and learning in higher education that can and does resist instrumentality.

Leoarna

I thoroughly enjoyed Mike and mine's first serious conversation about our book chapter. I came away from it seeing how the shared elements of our life-script thus far were going to help us in our writing.

Like me, Mike did not know he was going to be an academic, and had done plenty of other things with his time on the planet before he felt he could actually say he was one. This blend of practitioner and lecturer was something we mulled over at length, recognizing that it gives us a particular perspective on the HE classroom. Our disciplines prior to becoming lecturers were also ones that value democracy in the learning space and the active power of the learner to make his/her own choices; Mike in youth work, me in early childhood.

There was some light and shade between our stories of being HE students ourselves, but a narrative overlap in terms of feeling a little of what the academy likes to call 'imposter syndrome' (when I read professors on Twitter saying they feel it, I realize that everyone does, and so no one is the imposter . . .). We were both comfortable to be working at Newman, recognizing that elements of the approach of the place, the students who come here, the attitude of at least some of our colleagues, made the choice to work at Newman just that – a conscious choice. We both travel some considerable distance to work here, and do so part time, to allow for a life in other places with people we love. But we like the place, for all its flaws, and believe that the work we do here makes a difference.

As we talked, we remembered some of the things we had both read that had led us to think of the idea of writing the chapter to begin with. A rhizomous pattern emerged: Mike had given a paper at Newman, I had gone away and read some of his references because I could see overlap with my doctoral studies, I had shared them with my supervisor, and so the wheels turn. Zamojski, Vlieghe and Hodgson's work (e.g. 2018) stands out as a starting point. The basic premise appears to be that they are keen to sidestep the hole that critical pedagogy has dug itself into, and simply state that if we focus on doing good work in the classroom, good will follow. We cannot know whether we have educated for revolution, and we should avoid stating that we are doing so – because this is as dogmatic as the very constructs, such as neoliberalism or the market, that critical pedagogy is seeking to critique (Schwimmer, 2019). Holloway himself, whose legacy has in no small part shaped the thinking behind the title of this book, argues that rather than fight against capitalism, we should stop making it (2010, p. 256). Similarly, post-critical thinkers are arguing for us to act, consciously, in ways that do not (just) sustain the negative critique of the world as it is, (but instead) create hope through the doing of work that is performed with good intent.

In our abstract we set out to use the post-critical literature as a starting point for our written conversation, but it feels as if our experiences, rather than our reading, are likely to feature as our beginning.

Mike

We've had a couple of meetings now and I'm only just getting around to putting anything in to a document. I find it interesting, as I think I said when we last met Leoarna, that you have chosen to write as if to someone else. I'm sure we will need to decide on a format when we progress this work to the chapter. However, I don't want to just yet. This is not some statement of pseudo authenticity; I just think it will be easier for me if we write *to* each other as well as talk to each other.

That starting point mentioned at the beginning (where else?) is, I think, what we have been discussing so far. For me, the work I do has always been a seemingly natural progression from, or extension of, the work I did as a youth and community worker. My approach to teaching has always been informed by my experiences of working both with young people in informal settings and with youth work staff in training workshops. The beginning of my lecturing career saw me move from a local authority youth service to the local university. Having been involved in the design and development of a foundation degree in youth and community work, I went on to teach many of my former colleagues from Staffordshire. This, together with my own experience of qualifying during the 1990s in what was then a temporary portacabin behind Waltham Forest YMCA probably contributed to the sense I had, for many years, of not really being involved in a university at all. When I trained, the only students there were youth and community work (informal education as it was called in that particular institution) undergraduates and postgraduates; and when I taught on the foundation degree, I only taught youth and community work students. It was as if we were a discrete group of people who happened to be in a university building.

In recent years I have become increasingly aware that my youth and community practice was some fifteen years ago. A paper I delivered, 'How do you keep your teaching relevant when your practice is old and wrinkly', has now become part of *Teaching Youth Work in Higher Education* (Seal, 2019d). At first, this emerging realization was a cause for concern – what kind of youth and community lecturer can I be if I no longer have recent, relevant practice to call on? However, over time and greatly aided by my current doctoral exploration, I have become more comfortable once again with the identity of *educator*. I say 'once again' because it was an identity I held for many years while in the youth work field. This was, perhaps, as a result of the 'Informal education' title given to the DipHE I gained (I never actually studied for a batchelors degree). The 'education' I sought to engage in was not one of 'subject' and 'knowledge transfer' but one which was, as Mark Smith used to refer to in lectures at the George Williams College, conversation- or relationship-centred. Perhaps this is why I initially struggled to comprehend Vlieghe's (2016) plea for a 'thing-centred' pedagogy. But recalling instances in my practice when I have felt most useful, it was not, as I had previously thought, the times when I have helped young people stand up for their rights or 'stick it to the man' but when young people have been able to feel a deep sense of satisfaction in doing something they found meaningful (be that getting a skatepark built, going on an outdoor adventure or setting up a youth café). Perhaps this is the Rancièrian form of transformation through education to which Vlieghe refers. The 'thing' in each instance was the project, the experience or the ambition. Perhaps my 'thing' is, and always has been, education (pedagogy). Perhaps I engage in a pedagogy-centred pedagogy. There's something here about Gadamer's view of education as self-education 'through a conversational more than adversarial undertaking' (Cleary and Hogan, 2001, p. 520) as well, but I'll leave it there for now.

Leoarna

It was my birthday recently, and I was bought a copy of Rebecca Solnit's book *Hope in the Dark* (2016). It could be a book you just read, the writing is flowing, pleasurable, persuasive, but because I am involved in the writing of this chapter, I keep having to stop and make notes because the nuggets and gems are too good to not 'pin down'. For example:

> Hope locates itself in the premise that we don't know what will happen, and that in the spaciousness of uncertainty there is room to act. (2016, p. xii)

or

> Hope is only a beginning; it's not a substitute for action, only a basis for it. (2016, p. xvi)

In lines such as these Solnit is reflecting back to me very clearly what I believe I am doing when I am teaching. My interest in Buddhism demands a modesty of impact – I can only truly effect change in myself – so when I teach, I must do so without assuming that I can make a difference, direct the revolution, or have impact on an individual or group. I cannot know where the students will take what they discuss with me, and I cannot know whether what I have shared with them is useful, now or later. When I reflect on the teaching that I have most enjoyed receiving or participating in as the student, it has been of the kind where the teacher's love for the subject and their willingness to allow the students to find new interpretations of the material without egotistical agenda or being overly goal-orientated ('I *must* teach them this!') have worked in unison. Rogers declared more than fifty years ago that he had no real interest in teaching students anything that mattered to him, rather it was about honouring what mattered to them (1957b). I agree. This does not mean there is no curriculum in the classroom, no content to consider together; rather, that my sense of self as a teacher is not grounded in being able to persuade everyone else in the room to agree with me.

There is so much good writing out there that articulates the pain of the neoliberal era, that voices our fears for the impact of the market on the process of learning in higher education, on how it positions the student, on how it positions us as the staff working with them. Williams, in his conceptualization of the *Pedagogy of Debt* (2006) eloquently describes the various ways in which paying high fees, and positioning students as consumers has closed down opportunities and narrowed the nature of the relationship between student and teacher, student and institution, teacher and institution too. This rich description of the state of things as they are has been the contribution of critical pedagogy to our worldview, and it has genuinely served to trouble the way in which neoliberalism has become 'invisible to some' (Amsler, 2015, p. 41). But, if I accept the premise that Holloway (2010) explains – that in this era there is no grand revolution to have, capitalism is not about to end, and we must therefore work in the cracks and 'interstitial spaces' (Sutton, 2015, p. 45) – then my choice is either to drown in the hopelessness of living in an era whose politics and practices are so permanently at odds with my own or to feel hope about the good work I can do in those spaces, and trust that they will lead to good things for those I work with.

I want to do as Amsler suggests: to resist the 'totalising critiques of power [that] can obscure more nuanced insight into the real conditions of possibility in any historical juncture' (2015, p. 32) and instead feel the hope that Freire's work instils, when he invites me to recognize that I will likely not see the revolution come to pass, but that I should work towards it anyway (1997). I need to respond to Angela Davis's (2014, p.u.) plea that I/we 'have to act as if it were possible to radically transform the world. And . . . do it all the time'. So Brexit, child poverty, the refugee crisis, the threat of climate change and mass extinctions, the proliferation of polarized populist politics and ongoing wars – none of these things should deter me from my focus on doing good work in the classroom, that honours the agendas students have for the development of their own understanding and active citizenship. As a simple appraisal of the basic tenets of cognitive behavioural therapy would affirm, I have to act, and *then* believe, that 'it is possible to organize society in ways that enable people to lead dignified autonomous mutually engaging and collectively self-determined lives' (Amsler, 2015, p. 30). Humboldt characterized the university as a place where the knowledge remains *unfinished*, while Readings speaks of them as places where we can 'keep questions open' (2012, p. 27). Hopeful post-critical pedagogy, and the literature now shaping it, picks up that thread. As Sutton urges us, 'Progressive educators must not only mind the gap, they must also find the gap . . . discover for themselves the small spaces of praxis . . . in which human knowing, being and doing are transformed' (2015, p. 45). I believe that there are things we wish to 'maintain and protect; something of value to pass on' (Hodgson, Vlieghe and Zamojski, 2018, p. 18) and that hopeful practice within the university is a worthwhile endeavour.

Mike

I find your sentence 'When I reflect on the teaching that I have most enjoyed receiving or participating in as the student, it has been of the kind where the teacher's love for the subject, and their willingness to allow the students to find new interpretations of the material with egotistical agenda, have worked in unison' quite intriguing and somewhat relatable. The notion of 'allowing' the finding of new interpretations together with the acknowledgement of one's ego in the space is both slightly troublesome and reassuring. This is not to criticize your practice in any way, Leoarna. I'm merely interested in how the language we use might contribute to the construction of our own (and other's) worldviews. As McManus Holroyd (2007, p. 2) states: 'Language is pivotal, because it shapes all situations and experiences that we find ourselves in.' I'm troubled by terms that seem to relinquish power, yet at the same time hold on to it. In a similar vein is my perplexity of Hodgson, Vlieghe and Zamojski (2018) discussion of Arendt's (1968) expression of education as a gift. While the discussion is of this *gift* of education as good in and of itself without need for further justification is, I believe, to be celebrated as a positive challenge to a critical pedagogy they describe as both cynical (in its hatred for the world) and its utopianism (in its acknowledgement of unachievable ends), the notion of a *gift* still suggests an owner and a receiver of this education – arguably, perhaps, falling into Freire's (1996) banking model.

But without an exploration of actual practice, I am in danger of remaining in the realm of the cynical myself. With this in mind I am reminded of a seminar I was recently facilitating when the discussion turned to education. We were discussing approaches to teaching when some of the students were comparing my lectures to those of the two other staff members who run the module. There seemed to be some observations that, while all three of us are very personable, my approach was somewhat qualitatively different to the others. Students observed that when being questioned by the other lecturers, it was a one-sided exchange, with students being expected to give answers that would be further questioned or challenged, whereas my approach would be to be a little more conversational. In my session, I had begun with myself and my own experiences growing up as an example of ways in which gender is questioned or challenged. Some students on the day had commented to me that I had made myself quite vulnerable and was therefore quite brave. Students in the seminar were commenting on how I seem to be able to encourage a different kind of conversation and response compared to other lecturers on their courses. In talking about 'banking' and 'problem posing' education (Freire, 1996) I suggested that perhaps my experience as a full-time professional youth worker had afforded me the ability/confidence to step outside some of the traditional conventions that often see teaching as being a mere conduit for knowledge transfer. In relaying some experiences of training to be a qualified HE lecturer, I spoke about my difficulty in separating the human me and the human students from the teaching relationship, which could mean, therefore, that my approach is an exploration of my *relationship* with the subject rather than a reliance on how I can act as a conduit for the information about, or contained within, the subject.

This, I think, leads me to encourage students as humans to explore their relationship with the subject. The exploration of our own and each other's relationship with the subject then, perhaps, embodies not only what Freire (1996) describes as the 'teacher as student and student as teacher' and perhaps a kind of magnified conversation where, as per Gadamer (2013, p. 406), 'the common subject matter is what binds the two partners', but encourages a qualitatively rich *pedagogic* relationship deepened through the sharing of experiences of a particular phenomenon, subject or idea. Perhaps, as Rancière seemed to have done – Vlieghe (2016, p. 5) suggested that 'Rancière reports on what the labourers did in the little free time they had' – we get to know more about the humans in the room. This suggests a relationship-centred as well as 'thing-centred' (Vlieghe, 2016, p. 5) pedagogy. Perhaps my vision is of education as a shared experience rather than a process or a tool to be used for instrumental means and, in a post-critical paradigm, my approach to achieving that vision is ruled by the vision rather than the critique of the present system. An antithesis to Hodgson, Vlieghe and Zamojski (2018) critique of critical pedagogy: 'we are placed in a different reality than the one we want to achieve, and the process of getting there (i.e. education) is not ruled by that dream, but by the criticized present' (p. 10).

Leoarna

A few months back, my now eleven-year-old daughter Penny posed a question, while listening to the news on Radio 2 as we drove to school. The piece was about the quantity of plastic in the oceans, and she said, 'So, what *is* going to happen with all that?' In such moments our parenting philosophy comes sharply into focus: I want to be a realist, but my love for her means I also want to give her hope. I chose to speak about how science, when we give it support and resource, can find solutions to many things, and has done so throughout human history. This seemed to be the right answer, as she has ambitions of being a scientist herself. The conversation moved on to whether her PE kit was in the car and she was ready for her spelling test.

My later reflection on the conversation brought my commitment to, and my faith in, hope, as a 'method for living', into clear view. Balancing reality and hopefulness for children is one thing, and doing it for students in the university is another – but perhaps not so different. I have written with another colleague (Peters and Mathias, 2018) about hope and love in the context of our students, a pedagogical love that Freire's work seeks out in us and asks us to own (1997). This mix of hope and love is perhaps the thing that most takes us beyond the critical and into the post-critical: 'the pedagogue who acts out of love considers education for its own sake and affirms the world' (Schwimmer, 2019, p. 502). This is what I sense I am doing when I work with students.

In his reflections, my co-author Mike has spoken about how he is realizing that his work with students is at its most vibrant (that's my interpretation of what he says) when he is helping them to bring into realization a thing, an idea, a project, an event, that is in turn a representation of their hope for the world. Similarly, I feel that if I can help students overcome the 'thing' that most blocks their path, thus freeing them to learn, then that is as much pedagogy as is my teaching them a slice of content or a specific academic skill. I am, in those moments, holding *for* them an idea of who they can be if we can just overcome together the hurdle they face. Sometimes, things seem bleak to them, and they cannot see that version of themselves that I am choosing to believe is possible. Thus I am, I now see, engaging in an act of faith, I am operating as if they were just about to overcome their challenge and be the learner they want to be. Schwimmer (2019) suggests that for the post-critical pedagogic tradition, 'faith is important . . . because unlike knowledge, it engages the one professing it to commit to what is to come, even though it is unknowable and unpredictable, to act in the present, as if somehow it had anteriorly been proved or affirmed' (Schwimmer, 2019, p. 498). For post-critical pedagogues, the 'world as we know it is not a given' (Schwimmer, 2019, p. 500) and faith is the ingredient that allows us to sustain the hope for the future that is necessary if we are to act as we do in the present.

The baton of hope, borne out of faith that another way is possible, gets passed to us if we are open to it; for me it was meeting colleagues in my present institution, alongside the pleasure of time spent with my PhD supervisor, a man full of real and fervent hope for the university in the twenty-first century. In some of our earliest meetings he boldly and effectively critiqued social policy academics who I had until then admired, and his critique was grounded in what he found to be their *hopelessness*. For him, they had given in to the depressing reality of lived experience in the neoliberal age, and had abandoned the possibility of change, of revolution, of hope. He really meant what he was saying, and his own practice sees him living out his hope for the world. He instigated institution-wide change that brought genuine democracy to his university, and then, rather than sit on his laurels and enjoy the returns of this success, he moved on – to explore other equally profound ways in which the relationship between student and teacher could be reimagined. He offers a living commitment to the hopeful project, exposing me to ideas and to literatures that are guiding me now as I write my contributions for this hope-filled book.

As much as I can, I am trying to marry what I have come to wholeheartedly believe at a philosophical level about the importance of hope in the university, with what I actually do for the students I work with. In doing that, I am part of a collective; colleagues within my own institution, across the sector, and the people whose work I read, all focused on the project of maintaining hope.

At the start of this reflection I spoke of the moment with my daughter, and how my response in that moment was a matter of choice. I chose to share with her my faith in the possibility of a better future, and my hope of a new way of being, doing and living that is just around the corner. Solnit (2016, pp. x–xi) reminds us that we can either focus on the 'hideous economic inequality' that has come to characterize the last twenty years, or the hopeful among us can also see the same passage of time as a 'truly remarkable decade for movement building' (Solnit, 2016, xi). The growth of the post-critical literature is an authentic source of encouragement, to remain open to the idea that universities can be 'autonomous spaces where new beginnings are possible' (Schwimmer, 2019, p. 502).

Response from Joris Vlieghe

I have read Leoarna's and Mike's texts, or better, conversation, with great interest. It seems that the key feature they discern in a post-critical take on education is *hope*, and I would fully agree with this. By doing so they connect the post-critical with the critical tradition (which is firmly based on the idea that it is not necessary for the world to be as it is), but also takes a step beyond this critical approach: if we want to bring about a more hopeful future by continuously making ourselves and our students aware of all the wrongs of this world, we forget that we also can teach in a hopeful way by just paying attention to what we deem valuable (and interesting to work around in schools and in community education).

This is not to say hope is an easy thing, especially not in a world that oftentimes leaves little reason to expect a better future to arrive. This means, using the beautiful words of Isabelle Stengers (2002) that today

> [w]e have all the reasons we wish to despair – to think is to succeed in not following those reasons, one way or another. Thus I would say that hope is the difference

between *probability* and *possibility*. If we follow probability there is no hope, just a calculated anticipation authorized by the world as it is. But, to "think" is to create possibility against probability. (p. 245, italics in original)

Hope is the willingness to think against and beyond probability, that is, situating oneself in life such that cynicism never can have the last say.

Especially for this reason, hope could be called an 'educational attitude': in spite of the darkness that surrounds us – to refer to the title of Solnit's book which Leoarna thankfully brought to my attention – the educator must assume hope. She must display a particular stance and perspective, which is not the evident one to take. This is probably not so different from what Jacques Rancière (1992), one of the main inspiring authors behind the *Manifesto for a Post-Critical Pedagogy* (Hodgson, Vlieghe and Zamojski, 2017), claims when he says that the true teacher is the one who, in spite of all the good reasons one might have to think otherwise, has to assume an equality of intelligences and to act accordingly. One can only teach if one assumes that students and teacher share the same intelligence. Likewise, one can only truly educate if one starts from the conviction that there is no necessity in how we give shape to our world today and if one acts according to this particular conviction.

I would say that acting in such a way also comes with an attitude of *generosity*. Hence, I think I have a slightly different view than Mike when he problematizes the idea put forward in the *Manifesto*, that teaching can be considered a gift. I understand that this may suggest the Freirean notion of banking education. From a Rancièrian point of view, and developing further the idea that hope is at the heart of education, however, the opposite argument could also be made. If I assume equality of intelligences and I – as a teacher – consider something to be valuable, I must trust that others – and in fact everyone else – are capable of learning to appreciate, and maybe even to love, this thing of value. I should not keep what I find meaningful to myself (out of the belief that others are too unintelligent to make sense of it). Moreover, such a gift is a true gift in the sense that by giving it away, one is no longer in control. This can only happen against the background of the teacher's firm belief that others can go on with the world and that they can add new beginnings to the world. This makes education into a hopeful enterprise (cf. Arendt, 1961).

I see this generosity also materialized in Leoarna's and Mike's texts: this is not a traditional piece full of claims but an honest and at times searching and hesitating experiment to express what they hold dear in being educators. Their writing and thinking style is a matter of giving each other, and the readers, something to think about (rather being a matter of owning and claiming ideas). As we attempted to do in the *Manifesto*, they turn thinking about education into a never-ending and – above all – positive conversation. It is my hope we can continue this dialogue in the future.

Chapter Three

Perspectives on the Possibility of Hopeful Critical Pedagogies within Higher Education

Mike Seal, Response from Stephen Cowden

The classroom with all its limitations remains a location of possibility.
(hooks, 2014, p. 12)

I recently spoke at a conference on the tensions of trying to enact critical pedagogy within higher education. In comparing the pedagogic approaches, I noted that critical pedagogy is fundamentally democratic, informal, non-hierarchical with a curriculum determined by participants, that privileges the oppressed and their perspectives, and is committed to action (Seal, 2018, 2019b). Higher education, conversely, is often undemocratic, formal, hierarchical, with a curriculum determined by tutors or national bodies, often reinscribes existing privileges and is distant from lived experience (Seal, 2018, 2019b). Indeed, as Cowden and Singh (2013) note, higher education has long been criticized for its remoteness from the 'real world', culminating in the late 1960s student revolts demanding that higher education reflect the changes happening in the world. However, in present times 'living in the real world' has become serving the demands of the market, rather than questioning its legitimacy.

To compound these intrinsic issues, the penetration of higher education by late-capitalist thinking and structures is well documented, as are the difficulties this causes for anyone trying to develop a critical or 'radical' agenda. Such factors include the increasing domination of 'market logic' and 'managerialism' in planning (Ball, 2012; Zipin and Brennan, 2003), a neoliberal construction of knowledge as a 'form of capital' (Connell, 2013, p. 1), and that knowledge should be directed towards economic growth (Olssen and Peters, 2005, p. 330). Our language is changing; other authors describe how potentially radical concepts such as 'internationalization' have been colonized and rearticulated through neoliberalism as 'globalization' and constructed as the 'interconnectivity' of the world's markets, businesses, culture and people (McCarthy et al., 2009, p. 41).

The literature also details how neoliberalism and neo-conservatism have impacted on the ability of ground-level lecturers to meaningfully enact critical pedagogy, with the intensification of academic work (Davies and Bansel, 2005; Hartman and

Darab, 2012); the creation of a 'performativity' culture (Ball, 2012; H. A. Green, 2012); increased 'accountability' pressures (Bleiklie, 1998; Shore and Wright, 2004); heightened competition (Davies and Bansel, 2007; Nixon, 2011), the commodification and instrumentalization of knowledge and education (Ball, 2012; Bullen, Kenway and Fahey, 2010; Nixon, 2011); the hijacking of public spheres by corporate and militarized interests; and the 'increasing attempts by right-wing extremists to turn education into job training and public pedagogy into an extended exercise in patriotic xenophobia' (H. A. Giroux, 2018).

Writing on trying to enact critical pedagogy within education is not rare. Ira Shor is a key writer in this area; particularly notable is his *A Pedagogy for Liberation*, with Paulo Freire (1987), *Freire for the Classroom: A Sourcebook for Liberatory Teaching* (1987) and *Empowering Education: Critical Teaching for Social Change (2012)*. However, these focus on schools and the United States. As stated in the introduction, many contemporary accounts express a deep cynicism about being able to counter the ever-creeping hegemony of neoliberalism, neo-conservatism and new managerialism within higher education (Cowden and Singh, 2013, Van Heertum, 2006) and there are calls to abandon the attempt (Belton, 2014), or to say that an authentic attempt lies outside the academy (Neary and Saunders, 2011).

Others think that enacting critical pedagogy may be possible, but its ambitions should be more limited (Cooper, 2015), or that we should recognize critical pedagogy's limitations and refocus our ambitions, particularly for social change (Hodgson, Vlieghe and Zamojski, 2018), or concentrate on the power of critical pedagogy to counter the constraints of the financial and managerialist logics which dominate the contemporary university. The work of the Research in Critical Education Studies group at Lincoln University, particularly the work of Mike Neary, is also highly relevant, but again focuses on the erosion of critical education in new public universities.

So, the question seems to be, what is possible? And, if anything, at what level? I will argue that it is possible to enact critical pedagogy within higher education, even at a structural level, although the possibilities are limited. As ever, the real questions seem to lie at the intersection of structure and agency. I argue that in order to enact critical pedagogy we need to reflect on our motivations and intents and build practice architectures that enable critical pedagogy collectively. There is a need to have a community of practice, and not act in isolation.

Structurally, the questions are whether critical pedagogy can be part of the changing aims for public universities and whether SICPs can have structural influence. Debates about the purpose of a university have been conducted for centuries. For Humboldt (1810), a university was a community of scholars and students engaged in a common search for truth. For Newman (1852), we teach students 'to think and to reason and to compare and to discriminate and to analyse'. For Robbins (1963) universities had four objectives: instruction in skills, promotion of the general powers of the mind, advancement of learning and transmission of a common culture and common standards of citizenship. Recent Pearson debates (April 2018) asked whether the purpose of a modern university is to be the guardian of reason, inquiry and philosophical openness, preserving pure inquiry from dominant public opinions, or whether it has changed to a focus on social mobility, allowing more people to transform their lives.

Mahon (2014) usefully breaks down the functions of a university into knowledge and cultural production, civic responsibility and economic development. Knowledge-related functions include the acquisition of knowledge (Habermas, 1989), knowledge generation (Nixon, 2011), the dissemination of knowledge (Altbach, Reisberg and Rumbley, 2009) and public access to knowledge (Calhoun, 2006, p. 13). Knowledge functions are linked to the university's cultural role in society (Bleiklie, 1998), i.e. the transmission of culture (Habermas, 1989, p. 107), promoting cultural self-understanding (Parsons and Patt, 1973, as cited in Habermas, 1989, p. 121) and the continuity and creativity of culture (Calhoun, 2006, p. 10).

The second function is civic purpose (H. A. Giroux, 2010; Walker, 2002). Altbach, Reisberg and Rumbley (2009), Calhoun (2006), H. A Giroux (2010) and Walker (2002) see the university as being about the formation of citizens who can participate meaningfully in public and the formation of a society characterized by a healthy, 'inclusive democracy' (H. A. Giroux, 2010, p. 190). Mahon (2014) sees the university's role in offering a social critique as part of its civic duty (Bleiklie, 1998; H. A. Giroux, 2010; Shore and Wright, 2004), in that we should engage in public political debate (Habermas, 1989, p. 107), provoke public debate (H. A. Giroux, 2010; Shore and Wright, 2004) and frame public debate. H. A. Giroux (2010) places a large emphasis on the role of the public intellectual.

A third grouping of functions directly relates to how universities benefit the economy in preparing people for professions (Bleiklie, 1998; Calhoun, 2006; Habermas, 1989), the formation of professionals (Lee and Dunston, 2011) and providing products and research that are of economic benefit to the societies they serve (Bleiklie, 1998, p. 306), including the generation of new technologies and innovations (Calhoun, 2006). These functions are detectable in the current emphasis on impact within research, although many would see this as a constraining factor and in tension with the first two themes (Mahon, 2014).

However, H. A. Giroux (2010) contends that universities have 'largely abandoned' their civic purpose (H. A. Giroux, 2010, p. 186); Calhoun (2006) that universities have shifted from a focus on the public good towards 'the provision of private benefits' (p. 10). Bleiklie (1998) says that the focus of knowledge access, creation and dissemination has developed a narrow economic focus with what is good for the market and that we are 'educating people for the new economy' (Altbach, 2004, p. 5). However, Bleiklie (1998) concurrently argues that the other functions of the university are still relevant (each carrying its own 'layer of expectations') (p. 305). Indeed, in examining a number of UK universities' mission statements, words like civic duty, being there for the community, and even the words 'common good', are often foregrounded. However, in the strategic plan that rolls out these missions, we can see that community is often interpreted as the business community and the common good framed in economic terms.

Nevertheless, there is potential for leverage, in holding our institutions to account for realizing their mission statements and offering different articulations of these missions in the strategic plan that go beyond the economic, and re-own terms like civic responsibility and the common good. However, as I will go on to argue, this is difficult to do in isolation, and needs to be situated within a learning community, and one with critical pedagogy as its focus. Indeed, in our institution, the critical pedagogy group has very much influenced the development of the strategic plan, and then used it to justify research, pedagogic approaches and the setting up of a research and teaching institute within the university.

Whatever level of influence we can have at a strategic level, the question now becomes whether SICPs meaningfully have an impact on our students through our pedagogy. As a starting point we should perhaps reflect on our own motivations and intent as SICPs. Clark (2018) identifies SICPs as falling into four categories: those who do not know what critical pedagogy looks like in theory or practice, but quite like the idea and principles (aspiring critical pedagogues – my term); those who know the theory but do not really know what critical pedagogy is in practice, (theoretical critical pedagogues); those who consider that putting critical pedagogy into practice is not possible in the current higher education system (external critical pedagogues); and those who see enacting critical pedagogy as being not about their practice and implementation of it, but what others do with it in their practice (proxy critical pedagogues) (Clark, 2018, p. 985). In the critical pedagogy, we have certainly had all but external critical pedagogues as members, and whether it is possibly to enact critical pedagogy within the university has certainly been a tension we have lived, and a mirror we constantly hold up to each other.

Aronowitz and Giroux (1985) identify three types of intellectuals. Transformative intellectuals strive to make the 'pedagogical more political and the political more pedagogic' (Aronowitz and Giroux, 1985, p. 56), problematizing knowledge, both in its production and content. They also model reflection and self-critique and make learning relevant to students with an intent that they 'see themselves as social actors with . . . opportunities to engage in reflexive understanding of their own situation within the system of social relations' (Aronowitz and Giroux, 1985, p. 56). Critical intellectuals are critical of the social structures but remain consciously or unconsciously removed from social action. Accommodating intellectuals perpetuate the status quo (consciously or unconsciously). Finally, hegemonic intellectuals willingly and consciously perpetuate the status quo that typically benefits them and the dominant 'ruling' class they associate with.

These are interesting typologies but have the generalizing limits all typologies have. Combined, they are interesting. I have to confess that I find the types of external and proxy pedagogues somewhat problematic – and in my experience so do students. If external critical pedagogues do not think it is possible to enact critical pedagogy within HE, and make no attempt to link students to other possibilities, then why are they there? Without action, they seem to have ceased being critical pedagogues and become critical intellectuals at best. In saying that change is impossible in universities, they encourage students to develop such cynicism about their own contexts. Elsewhere I have written about the dangers of workers and lecturers instilling in people a sense of learned hopelessness, which is

> an informed sense of powerlessness, not one borne of ignorance of their potential or chances, but one that stemmed from knowledge of the limited nature of such chances. Young people were prone to turn this hopelessness on themselves or

their communities, become depressed, or lapse into conspiracy theories. (Seal and Harris, 2016, p. 123)

As for proxy critical pedagogues, I would ask why they do not see their role as enacting social action within the institution. Without action, theory remains theory. Even if they encourage and support students in engaging in actions, are they not conveying a message that it is possible to divorce theory and action. To my mind, proxy critical pedagogues are in danger of becoming, and encouraging others to become, 'rhetorical radicals' – not prepared to get their hands dirty by engagement in social action, preferring instead to leave this to others.

So to enact critical pedagogy as a SICP within the university, what are we to do?

Motta (2013, p. 123) gives some interesting pointers and principles for pedagogic practice within and outside of the classroom. First, we need to 'cultivate compassion and generosity, through the ethics of love and the politics of care, towards the complexities and complicities of student subjectivities'. She is calling for a new, or renewed, type of relationship to be had with students. This means engaging with our students' lives and, when needed, representing and advocating their complexities and subjectivities. This can be particularly important within higher education where the systems are designed for a particular kind of student who does not have such a complicated life (Parkes, Mathias and Seal, 2018). It may also mean sharing our own subjectivities, and vulnerabilities. As Tina and I will explore in Chapter 19, one of the central components of trust building, which is what many students valued in their relationships with university staff, is mutual sharing of vulnerabilities.

Motta (2013) then asks us 'not to assume that calling a space participatory and democratic means it will be, they need to be actively created with the students from the outset'. As noted in the previous chapter, students, and lecturers, may resist democratization. It is not what people are used to and carries with it responsibility. To enable others and ourselves to understand and embrace it, it needs pedagogic intervention. Also, higher education structures will limit this democracy (we may be able to negotiate the parameters of assessment, but we can rarely lose it). Mike and Helen in Chapter 8 will convey the complexities of such negotiations. This is not necessarily a limitation, but can serve as an example of the kind of structural resistance people will encounter in the world, the question being what compromises are possible before the endeavour loses integrity.

Motta (2013) also talks about '*la facultad*', defined as the 'affective awareness of dynamics of power and a nuanced and acute practice of empathy'. Elsewhere I have talked about the importance of breaking down notions of the classroom, challenging who is the learner and the learned, the nature of pedagogical relationships and who has the right to create knowledge. That the creation of knowledge is a process of co-creation needs to be emphasized from the beginning of the programme and integrated throughout. Lecturers should not privilege their own intelligence and insights, recognizing them to be inherently partial and contingent, and this needs to be named in the moment. To give an example, at a conference in Bangladesh on youth work in South East Asia, I asked why I – a white Western male – had been invited to open the conference. Was their indigenous knowledge (Smith, 1999), not a better starting point? I also publicly asked myself why I had colluded with being invited to speak.

Developing this idea, Motta's emphasis on empathy means that critical pedagogy in the classroom should be an intersubjective experience (Benjamin, 2017). Existential notions of encounter, and intersubjective notions of recognition (Benjamin, 2017; Butler, 2011), combined with elements of hooks's (2014) engaged pedagogue, seem relevant. It means explicitly working through the visceral, embodied experience of educational spaces and working to bring tacit, sometimes unconscious, processes into a learnable, theoretical framework (Harris, Heywood and Mac an Ghail, 2017), recognizing the performativity of this (Butler, 1990). Baizerman (1989) summed up this process of identity and meaning-making well, saying, in answer to what pedagogy is trying to instil in the student, that it is:

> developing the skills necessary to pierce one's taken-for granted, ordinary, mundane life so that one becomes aware of how the ordinary is constructed and how one is implicated constructing one's own reality . . . awareness of how one's biography pre-forms the present gives one the possibility of seeing in the moment its manifold possibilities, not simply what is there. Done well, all of this slows down the instantaneous process of seeing and making meaning. Once slowed, she can 'control' how she makes sense, and, in this way, come to be accountable to herself. (Baizerman, 1989, p. 1)

As stated, we should also name and explore power as it operates. This is not always an easy process. A commitment is needed to an honest, challenging exploration of views and personal identities – raw, often previously hidden, emotions and projections need to be absorbed, detoxified and rearticulated. Motta (2013) also calls for 'attentivenesss to the dissonances and discomfort experienced by individuals' recognising that such attentiveness can lead to 'transformation of such experiences into pedagogical moments not merely moments of reaction and conflict'. Such themes are central in order that students examine their social positioning and allow for both seemingly trivial and significant aspects of their own lives to be first discovered, named and then imbued with meaning. One way that power operates within higher education is through the tensions between support and professional staff, and academic staff, and this was played out continually in the critical pedagogy group, but the critical pedagogy group continues to keep working it through. This includes the tears, anger, guilt and fear that goes with such real exchanges, and makes for 'real' bonds.

Finally, Motta calls for 'epistemological disobedience' (Mignolo, 2009) in that we should disrupt norms of the emotional and bodily practices of the university, 'transcending the dualism between education and life' (Motta, 2013, p. 107). This means lecturers as well as students are encouraged to be open about their biographies, including discussion of professional challenges within their own practice, but also personal reflections on experiences as members of privileged hegemonic and marginalized and oppressed groups – often concurrently. Pauline in Chapter 15 explores how we can bring emotion back into the room, taking a feminist standpoint as a counter to more hegemonic masculine approaches.

We now need to consider whether it is possible to enact critical pedagogy as a lone SICP. Much of the evidence suggests this is very difficult, and perhaps not desirable to try (Kumisharo, 2002; Seal, 2019b). It is also often not effective; both students and the institution can see you as a tolerated 'maverick' who illustrates their liberal credentials, at best, or someone waiting to be picked off, at worst. Unless you are particularly high up in the structure, it is also questionable what strategic influence you can have. A common theme in the literature on critical pedagogy in higher education is the key role a strong learning community plays in fostering praxis. Mahon (2014) sees them as characterized by 'conditions of cooperation and commitment among a dedicated faculty' (Braa and Callero, 2006, p. 360); a spirit of trust and respectfulness (Gibbs, Angelides, and Michaelides, 2004; Hardy, 2010); concern for the creation of 'safe' spaces (Breunig, 2005; Hardy, 2010) (although we will explore the limitations of the idea of safe spaces in Chapter 19); a culture of mentoring (Gibbs, Angelides and Michaelides, 2004); a self-interest that is inseparable from the interests of humanity (Gibbs, Angelides and Michaelides, 2004); and scholarly dialogue and activity that promotes collaborative and individual self-inquiry into pedagogy (Hardy, 2010; Jacobs, 2008).

Newman's critical pedagogy group and the new Romero Freire Institute certainly seem to have these features, as we shall explore. In addition, we have made a commitment to action within the institution. Representation has been made to senior management on a number of these issues, with tangible results such as allowing time for professional and support staff to attend and develop their pedagogic practice. The group has sought to influence the wider culture of teaching at Newman. Critical pedagogy was a strand within last years' teaching and learning conference and was the basis of the approach to this year's conference, and the next has been expanded to two days. A collaborative organizing team of students, professional and support staff and academics ran it. In developing the new institutional strategic plan the leadership adopted some of the principles of critical pedagogy in running consultation sessions. The group was then asked to write the introductory section of the strategic plan, examining our 'human approach to pedagogy' articulating our pedagogic values.

However, a group cannot just exist in isolation, else it becomes just a different silo or place of retreat. We need to look at what internal conditions are needed for a critical pedagogy community of practice to flourish. Perhaps useful here is the framework of 'practice architecture' as developed by Kemmis et al. (2012, 2014). The theory explores how practices prefigure, and are prefigured by, the sites in which they are located, and how professional practices are enabled and constrained by those sites. As Mahon (2014) notes, extra-individual conditions, practices and individual actors interrelate and are enmeshed with each other in complex ways. She names a number of levels at which this operates – 'cultural-discursive' (such as university mission; discourses regarding pedagogy), 'material-economic' (such as allocation of staff to subjects; employment of casual vs. continuing staff; workshops spaces; staff meeting spaces; workload allocation; staff–student ratios; study leave) and 'social-political' (such as decision-making; surveillance measures; power attached to particular positions) dimensions of the social world (Kemmis and Grootenboer, 2008.)

Mahon (2014) conducted the only study to date that specifically looks at practice architectures that sustain critical pedagogy. Overall, she affirmed that groups like the critical pedagogy group and the institute are crucial. Collegial relationships and opportunities for collaboration within the academic community are essential as 'sources of solidarity, inspiration, information, and as sites of critical exchanges and stirring each other into critical language' (Mahon, 2014, p. 164). The critical pedagogy group and the Romero Freire Institute are uniquely made up of representatives from academics, professional and support staff, students, alumni and members of the local community. The institute has broad reach and acts as a bridge and mediator between student and community research, consultancy and evaluation, the scholarship of teaching and learning and academic research in higher education.

Mahon (2014) found other enablers to include student engagement, student feedback and positive student–teacher relationships. While it has taken two years, the critical pedagogy group now have active participation of students. John and Leoarna will explore in Chapter 11 how a precursor of this, the staff–student partnership, has been part of enabling a participatory culture with students. These partnerships have impacted at cultural-discursive levels (many participants felt that their project had had a direct influence over an aspect of the curriculum or wider student experience at Newman), material-economic (it has been both funded and attracted funding) and social-political dimensions (while some have said doors within the institution 'aren't open', while another sensed the projects were not yet routinely 'touching institutional structures'. The institute aims to help in facilitating this dialogue and aims to have reach at a senior management level, and so be embedded within Newman structures).

Another enabler is having opportunities to influence curriculum with 'opportunities for critical dialogue, building relationships, challenging assumptions, and drawing critical resources into the pedagogical encounters' (Mahon, 2014, p. 76). Exploring this potential has been a key aspect of the critical pedagogy group. Interestingly, we detected a lot of self-censoring from colleagues. A common call heard in relation to critical pedagogy, higher education and curriculum is that 'quality' structures do not allow for such innovation, with their demand for aims, learning outcomes, predetermined teaching strategies and set assessments etc. Yet members of the group had created empty modules, where student populated the curriculum and designed the assessment and even assessed each other – it was just that the learning outcomes, teaching strategies and assessment guidance needed to state that this would happen. Both cultural and political dimensions had been addressed – we had worked with Quality to allow these things to happen, and they cited us as example of good practice in turn. Similarly, Mahon (2014) talks about the importance of place, space, and information technology. Colleagues had found ways to negotiate times, student had come up with their own learning contracts, including aspects like time management and the place and spaces for learning. Tutors had also been able, through working imaginatively with e-learning, to enrol students as tutors so that they could edit and upload their own learning resources.

Mahon (2014) also says that research and scholarship are important. The institute has had a successful seminar series, involving students, academics and professional staff. Tina and I discuss the staff week in Chapter 19. It was attended by over fifty people from ten different countries and included support staff, students at all level and academics. It lasted four days and culminated in an exhibition, presentation/performance for all staff, including the vice chancellor. This book has been the logical next step, but we have plans for further publications and events. Mahon (2014) also suggests having relationships beyond the university environment as a source of sustenance and 'triggers'. Recently we supported a student who was encountering institutional barriers to putting on a local community movie night by providing a home for the night and a pedagogic justification for the endeavour.

Mahon (2014) also catalogues disablers including the intensification of academic work, the lack of (or diminishing) teacher–student contact time, challenges of online teaching, over-regulation and standardization of practice, promotion of technical, virtual, neoliberal constructions of pedagogic practice, and a shift from a critical and collegial culture to one of compliance and competition. There are certainly regular tensions and points of discussion within the critical pedagogy group. However, we help each other and highlight that people are not alone and there are different models of practice that can be invoked and articulated. For example, a recent day was given over to looking at the National Student Survey (NSS) and pedagogic practice. We were invited to participate and shape the day. It moved from showcasing those who had successful pedagogies (i.e. they had high NSS scores) to showcasing all, recognizing that NSS does not necessarily reflect quality. Similarly, a wish to explore why we had scored badly on our fairness criteria moved from deriding the Teaching Excellence and Student Outcomes Framework (TEF) and how we can 'game' the scores to a plan to explore with students what 'fairness' meant in HE, and how we could work on this together, and have meaningful dialogue.

Conclusion

Mahon (2014) provides a useful set of criteria for an institution to consider in supporting critical pedagogy, which I think is also useful for anyone considering setting up a community of practice around critical pedagogy.

1. Allow time (e.g. for reflection, relationship-building, scholarship, noticing, engaging in debate, democratic/inclusive decision-making, creating conditions of possibility).
2. Allow space for creativity.
3. Allow space for autonomy and flexibility so that educators can exercise professional judgement, be responsive, and respond appropriately.
4. Foster/sustain/allow the development of positive, productive, trusting relationships.
5. Encourage/legitimize/provide for critical dialogue and reflexive inquiry and conversation.
6. Provide opportunities for maximum engagement in community and opportunities to develop the capacity for critical pedagogical praxis through experience.

I think with these conditions, the right people and the right will, meaningful critical pedagogy is possible in higher education still. The interrelationship between the cultural-discursive, the material-economic and the social-political is nuanced and dynamic. We do not have delusions. Part of the reason that the institute happened is because we did not ask for any money. On the other hand, if we have institutional money we are always under the self-censoring threat that they can take it away (Alinsky, 1971). But we also thought senior management saw the value in it. Recently we wanted another round of face-to-face consultations for the development of the strategic plan (cultural-discursive). Senior management said they couldn't afford it and did not have time to do it, and just wanted online responses (material-economic). So we held our own meetings and fed into the online response, with the full knowledge of the VC, with whom we had built trust (social-political).

Response from Stephen Cowden

Mike Seal sets out to address an absolutely crucial question for anyone concerned with critical pedagogy: what spaces are there left for those who continue to deploy the methods and goals of critical pedagogy within today's marketized university framework? Henry Giroux and others have argued that one of the key impacts of marketization is to shift the civic goals of public education towards the idea of education as a business, reflecting the dominance of the idea of 'entrepreneurialism' in today's universities. Today's universities are driven and motivated by demonstrating their league tables on 'student satisfaction' and 'employability'. In his book *Capitalist Realism* (2009) Mark Fisher noted that this reflects the way the past thirty years have seen the 'successful installation of a "business ontology" in which it is simply obvious that everything in society, from healthcare to education, should be run as a business' (2009, p. 17). This profoundly ideological position now presents itself and is widely believed in and accepted as common-sense, which not only allows the privatization of previously publicly owned and accessible social assets and rights – hospitals, universities, care of older people etc. – but also obliterates the history of the way these social rights themselves were fought for by popular grass roots political movements. Alongside the obliteration of this history comes the enclosure of our political imagination, and nothing demonstrates this more than the way right-wing populist parties and leaders across the world – Trump in the United States, Bolsonaro in Brazil, Modi in India and now Boris Johnson in the UK – have become the beneficiaries of the despair and frustration people feel about the rampant inequality which has become a feature of capitalist societies. While the neoliberalization of social democracy which preceded this refused to consider any alternative to capitalism, we are now seeing the politics of the right gaining traction through appealing to people's frustration and resentment by blaming migrants and minorities for the problems people face; again, this is a politics which is unable to see beyond a neoliberal horizon.

Indeed, this populist rhetoric is very clearly accompanied by the ongoing drive of the competitive logic of neoliberalization and marketization through our public institutions and public spaces in new and entirely destructive ways. As this happens within public educational institutions, it will be accompanied by the foreclosure of critical spaces in classrooms. This is necessarily driven by direct censorship – rather it works through the control of the time and space in which educators have to work with students, including through the increasingly casualized employment practices used by universities. But marketization also involves the reshaping of the meaning of education in the eyes of students, so they come to see their own education not as personally developmental in the traditional humanistic sense, but rather as investment in their own selves as 'human capital' – and this links to ways university managements seek to grow their student populations through marketing metrics about employment and 'student satisfaction'. This reframing of student subjectivity and this reframing of the purpose of education can make it difficult for critical spaces to be opened up in class, and for students to become politically active in the way they have in the past. So if marketization needs to be understood not just as about structural institutional reorganization but also as about the reconstruction of student and teacher subjectivities around an 'entrepreneurial' ethos, where are the critical spaces in which this can be questioned or challenged?

I want to argue that alongside the commitment of teachers to the project of critical pedagogy in the classroom, where we need to use all the opportunities available to us, we also need to seek other ways of opening critical spaces. The ideas of critical pedagogy need to be taken into student groupings, lecturer unions and political organizations where they can provide a framework for an alternative vision of the university. We need to open spaces of resistance outside traditional classrooms – spaces of strikes, spaces of independent student organization around material questions such as housing, problems with debt, mental health issues, and using 'teach-outs' and other ways of taking critical education into the public space. These different spaces of engagement allow issues people face to be addressed not managerially as concerns of 'consumer satisfaction' but as the political issues they are, with a real presence in everyday life. These are all potentially spaces where students can break out of the pervasiveness of the discourse of marketization where they are the consumers of learning to a place where they can begin to see the potential of their own agency as creators of knowledge. The last industrial action our union organized surprised me for the way it provided unexpected contexts for conversations with students not just about the strike and the reasons for it but about the way they experienced the marketization of education. As one student said to us: 'I'm going to start my life in debt with money I didn't get to see and never had myself. It's like ghost money – and it's going to come back and haunt me for a long time'.

Chapter Four

The Policy Context of Higher Education

Resistance Is Possible

Sarah Parkes and Jane Beniston, Response from Neil M. Speirs

Introduction

Barnett (2000, p. 257) discusses that there is a 'fragility in the way that we understand the world' borne from the perpetual uncertainties and unpredictability's we experience. Underpinned by neoliberalism as a worldview, the structures and policy evident within the university sector reflect the market-driven approaches to social policy across the globe that pervade the very 'ontology of our everyday lives' (Martin in Downs, 2017, p. 61). Furthermore, the global university context of massification reflects a fundamental repositioning of the relationships between and within education systems and structures in society, in relation to the needs of the state and the global 'knowledge economy' (Parkes et al., 2020).

With the context of 'policy sociology' (Ball, 2017; Burrawoy, 2005), this chapter explores the historical background of the geopolitical climate; the developments in England that widened participation in higher education (HE) and the simultaneous rise of the problematic concept of student-as-consumer. Using policy sociology that critiques or legitimates the solutions that have already been reached (Burrawoy, 2005) enables us to uncover whose interests HE policy serves, and how this is operationalized in relation to reproducing privilege, inequalities and disadvantage (Ball, 2017, pp. 6–12). From within this context and our position at Newman University Birmingham as a faith-based, person-centred university, this chapter, and indeed this volume, expresses the need for – and possibility of – embodying resistance to neoliberalism and its managerialist relative, where a university education can focus on 'the importance of education for decision, for rupture, for choice, for ethics' (Freire, 1997, p. 44).

Scene-setting: The Context of HE Policy in England

From as far back as the late eighteenth century, the underpinning free-market ideology evident in successive English HE policies is foreshadowed in the rhetoric of Smith's

(1776/2014) laissez-faire attitude to economics and Bentham's (1789) utilitarian philosophies. Both argued for minimal state interference in economic systems but at this point, agreed that education should be state-controlled. A university education was at this time accessed solely by the privileged few that enabled participants to make contacts and fraternize in appropriate circles (Willets, 2017). As Matheson and Wells (1999) describe, for the wealthy elite the underpinning philosophy of university participation was not to attain economic independence through graduate-level employment but was seen as a way for those owning the methods of production to maintain the status quo. Indeed, as Gramsci later asserted, the hegemonic nature of education perpetuates the elite social and cultural norms in society (cited in Borg, Buttigieg and Mayo, 2002). As such, shared ideas or beliefs serve to justify the interest of dominant, capital-owning elite groups (Giddens, 1976, p. 583) that perpetuate class privilege and social inequalities (Bourdieu and Passeron, 1990).

During and as a result of the Industrial Revolution in the late eighteenth century, the nineteenth century saw concerns about the politically problematic nature of societal change. Ball (2017) cites this as due to the introduction of new manufacturing processes, the subsequent high migration into towns and cities, and the emergent urban and middle classes. The consequent focus on the provision of state intervention across the board was in response to a threatening of political stability 'manifested in crime, juvenile delinquency, changing kinship roles and gender relationships and general immorality' (p 65). Two divergent views emerged during this time according Williams (1984) regarding education. One saw education as a right for all people to enable them to contribute to the world, not just a privilege afforded to the elite. The other, though problematic in terms of the dominant discourses of the time, believed in a liberal education that fostered the development of free-thinking, values-based individuals. Such views were espoused by three key groups: industrial trainers, public educators and humanists (Gillard, 2018). The most powerful group – the industrial trainers – argued that industry needed a more qualified workforce, an argument that has echoed through time regarding graduate skills and employability. Indeed, professions such as law and medicine at this time established examinations to determine membership (Black, 1998). Here, then, the foundations of curricula for professions focused on establishing a vocation, that is, a suitability for a particular career.

The discussions visible within Smith and Bentham's philosophical positions were also inspired by the political radicalism simultaneously playing out across the English Channel. These were influenced by emerging philanthropic traditions, the evangelical movement of the Church of England and the philosophical work of Rousseau. Rousseau's (1762/1991) novel *Emile* was to have a major impact on educators' views of children and childhood, and profoundly influenced political theory and practice (Wokler, 1996, p. 1). Rousseau was the first to comprehensively attempt to describe a scheme of education corresponding to what he saw as 'nature' (Stewart and Mc Cann, 1967, p. 28). His ideas considered that education needed to allow the free nature of children and not be distorted by the unnatural limitations of civilization. Though influential and visible through state legislation in the nineteenth century in elementary education, this division of utility versus liberal education alluded to the possibility of a different type of university, where one might move away from vocation or profession to one where individuals developed their ideas and tried to make sense of the world. Indeed, our patron, John Henry Newman, in 1852 respectfully argued that professional or scientific knowledge cannot be the only sufficient end of a university education (2001[1907], Discourse 7:6). Rather, a university education should involve developing 'good members of society' with a 'clear, conscious view of their own opinions and judgements' (2001[1907], Discourse 7:10). Thus, the university as a place of higher education was now seen as a space for free speech, innovations and radical thinking (Neary, 2012).

The Journey from the Modern, Welfare States to the Neoliberal and Managerial World

Aside from the 1850 Royal Commission review of university provision derived from widespread complaints of an unrepresentative curriculum, state interventions in HE were largely absent during these discussions regarding the purpose of education in society. In 1905, the first Haldone Report established the idea of the University Grants Commission who advised government on grant funding and organization of the sector. This was followed after the First World War in 1918 by the second report, which created the Department of Scientific and Industrial Research (Kernohan, 2018).

Since the end of the Second World War, global post-industrial economies have been competing and trading knowledge rather than the methods of production (Ball, 2017, p. 25; Organization for Economic Co-operation and Development, 1996) through the expansion and provision of accessible university education (Parkes et al., 2020). In the UK, the early manifestations of this can be identified within the post-war rhetoric of the Percy (His Majesty's Government, 1945) and Barlow Reports (His Majesty's Government, 1946) that sought to provide opportunities for boys [sic] to return to university to utilize the ample reserve of intelligence, and allow for 'a doubling of the University numbers' (His Majesty's Government, 1946, Section 26). Latterly, the Kennedy (Her Majesty's Government, 1997b) and Dearing (Her Majesty's Government, 1997a) Reports argued that providing university-level education for a wider section of society was key to economic prosperity to ensure the UK could compete globally. Thus, in the move from private to public management (New Public Management) of higher education in the Thatcher years, the dissolution of the University Grant Commission was instigated. In its place the publicly funded Higher Education Funding Councils established across the UK meant that 'higher education was now unequivocally the subject of public governance' with concerns about the costs of running a mass higher education system high on the agenda (Shattock, 2006). Indeed, in Her Majesty's Government (1991) there was a call for 'proper accountability for the substantial public funds invested in higher education' where shortly afterwards in 1993, the Higher Education Statistics Agency (HESA) was established to monitor student performance to ascertain the return on investment. The Labour Government (1997–2010) followed suit and committed themselves to a policy of 'widening participation' to increase access and participation of groups who were, at the time, under-represented but could meet the needs of the knowledge economy. Indeed, drives to close access and attainment gaps for those perceived as disadvantaged in our society persist in post-2010 politics (Parkes, Mathias and Seal, 2018).

Such expansion required capital. The mechanism – student fees – has consequently turned a university education into a commodity to be bought and sold. Through a steady, progressive shift from state to market across the decades, 'consumer culture' (Ball, 2004), borne from the free- market economy, has been fully embraced. The UK Labour Government (1997–2010) reformed university funding through the introduction of tuition fees of £1,000 via the *Teaching and Higher Education Act* (1998), which in 2003 was extended to allow HEI's to charge £3,000. This position shifted again following the 2007/8 financial crisis, where in 2012 after the Browne Review (DBIS, 2010), the Coalition's (2010–15) 'Teaching excellence, social mobility and student choice' paper allowed universities to charge up to £9,000, removing state support for tuition at university. In addition, the Conservative government has further explicitly situated the university sector within the marketplace via the *Higher Education and Research Act* (Her Majesty's Government, 2017), creating instruments such as the Teaching Excellence Framework (TEF) to report back on 'performance', and a market regulator in the Office for Students (Doku, 2018). Such positioning places students at the centre as consumer, with the power to determine the educational products they 'buy' with the aim of producing a competitive HE market.

Within this context, the notion of widening participation is contested; it is viewed by some as an access and/or utilitarian discourse (Jones and Thomas, 2005) to drive the knowledge economy and improve social mobility where '*information* and *knowledge* replaces capital and energy as primary wealth-creating assets' (Ball, 2017, p. 19). Others, however, such as the authors of this book, understand widening participation as vital to improving social justice (Jones and Thomas, 2005) through education that promotes equality of opportunity and participatory democracy (Griffiths, 1998). Milojevic (1998, pp. 595–7) would identify this sort of work within her competing models of the university as cultural co-ordinator that educates people for citizenship; a place for exchanges and differences where oneness is replaced with multiple, shifting roles where the university acts as a resource for the local community through outreach work. These models situate the value of a university education as underpinned by a sense of the 'common good' for democracy to thrive that fosters critical thinking and self-awareness in those that participate (Newman in Collini, 2012, p. 50). Here, a university education focuses on 'the importance of education for decision, for rupture, for choice, for ethics' (Freire, 1997, p. 44), and thus, is interested in the development of a students' understanding of themselves and the world around them, their growth and flourishing – developments that are, by their very nature, ungovernable (Collini, 2012, p. 55).

The Problematic Nature of the Student-as-Consumer

Such a liberal, justice-driven vision is problematic for educators in a system saturated by discussions about 'value for money' in terms of employability within the current state-controlled yet student-funded education system; the 2018 Minister for Universities speech 'Delivering value for money in the age of the student' (Gimyah, 2018) and the House of Lords Economics Affairs Committee Report 'Treating students fairly: The economics of post-school education' (2018) make this plain. The former insists that universities keep a 'relentless focus' on value for money (Leach, 2013), whereby the latter's press release concluded that the current HE system 'offers poor value for money to individuals, taxpayers and the economy' (2018).

Rudd and Goodson (2017) assert that, following the financial crisis of 2007/8, neoliberalism has become an implicit series of 'central, systemic organising principles' within HE policy. This engages the sector in a perpetual and fundamental repositioning of HE, articulating policies of reform that permeate the 'roles, relationships and practices within institutions that enact policy, [changing] what people do and how they think about what they do' (Ball, 2008, p. 6). We can see this unequivocally expressed by the Browne Review (DBIS, 2010) that replaced maintenance grants with loans, and more recently by both the Coalition (2010–15) and current Conservative governments. The Coalition's 'Students at the heart of the system' paper (DBIS, 2011) and the Conservative's *Higher Education and Research Act* (2017) put much of the post-Browne review machinery into legislation (Kernohan, 2018), cementing the underlying ideology of student-as-consumer through the extension of tuition fees.

Williams (2009) talks of similar issues in the United States. He notes a repositioning of US higher education that in post-war policy perceived the unifying aim of university was the social good that, through higher learning, would strengthen the country (p. 92). Now, higher education is 'driven by individual competition rather than social cooperation' and 'democracy is a market; freedom is the ability to make choices from all the shelves' (p. 95). Thus, a student-as-consumer makes 'a personal investment in one's market potential rather than a public investment in one's social potential' that reflects a 'pedagogy of debt' instilling in students a sense that:

- Only the capitalist 'worldview' is viable.
- The state's role is to augment commerce.
- Higher education is a consumer service and about career choices.
- Your worth and hence value as a human is equal to how much you make, minus how much you owe.

What this promotes through policy, then, is a false consciousness generated in students to perpetuate the penetration of neoliberalism into the collective psyche, 'facilitating integration of the younger generation into the logic of the present system to bring about conformity' (Freire, 1993). Indeed, the aforementioned Lords' paper clearly demonstrates the inescapable value-for-money discourse surrounding higher education: 'some graduates may have been better off considering other higher education qualifications that were cheaper, shorter and *more relevant to the workplace*' (House of Lords Economics Affairs Committee, 2018, p. 5, our emphasis). Perhaps unsurprisingly within an economics paper, this neglects the value of establishing criticality in people's lives where the veracity of knowledge claims is evaluated (MacFarlane, 2017, p. 102) – something we would argue is highly valuable in the era of 'fake news'.

As argued elsewhere (Parkes et al., 2020), the expansion of the university sector, described earlier, and increased tuition fees replacing state support (DBIS, 2011) have positioned the student-as-consumer (Hursh and Hall, 2008). Universities consequently exist as a 'schizophrenic transnational business corporation' where competing, multiple communities within the organization cause a sense of fragmentation (Shore 2010, p. 15). Indeed, Olssen and Peters (2005, p. 1) describe how, globally, 'the traditional professional culture of open intellectual enquiry and debate' has all but been forgotten due to the increased 'stress on performativity . . . strategic planning, performance indicators, quality assurance measures and academic audits'. Furthermore, the TEF in England uses disputed sector-wide HESA non-continuation and completion retention statistics metrics, National Student Survey (NSS) results and employability data to stratify universities as being gold, silver or bronze. These explicitly position HE in relation to the market, propagating what Lilley and Papadopoulos (2014, pp. 972-4) call the 'biofinancialisation' of the university whereby the value of educational 'things, activities and spaces' are essentialized as 'the future monetary profit to be gained'. Accordingly, many universities are necessarily focusing in on issues relating to student attrition, continuation and performance as these relate to institutional income, reputation and therefore institutional sustainability. Thus, neoliberalism as a worldview that saturates social policy pervades the very 'ontology of our everyday lives' (Martin in Downs, 2017, p. 61) as university fees continue at around £9,000 per annum. Students thus arrive at university as 'well-tuned' consumers (Scullion, 2011), affecting their perspective and potential understanding of learning, teaching and studentship within higher education.

Gewirtz and Cribb view the nature of 'student-as-consumer' as akin to buying a house or stocks and shares rather than the idea of a consumable good; this is to them an investment that 'may yield dividends in the long term or lose its value' (Gewirtz and Cribb, 2009, p. 10). Nonetheless, this model returns us back to the question of whether a university education is about utility – both for the individual and society – in terms of the use of 'having' a degree in a subject or vocational area or concerning the act of 'doing' that develops and enables human flourishing. Fromm's (1976) theoretical work considered the challenges of 'having' rather than 'being', and links these to the extrinsic and intrinsic motivational drivers for action. This notion of 'having' is closely linked to extrinsic motivational drives (DeCharms, 1968; Lepper and Green, 1978), where students engage in an activity only for a specific outcome. Conversely, the 'potentially emancipatory' (Molesworth, Nixon and Scullion, 2009, p. 8) notion of 'being' – being a 'learner' or 'student' – is intrinsically motivating, whereby the activity is the reward itself (Deci, 1971).

The concept of 'having', or utility, is also reinforced by the current way universities are assessed in terms of quality. Writing back in 1995 Gewirtz, Ball and Boewe (1995, p.1) considered that in the market economy, if 'things go wrong the misguided consumers are to blame'. However, it seems that universities are viewed as the culprit not the student consumers who have specific rights. Policy and policy devices are in place to keep universities 'in check' and make sure they are providing 'quality' and 'value for money'. Indeed, universities are now measured by numbers of students recruited; the number in graduate-level employment (Destination of Leavers in Higher Education

– DLHE and Longitudinal Educational Outcomes data – LEO); and their research outputs (Research Excellence Framework – REF) and teaching, student outcomes and experiences via the TEF, NSS and nationally held performance indicators. Never before has the university been under such scrutiny in terms of what is called 'teaching excellence' (French and O'Leary, 2017), with such policy devices underscoring the commodification of and reinforcing the treatment of the student-as-consumer.

A policy device of particular concern is the NSS which supposedly 'measures' student satisfaction under the assumption that student satisfaction is/should be our aim. We can attempt to respond to student concerns within the classroom, but satisfaction within the learning environment should not be the aim. Learning should challenge, unnerve and trouble students as it represents an 'essentially creative and unpredictable process' (Delucchi and Korgen, 2002, p. 106) and so, satisfaction is not something likely to be part of this process. Furthermore, Prosser (2011, p. 46) states that using satisfaction ratings within NSS results to change practice may be 'counterproductive'. We need to be using the results to develop more understanding of the student experience and why they experience some teaching and courses more positively than others (Kuh, 2001) to enhance the quality of their experiences.

The student-as-consumer model, and all that it brings with it, is, to say the least, contentious. Gibbs (2010) considers that it is not the purchase of any particular teaching and learning experienced during study that is beneficial to students, rather, it is access to the university's reputation and the consequent social capital networks that prove useful. Yet, Scullion (2011) suggests that 'student-as-consumer' changes the lecturer into service provider, whereby the lecturer no longer challenges thoughts and ideas that consequently alter the nature of the student as learner and is dismissive of the transformative potential of a university education (Newman, 1875; Molesworth, Nixon and Scullion, 2009; Neary, 2012).

The 'student-as-consumer' is also at odds with encouraging learning for individual flourishing and independent thought (Newman, 1875) or the concept of 'deep learning' (Prosser, 2011) during degree study. It encourages passivity through a more competitive environment that depreciates open discussion and the sharing of ideas to deepen thought (McCulloch, 2009, p. 177). While the student-as-consumer positions knowledge recall or 'short-term reproduction learning' (Prosser, 2011) as desirable, it potentially limits the development of ideas on a more profound level. Indeed, Scullion (2011) argues that student-as-consumer enthuses students to satisfy 'whimsical personal tastes and preferences' rather than immersing themselves into the 'angst of deep learning'.

There is immense possibility in our lecture halls, seminar rooms and laboratories. Here, we can challenge and question the student-as-consumer ideology with considerations of adopting differing ideas, for example, the conception of students as 'co-producers' (McCulloch, 2009; Neary, 2012). This idea sees students as 'partners in learning' who participate in more of a community-of-practice model (Coffield, 2008, p. 7) though we acknowledge this as problematic too through its positioning of the lecturer as 'expert'. These approaches of partnership and co-production are supported by the National Union of Students. Indeed, written as a reaction to fees in 2012 the *NUS Manifesto for Partnership* (2012) calls for a way to use student power to work in partnership with academics and university staff. Thus, we must provoke students, academics and universities to resist the marketization of education from within the classroom to create new joint understandings. It is from within this context that Newman is well placed to consider alternatives borne from the neoliberal market place.

Newman University and the Need for Critical Pedagogy

Ball (2017, p. 64) encourages us to look beyond the 'periodisation' of history that describes specific changes in time, to instead view a retracing of policy to help think about the issues that they represent. 'Policy sociology' thus focuses on issues of equity and social justice and frames policy as both text and discourse – highlighting the use of language that constitutes reality. Policy here then is viewed as an unstable, contradictory process that constructs 'problems' to be resolved, which in the context of Newman concern the 'problem' of white working-class 'drop-out'; BAME attainment gaps; hard-to-reach or 'at-risk' students. Such an approach to policy is useful in Newman's context because of the University's commitment to and lived reality of widening participation embodied in pedagogies underpinned by issues of social justice and equality of opportunity. Indeed, for Newman University, pursing a higher education is viewed as a public good in and of itself; one that fosters critical thinking, self-awareness and the capacity to be affected and to affect others (Postma, 2016, p. 3): the current strategic plan endeavours to promote the growth of community members who are thus able to contribute to society wherever they find themselves (Newman University, 2014). Thus, our values base seeks to resist the definitions of our era from such policy instruments as the TEF and the Office for Students (OfS) that position individuals as in deficit in some way and are in need of 'fixing' somehow.

A critical assessment on policy language, instruments and technologies that perpetuates deficit thinking in HE is vital for Newman University. We are very much a 'widening participation' institution and unique in a number of ways. Located on the outskirts of Birmingham in England, we are a small, young, regional (or even local) university initially established as a teacher training college, latterly a university college and now a university. Underpinned by the values of respect for others, social justice and equity (Newman, 2014), around 2,900 students undertake their undergraduate and/or postgraduate studies at Newman University. These students are overwhelmingly local, with 91 per cent commuting from the southwest of Birmingham, adjacent 'travel to work areas' of Dudley and Sandwell and slightly further afield from Walsall and Wolverhampton (Newman University, 2019a). Though no formal definition exists for such 'commuting students', Donnelly and Gamsu (2018) acknowledge that students commuting to study are more likely to be considered 'disadvantaged' with regard to being 'the first generation in their families to enter higher education, have a lower income, be mature and be from an ethnic minority background' (Maguire and Morris, 2018, p. 6). Indeed, in terms of HESA measures regarding socio-economic backgrounds, the percentage of entrants from the lowest HE participation areas (aka quintile 1) are considerably higher than that in the sector at Newman. Additionally, over 80 per cent of Newman University students are defined as either from a Black, Asian or Minority Ethnic group, are mature or disabled (Newman, 2019b).

In a very real way then, how we work together with our student body requires careful consideration of our teaching and support practices that can enable their 'transition-as-becoming' (Gale and Parker, 2014). As argued elsewhere (Seal and Parkes, 2020), for a large majority of our student population, their academic self-efficacy is diminished against the established order of the university. They view their experience through a lens of natural inferiority; illegitimacy and displacement that bestows a sense of personal inadequacy and shame rather than structural disadvantage (Mallman, 2016, pp. 3–12), concomitantly, becoming fixed in their mindset regarding their own ability that perceives themselves as in deficit (Dweck, 2014). We maintain, then, that a process of perpetual inward institutional reflection on our pedagogies and institutional processes (Parkes et al., 2014) is always necessary to establish 'epistemological equity' (Dei in Gale and Parker, 2014, p. 748). This involves challenging traditional concepts of both knowledge and education to counter the hegemony that knowledge, and particularly theory, is something to be created or discovered by objective and neutral experts (Seal and Parkes, 2020). It involves uncovering 'new ways of thinking as situations change and evolve' (Seal, 2017, p. 28) through dialogue with each other (Cho, 2010, p. 315), and constructing possible futures (Braidotti, 2012) through an active and ethical democratic process (Seal and Parkes, 2020). It is here that critical pedagogy can serve as liberatory for our students and is the focus of this book.

The complexity of students at Newman thus necessitates careful consideration of our teaching and support practices, as well as reflection on issues of epistemological equity and hierarchies of knowledge. Data from the Realising Engagement through Active Culture Transformation Collaborative Development Programme (Beniston and Harris, 2017) concluded that we needed to move beyond the idea of 'involvement' and 'participation' to consider how knowledge and understanding of wider student engagement and ideas around student transformation can be realized. The concept of critical pedagogy suggests that this transformative action can be achieved as a result of changing pedagogical processes. Through an expanded understanding around the concept of critical pedagogy we facilitate a more collegiate and agentive approach to both teaching and learning. No longer having the teacher as the expert but 'through dialogue the teacher-of-the-students and the students-of-the-teacher cease to exist and a new term emerges teacher-student with students-teachers' (Freire, 1993).

We attempt to offer teaching and learning which provides space for 'transformative' pedagogy which goes beyond the individual towards collective change in what Massey (2008) terms 'activity spaces' (see discussion in chapters authored by Pete Harris and Ruth Roberts). Within these 'activity spaces' different models of pedagogy are possible. Through creating a collective community and a generative curriculum model, students become more aware of their own cultural identity and their own personal views (Ball and Pence, 2001, p. 122). Through this exploration, it argues for the intrinsic value and worth of HE to the individual, organization and society via the ways in which it develops a criticality towards knowledge claims: a way of being, knowing and acting (Lea, 2015, p. 114–18). This positioning necessitates pedagogy and approaches that resist enacting a 'prescribed set of procedures or rules' (Green, 2011, p. 120) legitimized by both internal and external systems to promote democratic engagement, meaningful dialogue and co-operative working with and between university staff, students and external organizations. This pedagogical change is not without risk, but, as this book explores in examples in practice, the belief is that this will be and has been worthwhile, both pedagogically and in a liberatory fashion to further develop relationships with our students.

The thinking of our patron, Saint John Henry Newman, continues to influence the ways in which we approach our teaching and learning. Our relationship with our students is based upon the foundation of 'an ethics of care' that resonates with feminist scholars such Noddings (2013) and Tronto (1993), who have drawn inspiration from Levinas (1987) and his ideas concerning the 'ethics of an encounter'. His starting point is how in Western thought knowledge readily becomes a will to *know* by 'grasping the Other' and so makes the 'Other' into the 'Same'. While this sameness does not allow for individuality or students-as-teachers, it yet still positions 'questions of otherness are at the heart of contemporary theory' (Tronto, 1993, p. 58) and offers some resistance to enacting the technicists' rules or procedures. We do not want to smother or grasp our learners, and part of our pedagogy involves reminding others that we are unavoidably part of wider relationships in which each one of us depends on others. Care as an ethic is recognized by us as a key component in all education and the bedrock of our practice.

The Time Is Now

Neoliberalism is now an underpinning organizing principle within the United Kingdom, as it is across the globe, giving birth to a competition-led and managerial state (Ball, 2017, p. 65). From the birth and consequence of industry and the ashes of the Second World War to the subsequent policies of the 2007/08 financial crash, this principle pervades our very lives. Explicit examples include the initial performance measure of the Higher Statistics Agency; policy instruments of the Teaching Excellence Framework that utilizes sector-wide metrics to determine levels of excellence, such as the NSS, Destination of Leavers from HE survey and HESA non-continuation and completion statistics. Additionally, the realignment of the Higher Education Funding Councils and Office for Fair Access into the Office for Students. These all herald an 'era of unprecedented scrutiny and focus' (French and O'Leary, 2017, p. 2) of institutions. Thus, when we ask ourselves whom does policy serve, we see that through situating HEIs as service providers to sell education to students, and subsequently producing 'employable' graduates for the state, it is clear that successive governments have penned and positioned HE policy in relation to the market (Parkes, 2018) rather than centralizing a higher education's intrinsic value and thus worth. There is hence no greater time to embrace critical pedagogic approaches, as discussed in the following chapters of this book, in the hope of creating an epistemological equity (Dei in Gale and Parker, 2014, p. 748) with our students; one that can go some way to challenge the systems that reproduces class privilege and social inequalities (Bourdieu and Passeron, 1990).

Response from Dr Neil M. Speirs

Higher education policies – hegemonic in nature – continue to impose the habitus of the dominant culture, while at the same time, a false consciousness gives the appearance that such policies are good for all, inclusive in nature. In the neoliberal society, we find that 'policy-making is reduced to the manipulation of focus groups, struggle to the mobilization of rival spin-doctors, and success to the acquisition of a lucrative consultancy' (Callinicos, 1999). We can recall Bourdieu (1998) when he noted that 'the neoliberal programme draws its social power from the political and economic power of those whose interests it expresses'. Therefore, those higher education policies that could be emancipatory in nature are instead twisted and disfigured to reinforce the dominant culture, indeed, even though 'education has fundamental connections with the idea of human emancipation . . . it is constantly in danger of being captured for other interests' (Connell et al., 1982, p. 48).

We know that 'the fate of workers, the jobless, and the poor hinges on the capacity of progressive political forces to harness the agency of the state to reduce economic inequality, bridge glaring social gaps, and protect the most vulnerable members of the civic community' (Wacqant, 2002). However, we are met face on by the suffocating neoliberal vision which 'dresses up the most classical presuppositions of the conservative thought of all times' (Bourdieu, 1998). While resistance is indeed possible and of course necessary, it is not easy. However, we must be encouraged by the generous and compassionate words of Freire (2004c, p. 55) when he says the 'most fundamental lesson is the one of non-conformity before injustice, the teaching that we are capable of deciding, of changing the world, of improving it'. However, hegemonic education policies seek, in their neoliberal way, to achieve 'the elimination of administrative or political barriers capable of inconveniencing the owners of capital in their individual quest for the maximization of individual profit' (Bourdieu, 1998).

But hope of resistance (Bourdieu, 1998) still exists, 'both in state institutions and in the orientations of social actors (notably individuals and groups most attached to these institutions, those with a tradition of civil and public service)'. As Giroux (2014, p. 194) points out, 'educators and others need to figure out how to defend more vigorously higher education as a public good' and 'educate students to be critical agents, to learn how to take risks, engage in thoughtful dialogue, and address what it means to be socially responsible'. The very act of teaching that injustice can be challenged is itself the beginning of resisting the neoliberal vision. We might then see a new generation that is critically literate and able to challenge hegemonic policies of all kinds, and act in compassion towards the working class and poor through the promotion of progressive political ways. But we must be aware of 'pervasive forms of public pedagogy that increasingly function to divorce learning from any vestige of critical thought' (Giroux, 2014, p. 195). Resistance is possible, and its compassion and hope must be alive in the hearts of educators. As Orwell noted: 'The moral to be drawn from this dangerous nightmare situation is a simple one: Don't let it happen. It depends on you' (Crick, 2004, p. 76).

Chapter Five

The Pedagogy of Partnership

John Peters and Leoarna Mathias, Response from Mike Neary

Introduction

Newman University, Birmingham, UK, is a small university committed to social justice and values-based higher education. Faced by the bleak prospect of rampant neoliberalism and creeping marketization in higher education (HE), we set out in 2014 to explore and uncover what gave us hope in, and about, our HE practice. In discussions led by the Academic Practice Unit, we sought to draw out what we thought was special and important about the HE we wanted to live. It quickly became apparent that the close human relationship between students and staff lay at the centre of our vision of HE for social justice. We therefore sought to articulate and enact student–staff partnership as a means of promoting democratic engagement, meaningful dialogue and co-operative working within and beyond our curriculum (GuildHE, 2015, p. 23; Peters, 2016). This enactment was underpinned through the designing and sharing of six principles of a 'pedagogy of partnership', informed by the work of Paulo Freire and others.

This chapter sets out the principles of our pedagogy of partnership; principles of shared hope, shared visions, respectful dialogue, co-investigation, co-construction and continuing transformation. It is important to highlight the inspiration we drew from the National Union of Students in the UK, who proposed partnership as an alternative to marketized HE, in addition to the clear debt we owe to Paulo Freire. Initially the principles were used to encourage project work, reviewed in a later chapter in this book, but we have begun to embed them in wider university practices – from development work to the classroom, to quality assurance mechanisms and strategic planning – all the time being mindful of not diluting their power and purpose. The domestication of student partnership, into tokenism, window dressing or synthetic 'student voice' activity is a constant threat, which our basis in Freirean principles helps resist. We continue to engage in reflective debate about how the pedagogy of partnership can best serve to underpin an authentic attempt at democratic practice in our university, and generate HE practice in which student and tutor, as 'student-teacher' and 'teacher-student' are 'jointly responsible for a process in which all grow' (Freire, 1996, p. 61).

The National Union of Students, *Manifesto for Partnership* (2012)

> Neoliberal doctrine seeks to limit education to technological practice. Currently, education is no longer understood as formative, but simply as training. I feel we must keep on creating alternative work models.
>
> (A. Freire, 2007, p. 4)

The National Union of Students in the UK argued strongly for student partnership as just such an 'alternative work model'. Their *Manifesto for Partnership* rejected both the traditional liberal idea of student as apprentice and the neoliberal idea of student-as-consumer (2012). Instead, they proposed the concept of students as partners, not just in learning but in the co-creation of knowledge and of the HE institution itself. To achieve this, they urged the need for 'a meaningful dispersal of power' (NUS, 2012, p. 8) and provided 'a statement of the folly of trying to sell HE to students when we can unleash the power of working *with* students to transform HE' (Peters, 2018, p. 182; Parkes et al., 2020).

In her introduction to the *Manifesto for Partnership*, Rachel Wenstone, then Vice-President (HE) at the NUS, stated:

> We have spent enough time condemning consumerism in education, and now we need to articulate the alternative. Student engagement is a great concept but it needs to be deployed to radical ends. Students as partners is not just a nice-to-have, I believe it has the potential to help bring about social and educational transformation, as long as we know what we are trying to do and we maintain a critical attitude about the ways the concept is adopted and used. (NUS, 2012, p. 1)

Unusually in policy discussion, Wenstone stressed the importance of going back to first principles and underlying values. As such, the *Manifesto for Partnership* sought to establish the underpinning purpose of partnership working, in terms of not only what it set out to achieve but also what it actively sought to resist. It therefore set out a vision of HE built on partnership, in opposition to both the consumerist model and the older liberal tradition.

We are all alive to the dominant consumerist model of HE, in a system where individuals are expected to find and pay high fees for their place at university. This is marketized HE (Molesworth, Nixon and Scullion, 2011). In this conceptualization, individual student consumers pay for a packaged, private good, sold by universities as HE providers. Such a model is increasingly embedded in legal provision, such as the growing invocation of the Competition and Marketing Authority in the UK as a judge of university provision, guaranteeing we provide 'what it says on the tin'. This model of HE does offer students a certain power, as customers who can express dissatisfaction and complain of poor service but:

> A narrative of 'competition' and 'choice' within a consumer model offers students a false and inflated perception of their power and encourages the mind-set of 'the customer is always right'. (NUS, 2012, p. 5)

This is not partnership, and nor does it capture the richness of being a university student:

> Conceiving of students as consumers is a thoroughly impoverished way of describing the relationship between students and their institutions, which ought to be one of mutual trust, care and respect. The power held by consumers is not the power to intervene and change things, it is the power to 'like' or to 'recommend to a friend', or to make a choice between five identical glossy marketing brochures. The consumer never grows, is never challenged, is never made to understand the vastness of the knowledge that exists and that has yet to be created. The consumer is not asked to imagine unthought-of possibilities. (NUS, 2012, p. 5)

If the consumerist model of HE, as a service sold to student customers, is impoverished then it is easy to fall back on the more traditional liberal idea of a university as a place where students go to be intellectual apprentices.

> This can be summarised as the idea that traditionally a student attends university in order to gain mastery of a particular subject area. Students spend time with experts in order to become closer to expertise themselves and teachers determine curricula because they know what they are talking about. (NUS, 2012, p. 7)

Of course, this model is also problematic, for both the limitations it sets on student power and the reductive vision of the HE learning and teaching relationship it represents. This is the 'students don't know what they don't know' view of HE, where students cannot and should not have a say in curriculum or pedagogic approaches because only academics understand the true mysteries of the subject and how it should be taught. While students are clearly not starting out as subject experts, they do bring knowledge and experience, including being experts in their own lives and learning experience:

> 'Equality' is as much about respecting each other's views as it is about having similar levels of knowledge. Taking the conversation seriously is the first step towards acknowledging known and prospective forms of expertise that students bring to the table. (NUS, 2012, p. 7)

This is education as the practice of democracy, not on the basis that everyone is equal in knowledge or power but based on the recognition that everybody has a part to play and a right to agency:

> At its roots partnership is about investing students with the power to co-create, not just knowledge or learning, but the higher education institution itself. . . . Partnership means shared responsibility – for identifying the problem or opportunity for improvement, for devising a solution, and – importantly – for co-delivery of that solution. (NUS, 2012, p. 8)

So, finally, the NUS-recognized student agency in HE comes with the provision that partnership demands students join with staff in taking responsibility for achieving the HE they envisage:

> Responsible student partners will not be satisfied with passing their demands up the chain and hoping that at some point somebody in charge agrees. Responsible student partners will work within the collective to determine what needs doing, why and how, and will work together with interested parties to make these imagined possibilities a reality. (NUS, 2012)

Student–Staff Partnership Spreads

Over the last decade, the idea of student partnership has been taken up with enthusiasm across English-speaking higher education globally, to the extent that by 2014 Healey, Flint and Harrington could argue:

> Engaging students and staff effectively as partners in learning and teaching is arguably one of the most important issues facing HE in the twenty-first century, (Healey, Flint and Harrington, 2014, p. 7)

while for Levy, Little and Whelan, 'the theme of staff-student partnerships reaches to the heart of debates about the values and role of the twenty-first century university' (2011, p. 2). We would agree.

Student partnership has quickly generated its own cannon including guides, frameworks, journal special editions and its own peer-reviewed journal – the *International Journal for Students as Partners*, which opened with a systematic literature review of the field (Cook-Sather, Bovill, and Felten, 2014; HEA, 2016; Bovill and Felten, 2016; Mercer-Mapstone et al., 2017). A recently produced bibliography of work on student partnership runs to fifty-four pages (Healey, 2019). Yet some of this work has demonstrated strong technocratic and domesticating tendencies, and the core question still remains:

> To what extent can power relations between staff and students be challenged and changed in HE given its prevailing ideological and structural characteristics, or are the barriers such that it is not possible to envisage wide-scale cultural change in the direction of genuine partnership? (Levy, Little and Whelan, 2011, p. 12)

In the face of established power structures and domesticating forces it would be easy to lose hope and give in to frustration and fatalism. But there is hope to be had. In 'acknowledging the fraught and siloed nature of HE, a partnership mentality stands to disrupt cultures of competition' (Cates, Madigan and Reitenauer, 2018, p. 43). Freire counsels us that 'Education, while not being able to accomplish all, can accomplish something. We have the duty to find spaces for action, of organising ourselves in those spaces' (P. Freire, 2007, p. 67). So student–staff partnership working provides us with possibility and the space to enact democratic education and transformational action within and around the traditional power structures of UK HE.

Why the Pedagogy of Partnership?

The term 'pedagogy of partnership' consciously echoes the title structure of many books by Paulo Freire (1996, 1997, 2004b) because the concept also consciously builds on his work. Like Freire, we believe education is an ongoing process and practice rather than a thing, commodity, product or package of subject knowledge. It is fundamental to being human. The potential is always there for us to learn; the potential is also always there for us to teach. Our education is ongoing and incomplete, unfinished and unfinishable (Freire, 2007).

Relationships between human beings are fundamental to this ongoing practice. These relationships of trust and mutual respect make meaningful education possible (Felten and Lambert, 2020). These relationships are not merely transactional or intellectual, they are rounded, emotional and complex. Whenever it is undertaken as a formalized activity, education is almost always social. Education is an act of love, a demonstration that we care enough about someone to pay heed to what they have to tell us or to invest time and energy in seeking to explain to them. The pedagogy of partnership foregrounds and lays bare the mutuality, collegiality, kindness, care and belonging that lie at the heart of any good educational practice. The pedagogy of partnership is also what makes a flourishing learning community.

In the pedagogy of partnership all are present to teach and to learn, to engage in scholarship and in action. This is not about being teacher-centred or teaching-focused, and it is not about being student-centred or student-focused; it is about fostering meaningful educative relationships between people who are present to learn and teach, to teach and learn. It is fluid and changing, the relationships develop as we learn from each other and teach each other, we teach and learn more as the relationships deepen. It is a space 'wherein competition is suspended and co-operation defines success' (Matthews et al., 2018, p. 2264). We practise partnership through engaging in democratic education and through engaging in partnership we practise democratic education.

The fundamental purpose of education is to 'be more' – to be more human, to be more humane, to be more present, to be more ourselves, to be more engaged, to be more aware (A. Freire, 2007, p. xi). Being more is to raise our consciousness of the world, our place in it and the possibilities and potentialities it holds. It is to grow and flourish individually and collectively. Education helps us realize our place in society and our role in shaping a better future for ourselves and our communities. This purpose is not a fixed end but a constant invitation to grow, develop, shape and transform.

The pedagogy of partnership, therefore, foregrounds human relationships at the heart of education practice. This is not to deny specific subject matter. People may come together to learn about history or chemistry, driven by their love of the subject.

Building partnership and mutual understanding is, in fact, easier if it can coalesce round both a shared joy for the subject and a respectful understanding of that joy in others. And, if the purpose of education is to 'be more' – to be more aware of our world and the potential of our actions upon it – then all subjects offer a lens on this. In the pedagogy of partnership, no subject is merely theoretical, all require application, and a consideration of their implications. Thus, history education is not just the study of the human past but a consideration of how we read and make sense of it as a means of being actors in our own history. Science education cannot be limited to the acquisition of an ever-growing body of knowledge but has also to consider the implications of that knowledge and develop wisdom and considered judgement in its deployment.

What the pedagogy of partnership does require is a realization that the people present define what will be learnt. They can do this consciously and openly or unconsciously and even covertly.

We think it is important that the always-political decisions taken about what to teach, why it is being taught and how to teach it, are laid bare, shared with students, and discussed by all interested parties. To fail to do so would itself be a political act of withholding. In informal and community settings, education might be issue- or action-focused from the outset. In more formal settings the action resulting from educational practice might be less obvious, but it is still vital to consider not just knowledge but also purpose.

The pedagogy of partnership is the practice of democracy. This is not to say that all are equal or have equal power or responsibility in a particular setting; as Freire points out: 'Dialogue between teachers and students does not place them on the same footing professionally; but it does make the democratic position between them' (Freire, 2004b, p. 107). Individual differences in knowledge, outlook and experience are what make collective education possible. All participants have some power and responsibility and everyone present has a right to think for themselves, share that thinking and, through doing so, has the opportunity to shape what happens, to learn and to teach, and, so, to grow and be more.

The Principles for a Pedagogy of Partnership

A pedagogy of partnership based on Freirean principles provides space and opportunity to live 'hope-full' critical pedagogy in UK HE. The six principles developed to help ensure that student partnership at Newman University was underpinned by Freire's ideals, rather than domesticating neoliberalism, are briefly set out here and can be summarized as; shared hope, shared visions, respectful dialogue, co-investigation, co-construction and continuing transformation (Peters, 2016; Peters and Mathias, 2018).

Shared Hope

As Freire states, 'hope is an ontological requirement for human beings' (Freire, 1997, p. 44). Without a 'shared hope' that things could be better, without '*critical optimism*' (Freire, 1997, p. 58), we are prey to fatalism and cynicism. In order to enact transformations, we must collectively believe in our transformational potential.

HE is about changing the world, our collective understanding of it and our place in it. As Nelson Mandela put it: 'Education is the most powerful weapon we have to change the world.' Talking through hopes, dreams and visions is fundamental to making this change.

Paulo Freire begins *The Pedagogy of Hope*:

> We are surrounded by a pragmatic discourse that would have us adapt to the facts of reality. Dreams, and utopia, are called not only useless, but positively impeding. (After all, they are an intrinsic part of any educational practice with the power to unmask the dominant lies.) (2004b, p. 1)

Some would reduce education to a transaction, just another service we buy; a ticket, not to hopes and dreams, but to skilled employment in the knowledge economy. Such a depleted, diminished view of education may promise the achievement of acquisitive personal goals – greater wealth, enhanced confidence, social mobility even – which are certainly enticing but which condition us to accept the world as it is (Giroux, 2019; Cates, Madigan, and Reitenauer, 2018). This is a world of money, market and competition, where my personal gain must inevitably mean your loss. In this world it is okay if more children are living in poverty, food banks are booming, xenophobia is growing and the planet is fast overheating, as long as I get the qualification and a small chance to climb imperceptibly up the economic ladder. Except that isn't okay, is it? We want a better world, for ourselves, our friends, family, neighbours, communities, for our children and their children. We would like life on earth to survive and thrive. HE can and does do that, it makes us question how things are, see the bigger picture, ask why and start to dream of better.

Shared hopes, dreams and visions may sound esoteric, but they are not, they are fundamental to HE and, in the current crisis, they may be the only thing that saves us. 'I have a dream' is one of the most powerful phrases of the civil rights movement because imagining something better helps us strive for it. Dreams of utopia are a strong thread in radical thought because they help us question the present. Imagining a better world feeds our hope and encourages us to work towards it, to make a difference and not accept things as they are (Mathias and Peters, 2018). 'There is no change without dream, as there is no dream without hope' (Freire, 2004b, p. 81). Building our hope strengthens our hand and gives us the will to act. Imagining a better world feeds our hope and encourages us to work towards them, to make a difference and not accept things as they are (Mathias and Peters, 2018). 'There is no change without dream, as there is no dream without hope' (Freire, 2004b, p. 81). Building our hope strengthens our hand and gives us the will to act.

As bell hooks put it in *Teaching to Transgress* (1994, p. 207):

> The academy is not paradise. But learning is a place where paradise can be created.

> The classroom, with all its limitations, remains a location of possibility. In that field of possibility we have the opportunity to labor for freedom, to demand of ourselves

and our comrades, an openness of mind and heart that allows us to face reality even as we collectively imagine ways to move beyond boundaries, to transgress. This is education as the practice of freedom.

Shared Visions

It is one thing to believe our world could be better, it is another to have an idea of what that better world might be like. The pedagogy of partnership therefore places great importance on establishing 'shared visions', which bring together our collective hopes and dreams. The sharing of these visions is important because of the collective and social aspect of educational practice; we seek to promote education as a social good of communal benefit. This may, to some, seem indulgent or even irrelevant to the demands of the modern world. If HE were about merely attending classes to get the notes, learn the stuff, pass the test, get the qualification and bag the graduate job, they would be right. But it is not. Our role as educators is not to produce 'oven-ready' graduates for the labour market but to help students 'be more'. This entails engendering the hope that things can be better, encouraging the vision to see how they might be better, and revealing the agency students have to make it so.

Again A. Freire states 'It is impossible to live without dreams' (2007, p. 3) and he charges us that: 'as progressive educators, one of our main tasks seems to be with respect to generating political dreams in people, political yearnings, political desires'. This he talks of as the creation of a 'pedagogy of desire' (2007, p. 5).

Respectful Dialogue

'Respectful dialogue' is central to Freire's work.

> Through dialogue, the teacher-of-the-students and the students-of-the-teacher cease to exist and a new term emerges: teacher-student with student-teachers. The teacher is no longer merely the-one-who-teaches, but one who is himself taught in dialogue with the students, who in turn while being taught also teach. They become jointly responsible for a process in which all grow. (Freire, 1996, p. 61)

This dialogue can be challenging for HE practitioners because it means letting go of control and hearing difficult truths from students. Yet, without listening with humility, we do not gain from diversity and will not learn to grow and 'be more'. Listening is the prerequisite for respectful dialogue. Hearing and listening to otherwise under-represented voices are the bases for promoting meaningful exchange. To do this we need to listen with humility, before leaping to debate and critique. This applies as much across all fields and forms of collaboration. Such approaches cannot avoid discussion of values and intentions (Peters and Mathias, 2018).

> Discussion a, disagreement and negotiation towards a set of shared values should be a hallmark of higher education. (NUS, 2012, p. 1)

Space has to be created to hear all voices and share our lived experiences. The concept of partnership working recognizes that our diversity is a strength because it brings together a vast range of experience, knowledge and understanding from which we can learn and on which we can build (Peters and Mathias, 2018).

> Dialogue is meaningful precisely because the dialogical subjects, the agents in the dialogue, not only retain their identity, but actively defend it, and thus grow together. . . . Dialogue is not a favour done by one for the other, a kind of grace accorded. On the contrary, it implies a sincere, fundamental respect on the part of the subjects engaged in it. (Freire, 2004b, p. 107)

If respectful dialogue values difference it also helps us think things through in relation to others and helps us live our values:

> This then is how I (and others) think about teaching . . . as practicing thinking with respected others (living or dead, present or absent) in conversations. Such conversations continue long afterward to provide good company when, in complex lives, we need to think through what we should do and who and how we should be. There are clearly both moral and political values in play when we think together, practicing rather than preaching equality and freedom, respect, and independence. (Minnich, 2003, p. 21)

Co-investigation

'Co-investigation' is a key aspect of the 'pedagogy of questioning' (Freire, 1997, p. 62). It provides the 'problem-posing' education of the 'pedagogy of the oppressed': 'The students – no longer docile listeners – are now critical co-investigators in dialogue with the teacher' (Freire, 1996, p. 62). This is a conscious rejection of the 'banking', instructional and commodified model of knowledge, which Freire called 'an education of answers', in favour of a model that educates curiosity:

> An education of answers does not at all help the curiosity that is indispensable in the cognitive process. On the contrary, this form of education emphasizes the mechanical memorization of contents. Only an education of question can trigger, motivate, and reinforce curiosity. (Freire, 1997, p. 31)

For Freire this meant collectively questioning the way the world is; why it is that way and whether it could perhaps be otherwise. Such critical curiosity can be about seeking to discover something new or turning to questioning our assumptions and challenging shared notions of 'common sense'. Again, it makes a virtue of diversity and listening to under-represented voices because these may well offer fresh and *challenging perspectives*.

Co-investigation describes the very nature of every joint research practice. However, it specifically sees the interacting partners as equal participants engaging in shared reflection through joint questioning, curiosity and rational exploration. Many different learning and teaching methods could form part of the co-investigation element of the pedagogy of partnership. It would include research-based learning, enquiry-based learning, problem-based learning, project-based learning and service learning. It can also, therefore, involve ways of working beyond the classroom and, at Newman, has often entailed engagement in development projects aimed at exploring the assumptions underpinning limiting university practices. Whatever particular method or focus is taken:

> Their uniting features are that they should be authentic, meaningful to those involved, active and collaborative. . . . There must be a sense of collective purpose and of pooling ideas. Critical curiosity can take many forms. . . . It is generative of new ideas, explanations and possibilities. (Peters and Mathias, 2018, p. 63)

Examples of university projects that have undertaken such co-investigation include those which questioned the Whiteness of the curriculum or explored the experiences of Black, Muslim and disabled students. They have posed the question: why does it have to be like this? And found that it doesn't.

Co-construction

Co-investigation then drives 'the *emergence* of consciousness and *critical intervention* in reality' (Freire, 1996, p. 62, original emphasis). Such intervention entails the 'co-construction' of possible solutions and better ways of being together. Addressing authentic issues will inevitably mean working towards producing meaningful changes that promote social justice and improve our collective lives. Thus, the pedagogy of partnership does not just help to deliver particular outcomes or improvements in understanding but also aims to be of social benefit, promoting a greater comprehension of how we can work together to take on greater challenges. It means caring about, and for, each other and should increase our capacity to collaborate effectively to achieve positive change. It both practises and strengthens our agency and our will to act.

Indeed, being committed to the co-construction of a shared vision is undoubtedly the path of the road less travelled. It takes much more work to listen and compromise than it does to either prescribe, or acquiesce to, the status quo. Felten et al. (2019) observe that 'deeply collaborative work requires openly acknowledging the liminal space partners are navigating and embracing the uncertainty and potential that it holds' (200). It requires a 'fundamental rethinking of the place of students and their agency' (Felten et al., 2019). This is not easy. As Cates, Madigan and Reitenauer (2018) warn, 'expecting agency from those at the bottom of power structures is a radical act' (p. 42). There is real progress to be made in abandoning any sense of entitlement or imposter syndrome, superiority or inferiority, and coming together to craft a genuinely synergistic construction of what HE could be.

An Ongoing Process of Transformation

If education is an unfinished and unfinishable process, then the pedagogy of partnership is an ongoing, transformative and collaborative process of being and becoming.

> It is not possible to be unfinished beings, such as we are, conscious of that inconclusiveness, and not seek. Education is precisely that seeking movement, that permanent search. (P. Freire, 2007, p. 87)

As such, the pedagogy of partnership values the asking of open questions above the provision of closed answers, the ongoing development of wisdom above the transmission of packaged knowledge, and acting in critical hope rather than adopting cynical fatalism. By its nature it cannot be contained in formal programmes and sessions. It will spill out into other aspects of study and life. As we discuss in a later chapter, both staff and students involved in partnership work have commented on the way it changes their approach across other settings and arenas. For example, working in partnership with students on Appreciative Inquiry changed the tone of the whole staff–student conversation for one institute (Kadi-Hanifi et al., 2014). Partnership is enduring and unconfined and, once experienced, there is no going back (Peters and Mathias, 2018).

The final principle is, therefore, that we are committed to 'continuing transformation'; an ongoing process of 'hope-full' action.

> In my view, 'being' in the world means to transform and re-transform the world, not to adapt to it. As human beings, there is no doubt that our main responsibilities consist of intervening in reality and keeping up our hope. (A. Freire, 2007, pp. 4–5)

Critiques and the Threat of Domestication

To return to the NUS *Manifesto for Partnership*, we noted earlier that Wenstone warned readers about the ease with which sharing best practice can become divorced from practice grounded in values, cutting its roots and killing the very purpose that gave it power.

> We say we want to celebrate and share best practice; that can no longer mean that which simply works well. Our practice needs to be underpinned by our values. An activity really should make the reality of education closer to our vision before we single it out as 'best practice'. (NUS, 2012, 1)

This has proved to be a fundamental risk to effective partnership working. At all times students and staff are 'operating in a space where teaching and learning have been metricised [and this has] significant implications for social relations [placing limits on] the kind of pedagogy and knowledge that is produced and valued in the space' (Matthews et al., 2018, p. 2198). The sector's preoccupation with conceptualizations of best practice, with being evidence-based, doing only 'what works', has the worrying consequence of limiting genuine exploration of the possibilities.

Wenstone also argued that we have spent sufficient time on critique of neoliberalism and the model of student-as-consumer that necessarily attends it (NUS, 2012). The time has come instead for us to reset the relationship between teachers and the taught. Eight years on, and the proliferation of further expressions of consumerism now shaping UK HE – TEF, the establishment of the OfS, the growth in the role of the Competition and Markets Authority and the NSS – juggernauts along, unabated. We are regulated, metricized, held accountable for the delivery of our product like never before. There has been more to critique – but this means there is yet more to *do*.

Reasons for Hope

How, then, to locate hope in the midst of this potentially suffocating layer upon layer of prescription, requirement and obligation? Zipke (in Scoles et al., 2019, p. 2) warns us of the 'elective affinity' between student engagement work and the neoliberal agenda. We might claim the pedagogy of partnership as the ultimate expression of student engagement, but the very notion of student engagement has been diluted, hollowed out through a plethora of synthetic initiatives that use student voice as a proxy for purposeful pedagogic relationships; this is the constant threatening domestication of such work of which we have spoken within this chapter. We become pessimistic about the possibilities of pedagogy of partnership as the critique of student engagement work grows louder. But, as Popova warns, 'critical thinking without hope is cynicism' (in Solnit, 2016, p. xii). How should we then set about locating authentic hope in our student partnership practices? What can our principled approach deliver in the face of this nihilistic picture?

One source outlining hope that is influential on this book is *Crack Capitalism* (2010) It is grounded in a tradition that blends Marxism, hopeful Freirean critical pedagogy and flavours of South American literature on educational democracy, Holloway has taken elements of Freire's work, and in turn inspired Neary and many others to keep on keeping on, to remain undeterred from the task of 'education for decision, for rupture, for choice, for ethics' (Freire, 1997, p. 44). In this text, Holloway acknowledges that the hope of completely eradicating capitalism (and its accompanying impacts upon HE) becomes ever harder to envision. But this is not, for him, a negative position that concedes ultimate power to the marketized forces shaping us. Our focus instead is on ensuring our actions do not recreate the inequities and injustices of the past. He implores us to 'stop making capitalism, and do something else, something sensible, something beautiful and enjoyable' (Holloway, 2010, p. 254). We must find the spaces, lever them further open, dance in the cracks, refuse to contribute to oppression and othering.

If we are to succeed in such a dance, and in locating and sustaining hope in our pedagogical practice, we need methods and strategies that resist the atomising and isolating effects of the neoliberal agenda as it operates in HE. Amsler indicates that it is 'possible to organize society in ways that enable people to lead dignified, autonomous, mutually engaging and collectively self-determined lives' (2015, p. 30), recommending that we are, to begin with, wary of the 'totalising critiques of power' (Amsler, 2015, p. 32) that obscure more nuanced pictures of resistance and creativity that abound across the gamut of HE practice. Throughout this book, we collectively argue that moving towards the form of 'educated hope' that imbues Freire's work, and finding a new iteration in the post-critical literature (see Leoarna and Mike Gilsenan in Chapter 4) is one solution to the challenge of doing meaningful work in our institutions. We would assert that the pedagogy of partnership is a form of HE practice that allows an authentic hope to flourish; it is a practice that, when underpinned by the values and principles we outline in this chapter, can represent a positive form of activism.

The pedagogy of partnership poses fundamental questions about the oppressive hierarchies that proliferate in our institutions. It forges connections and collaborations that would otherwise lie undiscovered, demonstrating the real possibility of achieving a 'radical collegiality' (Fielding, 1999) among all members of our learning communities. It can liberate staff from being characterized as neoliberal subjects (Cowden and Singh, 2013; Sutton, 2015) and students from being perceived as nothing more than customers. It can respond, in fundamental ways, to the ideals that underpin our very understandings of what universities are, and can be: unfinished, always being reimagined, always alive to the needs of society at that moment (Neary, 2012).

So, the pedagogy of partnership is a response to Holloway's call for us to immerse ourselves in 'human doing' (2010, p. 237). He shares everyday examples of large and small activism, speaking of them as 'cries of hope, projections towards a different way of living, attempts to do something better with our lives' (Holloway, 2010, p. 241). We assert here that the 100 or so student partnership projects we have witnessed reaching completion in our own institution stand as beacons of Freirean, Holloway-esque hope for all members of Newman. In living out our annual cycle of projects, we are operating on the 'premise that the world as we know it is not a given, that it is a construct, and thus, it is always possible to start anew' (Schwimmer, 2019, p.u.).

In Chapter 3 Mike Seal shares typologies that help us understand the approaches of self-identified critical pedagogues. The list includes those who believe that it is impossible to enact hopeful critical pedagogy within universities as they are currently conceived and managed. We do not hold to this view: rather, we acknowledge that while it can, as a hopeful critical pedagogue, feel impossible to be anything other than both 'in and against' the university (Harney and Moten, 2013), we equally think this makes it all the more important to (1) remain hopeful and (2) continue to act. As Holloway asserts: 'There is no purity here: we try to overcome the contradictions, we rebel against our own complicity . . . we try to direct the flow of our lives as effectively as possible towards the creation of a society based on dignity' (Harney and Moten, 2013, p. 257). Living out our hope is a moment-to-moment practice, as we recognize that we are part of a system whose operating principles we cannot condone but must often acquiesce to. It is necessarily messy, and in the spaces we lever open through an authentic pedagogy of partnership, we can acknowledge this messiness and seek solutions, together.

From Chartists, to Suffragettes, to Black Panthers and Zapatistas, to the student activism of the 1960s and modern youth movements such as those represented by the work of Malala Yousafzai and Greta Thunberg, turning hope into real and lasting change has often been the work of once-small groups of people. We think here of anthropologist Margaret Mead's oft-quoted incantation that we should 'never doubt that a small group of committed citizens can change the world. Indeed, that is all that ever has'. Hope remains politically, socially essential, and threads itself through the shifts we witness at global, national and local levels. Universities play a central role in shaping civic life, industry and our national cultural expression; those institutions that embrace a pedagogy of partnership are offering the communities and societies in which they are located a vision of how we can achieve change together through democratic practices. The exponential growth in partnership working that has taken place within HE contexts on every continent in the last ten years further confirms the possibility of 'alternative working models' that Freire believed could be found (2007, p. 4). At the very least, student partnership is 'responding to the problems of the student-as-consumer model' (Luo, Matthews and Chunduri, 2019, p. 134), operating as a vibrant example of how hope can be translated into action.

Response from Mike Neary

Leoarna Mathias and John Peters have set out a vision for the university life they want to live, organized around the practices of democracy, equity and social justice. This vision is inspired mainly by a programme for partnership set out by the National Union of Students in the UK and the work of Paulo Freire. Leoarna and John are arguing against the approach to liberal education where students are trained as the intellectual apprenticeships of academics. Their vision, which they call a 'hope-full' critical pedagogy, is organized around a values-based model for higher education framed by six partnership principles: shared hope, shared dreams, respectful dialogue, co-investigation, co-construction and continuing transformation. Their partnership of hope is grounded in an affirmative and appreciative view of higher education, seeking to energize what they claim to be people's essential humanity as the basis for cultural change in universities.

There is a problem with a values-based critique of liberal education as it is, itself, derived from liberal theory. The defining principle of liberal theory is that social relationships between individuals constitute the organising structure of society, in all their complexity, emotionality and power dynamics. For social liberals, human sociability has been disrupted by marketization, but can be restored through more democracy, community, mutuality, kindness, collegiality and love. There is much to commend the important work that Leoarna and John are doing with their colleagues and students at Newman, but a liberal critique of liberalism, even the social liberalism they express, avoids an engagement with the more foundational critique required to support the kind of educational transformations they desire.

Leoarna and John have pointed in the direction of a more foundational critical critique with their discussion of John Holloway's work later in their chapter. Holloway, after an 'open' reading of Marx, provides an historical materialist critique of liberal thought and action: there is no progressive social consensus to be empowered, rather society is riven by the contradiction between capital and labour, as the basis for class struggle. Social relations among people are determined by the capital relation: capital versus labour, and people are bearers of those relations. For historical materialism, the political and economic significance of value is not as a set of aspirational ideals;

but, rather, as the measure and substance of capitalist wealth. Value is extracted from human labour and the natural world in an exploitative and destructive process for people and the planet. The damaging nature of that relation is apparent in the stressful, exhausting reality of waged work in capitalist institutions, including the capitalist university, and the negative effects it has on domestic life. The nature of the contradiction between capital and labour means that it cannot be resolved; but, the cracks that the contradiction at the core of the capital relation reveals can be extended, and capitalism replaced with a new form of social wealth: a common wealth based on people's needs and capacities.

Cardinal Newman, after whom Leoarna and John's university is named, was the high priest of liberal education. In his book *The Idea of a University* (1852) he claimed the intellect as a privileged site of human activity that must be cultivated. The logic of Marx's historical materialism is that the intellectual should not be seen as a privileged site of human endeavour, but that intellectual and manual labour need to be reconnected, thinking and doing grounded in everyday life. Just imagine what kind of university that would be.

Part II

Hopeful Pedagogies in Higher Education

Part II A

Hopeful Pedagogy within Courses

Chapter Six

Early Years to Higher Education

Legacy and the Creation and Connection of Hopeful Spaces

Julie Boardman and Jane Beniston,
Response from Carol Aubrey

Introduction

In this chapter the authors play with ideas around critical pedagogy and pedagogical approaches, located now with students in higher education (HE) and look back to their experiences with young children and their families in early years settings. While on a research journey on our Doctorate of Education (EdD) professional doctorate many ideas seemed to 'come together' and this thinking has the potential to perhaps make useful and relevant connections for the reader. We were struck primarily by how our pedagogic practice in early year's settings has influenced and indeed provided the foundation for our pedagogy in a university learning environment.

Wahida, a current student on our Early Childhood Education and Care (ECEC) degree, has a lived experience of both. She was invited to contribute to this chapter and share her thoughts.

> Play is essential in early years. By giving the child the opportunity to play will, I believe, allow the child to exercise their rights, to have a voice, challenge, question and feel empowered to be a free/critical thinker and an independent learner.
>
> In later years, education becomes more structured and children are not given the opportunity to be critical thinkers. In my experience you are taught that there is a right and wrong for everything and this cannot be challenged. This restricts thinking which I believe is very important. In my opinion being a critical thinker comes with opportunities from the very start of your life. Being able to challenge, ask questions, disagree, I believe, are positive outcomes of being a critical thinker.
>
> When I was at college, it was very much the same as being in secondary education. There was no opportunity for challenging, the environment was structured. However, when I came to university, I was overwhelmed by the opportunity to have a voice, give my own opinion, challenge, question and not believe everything

> I read. Lectures and seminars are taught in a relaxed atmosphere with plenty of opportunities to think critically and reflect upon and to be an independent learner which makes me feel empowered. It has been difficult to adjust to as I was given little or no opportunity to be a critical thinker throughout my life which made it difficult to adapt to university expectations.

We believe that playing with ideas and possibilities is the thread between play and critical thinking, ECEC and HE. We believe both can only be facilitated through participatory pedagogy in hopeful spaces. Relationships, approaches, values and democratic working will be explored in predominantly female working environments in early year's settings and on an ECEC degree course.

Both authors are from a background in early years, subscribe to a critical pedagogical approach and are both studying on a professional doctorate or EdD. Reflexivity on the EdD revealed how our values and backgrounds and our view of the world form our pedagogy and determine our learning spaces. They underpin any question we ask about what we are studying or researching or 'teaching', and how we ask them. We ask of ourselves and others key political questions as put forward by Moss (2019, p. 51). What is knowledge? What is education? What is its purpose? What kind of society do we want? These are all the questions that Freire (2007) was asking in relation to 'critical' and 'pedagogy'.

Introductions

Our life history and personal narrative are of course relevant to all things discussed. Egan (1988) highlights that the story (a well-utilized pedagogic resource in early years) is the primary way we think about our lives and our worlds and therefore, a brief autobiographical narrative will be provided.

> I grew up as an only child, into a working-class home and environment. Around the age of ten my class teacher told me 'I was a clever girl' and I started to believe I was. This was both good and bad. It opened up in my imagination new possibilities, perhaps even university one day; however, it started to mark me out as being different. This is still painful to recall. Even at this stage, I was interested to discover a paper by Lucey, Melody and Walkerdine (2003) where this scenario of working-class women in higher education is explored. This feeling of not knowing quite how and where to 'fit in' has affected all aspects of my life including my closest relationships. (Julie)

> As one of a family of four children with two elder, clever brothers I began life thinking I was a boy! I was dressed in boy's hand-me-downs and played 'boys' games. It came as a bit of a shock when as I grew up, I had to act more like a girl! In today's world this may seem very stereotypical, but within a northern male-dominated family there were clear rules on gender identity. This idea of never quite being good enough pervades my life especially in my doctoral

study. 'Be more authoritative,' I am told, 'nod at the literature, don't let it rule you'. (Jane)

I am the eldest of two sisters. When growing up I really enjoyed going to school. I would come home and re-enact being the 'teacher' and my sister being the child. Since early on in life I knew I wanted to work with children. I achieved this by training to be a nursery nurse and worked in the profession for nearly twenty years. I am not sure which career path to take next but by going back into full-time education I feel my options are open. I might consider teaching in early years or carrying on studying and researching. I am particularly interested in researching childhood globally. (Wahida)

We all start from the position of wanting to make the world a 'better' place in some way. Understandings of what equals 'better' can vary depending on value positions. Pring (2000, p. 141) distinguishes between moral considerations which relate to general 'principles of action' and those which relate to the dispositions and
character of the individual. Moral practice is grounded in personal decisions borne out of personal subjective experiences and perceptions. We share Tierney's (2000, p. 546) view and goal that 'in a post-modern age [there is a need] . . . to break the stranglehold of metanarratives that establish rules of truth, legitimacy and identity'.

Boundary Crossers

We all recognize ourselves as boundary crossers. Lucey, Melody and Walkerdine (2003) argue that the process of educational success and social mobility involves crossing borders of social class, gender and ethnicity. Hybridity is a term they use to name a concept to explore the multiple layers of experience of subjects in this situation. They state that there are no easy hybrids and develop ideas around the uneasiness of hybridity in terms of social mobility, which stems partly from the difficulties of negotiating one's own emotions – negative as well as positive – that are aroused when aspiration and success mean becoming and being profoundly different to your family and peer group. The losses that are fundamental to and unavoidable in change, even when change is desired and with the enormous amount of psychological labour involved in transformation, are not commented on in policy debates (Thomson, Henderson and Holland, 2003). Unquestioned in contemporary social and educational policy and the widening participation agenda is the notion that upward social mobility is the desired outcome of social improvement.

The positive possibilities of becoming and being a 'hybrid' can be debated. Does having to exist between existing identities mean that the hybrid subject has the best of both worlds, or is 'forced to live in the interface between the two'? (Anzaldua, 1987 cited in Grossberg, 1996). We experience moving back and forth between competing identities. As a 'border-crosser' can we find a place and condition of our own and some stability? The transition of students to HE and their subsequent transformation on their 'journey' affects power and the dynamics in their relationships and can sometimes cause both internal and external conflict. This is rarely acknowledged.

ECEC/HE Settings

Early years settings and universities are social and cultural institutions. Dahlberg and Moss (2005, p. 2) suggest that they 'can be understood, first and foremost, as forums, spaces or sites for ethical and political practice'. They are positioned within a neoliberal context where *Homo econimicus* is the goal, and technical (rather than ethical and political) practice with performativity and predetermined outcomes is rampant.

Within the constraints of the political and financial context of HE, the small university where we work has a widening participation agenda and is driven by a desire for social justice. Our pedagogical relationships, because of our values and view of the view of the world, are based on participation and caring (Macartney, 2012). In HE, of course, it is adults not children that we support with their learning. The authors do not see our role as 'teaching' or 'lecturing', or regard ourselves as 'experts'. 'Standing back' is used as a pedagogical stance where priority is given to the engagement of the learner-to-be 'what-if' choice makers. We consider this central to learner ownership and engagement and a means to foster autonomy. This has allowed our learners to become decision-makers and manage the transition to becoming an independent learner as this is one of the key expectations of being a university student. Another closely related expectation is to be a 'critical thinker' where information, ideas and arguments are not taken at face value. Everything is questioned and analysed and students are supported to engage in being playful with ideas.

> Julie and Jane's background in early years reflects the playful aspect in our sessions which gives us the opportunity to be in charge of our own learning. The focus is on learning rather than teaching. Early on in our course, we were introduced to the idea of Foucault, that there is no one truth. I found this very different and unsettling to come to terms with. This led to ideas around critical thinking within higher education which made me realize my way of thinking is different to other peoples. I am still trying to understand what critical thinking means. At school and college, we were told what to think and not encouraged to challenge. This new position is empowering and scary at the same time. Thinking back to early years, children are encouraged or it occurs naturally to them to think critically. I feel more strongly than ever that adults should not interfere and dictate a child's thinking. (Wahida)

This 'stepping' or 'standing back' may be termed a pedagogical stance when working with children and an andragogic one when supporting adults. Sometimes the term 'andragogy', conceived by Knowles (1984) as 'the art and science of helping adults learn' is seen as something different to pedagogy but Knowles himself concedes that four of andragogy's five key assumptions equally apply to both adults and children.

The andragogic model (Knowles, 1984) asserts there are five issues that need to be considered and addressed in formal learning: letting learners know why something is important to learn; showing learners how to direct themselves through information; relating the topic to the learners experiences; an awareness that people will not learn until they are ready and motivated to learn; and, sometimes learners require help to overcome inhibitions, behaviours and beliefs about learning. The sole difference we see is that children may have fewer experiences and pre-established beliefs.

Assumptions about the active role in the construction of meaning and knowledge by young children's and student's learning in HE underpin this chapter, influencing its theoretical positioning and political intentions.

Relationships

Our relationship with our learners (whatever their age) is based on the foundation of 'an ethics of care'. This owes much to feminist scholars such Noddings (2013) and Tronto (1993), who has drawn inspiration from Levinas (1987) and his ideas concerning the 'ethics of an encounter'. His starting point is how in Western thought knowledge readily becomes a will to know, 'grasping' the 'Other' and so making the 'Other' into the 'Same'. Tronto (1993, p. 58), echoing Levinas (1987), concludes that 'questions of otherness are at the heart of contemporary theory'. Care as an ethic is recognized by us as a key component in all education and the bedrock of our practice.

Early years practice is influenced by the Reggio Emilia approach from Italy and Te Whariki from New Zealand. Carr (2001), one of the key authors of the Te Whariki curriculum, and Rogoff (2003) argue that learning and development are relational processes of cultural co-construction and are the 'transformation of participation'. Macartney (2012) suggests that learning as the transformation of participation involves a view of learning (and teaching) as being produced by children/students with a pedagogue engaged within a community of learners. Rinaldi (2006), associated with the Reggio Emilia approach, also speaks to this when she emphasizes the role of dialogue and interdependence in her view of learning. Her explanation of dialogue embraces having a capacity for transformation.... It is an idea of dialogue not as an exchange but as a process for transformation where you lose absolutely the possibility of controlling the final result. (Rinaldi, 2006, p. 184)

Our starting point has always been our view of our learners and our response has been strongly influenced by Loris Malaguzzi and his involvement with the Reggio Emilia early years approach (Cagliari et al., 2016, p. 397) where he states: 'All . . . whatever their culture, whatever their lives are rich, better equipped, more talented, stronger and more intelligent than we can suppose'. We believe that each human is born with enormous potential and makes meaning of their world in an active way from the start. How we view a learner – child or adult – has enormous significance, leading to choices which are productive, 'by which [we] mean they determine the institutions we provide . . . and the pedagogical work . . . undertaken in these institutions' (Dahlberg, Moss and Pence, 2013).

Pedagogy and Paradigms

Pedagogic practice is also determined by paradigmatic position. A paradigm is a 'set of belief systems, a "worldview"' (Guba and Lincoln, 1994) and a particular 'lens for seeing and making sense of the world' (Sparkes, 1992), and each paradigm is based upon its own ontological and epistemological assumptions. Since all assumptions are conjecture, the philosophical underpinnings of each paradigm can never be empirically proven or disproven. Ontology questions such as 'what is reality?' is the study of being (Crotty, 1998, p. 10). Epistemology is concerned with how someone knows something, and the value given to that knowledge. It is concerned with the nature and forms of knowledge (Cohen, Manion and Morrison, 2007, p. 7). Axiology is the name given to the values we hold. Our paradigm is a basic belief system and the lens through which we see the world. It affects our thinking about everything. The positions we hold are a choice which comes with responsibility because it colours our view and makes things seem self-evident and natural.

Dominant in education today is the positivist paradigm focused on 'quality', 'accountability' and 'dataveillance'. Positivism has a desire to control a complex and uncertain world, and in this way, it complements neoliberalism. Positivists share an ideology where 'everything must be scientized and reduced to the brute (value-free) data of mathematics for the purpose of control' (St. Pierre, 2012, p. 484).

Our pedagogy is based around social objects and we are reminded by Gray (2009, p. 110) that 'social objects are not like stars or stones, which exist independently of how humans think about them'. We believe that there are knowledges and truths, not Knowledge and Truth. We value complexity, uncertainty, context and interpretation. The values underpinning our pedagogy are forged from a desire to pursue the positives identified by Bauman (2000): tolerance of ambiguity, preference of complexity, and risk-taking, while living in 'liquid modernity'. Life is messy and tangled, explained by the choice of language we use to come to understand and know, so that different language provides a different reality. So, the central issues become those of understanding the conditions in which certain discourses or worldviews are privileged and how the distinctions they produce between true and false can be contested (Otto, 1999, p. 17).

As researchers, both of us have gravitated towards paradigms which challenge the basic principles of positivism. We have adopted similar epistemologies (how do you know something?), our knowledge of it, constructed with others in caring, ethical relationships. These paradigmatic positions have led to what might be termed a 'participatory pedagogy' throughout our professional and research careers in education. Our dialogical or relational aspect of education tries to embed participation within daily life (Bae, 2009). We conceptualize participation as a relational and fluid process 'where different intentions are met with respect and, and there is room for changing one's mind' (Finnis, 2011, p. 396).

Authentic Practice

As early years practitioners we needed to be creative in our pedagogical practice so children 'might be viewed as active subjects with rights and voice' (Moss, 2007, p. 37), and not, as the neoliberal climate suggests, data to be collected. We sought to cultivate a network of inspiring creative relationships, in the style of the inclusive, democratic Reggio Emilia pedagogy (Dahlberg, Moss and Pence, 2013). We argue that the legacy of this creative approach is necessary in higher education to enable our students to gain confidence and flourish as independent learners and critical thinkers. All of this may be termed 'compassionate pedagogy' (Taggart, 2016), containing both psychological and sociological connotations. He reminds us that 'compassion is simultaneously at the heart of social justice campaigns which seek to enhance the capabilities of oppressed groups and also at the heart of psychological understandings about the origins of the capacity to care' (Taggart, 2016, p. 173). We have endeavoured to be authentic in our practice and extend to our learners, to use Rogers' (1961) term, 'unconditional positive regard'. Freire (2017) and his idea of 'pedagogical love' also resonates here.

> The link between early years and higher education is very similar. In early years children are given the opportunity and experiences supported by the adult in a warm and trusting environment to learn freely and develop through their own play. This benefits the child to be a free thinker, learn independently, and feel empowered. This is very much similar to lecturers at university working in the same manner such as giving students the opportunity to be critical thinkers, learn independently, question, challenge and support students to be able to learn and develop through a supported network. (Wahida)

Play and Higher Education

This authentic practice has implications for the way we position ourselves in relation to children or adults, and knowledge itself. Of central importance is our facilitative, rather than authoritative, stance adopted in shared learning spaces with others. Thinking *with* others is central to this way of being. We believe that Lipman's (2003) model of thinking is useful in that it highlights criticality, creativity and care as key components. These components are all present when a child is involved in play and we believe need to be present in a HE learning environment. If we regard knowledge as provisional and constructed in communal dialogue and learning alongside others, then the teacher cannot be the source of epistemic authority. Importantly, specific relational conditions are required. Priority should be given to children/students understanding what they think, and why. There can be no hierarchy of status or power. All opinions must be respected and trust must be built so critique can be voiced in a non-threatening environment.

In early years, play facilitates epistemic justice because what the child thinks or discovers cannot be 'wrong'. We consider that in the HE environment the words of the lecturer must be open to a process of negotiated meanings and if they are accepted, it is because students find them 'internally persuasive' and not 'authoritative' (Matusov, 2011, p. 104). There is a need to act without epistemic privilege, the idea that we are in some way 'superior' with knowledge and wisdom and therefore exercise the power awarded by this. In HE we find that many students view themselves as consumers and this consumption is a culture resulting from schooling in the current neoliberal and performativity climate. We need to help them create and think for themselves, and facilitate their agency to break free from their conditioning and conformity. Being able to 'think outside the box' and independent thinking are often squashed in schools where the focus is on outcomes and conformity.

> At school and college, we were told what to think and not encouraged to challenge. This new position is empowering and scary at the same time. Thinking back to early years, children are encouraged or it occurs naturally to them to think critically. I feel more strongly than ever that adults should not interfere and dictate a child's thinking. (Wahida)

We consider that playing with ideas, language and possibilities is the thread between early years and HE. We believe both can only be facilitated through participatory pedagogy in hopeful spaces.

> The link between early years and higher education is very similar. In early years children are given the opportunity and experiences supported by the adult in a warm and trusting environment to learn freely and develop through their own play. This benefits the child to be free thinkers, learn independently, and feel empowered. This is very much similar to lecturers at university working in the same manner such as giving students the opportunity to be critical thinkers, learn independently, question, challenge and support students to be able to learn and develop through a supported network. (Wahida)

Playing with ideas at any age invites a view of 'difference' which seems natural and less threatening. So rather than ignoring and marginalizing difference, viewing politics/ethics/power as central to education involves recognizing and responding to the diversity and complexities that exist within education and society. We have only recently become aware, through reflection as part of our doctorate study, that we were embracing the tenets of critical pedagogy as early years practitioners through our way of 'being' with the children and their families and the team we were part of.

Final Thoughts

Homo economicus, the product of neoliberalism, needs to be replaced with the daily reality of *Homo et Femina ludens*: man and woman the player, able to reflect on and play with ideas on the 'diagnosis of our time' (Mannheim, 1943). We need to think about the social, cultural, economic, political and technological conditions in which we are living, in order to create a relevant education for all and a better life and world. In both early years settings and the HE environment we have sought to create a hopeful playful space where:

Politics and ethics come together in an approach to education which rejects the regulatory bonds of developmental classifications and education as transmission and normative outcomes, and which emphasises the importance of otherness and difference, connectedness and relationships. (Dahlberg and Moss cited in Rinaldi, 2006, p. 15)

We concur with Moss (2019) that education is first and foremost a political practice where choices have to be considered and reflected on. It is underpinned by a strong ethical dimension about what a good education is, and can be, facilitated by relational pedagogy. We worked in early years as practitioners for fifteen years and were driven by wanting to contribute to challenge injustices in society. That same drive has stayed with us throughout our career in education and resides with us now in our work as lecturers in Early Childhood and Care in HE. Educational settings do not function in a 'neutral' way and some suggest that the way they operate reproduces and/or resists inequality and exclusion (Moss and Petrie, 2002; MacNaughton, 2005; Rinaldi, 2006).

A new epistemology is needed in which the present is deconstructed and the future is reconstructed mirroring early years practice. This utopian thinking also needs hope and a willingness to act. Resistance to the neoliberal positivist view is possible if we work alongside others and consider new possibilities together in 'playful hopeful spaces'. Politics and ethics come together in an approach to education which rejects the regulatory bonds of developmental classifications and education as transmission and normative outcomes, and which emphasizes the importance of otherness and difference, connectedness and relationships (Dahlberg and Moss, 2005). While we wait and work for the future, post-critical pedagogues (Hodgson, Vlieghe and Zamojski, 2018) choose to celebrate the present. We also celebrate the present and seek to create playful spaces and pedagogies to encourage learners of all ages to dance in the cracks between liminal spaces.

Chapter Seven

Widening the Cracks

Co-constructing Learning within Dialogical Spaces

Jane Beniston and Debbie Harris, Response from Dr László Varga

Introduction

Newman University is a Catholic university located within a suburb of Birmingham. Currently there are just under 3,000 students with 76 per cent attending on a full-time basis, and 24 per cent on a part-time basis. Of the students, 77 per cent are female and 23 per cent are male. In terms of ethnicity, 56 per cent are white, 10 per cent black, 25 per cent Asian. The remaining 9 per cent of students are of mixed heritage or have not declared their ethnicity. Over twice as many students declare themselves to be Muslims as declare themselves to be Catholic. An overwhelming majority of students are from areas which have low or very low participation in higher education (HE). Of the students, 93 per cent are classed as commuter students, that is, their term-time address is the same as their permanent address. The general student corresponds to the adage of being 'hard-to-reach'; however, Newman is seen as a thriving community, albeit not a residential community.

The culmination of all these factors do, however, present their own set of challenges around student participation. Data from the Realising Engagement through Active Culture Transformation Collaborative Development Programme (Beniston and Harris, 2017) concluded that we needed to move beyond the idea of 'involvement' and 'participation' to consider how knowledge and understanding of wider student engagement can be developed. From this research study, it would appear that there are certain barriers to students engaging more widely within the institution. These concern lack of communication, work commitments and, within this institution, being a commuter student. We also need to consider the unique identity of students at our institution. It was with this mind that we developed student-led modules to meet the needs of our diverse students.

Working within a university which recruits a diverse cohort of 'non-traditional' students, two senior lecturers critically reflect on how pedagogical approaches have been adopted to develop co-constructed learning (Freire, 2000). Drawing on theoretical perspectives from Giroux (2006, 2011), and Freire (2000), two student-led modules at

Levels 5 and 6 were developed within an Early Childhood Education and Care (ECEC) degree programme. Students studying on this programme are predominantly female, Muslim, 'commuters' (Jacoby, 1989) from disadvantaged backgrounds. Such students have been 'problematized' in discourse of late (Thomas, 2012; Donnelly and Gamsu, 2018) but this chapter hopes to explore the engagement, power and independence of these students.

This chapter will explore how experienced tutors on the ECEC programme considered the idea of critical pedagogy (as defined in Chapter 1) and how this thinking translated into the delivery of two modules based on this approach. It will focus on dialogic practice, and relational pedagogy, which enabled students to engage in collaborative dialogue to plan and deliver the content of the modules. The chapter will also consider the student role in the assessment process. A 'generative' curriculum, taking ideas from Massey (2008), enabled student voices to lead on module development and this chapter will therefore reflect upon the experiences of students and consider as to how this approach to critical pedagogy enhances both the students' and tutors' experience.

Contemporary Issues in Early Childhood

The module 'Contemporary issues in early childhood' is one of the second-year optional modules that we offer on the Early Childhood Education and Care BA (Hons) degree programme. Students undertake this in their second semester alongside core modules. This module has been taught over the last five years and has been labelled as 'student-centred' and 'student-led'. Although this seemed innovative at the time in terms of promoting individualized learning (Khan and Gabriel, 2018, p. 36), and ensuring 'student voice', a deepening understanding around the concept of critical pedagogy has enabled us as tutors to reflect on how to develop a module that facilitates a more collegiate and agentive approach to both teaching and learning. Relational pedagogy (Papatheodorou and Moyles, 2008, Hedges and Cooper, 2018) and a dialogical approach (Freire, 2006; Darder, Torres and Baltodeano, 2017, p. 389) were facilitated through the module. The premise is that these approaches would align with our aims for an ECEC graduate, which focus on developing students' critical knowledge and understanding relating to early childhood issues, enabling them to demonstrating thinking with ambition and empathy and equipping them with skills to enter the workforce, ultimately enabling them to contest inequality, and identify and challenge social injustice.

The planning of a curriculum is a people-orientated process. Maimoudi, Khoshnood and Babaei (2014, p. 90) state that, from a Freirean perspective, the student, as well as other stakeholders, has active participation in the construction of the learning. This was something that, as tutors, we were keen to engage with and resonates with work undertaken by colleagues within the next chapter who undertook a similar pedagogical approach with four cohorts of students in their foundation year. 'Generative themes' (Freire, 2006; Ledwith, 2011, p. 101) were used with the small group of students to structure the module and these themes provided the framework for ten weekly sessions. Themes were selected that students had an interest and/or a concern around within the early years sector and included 'Men in early years', 'School readiness', 'Assessment' and 'Mental health'. The only 'condition' was that the theme needed to meet the remit of being a 'contemporary issue'. There were themes that, as a tutor, I felt it would have been interesting to include; however, in order to avoid what Ledwith (2011, p. 100) calls a 'cultural invasion', where the content and delivery of the module imposes the seemingly dominant societal or tutor's views and beliefs 'on to' students, I had to learn to let the students take the lead on this. Then as a group, we negotiated the final teaching framework for the module. Once this was in place, a problematizing approach (Freire, 2006) was taken where we discussed what strategies could be undertaken in order to develop further knowledge, understanding and criticality of the issue together as a learning community. The strategies that emerged ranged from all students agreeing to source resources such as journal articles, relevant reports, video clips, on a weekly basis, to some students wanting to design presentations in order to use these materials to lead on and facilitate the sessions. This approach moved students from a passive to an active role – from 'cheerful robots' (Giroux, 2011, p. 3) to being more agential in their own and others learning in a 'generative-theme orientated classroom' (Darder, Torres and Baltodeano, 2017, p. 387).

Student Voices

> Students provided varied academic sources and produced PowerPoint presentations on their chosen topics to present the whole class. This encouraged us to discuss and think critically with other students. (Suhella)

> I enjoyed this way of working as when we are given reading material for other modules, even though we are given freedom to use other materials you have to try and use the reading material provided as they link more to the topic, but within the Contemporary Issues module we were able to provide our own material, we had more freedom. This was particularly enjoyable for me as some materials I bought to lectures, the lecturer did not know about so it made me feel happy that I was able to provide some reading material that the lecturer would find interesting outside of the lecture. (Amandeep)

Relational Pedagogy: Role of the Tutor

Relational pedagogy, which was discussed in more depth in the previous chapter, is a term more frequently used within early childhood pedagogy, as opposed to higher education. It draws on Vygotsky's (1978, 1986) thinking around social cultural theory and constructivism (Papatheodorou and Moyles, 2008) and the pedagogical relationships between children and teachers. These ideas, however, can be easily translated to pedagogical practice within higher education and in fact were key to the success of the module. The role of the educator needs careful consideration in critical pedagogy. Relativistic epistemology beliefs (Brownlee, 2004, p. 4) around teaching and learning when designing the module were based on the view that knowledge is an interactive process, through which problems are posed, that there is not just 'one truth' and that teaching is not just based on transmission of knowledge (Darder, Torres and Baltodano, 2017, p. 398). There was alignment with Freire's thinking of a more 'egalitarian model' where students act as partners with their tutor in order to develop a shared understanding and transform their reality (Sheldon, 2017, p. 91). To identify with Giroux and Giroux, (2006, p. 30) it was vital to consider a type of pedagogy where the focus of teaching is not solely driven by what is needed to be learnt in order to pass an assignment, and where the learning is 'regulated by the teacher's efforts' (Luhmann, 1990 cited in Sheldon, 2017, p. 92), but provides a space for students to reason, and understand through dialogue and critical engagement. This was not necessarily a comfortable way of working with students initially; it required risks to be taken, particularly as the onus was on students to prepare the materials for each session, and attend each session. It was not known if the students would engage with this mode of working when the responsibility was extended to them, and as a tutor who systematically plans and creates resources for students it was not easy to arrive at the teaching room without a planned session. It required, as Ledwith (2011, p. 101) states, a belief that the students had the capacity for both action and reflection. As a tutor, I wanted to force the 'teaching genie back into the bottle' (Pinar, 2015, p. 92) where traditionally the teacher is viewed as the 'key agent in the process' (Sheldon, 2017, p. 92), instead moving to a model which emphasized student agency. It was important that learning was meaningful and which, according to Freire, should be 'critical, rational and transformative' (cited in Serrano et al., 2018). The intentions for the module aligned to ideas around authenticity in learning cited by Serrano et al. (2018, pp. 11–12) which focus on identifying and acknowledging the impact of power relationships between students and tutors in the educational process, and reshaping this relationship. This concept of breaking down the teacher–student power imbalance is also explored further within the next chapter.

To put this into practice, the first session of the module saw discussions undertaken around the experience, knowledge and sharing of 'power' in the classroom. To encourage this, it was important that as a tutor I sat with the students and did not 'lecture' from the front. Democratic relationships were developed with the students, bearing in mind that the students were known to me from other modules that I had taught them. The discussion on democratic relationships was based on ideas of mutual trust and respect and of equality between the tutor and the learner where the role of the tutor and student are interchangeable. This is viewed by Ledwith (2011, p. 101) as a horizontal model of pedagogical practice where the traditional power imbalance between tutor and student is readdressed through dialogue between 'equals who are mutually engaged in a process of critical inquiry,' and according to Freire (1972b, p. 54) strives for the 'emergence of consciousness and critical intervention in reality'. This relational pedagogy focused on three parameters as cited by Brownlee (2004, p. 15) and crucially underpinned the philosophy of the Contemporary Issues module. These were:

- Showing respect to the student as knower.
- Providing learning experiences that relate to the students' own experiences.
- Articulating and facilitating a constructivist approach to learning by emphasizing meaning making rather than knowledge accumulation.

Student Voices

> It was interesting working as students who were leading the content of the module with lecturer support as we were able to choose the topic that we were interested in and be able to find out more about it. There was enough time to discuss and present without rushing through everything. Students were able to present their information but also had the support from the rest of the group as well as the lecturer which enabled everyone to take part. (Heleema)

> I thoroughly enjoyed being able to co-lead the module with the lecturer as it allowed me to have a little more control on how the module was structured. This was very effective within my learning as I was able to learn how to produce a lecture and present it to the rest of the group. (Amandeep)

Relational Pedagogy: Spaces to Belong?

Much has been written about students needing to feel a 'sense of belonging' to their institution (Trowler, 2010; Thomas, 2012) and within this relationally centred approach the emotional engagement of students was significant. Brownlee and Berthlesen (2005) refer to the work of Watts and Bentley (1987) where students who are asked to reflect on co-constructed ideas openly may find this a threatening task. Therefore, the pedagogy of space needed to be seen by students as supportive and empathetic to their needs and providing an ambience of 'mutual caring' (Ledwith, 2011, p. 54). The space for teaching and learning was negotiated with students for this module in terms of where we as a group should sit, how the room should be set up, providing an environment based on mutual respect where students felt able to discuss subjects freely and with agency. Berthlesen, Brownlee and Boulton-Lewis (2002, cited in Brownlee and Berthelsen, 2005) identify this as 'connected teaching' where there is 'a balance of relational and impersonal modes of knowing where students access their own experiences', in this instance relating their experiences of practice to the themes being discussed and 'engaging with the perspectives of experts'. In this case this involved engaging with material and resources found and also the knowledge and experiences of knowledgeable others within the group.

Student Voices

> I was able to support others as well as receive support from the rest of the group. (Haleema)

I think it was important for students to have support, particularly as this was our first student-led module. (Suhella)

As I mentioned before, I really enjoyed how the lectures were run as the lecturer gave us more freedom that they normally, do. They allowed us to work in more of a team as we structured the module together. (Amandeep)

Dialogical Practice

The tutor–student co-relationship is the basis of both a communal sense of learning and dialogic practice. Freire (2006, p. 81, 1972b, p. 65) discusses extensively the importance of the use of dialogue with students, moving them from 'docile listeners to critical investigators in dialogue with the teacher'. The dialogue can be viewed as a focused and purposeful conversation (Darder, Torres and Baltodano, 2017, p. 389) which Freire (2006, p. 84) views as 'dialogic problem posing'. He goes on to explain how this approach views the questions and not the answers as central to this method of education, with the use of open-ended questions providing students with the opportunity to co-construct learning, critically analyse situations, reflect on their own realities and consider them from a different perspective (Darder, Torres and Baltodano, 2017, p. 383). Freire's belief stems from the premise that dialogue needs to be capable of generating critical thinking; without dialogue there is no communication and 'without communication there can be no true education'. Dialogue in the form of questioning, reflecting and analysing, was significant throughout the module, problematizing issues specific to the early years workforce, and both the wider education and political agendas.

This way of working enabled us as a learning community to reflect on the dominant discourses, locally, nationally, internationally and, importantly, from a cultural perspective, and reflect on implications for practice. Mayo (2004, p. 93) cites Freire's legacy for radical education that 'for all their competence and authority, teachers must be humble to relearn that which they think they already know from others and to connect, through learning . . . with their learners' lifeworlds'. This was the foundation on which the dialogical approach to the module was based and such discussions helped students and the tutor to challenge assumptions, and to exchange and develop ideas in a group context through the facilitation and scaffolding of learning.

Student Voices

This style of learning has had an impact on student experiences as students were thoroughly motivated to prioritize and prepare weekly tasks, providing varied academic sources for each theme. (Suhella)

It [the module] allowed us to develop our confidence in presenting in front of a group as well as helping to improve our research skills. (Haleema)

I chose to study men in early years, so as well as another student I provided a PowerPoint presentation on the issues of men in early years and how we could tackle that issue in practice. I was able to work with people I have not worked with or spoken to before in the group and because of that I am now in regular contact with them which has helped me to gain confidence in socializing with more people that was a barrier before. The module has also supported me to become more critical which has had a huge impact on my role as a student as I am able to use the skills learnt within my assignments and more importantly within my dissertation. (Amandeep)

Challenges of Assessment

The concept of critical pedagogy also suggests transformative action as a result of this pedagogical process. However, in the current climate of accountability, compliance and quality assurance processes, students on this module were still exposed to and constrained by the requirements of assessment. An assessment that had been predetermined prior to delivering the module and where students to some degree had to 'reproduce knowledge in order to fit in with conventional approaches to assessment' (Beckman and Cooper, 2013, p. 17). There were obvious tensions here between what Giroux and Giroux (2006, p. 1) identified as democratic values and market values with a module that had encouraged students to believe that 'they are indeed individuals, while simultaneously they adhere collectively to the dictates of the market place. In this way mass forms of standardisation can prevail' (Darder, Torres and Baltodano, 2017, p. 101). In order to redress the balance somewhat, peer feedback was introduced and formed an element of the final feedback, but not the mark, perpetuating the ideas of the power of domination of traditional education (Freire, 2006). We had, on reflection, 'opened' the cracks but, still feeling constrained by the bureaucracy and lecturer-led assessment requirements, we decided to 'widen the cracks' further and introduce a totally student-led module with more student autonomy around assessment and a generative curriculum.

Critical Reflections on Early Childhood Education and Care

At Level 6 of our ECEC degree programme students have a range of mandatory and optional modules while also carrying out a research-based dissertation. A new student-led module was introduced which would allow students control over content, structure, assessment topic and method. Students also had complete control over the virtual learning environment for this module which was unprecedented at Newman.

Students were introduced to this module through the concepts of pedagogical approaches adopted to promote co-construction of learning (Freire, 2000) and a generative curriculum model (Pence and McCallum, 1994; Ball and Pence, 1999). This model is based upon mutual learning, sharing of skills and a collaborative construction of concepts and curricula based upon Freire's (1995) notions of generative themes. Students initial responses to this module were mixed.

Student Voices

> After the first session I felt confused about what was expected, and worried about how lecturers would assess each piece of work fairly as they would all be produced so differently.
>
> Having total ownership over the assignment surprisingly made me feel more out of control – because there was little guidance or structure to start with. (Meg)

> When the design of the module was explained to us, my first thoughts were, this is not going to work. (Chloe)

> My initial thought was 'Oh no! How on earth am I going to do this module?' I felt extremely anxious as I am the sort of person that appreciates guidance when I am facing unknown situations. I did not know what to do or how to do it and those initial feelings left me feeling really emotional and a little out of my depth. (Nikki)

Generative Curriculum

One of the strengths of the generative curriculum model, according to Ball and Pence (2001, p. 122), is that learning occurs 'all ways' through a diversity of cultural perspectives and voices. Khan and Gabriel (2009, p. 30) support this, commenting that this particular pedagogical approach enables students to use their own experience to develop ideas in a group context, providing a 'means of collective empowerment, both intellectual and practical', unlike a lecture that more often than not contains only the lecturer's voice and perspective. Budd, Kell and Humphry (2015, p. 24) consider that the development of any curriculum is not a neutral process but one that privileges the knowledge practice of a particular social group or in this case a particular lecturer. Students experienced this in different ways.

Student Voices

> I was able to express, my views and experience on the range of different topics that was brought forward in each week. It also allowed for me to express my interests, which then made people feel comfortable to ask further questions. (Chloe)

> I raised my own issues and shared my experiences which explained why I had issues regarding the topic. I was also given opportunities to engage in conversations and debates with other students within the module. I particularly enjoyed this as I was able to support ideas, giving my own thoughts and disagree with ideas, giving my own critical opinions and experiences. (Amandeep)

Students were asked to identify what mattered to them within the early childhood context and generate themes for discussion within the sessions. They were then given time and space to develop what the sessions would look like, how they would be structured and who would lead them. This was done without lecturer management, intervention or interruption. Fisher and Cordeiro (1994, pp. 2–7) suggest that there is the continuous interplay between content learning and process learning within this pedagogical approach. This can be risky and was, but also has the potential to be generative, productive and transformational (Khan and Gabriel, 2009, p. 31).

> I enjoyed some of the lectures. But some I did not, as there were times where some students did not give 100 per cent of their contribution. This was quite frustrating as we were not able to express our opinions and experiences in a lot of detail, as we were not given much background information or any presentations in order to understand students' reasons for these issues or their opinions regarding the issues they were raising. However, there were other students who gave their all in the lecturers where you were able to understand and learn their opinions and give your own thoughts. (Amandeep)

> Generating the curriculum and planning sessions was the hardest part of the module I think, as we were all at different stages at different times and everyone wanted all sessions to be relevant to them. (Anna)

Transformative Pedagogy

This module provided space for 'transformative' pedagogy which goes beyond the individual towards collective change in what Massey (2008) terms 'activity spaces'. Within these 'activity spaces' different models of pedagogy are possible. Although creating a collective community, Ball and Pence (2001, p. 122) highlight that, through a generative curriculum model, students become more aware of their own cultural identity and their own personal views. Through cooperation and collaboration students understand how these relate to the views of others from both outside and inside their communities. These new understandings may lead to ontological changes and a kind of transformative pedagogy.

Student Voices

> I found it hard at times to try and be collaborative and less competitive, for example when I found a good journal article, I didn't want to share it with anyone (ok I am selfish!). I had to remind myself that the rest of the group's success doesn't take away from mine and we can all do well. I stopped being a resource hoarder and added things I found helpful to the virtual learning environment (VLE). Having to work collaboratively changed my outlook as a learner; I had to try hard to be less competitive and to want to contribute to help other people do well. I think throughout school, and previous years of FE and HE as well, competitiveness has been encouraged, so it was difficult at first but also enjoyable to make myself challenge my own feelings on sharing resources and working together. (Anna)

> The module has had a positive impact on me a learner. It has been positive as I am now more aware of issues and have the confidence to be more vocal about issues

that I do not agree with. I also have become more critical which is a skill that I can bring to my assignments, especially my dissertation. (Amandeep)

The module was a great way to get to know more about the experiences of others in the group and to understand what areas of ECEC they were passionate about. Collaborating as a group meant that discussions and 'debates' were developed; listening to the beliefs of others gave me the chance to reflect on and consider my own opinions regarding issues in practice and policy. Being able to hear other people's opinions on different topics which challenged my own was really valuable to support my own reflections. (Meg)

The module definitely helped me in my last few assignments on my degree because I actually received the lowest score of my whole degree on this module. It made me realize how much I rely on the lecturer's module information and guidance and I feel that the outcome of this module enabled me to be more independent in the remaining modules rather than relying on the lecturers supplying everything. It makes me wonder if I had done this module in my second year if I could have achieved higher marks from that point. I also grew in confidence throughout this module. It definitely throws you in at the deep end but upon reflection I think there was valuable personal learning that took place by completing the module. (Nikki)

Personally, this module made me feel like I can take more control and made me feel like my interests can be put into action. It also helped to develop new relationships with my peers. As a learner I feel it made me understand critical analysis better, as I always struggled to understand it. It also helped me develop my knowledge more on a range of subjects, some I have never considered. No matter how the themes were delivered there was room for open discussion and also debates, which one in particular got into a lot of depth. A memory that will not be forgotten any time soon. (Chloe)

Conclusion

Within this chapter, we have attempted to provide an authentic reflection of both tutor and students experiences of engaging with critical pedagogy in two particular modules. This journey was not without risk, but on reflection we believe that this has been worthwhile, both pedagogically and in further developing relationships with our students. We would ask you wherever and whoever you work with to consider your own relationships and consider if there are other ways of doing things; it is only by questioning and reflecting on our day-to-day practices that we can look at the past and understand more clearly what and who we are so that we can more wisely build the future (Freire, 1993).

Response from László Varga

'An ounce of experience is better than a ton of theory' (J. Dewey). Co-constructing learning is considered a new development in effective learning. Working together, looking at things from a different perspective, being able to really listen to each other, communicating and informing, accepting changes and dealing with these changes in a flexible way, thinking and acting in a creative manner, making use of the possibilities of each individual... these are just some of the skills developed within constructing learning.

Thinking, knowledge and problem-solving will be the new educational basics of the twenty-first century. 'Widening the cracks: Co-constructing learning within dialogical spaces' is a very comprehensive and detailed chapter. The layout of the chapter is well presented to allow the reader to see the concept from the point of view of student and of lecturer. This brings a wider approach to the concept and makes it easier to follow and comprehend. In addition, providing students' experiences in the paper points out the real value of supporting individuals' to bring out their own voice. This chapter is very valuable in terms of raising awareness for both students and lecturers in terms of focusing on the learning and teaching process, rather than purely information received. Using a new method in teaching can be challenging for both parts but also very rewarding in the longer term. Thank you for taking the initiative and trying out the method while teaching.

This student activity-based education is a commitment to ensuring a high-quality, culturally and linguistically responsive and equitable education to support the well-being and achievement of every student. All students should feel that they belong to an inclusive classroom so they can best learn and succeed. Constructivism learning theory means that students generate knowledge from their experiences, construct knowledge for themselves; that is, students build themselves up, so we can talk about the 'self-made student'.

The concept known as self-authorship and social constructivism in education is inseparable from quality education. Quality education can only be achieved if the needs of all students are addressed so that each learner is allowed an opportunity to succeed. Teachers are crucial in determining what happens in classrooms and there are those who would argue that the development of more inclusive classrooms requires teachers to cater for different student learning needs through the modification of, or divergence from, the curriculum.

We all know that every student is unique and different. They have different abilities; they learn in different ways and at different paces. Inclusive, learner-friendly and barrier-free environments should therefore be created in every school and community throughout the world so that all students will be enabled to develop to their full academic, social, emotional and physical potentials. It is important to remember that a student's academic potential cannot be developed separately from the social, emotional and physical potential, as these are interdependent aspects of a student's development. Individual support should primarily be given by the class teacher. However, s/he may also need assistance from school-based and itinerant resource teachers to ensure that the students concerned receive quality support that is based on their individual learning needs.

The goal of this research is to describe and explain basic phenomena. In teacher education the dissemination of general knowledge relevant for teaching and learning is based on the assumption that practitioners will make productive use of such knowledge.

The new practice of co-constructing learning within dialogical spaces thus needs to become the object of further research.

Chapter Eight

Preparing for an Unexpected Journey

Exploring the Experience of Teaching Critical Pedagogy through Critical Pedagogy

Helen Bardy and Mike Gilsenan, Response from Christine Smith

Introduction

The analogy of 'journey' is somewhat appropriate for this chapter as it represents several concurrent and successive travels along educational and research routes. Destination, however, is perhaps more problematic as the intentionally open-ended nature of the critical pedagogy module is an inherent challenge to an education system that requires measurable learning outcomes and quantifiable achievements. The piece will take its own journey (and at the time of writing we do not know what the end point will look like) that considers narrative provided by two groups of students through interviews and, to a lesser extent, recordings from our own reflective discussions on the experience of being the lecturers engaged in this module over the four-year period. Both the interviews and reflective discussions make reference to virtual learning environment (VLE) forums which, presented chronologically, reflect both temporal and qualitatively developmental journeys we have had the genuine privilege of making, alongside (sometimes behind and sometimes ahead of) the students. Despite the seemingly pleasant imagery being conjured here, the journey has not been without its roadblocks, stalls, accidents and breakdowns but all fellow travellers have now moved on to different ventures. It is intended that there be a full written research document in which some of what is discussed in this piece may be further interrogated, but we are approaching this chapter as another separate but related voyage.

The intention of the module in question is to offer the space for students to engage in what Brookfield (2005, p. 13) refers to as 'ideology critique', which is: 'the ability of individuals to disengage themselves from the tacit assumptions of discursive practices and power relations in order to exert more conscious control over their everyday lives' (Marcuse, 1964, p. 24 in Brookfield, 2005, p. 13). The module is, from the outset, completely given over to students to determine how it is taught, what specific content is explored, how it is assessed and what the criteria for assessment are. Located in the second semester of the second year within the youth and community undergraduate degree, which is professionally accredited and unapologetically from a critical theory standpoint, the module (at its inception) intended to provide the students with: an understanding of critical pedagogy, namely the work of Paulo Freire and others; an experience of dialogical education, which was somewhat different to how other modules in their programme operated; and finally, underpinned by Meyer and Land's (2005) notion for 'threshold' concepts and Seal's (2019a) idea of 'threshold praxes', transformation in their practice as professionals. Students, in Level 4, acquired some understanding of the work of Freire with particular reference to dialogical approaches in youth and community work. Indeed, Freire's approach has been synonymous with the youth and community work curriculum for practitioners for several decades. While authors such as Giroux, bell, Kincheloe and Ellsworth have furthered and critiqued his work, Freire is still relevant, we would argue, for professional youth and community workers. Utilizing this body of work helped students to: reinforce concepts and ideas that they had been introduced to in their previous modules, provide clear examples of criticality and offer another way of viewing youth and community work.

The dialogical approach is further underpinned with explorations of concepts such as hegemony, intersectionality, cultural and social capital, as well as practical applications such as learning the art of listening, sharing, negotiating and working collectively. What has arisen to a greater or lesser extent in each year, as we have attempted to embark on a truly democratic learning journey, is an inherent tension between a qualitatively fruitful and valuable learning experience and the institutional requirements (and sometimes individual desire) for a numbered grade at the end of the twelve-week period. However, rather than view this tension as an insurmountable conflict of ideologies, we try to recognize it as the reality that necessitates a critical pedagogy. This reality has been borne out in a range of themes we are beginning to identify as the research progresses.

After the introduction in the first week, the module expects the students to generate the content, facilitated by the staff. It needs to be noted that we don't see ourselves as lecturers here, more as fellow learners, although we recognize our place and power are different to the students (we are not one of them!). Students on this programme are not alien to experiential learning but, in offering merely a shell of a module within which they create the learning journey and negotiate the assessment, there is a qualitatively different experience to modules which are more content-driven. Offering the steering wheel for students to direct us on our route means that, from the outset, the balance of power is, if not shifted outright, at least questioned and challenged.

Some Preliminary Findings from the Group Interviews

Inevitably, one of the areas that students discussed in some detail is the influence or qualitative impact that the experience has had on them, both in personal and professional life, and this we shall discuss. However, impact as a concept tends to fall within the marketized paradigm in which education currently operates and our desire here (as the introduction suggests) is to explore the process, an educational travelogue if you will. So, travel versus impact will be one of the themes explored in this chapter. Others embarked upon will include: ethics – do we have the right to engage in such experimental approaches?'; and freedom – is the process liberatory for all or are we as lecturers implicated in the hegemonic power of education? The chapter alludes to a somewhat organic development of the teaching approach over the four years that allowed for a model of critical pedagogy which enabled the students to bring their lived experiences alongside theoretical concepts and in turn became, to varying degrees, perhaps a kind of lived theory.

Students' Perspective on the 'Process' (Travel Versus Impact)

It is fair to say that, perhaps, in the earlier iterations of the module, we had underestimated the anxiety caused by fully giving the module over to the students. Having discussed the purpose of the module at its outset with students and given the discussions of Freirean approaches to youth and community work at Level 4, we may have envisaged a greater 'buy-in' and less resistance. Whether the tensions created were a result of resistance or vice versa, it is difficult to ascertain, but it was particularly evident in the second cohort. Observing what we understood to be the group falling into familiar teaching processes – such as organizing workshops for the following weeks, arranging guest lectures and, in particular, spending much of the sessions designing assessment processes and criteria (although fully negotiated) – we took the decision to suggest they focus not on the assessment at the end, but engage with what they saw as the *process* of critical pedagogy. On reflection, students from that cohort saw this as a key moment of seeming contradiction.

> . . . time was always restricted . . . there was always a time limit on, you know, how long we had, when the assignment had to be in.
> Exactly and we started planning what we needed to do each week.
> I felt like the end bit was just so rushed.
> But it was rushed because we spent all them weeks prat arsing about.
> . . . not focusing on the end bit . . . this is what drives me insane, how can you not focus on the end bit when, we're already getting graded . . . on what we produce in the end?

The group began to reflect on how the process of the module might, therefore, have been given greater priority and perhaps some legitimacy. However, interestingly, this was still articulated using an outcome-focused discourse.

> . . . the process when we was doing different stuff each week and we planned what we was going to learn about, I found that more relevant to me and my learning. I feel like what we got graded on in the end really, I'd have preferred to be graded on . . .
> Everything . . .
> If the weekly process resulted in something . . .
> Like a mark or something.
> An evaluation of how we'd been throughout the whole process, not just on what we'd done on that last day.

Nonetheless, despite the articulation in terms of outcomes, there was also some attempt to understand, or grasp, the value of what might still be remaining tacit ('No, I'm not saying there wasn't learning') but that, perhaps, we as staff might have been in a better position to articulate the learning through our observations and assessments.

> . . . but what I was saying is, like, I would agree with [name], if that process had have been like throughout those weeks . . . even though you and Helen weren't involved in, like, you were there but could have been writing notes down on, like, each of us, like, on our journey.

There was some articulation of the intrinsic value of the process and that what is learnt might not always be, or need to be, defined in terms of outcomes. Moreover, perhaps, there was a frustration that the outcome might not adequately reflect the value of the whole university experience.

> I think that's what annoying, I don't really care about my grades to be honest cause I'm learning anyway, I'm doing the best that I can . . . but I feel like the mark from that frustrated me because it was based on reflections which I'm crap at and I know during them weeks there was relevant points that I'd made or participated in, you know?

Other students had similar struggles with process and articulated it as a paradox. Some of this frustration, however, might arguably be down to the need to attend to the process with other people. That said, there is some attempt to identify or name what could be viewed as tacit understanding. Enlightenment was the word used to encapsulate this.

> I personally thought you were torturing the life out of me if I'm completely honest because I had to . . .
> It's a paradox, there is the paradox in critical pedagogy.
> I've never known a course where I would walk out of the building and I'd rant about the infuriating people I studied with and how idiotic they were. I was quite brutal to some but that's because I don't deal in fiction I deal in fact. I like facts, I don't . . .
> And then you've got opinions
> . . . and its . . .
> Frustrating is the word, frustrating.
> That's a bit egocentric isn't it?
> Well maybe, but you know.
> Yea but what you were talking about is how you were feeling, or well, who you are and how you were feeling during undergoing this process of doing this critical pedagogy module.
> It's a bit like enlightenment. Not at the time, once I felt like . . .
> Not while you're going through it but at the end of it. Enlightenment is never an easy process anyway is it, you don't wake up one day feeling enlightened.

> At the end of the process, once it was all done and dusted and out the way and I was able to sit there and think about it without stressing, yea, but at the time . . .

Students' Perspective on Freedom

Some of what was articulated could be viewed in terms of struggles with freedom or struggles with levels/types of freedom. This module was the first of a number that really began to offer the subject, direction and framework for assessment open to the students.

> I think the other point was as well, because every other module we had was lecturer led, we really struggled to, kind of, take it over for ourselves.

It appeared that the freedom offered was initially replaced with familiar structures whereby students were co-opted to take on the role that is traditionally associated with the lecturer.

> Banked yea but we are already in a process where we are expecting to be banked because that's all we know in the education system.
> Even when you guys were in the room, even when you said don't even, like, forget that we are there, we struggled to forget that you were there and even when you left the room, we still struggled because the class then appointed lecturers so they appointed me and [name] then to do what you were telling us to.

It was mooted that what might have been experienced was to some degree a fear of freedom which led to the two being co-opted but this notion did not entirely suffice.

> I don't know if it was that, scared of freedom, or it was that we didn't know what to do, I think that was the main, didn't know where to start.
> I think it was a mixture of both to be honest wasn't it. People, I think, me personally, I think I was scared of freedom cause I like control, I like to know where the boundaries are
> Yea cause I suppose it's on a micro level isn't it cause not knowing what to do, being uncertain about what you should be doing can lead to a level of anxiety can't it.

However, some ambiguity about the notion of freedom in this context was evident, in that freedom, to one person, aligned with having clear boundaries within which to work.

> Yea that is freedom if you think about it because if you're given an assignment brief you know what you have to do in a sense that you have freedom in how you do it but you've got those base-lines which is what you do.

And so, from this ambiguity about what constitutes freedom, there was a rearticulation of the sentiment expressed through one of the VLE forums.

> But then was it real freedom anyway because we still had to do the assignment at the end and the assignment had to be in relation to how you wanted it to be, how it basically has to be marked?
>
> Did we have freedom? Did we really? Or did you give us freedom to a certain extent and make us believe that we had freedom but in actual fact it wasn't freedom because then we had to produce an assignment which had to be produced in some sort of certain ways to give us a, a mark.

Interestingly, when the discussion recalled, from the VLE forum, that somehow the lecturers might have been implicated in this pretence of freedom:

> ... at the time it was, it was voiced in such a way ... they were real feelings you know and it was the reality ... it was the situation but at the time it seemed like some of you felt that we had
> Tricked me, that's how I felt.

There was a recognition of the parameters within which we, as lecturers are confined.

> Cause sometimes you two really had no choice cause although you would say you were leaving us to it, in the end you have a job to do.
> And you have to get us through, well, support us in getting through this course and in order for us to prove that we can do that we have to submit some work.

A further interrogation of freedom emphasized the related notion of choice, and one group recognized the tension in this freedom of choice between the collective and the individual.

> But that's what I'm saying about the pedagogy, cause we kind of had a choice, that's why I think we got so pissed off. It wasn't a tough shift you've got to do what it is 'cause...
> But then that's what I was saying, did we really have a choice?
> No, no but it was that fact that we could
> We did have a choice
> Could have chose not to but it didn't happen, it still didn't happen regardless anyway
> We had a choice collectively we just didn't necessarily get our choice that individually we wanted,

Another group recalled the sense of frustration at the individualized learning approach taken and the accompanying lack of group cohesion.

> None of us really knew our arse from our elbows at the time I don't think and it was a bit like 'what we doing then' and you do have the . . yea it's easy to shut down and I think that's probably why it dragged out so long. Cause we didn't seem to get it until the critical discussion, do you think?

Ethics: Dangers of the Experimental Approach

At the time of assessment, one cohort had a particularly difficult experience.

> I had you and Helen come and speak to me. I cried, do you remember, I cried into my cardigan. I never cry, though I did then, and I weren't even involved in the whole heated thing
> We were shattered we were absolutely shattered.
> It was cause it was going on so long.
> I sat out, I think I said three things.
> You didn't, you sat on the floor next to each other.

The circumstances surrounding assessment had already caused some frustration which was articulated quite vehemently on the VLE forum. There seemed to have been some misinterpretations (some perhaps genuine and others opportunistic) about whether the assessment was even going to take place. The group had arranged to undertake an assessed seminar; however, one person reached a point of complete refusal to engage in any assessment on the grounds that it was not in the spirit of critical pedagogy. Adding to the anxiety was the fact that, for this component, the mark would be given to the group rather than individually. The rest of the group had agreed to participate in the interests of the collective endeavour, and it was viewed by the majority that this person's actions were quite controlling and not in the interests of the group. There had been tension with this individual previously and this behaviour was, arguably, a continuation of that.

> It was a few times that we were being oppressed as a group. Yea and that's why I think it built up.

Students' Perspective on Power

The gravity of the lecturer's words became apparent in both group discussions. One discussion group centred on what could arguably be an innocuous question by the lecturer merely aiming to encourage students to think further but, with the seeming power imbued upon them, the interpretation was more one of a suspicion of being on the wrong track.

> Shall I tell you why I think that way Mike, so when we set ourselves into those groups, do you remember? And we'd all said and we were all getting on with it, Helen came in and . . . instead of being like 'ok yous lot, you know what you're doing, get on with it, blah blah blah' she almost threw a spanner in the works.
> It was kind of like, don't quote me but kind of like, 'are you *sure* you want to do that'? and that was it. Why? What's going to happen if we do that, we can't do that now, so we was like . . . something was going to happen that was really bad if we do it that way.

Another recounted a lecturer in a previous year's module and their opinion of how one should approach the work of Freire.

> [Name's] words were though 'don't even start looking at that critical pedagogy'.
> Yea, 'you won't be able to understand it'.
> Don't even start reading it, he said, 'don't be reading that book yet' which personally, automatically made me absolutely petrified of the book...

Preliminary Findings from Reflective Discussions

Travel Versus Impact

Our tentative discussions seem to be revealing that this focus on the journey rather than the outcome (while recognizing the very real requirement for outcomes) could be counter-cultural to the current practice expected in higher education today. So, to be given the 'freedom' by our institution to be able to engage in a module with no discernible curriculum in such a regulatory environment (Competition and Markets Authority, Office for Students and the Higher Education Academy's Teaching Excellence Framework) shows that there is a great deal of trust in such 'hopeful pedagogies' at Newman University at least.

Discussions of dancing in the cracks between process and outcome brought to mind Prochaska and DiClemente's (1984) model of change. One of us had utilized this model in youth-work practice focusing on drug use in the early 1990s and, although its focus is on individual behaviour modification, it resonated due to its applicability in bringing to mind, in students, things that they may not have contemplated prior to this experience. There was an emerging idea that in focusing on the process of a learning journey and encouraging 'problem posing' (Freire, 1996), we were somewhat pausing or holding them in the pre-contemplation and contemplation stages for quite a prolonged period. It seemed that this *holding* of the process allowed for quite a deep level of thinking about the purpose of education (more latterly considered in Zamojski's (2015) instrumental, critical and post-critical terms) and a threshold crossing which has informed practice for some in later years. Once students had shifted their focus from an instrumental notion of education, they seemed to be able to engage with the tensions in their fieldwork (youth and community work practice) between outcomes (required by funding agencies for example) and inherently valuable learning experiences for young people. This does perhaps need further exploration and verification, but we have observed, in the university environment, that this process has led to a more considered approach, for some, to the subsequent predominantly self-directed modules in their third year of the degree.

Of course, the behaviour-modification model mentioned earlier highlights the paradox that we may be utilizing our positions of power to modify student's behaviour and, perhaps, deep-rooted values. Why shouldn't they perceive education as an instrument for career progression? Is this not valid? This indeed maybe the case, but given our extensive informal education background we are hopeful that the relationship we have built with students is quite deep, honest and dialogical (perhaps despite, or upon learning from, the experiences articulated in the interviews mentioned earlier) and, as per Amsler (2013, p. 74), includes 'the embodied, situated, everyday processes of learning and becoming'. We are hopeful, too, that students can engage with us not in *techniques* but in 'a mode of cultural production and a type of cultural criticism that is essential for questioning the conditions under which knowledge is produced' (H. Giroux, 2004, p. 64). We hope that this cultural criticism through dialogue prevents us becoming dogmatic in our status and teaching.

Ethics: Losing the Richness of Experience

Reflecting on the VLE recordings and the subsequent content mapping (summaries of recorded sessions noted down on long pieces of wallpaper) we recalled some of the difficult times (mentioned in the interviews mentioned earlier). During the process of mapping the content it became apparent that we had started to focus on assessment at the halfway stage of the module, about six weeks in. This observation and subsequent discussion about the conflict informed us of the necessity to tell students that we would not set them up to fail and reassure them that attention to the assessment would be given later in the module. However, including this discussion and effective safety net, while intending to encourage a focus on process, seemed to remove some of the anxiety and render tensions, articulated earlier, abstract. The educational outcomes–focused environment in which we operate was no longer a threat and the module had shifted unintentionally but unavoidably from the 'critical' to the 'instrumental' (Zamojski, 2015). It seems that the experience of those early years cannot be replicated now that we are aware of the potentially traumatic effect of not reassuring students that they will be afforded the time to focus on assessment. While this needs further interrogation, it seems that because we cannot forget our own experiences, those of the students and the consequences of what was to follow in the learning and assessment, there is something qualitatively different (and possibly inferior). We ourselves have crossed a threshold which we cannot unlearn.

Change Through the Pedagogical Relationship

Reflecting on the notion of 'change' through the process of education, whether that be viewed in terms of transformation, thresholds or in more psychological terms as per de Houwer, Barnes-Holmes and Moors' (2013) functional definition, it is clear that we have observed a change, or students have articulated a change, in values and behaviour. We have seen some of this change in behaviour lead to action in practice and it is perhaps due not only to this module but the nature of the course which comprises predominantly compulsory modules run by a small team of staff. Such an approach allows for continual inter-modular reference which may not be possible on more disparately taught programmes made up of modules from a wider pool. This experiential module, within a small programme, informs a pedagogical relationship which, while costly for an HEI, is philosophically quite profound. We journey with people in their, and in our, learning.

Response from Christine Smith

In this writing space I want to consider what lines of inquiry are made available if we explore teaching critical pedagogy through the role of a post-human lens. In particular, I want to think, with this chapter, about the role of concepts and what might be a key ethical consideration in how we make educational relationships locally and contextually and as part of wider international movements in battle for the soul of the university (Ball, 2013). In the contemporary landscape, and in thinking about critical pedagogy, this raises questions explored in the chapter about how teachers working with critical pedagogy hold the tensions inherent in role and purpose across 'domesticating', 'disciplining' and 'emancipatory' agendas for practice (De St Croix, 2018) especially at 'key moments of seeming contradiction'. Bardy and Gilsenan explore key concepts that in their analysis shape and underpin dialogical approaches including hegemony, intersectionality and cultural and social capital. Deleuze and Guttari (1994) explore the significance of working creatively and innovatively with concepts by 'plugging them in' and seeing where they go and what they do. Concepts understood in this context are orientated to making a difference and understood as 'performing' (Gale, 2018) in producing and shaping teaching practices.

Knowledge in this regard is not superimposed by an external other but generated from within all those engaged in the teaching process or 'journey' as described by Bardy and Gilsenan. This perhaps provokes a troubling of their claim in the chapter that 'we [lecturers] are not one of them' when talking about students engaged within the module. The concept of intra-action (Barad, 2007) is a useful way of reframing and navigating Bardy and Gilsenan's exploration of the relationship between students and lecturers. The concept of intra-action as a productive tool provides a way of orientating practice meaningfully with teachers, students and with policy and discourses. This opens up opportunities to think differently about the ethical dilemmas that the 'journey' through a critical pedagogy can throw up, including the inherent power vested in the role of lecturers referred to by Bardy and Gilsenan.

Through this lens, our ability to act as students and lecturers in intra-action becomes a perpetually 'unfolding' act from within relationships. This makes it possible to re-see our teaching practices if we begin to understand the knowledge making process as developing intra-actively in co-constitutive ways and in relationship with each other. Such an orientation to educational relationships implies an actively engaged, emergent intra-active and relational role for the lecturer situated in higher education and it begins to make it possible to make visible the 'affects' and ethics of constructions of power and knowledge (Braidotti, 2013). Ethics in operation through the process of educational relationships can therefore be understood as emergent and processual (Coleman and Ringrose, 2013, p. 11). This offers a way of deepening teaching practices in relation to discourse, ideologies and power and consideration of the way in which different subjectivities are constituted and affected through 'the journey' and a questioning of 'what is being made to matter and how that mattering affects what it is possible to do and to think' (Davies, 2018, p. 121). The concept of diffraction may also be useful in creating openings for new understandings of educational practice and new ways of becoming as a practitioner, which focus attention on how differences are materially constituted and come to matter; interfere with common notions of relationality, self and practice; and invite continuous (re)configuration (Hill and Fraser, 2017, p. 13). Material engagement through diffractive practices can 'disrupt artificial boundaries between theory and practice and interfere with unjust practice to establish new ways of thinking' and produce different approaches to practice (Spector, 2015, adapting Barad's diffractive methods cited in Hill and Fraser, 2017, p. 4).

Chapter Nine

Academic Identities

Conversations across the Cracks

Roger Willoughby and Parminder Assi, Response from
Marina Tornero Tarragó

Introduction

The academy in late modernity continues to be a site of multiple contests. One such skirmish broke out for us in 2014 (Jones, 2018), when seven people, three students and four academics, collaborated in a modestly funded small-scale research project reflexively investigating the ethnic representativeness of the curriculum that said students studied and said academics delivered, at least in part. The students volunteered for the project, proposed its focus, conducted the fieldwork research and wrote-up and disseminated the results. The collaborating academics for their part contained and catalysed the process and would through varying efforts seek to champion the spirit of the research over the ensuing years. Such a demarcation is too neat, but it offers a possibly useful heuristic with which to begin. The synergy that developed in the project was considerable. It was, we argue, a reciprocal liminal process through which all the principal parties were to some degree changed. In the context of our considerations of togetherness, this deserves a brief preliminary discussion.

Containment, Transformation and Collective Praxis

Our understanding of the synergy that emerged in our working together rests on various foundations, one of which is the concept of containment and the dynamics of the container–contained relationship (Bion, 1959, 1962a, 1962b), and a second is the notion of collective praxis (Smith, Salo and Grootenboer, 2010). In his psychoanalytically inspired formulation, Bion advances a model in which primitive inchoate mental states (proto-thinking) require an other's receptive mind (or 'reverie', in Bion's terms) to transform them qualitatively before both contents and process can be internalized, thus building a capacity for thinking and for the understanding and tolerance of feelings. Here, the container–contained model offers an idea of a resilient interpersonal and intra-psychic dialogic learning process. This process of containment is essentially a meaning-making activity, which will inevitably be coloured by other factors such as the character of the relationship between the parties and the ebb and flow of our emotional lives and our subjectivities in all their complexities (Bion, 1963).

Smith, Salo and Grootenboer's (2010) discussion of collective praxis resonates with this view, albeit in different language, in its foregrounding of mutuality, authentic collegiality and commitment within a non-hierarchical communicative space as one means of sustaining creativity, academic vitality and productivity in what may be a less than hospitable environment. Part of the challenge here is in how we might sustain our being, our existential selves and an openness to others (something Hegel, Martin Buber, Kojève, Honneth and others working within the Continental tradition in philosophy have had much to say about). While Smith, Salo and Grootenboer's (2010) work reported principally on relatively elite networks of academic staff, augmented with an occasional doctoral researcher, our work goes beyond these parameters to encompass work with undergraduate students as partners in research, curriculum development and pedagogic praxis.

Broadening the Curriculum

Among the outputs that ultimately flowed from the project were recommendations to broaden or enrich the curriculum underpinning the programme through increasing the international ethnic and gender representativeness of its literature base and to diversify pedagogic examples of praxis and educational outcomes. These were not unusual challenges to curricula within the academic zeitgeist, wherein, sometimes pejoratively, dead white men (Hughes, 2006, pp. 348–9) supposedly still exert a zombie-like grip on the minds of the living. Thus, elsewhere, others were voicing similar ideas, in, for example, the panel discussion 'Why isn't my professor Black?' at University College London (UCL, 2014; Jahi, 2014), the subsequent 'Why is my curriculum white?' student campaign, also there (Peters, 2015; Andrews, 2016), and more recently the 'Rhodes must fall in Oxford' campaign (RMFOxford, 2015), all arguably part of a wider movement seeking a decolonization of curricula (Jivraj and Simpson, 2015; Le Grange, 2016; Heleta, 2016; Kennedy, 2017).

The particularities of each situation are important. So too in our case. Our student researchers came from Pakistani and Bangladeshi ethnic backgrounds. This created particular resonances within the matrix of our work group, which were heightened by events on the world stage, on the British national stage and locally. These included, among other things, the campaigns of al-Qaeda, so-called Islamic State or Da'ish, and their affiliates, on the one hand, and the ongoing Israeli–Palestinian conflict and the persecution of Rohingya peoples in Myanmar, on the other, in the global context. In Britain, on the one hand, the government was rolling out of an educational policy on promoting 'fundamental British values' and its anti-radicalization Prevent strategy, while, on the other, there was a rise in Islamophobia, xenophobia and hate crimes. Locally, there was the so-called Trojan Horse affair, a fake plot to Islamize schools in

Birmingham. For their part, the ethnic backgrounds of the staff were Indian, Irish-American and white-British, which all carried their own inevitable resonances.

Why had these *particular* students, out of all those on our programme, stepped forward to work with us? Their own overriding response centred on the concept of leaving a cultural legacy: a sense of connection or togetherness with future generations of students. Within our own institution the student body is ethnically diverse. Considering just those students enrolled on our programme over a five-year period (435 students from 2010/11 to 2014/15), an examination of demographic data showed 36 per cent defined themselves as coming from a Black and Ethnic Minority (BME) background, with British-Pakistani students forming the largest single cluster therein (15%). How did these students fare on the programme itself during this period? Using degree classifications as a *very* crude proxy of academic achievement, and just considering those who achieved either first-class or third-class and pass degrees, white students *appeared* disproportionately represented among those gaining firsts (78% though they comprised 64% of the student body), while the preponderance of *some* BME students was conspicuous at the other end of the classification spectrum (46% though they comprised 36% of the student body). Notably, Pakistani students appeared evenly distributed across these classifications. We do not wish to make too much of these patterns as yet (further statistical analysis is needed), but merely wish to note them here as perhaps bearing on the question of the potential differential impact of the curriculum on student achievement across groups and as more general food for thought. This attainment or awarding gap is something the British Office for Students has now identified as a national issue to be addressed as a priority (OfS, 2020; Amos and Doku, 2019; Dale-Rivas, 2019; Akinbosede, 2019; Mountford-Zimdars et al., 2015).

With students themselves soliciting curriculum development, indications that some sections of the student body were failing to thrive on the existing curricular diet, and our own commitment to a praxis based on togetherness, we disseminated project recommendations to review and revise reading lists and praxis on existing modules and developed two new innovative optional modules, titled 'Education in Birmingham' and 'International education', to run in the second and third years, respectively, of the undergraduate programme.

What follows focuses substantively on what we have so far learned through the latter efforts. We will explore three themes: recognition of the sociopolitical context, situated learning in Birmingham and some of the challenges of assessment.

Recognition of the Immediate Socio-political Context

Education is commonly regarded as one of the key ways through which 'society transmits its accumulated values, knowledge, skills, attitudes and customs from one generation to another and influences how an individual thinks, feels and acts' (Mortimore, 2013, p. 3). There is a wealth of literature on how educational theories, content and practical activities influence, reflect and embody differing societal values

(Halstead and Taylor, 1996). Similarly, Bourdieu and Passeron (1990) suggest ways in which education is implicated in the reproduction of society (Sullivan, 2002), through fostering the transmission of certain cultural values.

The International Education module, subtitled 'Global diversity and educational inequality', is explicitly surrounded by such values given the degree to which the current political climate seeks to influence the English education system. Headline initiatives here include the controversial policy to 'put the promotion of British values at the heart of what every school has to deliver for children' (Gov UK, 2014), in order to promote social cohesion on the one hand and support the anti-radicalization and counter-terrorism Prevent strategy on the other. British values are defined in the government legislation as centring on: 'Democracy, rule of law, equality of opportunity, freedom of speech and the rights of all men and women to live free from persecution of any kind' (HM Government, 2011, p. 44).

Nonetheless, others cogently argue that such purported British values are actually universal values, values which are inclusive and non-negotiable (Bari, 2014). Given the globally connected, multi-ethnic, multi-religious nature of much of Britain, according differential rather than equal recognition and esteem to bona fide groups essentially perpetuates power relations very much akin to that between colonizer and colonized groups, with the latter invited to adopt an essentially subaltern position (Gramsci, 1971; Guha, 1982; Spivak, 1985). This hegemonic hierarchical structuring in Britain, a country that has been traditionally riven with social class distinctions, is no surprise. Seriously voicing this in the academy, however, potentially gives rise to considerable cognitive dissonance for some students. This is particularly so for those aspiring to careers within the state education system, which is substantially dominated by neoliberal policies. The entailed regulatory practices all too often disempower students and teachers, the demands for compliance in exchange for position subverting agency and compromising integrity of praxis. Such dissonance is, of course, intersectional, as Crenshaw (1989) would emphasize, with gender and class divisions for example further problematizing the desire for authentic collaborative togetherness.

This dissonance was further magnified locally in Birmingham by the previously mentioned 2014 Trojan Horse affair (Holmwood and O'Toole, 2018). With Da'ish campaigns in the Middle East and elsewhere in the headlines, as well as well-founded concerns about terror attacks on the British mainland, an alleged plot by 'hard-line' Muslim 'Islamist's' to take over some Birmingham schools became breaking news. The Trojan Horse letter appeared in March 2014, claiming that some schools in Birmingham 'had been deliberately targeted by Muslims standing as school governors in order to replace school leaders with heads who would adopt a more Islamic agenda in running the schools' (House of Commons Education Committee, 2015). This swiftly led to Birmingham City Council and Department for Education inquiries into the stories and snap inspections at fifteen schools. Such regulatory gaze came hand-in-hand with a prejudicial preformed transference and hegemonic narrative about the supposed failure of multiculturalism and its subversion by radicalized Muslim separatists, which was widely and largely uncritically reported in the media. It was only in mid-2017 that the cases were abandoned following the emergence of clear evidence of abuse of process (Holmwood and O'Toole, 2018). It was rich and powerful material, in relation to which some of our students were insiders with various ties to the schools involved and all had a view. Seminar discussions inevitably revealed disconnections, mistrust and misunderstandings among participants, the recognition and dialogic working through of which facilitated collective praxis (Smith, Salo and Grootenboer, 2010).

In the classroom this process involved considering with students the contemporary socio-political context as inherently linked to collective histories, which of course included consideration of the rise and function of education systems internationally, particularly through the conceptual lenses of imperialism, colonialism, globalization and gender. Taking just colonialism here as illustrative of the challenges these concepts entail, its reach is substantial given its recurrence across world history. By the 1930s its European iteration at one time or another stretched across over 84 per cent of the world's land surface (Loomba, 2015; Rizvi, Lingard and Lavia, 2006, p. 250). With education as a key agent of past colonial control (Gramsci, 1971; Viswanathan, 1992; Andreotti, 2011; AbuHilal and Abu-Shomar, 2014), contemporary education often continues to obscure and perpetuate colonial legacies (Dei, 2010; Dei and Simmons, 2010). Here teacher and taught risk becoming proxies for the colonial master and subject, while traditional education itself arguably bears some of the hallmarks of a colonizing discourse (Dei and Simmons, 2010; Hoerder, 2014).

We thus raise the question of the extent to which these living educational legacies, which shape identity (Fanon, 1952), social relations, freedom and various forms of discrimination (Gilroy, 1987; Mac an Ghaill, 1988; Pajaczkowska and Young, 1992), for example, persist in impacting on contemporary educational experience and attainment. Their impact on recent socio-political and cultural contexts in Britain, including Brexit, is another story.

Situated Learning in Birmingham

One of the key findings of the initial research included the desire for a locally based representation of education, exploring local theory, research, praxis, institutions and educational trajectories. This expression we saw as intimately related to the preceding discourse on power, with its implicit critique of relations between the metropolitan centre and colonial margins, prominent dimensions in both colonialism and contemporary globalization. One effort to meet this desire was our construction of a second-year undergraduate elective module titled 'Education in Birmingham'. Staff were enthusiastic about this development, designing the module to incorporate content such as Paul Willis's landmark 1976 study *Learning to Labour* about disenfranchised youth in 'Bricktown' (Birmingham), the progressive Steward Street School experiment (Burke and Grosvenor, 2013), the Trojan Horse affair (Holmwood and O'Toole, 2018), through a host of studies of gangs, child protection tragedies, terrorism, diversities and flagship initiatives.

Exciting stuff you might think. We thought so. Yet, when the module was actually offered, very few students enrolled and, as a consequence, it was deemed under the university regulations to be unviable to run. How might we understand this apparent falling away of interest? For example: were the responses in the initial research on this point overblown? Were the alternative module options just more attractive? Had we failed to adequately promote the module? Was it, in some way, perceived as a step too far? Were the university regulations on module viability partisan and the institutional climate rather lukewarm in this context? While the reasons behind the lack of take-up and institutional shelving of the module are likely to be complex, our experience of student struggles on the International Education module with formative ethnographic fieldwork across the region was suggestive. This latter activity was a further way in which we sought to achieve the curricular ambition to rebalance academic attention towards the local.

Assessment, Ethnography and Risky Practices

The International Education module offers students a comparative interdisciplinary perspective on the topic. We adopt an explicitly compound focus, examining indigenous educational practices in England alongside case studies of education elsewhere (e.g. Israel, South Africa, Pakistan, Finland). At the same time we strive, like C. Wright Mills (2000), to make the familiar strange, illuminating markers of ethnic diversity and otherness that exist often quietly in the indigenous scene. In an effort to achieve this in a grounded manner, students on the module are tasked with undertaking an ethnographic walk (O'Neill and Roberts, 2020) in pairs or small groups, the findings from which experience they are to subsequently report to and discursively unpack with the class.

The material thus gathered, captured often in the form of photographs, sometimes snippets of conversations, reported associations and subjective affect states, etc., is sometimes very rich indeed.

Our first example was a photograph of a language school advertisement incorporating a 1939 British motivational poster ('Keep calm and carry on'), that resurfaced in 2008 to become an anthem for austerity resilience and was quickly adapted to serve a plethora of other markets (Hatherley, 2017). In this case it was being pressed into service to sell English language lessons. Trading on the imaginary, on nostalgia for a lost heroic identity and an injunction to manage, if not repress, feelings in the face of adversity (the stereotyped 'stiff upper lip'), the advertisement resonated widely in the seminar. The conversation thus touched on national identity, esteem, a new (linguistic) empire in which English is dominant, commodification, marketization, McDonaldization, inter-ethnic tension and the decline of minority languages among other issues. As such, the image engaged the seminar in a joint (Freirean) enterprise in an accessible and visceral way, in part as this student-produced resource, a found object, was embedded within the local community.

Some students were able to document changes of use in local buildings and in this way chart changes in community ethnic demographics, while opening up conversations on migration, community cohesion, racism, xenophobia and co-existence. Two photographs, for example, partly illustrated this in their depiction of a former public house in Bordesley Green, Birmingham, which more recently became an Islamic Centre and mosque. Such sites, while of course often encompassing learning establishments of varying degrees of formality, offer grounded insights into the lived lives of communities which are also served by mainstream educational provision.

This is important in contributing to the professional formation of aspiring teachers, or indeed other human services professionals, sensitizing them to a sample of issues their future constituents may face and helping to consolidate empathic resources and understanding of affective and broadly psychosocial dimensions in the process.

Our third student example was an image of a war memorial commemorating local soldiers who died during the Anglo-Boer War of 1899–1902, just one of several war memorials that have featured so far in students' documentation of their localities. Such memorials engaged us in discussion of the age of empire and colonization, of politics, ideology and power, of identity, of social class, of personal troubles and public issues. In the contemporary multi-ethnic context, such sites of memory are potentially ambiguous signifiers, sometimes representing triumph and defeat to different members of the same class; as memorials to the dead however, to other young local people who lost their lives from violence or disease, they were also moving human sites evoking a greater degree of togetherness.

In considering such material, we, as teaching staff, did not necessarily have advance warning of the nature of these offerings to the class or their potential relevance or meanings. Neither did others in the class. Yet *these very features* offered opportunities for students and staff to encounter each other and each other's work afresh within a local, national and international context and to engage in a meaning-making process. Such engagement was often fraught with hesitation and uncertainty, which process ultimately required emotional and intellectual containment (as Bion might talk about) for deep learning to evolve. Staff were at times viewed with scepticism or confusion: were we simply indulging pet ideological views rather than engaging in serious praxis? Were we inviting them to join us in some sort of risky practice (Enright et al., 2017), jeopardizing crucial final-year grade possibilities? We would regularly need to engage with subaltern silence (Spivak, 1985) or politeness in response to ethnographic offerings, posing our own questions or thinking aloud to scaffold discussions and shore up confidence.

That this was so ought, in some ways, to be no surprise. Our students are facing a high-stakes assessment within the hierarchical marketized university system, well aware of its inherent inequalities, where others hold the structural power to mandate assessment modes and focus, where commodification is commonplace, and where attempting to anticipate-and-satisfy covert staff expectations in assignments is sometimes believed to be a sine qua non for securing good grades. These tensions were equally, if not more, evident in moving from the formative- to the summative-assessment component of the module. Here again student uncertainty emerged, particularly over our encouragement to further develop their formative ethnographic work into a more comprehensively written-up paper. There was increased checking and validation seeking over submission foci. Some students opted for 'safer' alternatives, such as mainstream comparative analyses of two national education systems. Others were able to sustain their earlier dialogic engagement, despite its uncertainties, and emerge perhaps not with higher grades but with an enhanced degree of filiation or togetherness.

Conclusion

In moving from research, through curricular development to a praxis that incorporates further joint research, we have here sought to build on the previously discussed notions of containment and collective praxis. Our construction of potential spaces for exploration, alongside conceptual support and emotional encouragement, was important throughout. As with Smith, Salo and Grootenboer (2010), the endeavour has been productive, sustained and creative, though its extension into pedagogy has highlighted more interpersonal and systemic uncertainties.

This again is unsurprising. A majority of our students are on a trajectory into teaching and the developments here are to an extent disruptive of some of the mainstream models of transmission legitimized in ITE programmes, which model practice 'inauthenticity' (Freire, 1970; Glass, 2001). Focusing here on togetherness, intercultural learning and the promotion of opportunities for fostering empathy, through dialogical, democratic engagement, facilitates – we argue – the growth of important human and professional capacities (Kemmis and Carr, 1986, p. 190).

Response from Marina Tornero Tarragó

I welcome this paper from Roger Willoughby and Parminder Assi and I have personal experience of working with them during May 2019, when I contributed sessions on education, internationalism and bilingualism. The range and scope of courses in education and multi-professional practice at Newman University extends student engagement beyond the familiar narrow notions of academic engagement to embrace collegiate membership of social and learning communities in higher education. The curriculum is focused on the interrogation of educational policy and practice for greater social justice, equality and inclusion.

During my visit I contributed to the module 'International education: Global diversity and educational inequality'. In this work, active student participation is central to teaching being based around close discussion of material and experience. The group Parminder kindly invited me to participate with was keen on learning new perspectives about how the co-existence of languages and cultures in the same country very frequently leads to struggles, especially for minorities. This has happened in the past in Spain, the country where I come from, with Basque and Catalan, languages that were severely repressed during the Franco dictatorship. In their text, Parminder and Roger describe a 'hegemonic hierarchical structuring in Britain, a country that has been traditionally riven with social class distinctions', and that is relatable to many other countries, including Spain.

Midway through the module, students undertake an ethnographic walk to critically explore a chosen area of the environment, the results of which are presented in the module to deepen understanding of sites of contest and the ways in which history and ideology are reflected in our everyday urban geography.

It is encouraging to see that student experience and engagement is reflected in this paper and that the learning, teaching and assessment processes used serve to foster a sense of belonging using dialogical and critical pedagogical approaches which recognize student expertise and experience. For instance, the use of visuals in class to provide examples of – and assist in exploring – the topic provides the students with meaningful tools with which they can connect immediately as it is basically the language of their generation, as discussed by writers such as Buckingham or Livingstone in their work on the concept of 'media literacy'.

Letting them learn through pictures that, moreover, they have taken from their surroundings (such as the sign of 'Keep calm and learn English' or the change in patterns of use of a local building) link them to their reality, since one of the most illuminating factors of this module is the capacity it holds to make young people understand the diversity they live in and have a critical, mature position about it. The students are, thus, experiencing an immersive learning.

Roger and Parminder have taken an initiative commenced as a 'Students as partners' research project in 2014 to increase opportunities for collaborative learning which exploits the diversity within the student population. The work to incorporate multiple perspectives by including the ideas of Black and Asian thinkers and academics from local, global, past and present is very clearly represented. I wholeheartedly commend the curriculum and assessment design of the work done by Roger and Parminder which enables students to identify and relate learning to diverse experiences. It is very satisfying to see this ongoing work being developed into this text on critical pedagogy.

Part II B

Hopeful Pedagogies within Structures

Chapter Ten

The 'Rehearsal Space'

Viewing Induction and Transition Work as a Critical Pedagogy Practice

Leoarna Matthias and Sarah Parkes, Response from Liz Thomas

Introduction

This chapter explores why we are drawn and motivated to work within transition and retention spaces at Newman University. Through enacting critical pedagogy, we aim to value the hopes, fears and humanity of every student who enrols at the institution. We recognize that forming genuine relationships with students, and creating democratic spaces for them, can enable them to flourish on their own terms while they are members of our community.

Our experiences and understandings are presented here through a series of individual reflections and commentary on our own contexts, motivations, values and attitudes that disable/enable practice. Our focus is on practices – such as those delivered prior to entry (Parkes, 2014) and during the first year (see Parkes et al., 2017), as well as those moving between academic years – that aid students new to the institution to become socially and academically integrated (Thomas, 2002; Tinto, 2006; Yorke and Longden, 2008). Such practices draw upon a particular understanding of the challenges student's face in feeling both that they belong to their university community, and are prepared for the challenges of completing their studies (Thomas, 2012; Thomas et al. 2017; Jones, 2008).

Contexts and Motivations: Public and Private Landscapes

Sarah

The widening participation (WP) policy of the New Labour Government (1997–2010) in the United Kingdom (UK) shaped much of my thinking in my early widening access and retention-related roles in higher education (HE). Though contentious (see Hursh and Hall, 2008; Stevenson, Clegg and Lefever, 2010 or Sheeran, Brown and Baker, 2007), WP sought to widen access and participation of groups who were previously under-represented in HE. I was and still am wedded to the view that WP is vital to improving social justice and mobility through institutional, sectoral and individual transformation. In 2009, I created a discrete pre-entry course, and on-programme activities, for students studying a Certificate in Higher Education, to assist their transition. These resources and activities were envisaged as spaces that developed academic literacies as the students moved into and through university, creating knowledge as they attempted to understand their experiences (Driscoll, 2000) and connect with each other to foster a sense of belonging (Parkes, 2014). It was, however, the work of Quinn that developed my thinking about the complexities of transition, particularly the socio-cultural influences on working-class 'dropout' (2004) and notions of the self (2010). Thus, in developing my own practice I have moved towards encouraging students to practise their academic study skills, while in parallel, engage in other, more personal activities designed to support interpersonal relationship building.

Leoarna

Sarah's initial 2009 programme became, over the following decade, the Higher Education Academic Department's (HEAD) suite of programmes, open to all students new to the institution. I took on the delivery of these programmes in 2017. Sarah had also initiated other curriculum shifts within the university in line with the thinking she articulates earlier, and I have endeavoured to continue that work.

If HE has experienced a fundamental change in the nature of the student body inside twenty-five years, we have also changed many elements of the task of teaching students. For me, HE can hold onto a John Henry Newman-esque vision of the public good of degree study, while also becoming the 'multiversity' of which Collini speaks (2012). At the heart of all comes the instruction from Ausabel to 'know your students and teach accordingly' (1968, p. 6). When I marry this with the moral obligation to enable student flourishing that comes with us having accepted them into the university (Thomas, 2012), I find myself at the starting point of transition pedagogy (Kift, Nelson and Clarke, 2010) in the institution.

I tend to believe the old adage that you can't know where you are going if you don't know where you have come from. The UK's higher education sector has a long, long history, and making sense of its simultaneously glacial pace and lightening quick progress really helps me to navigate the work I am involved in (Barnett, 2007). Universities drive us forward, making discoveries, finding cures, revealing the state of things. They also lean towards a reverent archiving of the past, and a reluctance to shift when the times they are a-changing. My eyes are open to the absolute necessity of the university to reinvent itself at any given moment. There is no purpose in lamenting the past; our task instead is to embrace the unfinished nature of knowledge (Freire, 2007; Readings, 1996 in McLean, 2006), and to engage in the co-construction of possible solutions to the challenges faced in the here and now (Neary, 2012). Critical to this endeavour is the removal of all sentimentality for our institutions, given that it has the potential to b(l)ind us to their shortcomings.

In the latest attempt to make universities move to the music of government – the establishment of the Office for Students (OfS) – I see a depressing hollowing out of educational experience through regulatory means that Sarah and Jane Beniston discuss in Chapter 4, but also an opportunity for white-haired radicalism. If we can use the leverage of OfS demands upon the institution to do meaningful, genuine transition work with our students, that promotes their flourishing on terms that they, not government, determine, then I am OK with the neoliberal policy creep. I recognize I am unlikely to see an end to the capitalist model (Holloway, 2010) but that does not mean that I cannot 'dance in the cracks', find the spaces in which to do good work, to invest my energy and time in authentic relationships with my students, as Mike Gilsenan and I indicate in Chapter 2. Policy will most likely always seem to be to be travelling in the opposite direction to what my instinct says will work (Mathias and Peters, 2018), but I enjoy the intellectual and emotional challenge of remaining hopeful in the face of it (Freire, 1997; Solnit, 2016).

Sarah

Transition and retention are tricky concepts. The English definitions of retention are:

1. The completion (or success) rate: the proportion of starters in a year who continue their studies until they obtain their undergraduate qualification, with no more than one consecutive year out of higher education.
2. The continuation (or retention) rate: the proportion of an institution's intake which is enrolled in higher education in the year following their first entry to higher education (on an undergraduate course) (National Audi Office – NAO, 2007, p. 5).

Colleagues and I have discussed (Parkes, Mathias and Seal, 2018, p. 74) how these definitions of retention are problematic, not least because they imply an ownership of the student, rather than reflecting their agency and autonomy as individuals. So, while I use 'retention' in my everyday working world, my retention-related practice is underpinned by a particular view of transition: principally, the sense that transition involves a perpetual process of *becoming*. Such 'transition-as-becoming' (Gale and Parker, 2014) resists positioning students within a linear progression or 'qualitatively distinct stages of maturation' (p. 738). Rather, it offers a transformative discourse that values the diverse knowledge(s) and ways of knowing that students already have (Gale and Parker in Parkes, Mathias and Seal, 2018, p. 76). Thus, transition within an increasingly diverse student population is about recognizing the student in front you and valuing all that they bring to the university.

Newman: The Place, The People

Sarah

The fact that Newman is a relatively small university (circa 2,700 students) has meant that for someone in quite a junior role, I have been able to get involved in activities that elsewhere may have been beyond my remit. Through working collaboratively within a hybrid role (see Parkes, Cousins and Blackwell-Young, 2013), I was able to start informal conversations with like-minded people. Indeed, my first 'project' was a collaboration with a fellow academic colleague interested in transition issues from a pedagogical viewpoint. This led to our involvement in the second phase of What Works (Thomas et al., 2017) that attempted to consider how Newman could embed Kift, Nelson and Clarke's (2010) notion of a transition pedagogy within programme design. I've become increasingly aware that the external context for Newman, with an increased focus on HESA statistics, the Teaching Excellence Framework and the arrival of the OfS, has created the environment for transition and retention work to be taken far more seriously than when I first arrived. A continual frustration prior to 2015 had been a perceived reluctance for embedding this work into our programmes, even when the university seemingly embraced the notion of a 'transition pedagogy' to scaffold learning (see Parkes et al., 2017). Work supporting students in their 'transition-as-becoming' (Gale and Parker, 2014) has not always felt a serious focus within the institution's access agreements until around 2016: these documented how institutions spent their fee income which largely focused on spending relating to access, rather than 'success' in HE. Until then, the intersectional nature of disadvantage experienced by our students appeared to appease any pressures or desire to take such work seriously. Indeed, on reflection, my early work felt tokenistic and a bolt-on, rather than successful at embedding different attitudes to practice within programmes.

Leoarna

I think Sarah has experienced highs and lows in the pursuit of better transition-enabling practices within the institution, and she is always modest, humbly so. But her shoes felt big to me, when in January 2017 I took on my first educational development, third-space role that she had vacated. When we talk about this, we usually end up observing just how much I have been able to benefit from the shifting HE climate, now there is policy- and market-driven traction to do things that she always wanted to – but was resisted. In essence, I feel like I make progress in the wake of her having put all the really hard miles in in the training room.

The demands of the OfS are no doubt based on a moral view that universities should be inclusive, and a slightly less moral perspective that they should also provide value for money. But their insistence on such principles does create space for a new type of conversation within the university. When there was no compulsion for colleagues to change the way they did things, some travelled with Sarah, and some did not. A postcode lottery of experience for the student ensued. This is now directly at odds with what the OfS is asking of us, and I use this leverage – arguing that we should change practices, not only because scholarship, research and evidence say we should, but also because our existence as an institution is under threat if we do not. Carrot *and* stick. Hopeful critical pedagogy is not so lofty that it cannot squeeze good work out of the pragmatism of circumstance.

Why Are We Drawn to This Work?

Sarah

I am drawn to working within undergraduate student transition because of my own, continuous journey through higher education. My entry into higher education employment was unintentional, beginning with my own voyage as a 'first-generation entrant' from a 'low socio-economic background': that is, I came to study in my mid-twenties; my parents did not experience higher education themselves and have worked in relatively low-paid jobs all their lives. I left school with two A-Levels and no tangible encouragement from my family to pursue a higher education. This is not to apportion blame but to recognize that the social and cultural capital needed to navigate the university system were absent. I did, from the age of eighteen, have a successful career in retail that saw me working in a variety of settings and with a diverse range of responsibilities including delivering training. This period was, however, frustrating and left me wanting to affect life differently. I started to consider a teaching career, not least because my training was positively received. I now realize this was the beginnings of my uneasiness of existing in a 'for-profit' environment, and an increasing questioning of the world around me that evolved into a desire to be involved in something more hopeful.

Leoarna

While I was at university, I had a strong sense of wanting to work in one, and an equally strong sense of not being worthy or clever enough to do so. I carried a predictable dose of imposter syndrome, born of my awareness of my working-class, single-parent origins, and their incongruence with the deeply privileged climate of the northern, red-brick, Russell Group institution I found myself in, before any Baker–Blair HE massification programme had really taken hold. While studying law I chose to focus on the more theoretical and academic content, rather than practice-based elements of the module offer. This led to some great small-group teaching and learning experiences, with time spent in tutors' rooms discussing the materials and exploring concepts; conversations grounded in relational pedagogy, operating in an educationally near-democratic space. I knew what good teaching looked like, and felt like, and I knew it was based in relationships, discussion, connection, and my own views being valued.

Sarah

As an undergraduate student I volunteered as a student mentor, running workshops with small groups of young people to encourage and support them to embark on their own higher education journey. My motivation for this derived from wanting to share my desire to expose but also generate a sense in others of uncovering an 'authentic self': a self yet undiscovered, looking for its own voice and seeking representation (Burke and Hayton, 2011, p. 9); one that 'is free from social structures . . . and able . . . to make itself anew' (Francis and Skelton, 2005, p. 319). Latterly, rather than take up my place on a PGCE, I accepted a full-time paid role as Widening Access Officer that involved working with schools, colleges and community groups to promote access to HE among disadvantaged people. I recognize my desire here was to compensate for the 'inescapable selves' of those imprinted with and bound by characterizations of gender, ethnicity, ability or class (Quinn, 2010, pp. 16–17).

Leoarna

I am at the same time both like the students that we work with at Newman, and unlike them. As a new undergraduate I shared their doubts about my own academic ability and felt I didn't belong. In my first three months I felt 'othered', realizing everyone had been to public school, completed the International Baccalaureate, done a gap year somewhere interesting and exotic. Why was I there amongst them? My headmaster had told me that 'people like us don't go to those places'. I was determined to prove him wrong, but still felt excluded upon arrival, sensing that someone would find out I wasn't clever enough pretty quickly.

I am unlike them in that I did not endure the financial pressures they experience, and I did not start my working life with significant debt, as they now do. I was not constantly pressed to say what I was going to do after my studies. And whether or not I entered 'the graduate job market' – whatever that is – didn't seem to matter so much. I now share this story with Newman students; it gives them a point of contact that allows them to trust me but also to acknowledge their own challenges (Carruthers-Thomas, 2019); then we can begin to work on overcoming the hurdles that litter the path of their progress.

Sarah

My dissatisfaction with notions of the 'authentic' or 'inescapable' selves surfaced as resistance to the dominant deficit discourse of transition that views identity as bounded (see Parkes, Mathias and Seal, 2018; Parkes, 2018). My view – and why I continue to be enthralled by this work – is to perceive identity as akin to the *Wunderkammer* or wonder cabinet (Maclure, 2013, p. 180). Such cabinets – like ourselves in thinking through our wants and desires – are made up diverse treasures with a 'syntax of unanticipated associations' (Lugli in Maclure, 2013, p. 180). They are continually changing, never congealing into 'fixities and definites' (Coleridge in Quinn, 2010, p. 22). Similarly, Quinn's idea of the 'un-self' is represented as a becoming between multiplicities (Tamboukou in Quinn, 2010, p. 18): a becoming that is constantly dissolving, diffusing and recreating (p. 22). This is at once viewable as transformation *and* oppression: as subjectivity engaged in a perpetual process of flux (p. 18). Thus, I am drawn to this work because I view the students I work with, my colleagues and myself as 'unselves'. This enables me to acknowledge the power of education to both transform and simultaneously oppress, allowing a questioning of our structures and institutional activities in order to transform them (Freire, 1972, p. 12).

Values and Attitudes

The Values That Drive Our Practice

Sarah

My approach to transition work at Newman is founded on a belief that knowledge of how students are empowered or confined should not focus on discourse of 'lack', but potentially explore how power management and power relations affect their respective *becoming*. Indeed, Foucault's (1990 [1979], p. 93) discussion of how power exists everywhere is useful in this respect, particularly in relation to student transition. Thus, student transition (i.e. transition-as-becoming) concerns itself with the circulation of power effects (Braidotti, 2012, p. 171) across the spectrum of interactions and contexts of students arriving in HE.

So, while I recognize that HE can be a site of social and cultural reproduction, it nonetheless has the potential to develop 'an ethical subjectivity that . . . resist[s] and overcome[s] neoliberal subjectifications' (Postma, 2016, p. 3), enabling transformation and empowerment through co-exploration of the 'realities' present within the lifeworlds of others (Ball, 2007, p. 116; Freire, 1993, p. 106). As such, I see HE as a part of society that can facilitate change and/or preservation at the structural, cultural or individual level (Buckley, 1998, p. 128). Work that supports student transition is inextricably entwined within the cultural, economic, social, imagined and, thus, relational contexts of students (Quinn, 2004) and the institutions within which they study, and needs to go beyond homogenous identity constructions.

Leoarna

It is natural enough for us to locate the growth of our values in our formative experiences. In very simple terms, my experience as a working-class woman from the state school system and a single-parent family informs my values, as does the psychotherapeutic literature and Buddhist practice I discovered in my early twenties. Other more eloquent writers have considered how class defines our access to education and privilege (Reay, 2017) and while I recognize that some commentators would reject 'class' as too crude a prism through which to view society, my sense of my working class-ness shapes my own experience of the world and gives me legitimacy in feeling angry and motivated to work for change.

Self-awareness and personal reflection are front and centre for me, and having trained in Rogerian therapeutic practice during the 1990s, I see now how psychotherapeutic knowledge enables me to establish clear boundaries between myself and my work, frames the empathy through which I can see both the potential of the student in front of me, and recognize the hurdles to their progress. While there are fundamental differences between the role of lecturer and therapist, this knowledge/practice sees me believing in the potential of everyone who ever stops me in the corridor, or sits in my office, calling on me to clear the decks and give them my full attention in order that I facilitate their becoming.

Finally, I see my Buddhist practice as another dimension to my understanding of human psychology. Buddhism emphasizes how much we cannot, in the end, influence or direct others, only ourselves (Chappell, 2004). Thus, we should do good work in the here and now, and trust that it will benefit our students, though we may never know the nature of that benefit. For me, there are echoes here of the post-critical notion that we cannot know what our students are learning from us, and so we must act ethically and trust that the outcome will be positive, as Mike Gilsenan and I indicate in Chapter 2.

As a relatively low-status academic, in a low-tariff institution heavily reliant on student fees for income, conceding to the inevitability of market logic (see Mike Seal in Chapter 3) and acquiescing to customer-driven bureaucracy is a route to one version of the easier life. But Lipsky (2010) has long reminded us that the values-driven discretion we can operate at the university coalface gives us more power than that; we can fashion the Street Level Lecturer from his seminal work, and recognize how much her values can free her up to take risks. We remain a long way from knowing the most meaningful paths to learning within HE, and powerful forces are arguably operating to take us further from, rather than closer to, a climate that promotes authentic and impactful learning experiences for all. At this point, my values are there to indicate the way forward; our task is to keep on contributing, to keep working harder, pursuing what we believe through careful self-reflection, to be appropriate transition practice for the students in front of us.

Doing Critical Pedagogy, Being Critical Pedagogues

Sarah

It is really only in the last five years, but particularly the last three years designing and teaching on the foundation year, that I've recognized how powerful embracing a hopeful approach to pedagogy can be. I resist deficit approaches when enacting a transition pedagogy that can contest the 'value for money' discourses that appear to pervade societal understandings of university study (see Parkes et al., 2020). This remains difficult, particularly when working in roles that also require an element of collusion with the system. Yet, without collusion, how can we understand or subvert the hegemony represented within any system?

The discussions of critical pedagogy within our group (see Mike Seal's Introduction) have prompted thinking on how we intuitively use spaces to speak with/to students and staff about themselves and their own journeys. The idea of 'rhizomic working' (Deleuze and Guattari, 2000) – in that we never know how or where the conversations we have might lead – is key for me in how to do this work, especially if it is to avoid tokenism. The most valuable work I have been able to complete has been through the relationships I have built; the seemingly random yet serendipitous conversations and connections between and within my own interests, those of others and those of the institution.

Leoarna

In the neoliberal world, the value of academic labour is highly contested, and the atomizing, dehumanizing effect of the market endures. We need to work 'much harder' (Neary, 2012, p. 146) at finding new ways for the academy to thrive, for 'social knowing' (Neary, 2012), and knowledge production, to be democratized. Neary was lauded for his work in creating Student as Producer at Lincoln, but no sooner was he out of that project and into another – the establishment of university co-operatives. He sets us a humble example – to never think that the work is done, to never sit back, to *unlearn* as fast as (you think) you have learnt. I am an insecure academic labourer of the kind much documented these days. I operate on multiple fixed-term part-time contracts and need to pedal hard to demonstrate my impact in order to argue for a continuation of my time at the university. And yet, I love my work, the learning *and* unlearning.

Together

Hopeful critical pedagogy, where it meets our shared thinking about transition and retention, motivates us to understand the challenges our students face, rather than expecting them to adapt to the institution. It calls on us to distil scholarship, research, data, evidence, and best practice exemplars from across the sector, so that we and our colleagues across the university live out welcoming and supportive HE practices. Ultimately, it demands that we remain committed to the unfinished and reflective task of finding new and better ways to facilitate student flourishing, of aiding our students to experience the 'emancipatory project' (Winn, 2015, p. 20) of degree study.

Response from Liz Thomas

This chapter charts the development of transition activities designed to empower non-traditional students to succeed in higher education. Initially these interventions were designed and implemented by a comparatively junior member of staff, by Sarah's own admission, and were positioned 'in the cracks'. Slowly, the merit of being student-centred, and listening and understanding their perspectives, and their strengths and weaknesses, has been recognized within the contemporary higher education context, and these activities have become more mainstream and embedded into the student experience at Newman, and beyond. Transition is increasingly seen as a process of becoming and belonging, and there is a growing tendency for practices to aim to empower students through authentic relationships between staff and students, and with peers, developing the capacity of students to equal members of an academic community, and offering relevant curricular experiences (Thomas, 2012). The reflective accounts from Sarah and Leoarna demonstrate an enduring commitment to these values and a genuine enactment of a hopeful pedagogy, as they have developed their own thinking and practice to allow students to build on their strengths and become successful. The journey at Newman is broadly echoed across the field of widening participation in England.

In the early days of widening participation in this country much of the work was focused on 'raising the aspirations' of young people, to make them want to enter higher education, as opposed to the worlds of vocational training and work. The dominant discourse framed these potential students as being in deficit, they were viewed as lacking (any) aspiration or of holding low aspirations; there was a blindness to the ways in which these aspirations had been constructed and constrained by the education system and other social processes. This resulted in an approach to widening participation akin to 'cream skimming' – identifying and nurturing the anomalous 'gifted and talented' working-class students to enter into an unreformed higher education system. As the widening participation agenda proceeded, the demand for such students outstripped supply. The next approach to emerge therefore framed working-class students as effectively having a double deficit, lacking both aspiration and academic achievement – and indeed academic ability. Remedial interventions flourished, and as the national agenda turned towards not just access, but retention, bolt-on interventions to fix-up gaps in students' academic skills were introduced. It is only more recently that the need to transform higher education institutions themselves has gained more recognition – and this work necessarily relies upon the more radical views about the purpose and approach to education, and many of the values that underpin critical pedagogy and the practices described in this chapter (Jones and Thomas, 2005).

The higher education sector currently finds itself in a curious place, driven by market forces, but drawing on more radical pedagogies to meet student needs. The latter, however, is sometimes compromised by the very instrumental approach that students are forced to take, to earn the best grades to secure the well-paid graduate jobs that will enable them to pay off their large student debts. While critical (/hopeful) pedagogy focuses on students' discovery and transformation, many current students find themselves focused on the end goal – i.e. a first or an upper-second and a professional career. It will be this context that presents problems for the further development of progressive pedagogies, as much as well-established institutional practices.

Chapter Eleven

'Very Much a Democratic Thing'
Enacting the Pedagogy of Partnership

Leoarna Mathias and John Peters, Response from Gill Gilbert

Introduction

In Chapter 5 we discussed the development of our Freirean approach to student partnership, including the identification of six principles that now guide the partnership work we do at Newman. This chapter will, through a consideration of the data generated in a recent evaluation of our scheme, consider the application of these principles, and how effective they are at generating student partnership projects that actively promote hopeful practice within the institution.

How Partnership Happens at Newman

Newman's student partnership projects (hereafter, the projects) are open to all. A call for project applications is put out across the institution in the early part of the autumn semester, and those interested attend a preliminary meeting to gain an understanding of the application and project delivery process. Applications are reviewed by a university committee containing a balance of academic practice and professional services colleagues, and student representation. Once the panel has determined which applicantions have met the criteria, feedback is given in terms of any amendments that are needed. Successful projects then gain funding for the student partners, to facilitate their participation.

Staff across the institution and students from every year of study and all academic subject areas opted to participate in the projects during the first three years of their operation. Some partnership teams had only one staff partner and one student partner, others were much larger. Participants across the projects are brought together in ongoing meetings throughout the academic year, where progress, challenges and outcomes are shared. The yearly cycle culminates in a Celebration Day, during which all projects are shared and ideas for taking outcomes forward are considered.

Project funding strands support academic partnerships, focusing on aspects of the student learning experience; research partnerships, to undertake disciplinary research activity; and community partnerships, intending to undertake aspects of service learning. Ideas for projects ideally come from the students themselves, but there are, each year, a mix of those that are student-generated or staff-generated. Individual projects have sought to address a wide range of issues, including means of engaging more students in democratic activity, the whiteness of the curriculum, realigning assessment practices and bringing young school children from working-class communities into the university. This has been done alongside more traditional work, such as researching student motivation and transitions, editing books, co-ordinating conference presentations and publishing in academic journals.

At the time of writing the projects are entering their seventh year, with over 100 projects completed, including a number that gained external funding from the UK Higher Education Academy and the Higher Education Funding Council for England. In early 2017 the authors gained ethical approval from the institution to conduct a series of focus groups with staff and student participants in the projects at the university between the 2014 and 2017 cycles. We then analysed the data through the lens of the six declared Freirean principles, outlined in Chapter 5. In the following discussion staff and student participants are given numbers P1 to 15 and SP 1 to 3 respectively.

Shared Hope

Student partnership has the potential to become 'a space wherein competition is suspended, and co-operation defines success' (Matthews et al., 2018, p. 2204). In challenging the implicitly hierarchical structures of the institution, the projects foster a new approach to relationships between students and staff, and from this, springs hope; hope for new ways of doing the work of the university. Participants in the focus groups here at Newman, both staff and students, attested to a clear sense of how the projects can work to challenge the power differentials that are inherent in the terms 'lecturer' and 'student', and can instead contribute to the creation of a learning community. P11 spoke of partnership working as a tool that 'removes the power differential and means you are actually sharing ideas and co-constructing knowledge'. SP1 described the pleasure of being referred to as a 'colleague' by her staff partners.

While many acknowledged that at present, the projects are working in 'pockets' of the university, rather than at an institution-wide level in the fullest sense, staff and student participants alike felt that individuals, and individual subjects and processes, were benefitting from partnership working. As P4 observes, the 'aim seems to be to get students to work with staff on a level that is not simply pedagogical... [but] something approaching an equal footing', while P3 agrees that they are 'modest *and* making a real difference [and] that should not be overlooked'. Here, then, is a sense of students and staff demonstrating a capacity to 'author their own lives' (Neary, 2015, p. 68 in Lea, 2015; Baxter-Magolda, 2012). There is shared optimism for the potential of the projects to enliven hope of constructive change through this realignment of the relationship, and the discussions suggests that, once they have been through the project process, students come to a more explicit recognition of this shared hopefulness; they become 'open to other explainings' (Neary, 2015, p. 168 in Lea, 2015) and alive to their capacity to 'produce forms of knowledge [they] do not know yet' (Freire, 1997, p. 31). Thus, hope is becoming a feature of the operation of the projects.

Colleagues were able to articulate a real shift in their own pedagogy and self-identity as a result of taking part. In doing so, they indicated a relationship between personal transformation, and the contribution this was, in turn, making to the institution. They had thus embraced the capacity of the projects to 'interrupt power imbalances' (Lather, 1986, p. 208). P2 shares how it has, for her, 'informed her knowledge and understanding of different ways of engaging with students', (bringing about a new research interest in student engagement) while for P11, it has made her consider 'how important it is that we help our students understand the wider value of research for influencing change'. In this, the participants begin to articulate 'pedagogies of possibility [which] aim to foster in students and teachers/researchers other ways of doing, being and thinking' (Motta, 2013, p. 86 in Cowden and Singh, 2013). In locating such possibility and alternative understandings of the structures shaping experience, students and staff alike drive hopeful change within the university.

Shared Dream

Student partnership has the potential to rebalance an institution, providing a forum in which the institution can be reimagined. Our focus group participants felt the projects had made a significant contribution to a shared dream of the university as a place where 'political moral practice' (Giroux, 2011, p. 174) occurs. P2 observes that the projects have been, and are, 'very much a democratic thing . . . and I think they found that quite empowering, and it was about seeing them flourish'; while P10 believes this is a method of working with the student body that allows staff to 'empower, engage, and get people to participate', echoing Freire's belief in the need for 'continuing hopeful inquiry' (1996, p. 53). There is investment in the idea that the projects put 'students at the centre' (P8) of the work being done, that 'they have expertise in being a student and the perspective that brings' (P5). This is a direct challenge to other models of university study, such as approaching it as academic apprenticeship, serving as a rejection of the 'banking model' (ibid.) of education of which Freire was so critical.

While one participant expressed concern about the positioning of the student as 'God' in the current marketized higher education context (P3), others spoke, in contrast, of the satisfaction of seeing 'the personal growth of some of the students' (P13) and the degree to which they found the 'students so inspiring' (P11). Some commentators argue that the modern student in the neoliberal institution is at risk of being unreceptive to the idea of contributing to the ongoing transformation of higher education (Matthews et al., 2018; Scoles et al., 2019), but aspects of the focus group discussions suggest that students are willing to act in ways that 'interrupt [the] consensual discourse' (Neary, 2015, p. 168 in Lea, 2015), creating new knowledge through a greater acknowledgement of what they know and can do (Freire, 1997).

Newman University offers payment to each student partner who participates in a project. This is a less common aspect of the student partnership model currently at work in the UK and elsewhere (Mercer-Mapstone et al., 2017) and gave cause for a good deal of debate during the focus groups. For some, including the majority of the student participants, payment represented a significant encouragement, a critical factor in engaging their interest in participating. For P5, 'the fact that they are offered payment and recognition in that way meant that they could justify to themselves the extra time they would spend on it; it allowed a further deeper collaboration', and for SP1 'the incentive that you are going to get paid for it, is an extra dimension that makes it worthwhile'. P8 sees payment as a way of avoiding entering into an 'exploitative relationship'.

In an era in which the student has been 'increasingly commodified as an economic resource' (Tymms, Peters and Scott, 2013, p. 260), discussions around payment of students are coloured by what Williams has elegantly called 'the pedagogy of debt' (2006). Newman has a profoundly diverse student population, with many of our students coming from low-higher-education-participation areas, and being the first in family to enter a university. They complete their studies alongside a range of other substantial commitments, including paid work, caring and parenting. If we mean what we say about creating democracy, we need student involvement, and payment is one clear way of encouraging students to feel they can devote time to this work. We hold to the idea that payment facilitates, indeed, ensures, student participation in the shared dream, that might in turn lead to such democratic tomorrows – while also avoiding thin, morally questionable and neoliberalized versions of student engagement (Matthews et al., 2018; White 2018; Scoles et al., 2019; Luo, Matthews and Chunduri, 2019).

Respectful Dialogue

Many participants articulated their enthusiasm for how many different 'types' of members of the university community had had an opportunity to take part in the dialogues that occur within the projects. Professional staff from the institution were well represented within the focus groups, and one, P12, expressed a sense that such employees can 'feel side-lined and not part of the institution', but that the projects worked to remove this feeling. Similarly, members of under-represented groups within the student body found a voice within the projects, with reference to Newman's 'widening participation' student demographic, made numerous times within the discussions. Given Newman's position as a Catholic university (which in turn attracts members of other faiths to study at the institution in significant numbers), it is relevant to note that students said that they got involved as, for example, an 'interpretation of their Islamic faith' (P1). P3 goes on to observe that in terms of the types of work undertaken in the projects, it has 'been a strength in these first few years . . . that more or less anything on the spectrum was given a chance'. But while P12 warns that 'saying everyone can take part is not the same as ensuring that they all can', echoing Antonucci's plea that we do not interpret access to participation as a 'proxy for equity in HE' (2016, p. 22), P11 has faith in 'the ethos of Newman that everybody is equal' as a driving force behind the perceived success of the projects. Thus, voices from across the institution participate in the dialogue inherent within the projects.

Questions about which projects were successful in gaining approval were posed during the focus groups, as were concerns around whether work and caring commitments, or cultural barriers, may mean that the pool of potential participants has nevertheless been 'narrower' (P3) than we would hope. Nevertheless, to a greater or lesser degree, participants recognize that they have an opportunity to 'fundamentally change the terms on which teaching and learning take place' (Bell, 2012, pp. 47–8), to operate in a space where 'people think together and keep questions open' (Readings, 1996 cited in McLean, 2006, p. 14). They have felt the 'generosity' and 'respect' inherent in the relationships they have built through such respectful dialogue (Freire, 1997, p. 86) – the 'ethic of reciprocity' in action (Cook-Sather and Felton, 2017, p. 171). Ultimately, the project participants have a sense of engaging in dialogue, not only with each other but with the institution itself.

Co-investigation

Many participants articulated their enjoyment of, and pride in, the process of investigation undertaken through the projects. While staff varied in their response to the idea that partnership working was, or was not, like other elements of their teaching, the majority indicated the pleasure they took from this 'new' way of working: 'I still hold now that it was really enjoyable . . . on that pure level', states P1. The investigation process brought about individual and collective benefits that felt tangible to most; they spoke of the development of research and other skills, of influencing university processes or curricula, of contributing to the employability of students, and of seeing students gain a greater understanding of the machinery of academia. We might argue that some of these benefits are more closely aligned to Freire's hope that we 'continue the struggle for democracy [in our] institutions' than others (1997, p. 60), and we must be wary of institutionalizing the student – or the staff member. Through co-investigation we seek to bring awareness of how all are simultaneously 'themselves *and* the oppressor whose consciousness they have internalised' (Freire, 1996, p. 30) and thus avoid the language of participation as 'domestication' (Peters and Mathias, 2018, p. 55) creeping into the projects' terrain.

Responding to the motivation of students who express a desire to transform an aspect of the student experience was important for some staff partners, if not complex. Irritation with the constraints of the project timescale deadlines, which are partly dictated by the fiscal and academic year, were a concern, but this was often seen as a reason to launch follow-up projects in the next academic year. Perhaps, ultimately, students themselves were best placed to articulate the benefits of having participated in the co-investigatory process of student partnership. As SP3 asserts, 'Knowing within myself that . . . this will be the foundation for future ventures that I take, and that I have been part of this research that has been fundamental in changing the institution . . . it sort of gives you a warm fuzzy feeling!'. Here, the student voices elements of both instrumental and progressive views of the purposes of higher education, but critically, she has not lost the desire to 'persevere' (Freire, 1997, p. 63). She has engaged in the often-difficult process of co-creating knowledge and has felt 'the joy that steeps it' (Freire, 2004b, p. 69), recognizing that we can build tomorrow through 'transforming today' (Freire, 2004b, p. 56).

Co-construction of Solutions

Staff and student partners alike were keen to see their project either gain traction within the university, or achieve a tangible output, such as a journal article or academic conference presentation. Participants whose projects fell into the latter category tended to express higher levels of satisfaction with their participation than those who had endeavoured to effect change upon an aspect of the university's functioning: again the possibility of collapsing into the language of partnership as domestication hovers in the wings (Peters 2014; Mathias and Peters, 2018). This left both student and staff participants sensing that Newman was 'absolutely not at the stage' (P3) of finding ways to bring *all* the collective messages coming out of the projects fully to bear on processes, management or the university's leadership and functioning. Participants wrestled with whether it was better to take the approach of allowing a 'thousand flowers to bloom' (P1) (in which very little constraint is placed upon projects in terms of what qualifies as an outcome), or for there to be a more 'co-ordinated' (P3) approach, striving more explicitly to bring about institutional change.

Nevertheless, there appeared to be widespread agreement that if the projects could have a 'life beyond', that would be 'fantastic'; at the same time, an equal sense that the projects 'can't always change things however much you might want [them] to' (P11). There were modest indications that the projects were helping to find solutions to some issues faced by the university community. And at an individual level, there was agreement among participants that the students can very much be the 'experts', who can 'teach us things about their experiences' (P1). Freire again helps us here as he urges us to 'not leave for a random tomorrow something that is part of my task as a progressive educator right now' (1997, p. 75). We are only part way along the path towards a new settlement between lecturer and student, institution and state; even if our efforts sometimes falter, the hopeful pursuit of co-constructed solutions must be our mantra.

Continuing Transformation

Ultimately, the projects were viewed by both staff and students in overwhelmingly positive terms and are now seen as integral to the life of the university, as 'part of a continuum . . . of different ways of engaging with the student' (P1). While we should be wary of the colonization of the word 'engagement' as a consumerist tool in higher education (Neary and Saunders 2016; Scoles et al., 2019), the projects at Newman have enabled staff and students to get to know each other 'on a different level' (P3). For some, they have 'opened [their] eyes up to the sorts of things we can do with students' (P2). The projects have 'completely changed the way' some lecturers teach aspects of their modules (P10) and have 'helped to transform ... [and] certainly helped reflection and also a sense of belonging' (P11). One student participant considered the role of the projects, not just for herself but for the wider higher education community, stating:

> We are in a generation where education is changing, and it is beginning to really turn on its head, and it is not so much this student–lecturer thing; and I think this idea of students being researchers right from their degree is maybe where university and degree level education is heading ... and I think it is a really fantastic way to break the hierarchy. (SP3)

Here, then, a recognition by the student of the possibilities of democratic potential in partnership working. We must 'watch out' for the 'insidious capacity' of dominant political discourses to convince us that 'education is neutral' (Freire 1998, p. 90; Luo, Matthews and Chunduri, 2019), and instead create opportunities for genuine participation in institutional life. Ultimately, we can acknowledge that we, and the project of higher education itself, are 'unfinished, but we have made ourselves capable of knowing ourselves as such' (Freire, 1997, p. 93). The projects articulate a continuing transformation, a sense of belonging to something larger than oneself, to a moment of possibility.

Critiques of the Projects Within the University

There were some examples of disillusionment among the research participants. They had initially believed that the commitment to financially supporting the projects meant that the university was somehow invested in them and might respond to their content (if it had something to 'teach' the university about itself). In some cases, following their project, participants came to feel this was not the case, and were frustrated by the resulting lack of institutional change, as they perceived it. For P8, 'my assumption was naively that the willingness of the university to pay for this represented some commitment to the output'. SP1 expressed disappointment that she had been encouraged to think that her report would 'inform [an] aspect of the life of the university; ... [but] those channels, they just seemed to stop or fizzle out'. Thus, there is work to be done, in fully realizing the transformative potential of the projects to Newman's benefit. At this juncture Freire (2004) reminds us not to allow hopelessness to become 'a programme', echoing Lyotard's invitation to maintain 'incredulity towards metanarratives' (1984, p. 14). While we can acknowledge that educators 'feel contractions in already-cramped spaces for critical work as political cultures harden' (Amsler, 2015, p. 15), if the projects are serving to raise staff and student awareness of the forces oppressing them, then they are also fulfilling a Freirean purpose of consciousness-raising.

Conclusion

We have presented the findings of this research numerous times at academic conference. We have often noted the genuinely warm response from our colleagues working in much larger institutions as to how our principles-based, student partnership project scheme has gained such traction within our small university. In turn, we reflect on how more than 80 per cent of our students belong to groups under-represented in higher education; on how more than 90 per cent of them commute up to an hour and a half each way to reach the university; on how many have parenting, caring and employment commitments to negotiate alongside their studies; and how many are first-in-family students, or are possessed of complex educational biographies that have the potential to deprive them of traditional social capital (Parkes, Mathias and Seal, 2018). And yet, the projects have become a route through, as both a 'disruptive ethos and messy human relational process of partnership praxis' (Matthews et al., 2019, p. 281) *and* a central pillar guiding our strategic intentions. As the most recent iteration of our Access and Participation Plan declares:

> our students bring a diverse wealth of lived experience with them and this has implications for the nature and ethos of Newman's teaching . . . Our pedagogy of partnership seeks to ensure we teach and learn with our students, working together to make a difference for our students and community. (Newman University, 2019d, p. 1)

In small and large ways, principled student partnership, grounded in a hopeful Freirean pedagogic approach, has come to be embedded within the life of our university. Together, we affirm the possibility of doing the work of HE differently, of moving beyond cynicism, and celebrating the good work done here and now.

Response from Gill Gilbert

Participating in Student–Staff Partnership

I became involved in student partnership at Newman in my final year as an undergraduate and have continued participating in the projects during my Master's Degree. All students (and staff), if possible, should take up opportunities to participate in projects, and every effort should be made to avoid it becoming a clique of those in the know. Student participation can be widened by encouraging experienced project-participant students to work alongside students new to them. The projects should be promoted as a safe space to develop outside of your comfort zones and it is vital to communicate effectively 'what's in it for the students' to encourage engagement from year one and two students (e.g. that it supports the dissertation process). Student partnership is about sharing ideas and constructing knowledge together, and initially I anticipated power differentials. However, my experiences provided equal partnerships, and in some elements of the projects I took the lead by choice rather than delegation from the staff partner. Student partnership is not necessarily about student empowerment, as this suggests the powerful have some power to share with the powerless and hand it over. Instead, the aim is to raise consciousness within those that are seemingly powerless to help them recognize the power they held all along (as Leoarna and John describe in the chapter).

Payment of students for participating in the projects is an important aspect and demonstrates how the institution values my contribution. It helps me justify the time I devote to these projects rather than undertaking other paid work. The payment does not necessarily break down into an hourly rate, as often students will spend more time on it than the advised fifty hours, especially when you are passionate about the project topic. Being paid for the project may be an initial incentive, however it often ends up being the 'icing on the cake', with the social interaction with others taking part in the programme becoming the more memorable and most valuable element. In addition, participating in the projects, and being paid for it, has led me to participate and volunteer in other projects within the institution and community; all of which help develop my personal skills that will serve me beyond my time at university.

To help students feel a sense of completion in the projects, there could be a process or space to support the implementation of the project recommendations. Some outcomes may be quick wins that students can implement themselves. However, as Leoarna and John point out, there are hierarchal challenges that exist within institutional framework that can hinder the path to making change happen. Partnership is at risk of creating spaces for democracy only for this to lead students to the end of a 'process', looking over the edge of hope into an empty crevice of despair and frustration, where the powerful still reign and the student voice is once again silenced. Providing follow-up support for students and staff, which includes support from the institution's decision-makers, would further endorse the institution's commitment to the values of working in partnership.

Chapter Twelve

Foundation Years

Undoing Discourses of Deficit

Pheobe Hall, Kace McGowan, Leoarna Mathias, Samantha Snelleksz, Sarah Parkes and Mike Seal, Response from Sarah Hale

Introduction

Newman University Birmingham had its first intake of students onto the foundation year programme in Autumn 2017. Foundation years across the sector are designed to open up higher education opportunities for people who have had a gap in education or who do not have adequate prior qualifications to enter onto a three-year undergraduate degree. Foundation year students are very much viewed as 'widening participation' cohorts. In this regard as discussed elsewhere (Parkes, Mathias and Seal, 2018), the programme at Newman in design resists the dominant deficit discourse of undergraduate transition, and instead, focuses on what is within our control at the university to influence, 'chang[ing] ourselves rather than wishing for a more homogenous or traditional student body' (Thomas and May, 2011). This means that we do not assume that students have failed in the education system, but that the formal educational and/or societal structures and systems within their experience up until the point of university study have failed them. Embedded within the curriculum of this new foundation year is an unequivocal invitation to students to challenge the structural inequalities that had previously operated to constrain their educational choices, in the full knowledge that contemporary university education colludes and perpetuates such structures (see Thomas, 2002 for a discussion on the role of institutional habitus).

We argue that foundation years should thus seek to support the perpetual process of our students' becoming; the constantly dissolving, diffusing and recreation of their subjectivity that is engaged in a perpetual process of flux (Quinn, 2010, pp. 18–22). Between 2017 and 2019, the foundation year(s) have adopted a particular approach to curriculum and the delivery of the programme through a commitment to the principles of critical pedagogy. This approach, unlike many traditional approaches to 'study skills' or deficit models of student development, seeks to develop an awareness of the subtle injustices legitimized by the current education system: what Paulo Freire calls 'conscientization' (Freire, 1972) to promote democratic engagement, meaningful dialogue and co-operative working.

Given this context, the staff working at Newman, in particular those of us involved in the foundation year, are privileged to witness the nature of our students' experiences; their emergent academic identities that brings together with it, an appreciation of the complex trajectories towards degree completion. Taking a Freirean approach also facilitates staff and student interaction, enabling students to develop critically and academically, and staff to better understand their students (Thomas and May, 2011). Students therefore have been actively involved in the evaluation of the programme throughout. The learning we share here from working with our students includes vignettes from three 2017–18 foundation year students, P and K, and a 2018–19 student, S. They are all working-class white women whose ages span late teens, mid-twenties and mid-thirties.

We begin this chapter with student vignettes exploring their experiences of navigating university study via the foundation year. Having considered breaking them up into themes and adding our own analysis, we ultimately decided against this approach: this potentially reduces and dilutes their narratives and the flow of their accounts. In addition, their reflections contain enough analysis of their own. We then draw the chapter to its conclusion through sharing our learning around working with the 'Newman student' while exploring the ways in which we embed the foundation year alongside other strategic work in relation to student transition, retention and success.

Student Vignettes

K

The idea of coming to university terrified me. I felt that education was not for me, or more accurately, I was not for education. Due to having dyslexia, I was regularly referred to as 'lazy' throughout primary school. Before joining the foundation year, I would have described myself as a 'slow learner', and most certainly not an academic or an intellectual. I never finished school, however, I spent most of my life in some sort of part-time education, but at lower levels. I wanted to progress and move forward but did not think I could achieve higher than Level 2 qualifications. I acquired my English GCSE in a matter of weeks before starting university, which gave me the boost to enquire about university for later in life although, I ended up starting university that semester!

I had no idea I was going for an interview at university. I thought it was a tour and a casual discussion to answer a few of my queries, but I left being accepted onto the course! I was surprised; naturally, and so petrified I cried on the way back to the car. My main fears were:

(1) Commitment: I had never committed to anything really for longer than a year, and a four-year degree took me to the very end of my twenties! Would I be able to stick it out?!

(2) Financial worries: I had never paid for my education before. Being on a low income and coming from a low-income family, I was immediately in fear of this huge loan and the added pressure that added to passing all four years. A bigger financial issue that came to fruition when I started my course, was how I was going to financially support myself.
(3) Support: I am a complex student with complex needs. I had heard horror stories of universities leaving pupils like me treading water until they eventually had to drop out.
(4) Ability/capability: I had just got my English GCSE at the age of twenty-five, and my maths a few years prior. I did not feel well equipped to accept a place on a university degree course.

I remember walking down a corridor and bumping into my tutor and head of course on the way to his lecture. He asked me how I was, and I remember quite fervently accusing him of being responsible for me having an existential crisis. His response stuck with me to this day: with a smile on his face he replied, 'In the nicest possible way – good! Because that means we are doing our job properly!' I had regular existential crises on the foundation year, but our lecturers were so welcoming of the questions that came from me wrestling with these big topics and ideas. It felt like such a joint learning experience. Staff and students all bounced ideas around, and there was no fear of asking questions.

It made me angry; all the injustice, heartache and suffering I experienced throughout my education. It was not because I was not capable – it was because the education systems were flawed. There was psychological damage that had hindered my development until the foundation year, and now I want to achieve high and find a way to make a difference. I no longer doubt my intelligence, and I repeatedly try different angles and strategies to overcome any obstacle thrown my way.

During the second semester of the foundation year, we looked at the Paulo Freire's *Pedagogy of the Oppressed*. Again, I sent an email to my tutor expressing that I did not understand why we had to look at it, saying something along the lines of ' I knew I was oppressed from when we looked at it in the first semester and now it's just making me feel hopeless'. She said I had a very good point and, consequently, did a lecture on the issues I had raised. It made me feel like I had something to contribute, like my thought process and reasoning seemed worthy, equal and relevant.

The genuineness, approachableness and openness of our lecturers had a huge impact on how I felt and still feel as a university student today. During the educational timelines, our lecturers shared their struggles through education and some of their background. I saw them as role models: people I believed in, people who came from similar places and had similar stories as me. The educational timeline also created this deep incomparable comradery and peer support that I still rely on today with my foundation year peers. The thinking theoretically presentation was a significant point for me. It allowed me to see that my ideas were interesting, worthy of expression, and of academic relevance.

Sadly, I have not enjoyed my subject specific years as much as I enjoyed my foundation year, and I regularly feel those feelings of self-doubt, imposter syndrome and inability creeping back in. However, I have found some allies within the subject specific staff, and the foundation year set me up well to prepare for these feelings. When my capabilities were questioned by staff members who had not worked directly with me, in my mind I knew I had educated staff members who did know me, had seen my work, and they did believe in me. So, I stood my ground. I felt that I had as much of a right to be there as anyone else. I felt I was just as capable as anyone else, and more passionate than most! I plan to do a doctorate now, which would have been unfathomable before the foundation year.

Thanks to the foundation year, for the first time in my life, I have finally mustered up some self-worth. I was always stubborn, but self-worth gives that stubbornness purpose and shape. Although I was not prepared for my specific subject by the foundation year, I was prepared for academic writing; politics and procedures; manoeuvring the campus; knowing what staff to speak too regarding different enquires or issues. I have a goal and I now know that I have the intellect, skills, perseverance and self-belief I need to achieve it. After I completed the foundation year, I was still given opportunities for further professional development. Speaking at a conference hugely improved my confidence regarding public speaking and gave me first-hand experience of networking. While being a foundation year mentor gave me experience, responsibility and the chance to help new students with the knowledge I had gained.

P

Before joining the foundation year at Newman, I was always a 'giver-upper'. Meaning that with education if I couldn't do something, I would always walk out of my lessons, refuse to do any work or just not attend those lessons. There were times at A-Level where I would go to a mock exam, which was rare, and sit and write nothing but my name because in my mind it was better to not try than to fail. Both parts of that mindset were wrong. Firstly, it is definitely better to try, and secondly, passing was certainly an option: I was not always going to fail. I didn't see myself as academic and I thought that was a terrible thing. The only way to be worth anything was to be clever and get good grades, and between sixteen and eighteen years old I only knew my worth by grade: it wasn't just a grade for my work but a grade for me.

I thought education was the 'be-all or end-all' of everything and going to university meant I would be somebody. I didn't think I belonged there; I had not earned the right to be there. After failing my A2 subjects I was a failure and I was destined to be nobody. Along with ill mental health and low self-esteem I was willing to do anything to feel some worth, so fighting for uni through clearing meant everything. University to me seemed like the place people went and got better, I thought it was a magical place and things would instantly be better. I viewed them as all the same as Oxford, as I thought that was where I wanted to be.

Since being at Newman my view of myself has changed a lot in several ways. I realised I was capable; I wasn't always going to fail and it didn't matter if I did fail as my worth is not based on a grade. This began to change slowly but all at once! Before I knew it, I was confident in academic work; I was excited to go to a lecture and was willing to stay there. The first time I remember it changing was seeing mature students in the classroom with me. This told me that people survived without uni, so even if I did fail, I would to. People had lived amazing lives and had families: this reassured me that failing wouldn't make me a failure. Then we did an educational timeline allowing me to be creative, which opened my mind. I could tell people my story in a way that felt true to me, not an exam spec. It was something I was interested in and cared about. This also gave me the chance to get to know staff and students, and relate to each other. Relationships in the foundation year helped with changing my views of uni and me. We encouraged each other and it sparked ideas and thoughts.

The foundation year at Newman was valuable to me because it gave me another chance to find and learn about myself and my capabilities. I was learning about subjects without realizing I was learning. It changed the definition of learning for me. It was delivered through discussion; it was very student-led but guided very discretely by lecturers. We would have discussions and debates with each other which helped us think about things wider than our own opinion. Tutor groups were really valuable to me. It gave a chance to talk about anything worrying you or the things you were struggling with in a smaller close-knit group. You felt heard in that group and to me that was special. That made me realize: people actually care about what I have to say. It gave a chance to learn about opinions of others and use your own voice too. This became a powerful part of the foundation year for me. This has helped me in my subject because it has made me challenge ideas, thoughts and theories, which not only expands my knowledge in that area but enables me to write critically and evaluate theories better in academic writing.

I am a better independent learner because I don't doubt myself. I can sit at home and work on an assignment and remember that I am capable and I won't always fail. My mindset towards my academic abilities has changed which makes me more confident, therefore I can write more confidently. I will not always question if I am on the right lines, I trust myself that I can do it. This reduces my stress when I'm working on assignments or in exams, therefore, I can get them done with ease and in less time, which is great for any student. I still don't see myself as 'an academic' but I don't think this is a bad thing anymore, I think this comes from my attitude towards education changing. For example, I don't think failing is the 'be-all or end-all' anymore, therefore I don't hold a fear of failure. The idea that I still could fail is there but the idea that I could pass is too. I don't feel that university is the only thing to give me worth or self-esteem, but it is an important part of my life that I gain pride from. It's something I work for and earn, as opposed to something I need to make me feel worth.

S

Before I made the decision to apply for university, I believed that my educational days were well and truly behind me, accepting the fact that I was probably now too old. Following what to me was a life-changing event, I decided to rethink my educational status. I applied and was successful, surprisingly I was very proud of myself for achieving entry and the staff believing I had the capabilities to acquire a degree.

Until the point of enrolment, I experienced no nerves and didn't think too much of what I was letting myself in for. It was at enrolment that reality hit. Surrounded by considerably younger people I did doubt myself and I did think 'were my critics right? Am I too old?' Fortunately, despite these feelings I pushed on. The longer I was at university during the foundation year, the more I settled and began to feel I had made the right choice. Ultimately, the feeling of intimidation, whether it being the eldest on campus or the size of the campus, I knew I had made the right choice. Looking back, I am grateful that I was able to access university education at my age, and with the adequate qualifications that I had. Attending the foundation year helped me improve immensely, giving me good basis to further my educational journey. I felt better equipped to start year one of my degree, having built a good sense of what was expected of me.

The tutor group gave us an opportunity to discuss anything we were struggling with in a smaller environment, and not feel intimidated that you shouldn't really ask. Feedback to me was also fundamental in my development, I found it very useful to have my work marked and structured feedback delivered. This gave me stepping-stones, ideas to build on and things that I may have been good at. I always remember being really excited to get my marks and read staff feedback. This was a tool to me, as I had created a spreadsheet with all received feedback and always tried to use it as a basis of how to develop my work for the next piece.

Without the foundation year, starting in year one without previous experience would have only ended in disaster. I would not have had the confidence or the ability to grow and feel I could achieve. Foundation year provided me, having been out of educational environments for a very long time, with the skillset and importantly the mindset to be able to produce work of the standard that was expected at university level. In year one I found that tutors spoke as if the students already knew what they were doing and expected to already be at a level of competence. Had I not taken part in foundation year I feel I would have quit in the first few weeks of year one, simply because I wouldn't have understood the terminology and the basics of what was required of me. Simple things like formatting, how to structure an assignment and referencing.

At the point I am now in my educational journey, I have a totally different mindset and would encourage any mature student to apply and follow their passion. Age is not a barrier, if anything it's an added bonus as you have lots to draw from and still lots to gain. My ability levels have in many areas increased to a point now that I feel comfortable in a lecture, and when tasks are requested, I may not have the answer straight away but I am confident to know where to start. I understand the importance of research and how to gather useful articles or books from different sources. The library is no longer scary, and I also can happily find my own information or direction I want my essay to go, independently and not be reliant on a tutor to advise where to start and lay things out step by step.

Being at university has allowed me to believe in myself and trust my ability. I know I have the right to be at university and my work is proving that I am capable. Moreover, my written work in a professional capacity has also improved, my language is more professional and appropriate. I am proud that even after various struggles that have challenged me along the way, I have managed to overcome them and rise to my challenges.

Conclusion

Looking at the vignettes in the chapter, Foundation Years aimed at widening participation appear to need inclusion of a concrete set of aims that:

- Deconstruct and reconstruct students' previous educational experiences to resist internalized deficit thinking and negotiate the resources students will need to traverse higher education.
- Explore, deconstruct and reconstruct concepts encountered on the course including the language of higher education.
- Develop student confidence, self-belief and resilience to be able to traverse the landscape of higher education.
- Develop knowledge generating spaces that are actively and mutually constituted to challenge those 'banking' models of education.
- Discuss and co-construct student (and tutors) 'possible selves' that are drawn from and relate to past and future representations of 'self'.

The question then becomes what necessary pedagogic approaches are needed to achieve these aims. Elsewhere (Seal and Parkes, 2020), we have identified the characteristics of these spaces in that they:

- Are visceral, pedagogic and liminal, rather than safe, though certainly not dangerous.
- Have an emphasis on deconstructing power both inside and outside of the space, and on the concept of knowledge and its creation.
- Have a process framework of intersubjectivity, encounter, recognition and working in the moment.
- Emphasize the cultivation of hope and a future orientation, recognizing an equivalence between reconstruction and deconstruction.

There are also some structural features of Newman's current foundation years that intend to work with the characteristics and aims seen earlier and are worth discussing here.

Interviewing Students

Historically, we have had a policy of interviewing all potential students. This is not explicitly to test whether people can come on the course, but from the outset aimed to engage with the potential student and undo any fears they have about education in general and higher education in particular. Students reported that coming to interview, seeing the university and meeting the staff was one of the significant factors in persuading them to come to university. Indeed, pre-entry activities, such as extended interviewing, can increase the likelihood of a student successfully progressing in HE through generating an early sense of belonging (Thomas, 2012; Thomas et al., 2017; Parkes, 2014). For recruiting universities such as Newman, it could be argued that interviewing is an unnecessary burden, and a quick offer of a place at the university to the student results in an increased likelihood of acceptance. We would argue this is questionable. In our experience of interviewing, the conversion rate has been high at circa 40 per cent and actually the highest for any course with significant numbers. For the first two years of the foundation years, there was a direct correlation between those who were not interviewed and those who did not subsequently engage, and this has proved to be the same in 2019/20. We also achieved an enrolment conversion rate of 95 per cent and rising, compared to the average of the institution of 80 per cent. We would state, therefore, that interviewing students is a key 'first step' of building a relationship with them that, concomitantly, supports student transition.

Modules Deconstructing Education

Our foundation year consists of six modules (Parkes, Mathias and Seal, 2018) and within a number of these we aim to facilitate a process of deconstruction and then reconstruction of knowledge and power that investigates what universities are, who they are for and how they are structured. Indeed, within the portfolio assessments, three items specifically aim to provoke discussion on the nature of our understandings of the world. First is an educational timeline, which both students and staff produce to deconstruct their experiences of formal education to date. For the students, this leads later to essays and presentations that examine what is needed to be successful at university and challenges them to consider their views on what constitutes knowledge, education and learning.

The second is a presentation called 'Thinking theoretically' which recognizes that students have their own theories and ideas about the world. Third, students produce a glossary of words and concepts from HE as part of the Semester 2 portfolio. On one level this helps them understand the terms they will encounter, yet also allows contestation that illuminates the political project behind the use of words. This challenges and deconstructs language: a central component of critical pedagogy (Freire, 1972). Students thus unpack and deconstruct academic language in recognition that it can make people feel excluded, and be an exercise of power, even if inadvertently.

Student-centred Tutor Groups

Mediating and working through these experiences thus requires an approach that enables teaching staff to respond according to the needs of a student group in any given moment. Our approach is influenced by a combination of the Swedish Folk High

School Grundtvig model of education, critical pedagogy and Tavistock experiential group work. This has translated into a three-hour student-led tutor group that is responsive to student need, rather than requiring delivery of predetermined, set content. Evaluations and student partnership work reveals that students see this as one of the transformative elements of the course that makes their experience coherent and provides a space for them to work through their previous and current constructions of themselves and their education. The role of a tutor in these groups is to:

- Monitor the time-bound nature of learning experiences.
- Keep the group on the task of examining a broad curriculum, facilitating the deconstruction of previous and current educational experiences and offering observations on group processes.
- Act on the students' will, self-belief and efficacy including their will to engage, challenge themselves and others; and their wish to learn, encourage and affirm students' intrinsic ways of knowing as legitimate, but that perhaps need to be clarified and articulated.
- Aid students to understand and deconstruct both the language and concepts behind the arguments they use.

Issues of Progression

Foundation year continuation and progression rates are fodder in the 'value for money' discourse that now pervades the English HE sector, as discussed in Chapter 3, and as the Augar review's (Department of Education, 2019) questionable commentary on foundation years clearly demonstrates. For a university such as Newman, this raises tensions between the drive to further generalize the foundation years through amalgamating discipline streams into one, and the desire for more subject-driven content: it is certainly hard to do both. First, what level of grounding in a subject canon of knowledge do students need on a generic course? Foundation years generally allow for students to change courses and build-in an experience of the course they are going to do/thinking of doing in subsequent years. It certainly seems pertinent to at least get students used to what the content and nature of the subject area would be. K certainly did not feel prepared by the foundation year for what the study of psychology entailed:

> I underestimated how much of a science it was. I was not preparing myself to become a scientist but a psychologist, which in my mind were very different things. I was massively unprepared for the level of statistics on my course. Statistics is like no other subject I have experienced. I feel I spend very little time studying what I thought was psychology, and an insane amount of time on scientific methods, research methods etc. I feel that being more aware and equipped for this would perhaps have changed some of my feelings about my first year in my subject.

A second tension is the extent to which it is a foundation years role to induct students in the pedagogies and style of teaching that course teams have, or that the subjects should change their pedagogy. Some university subjects argue that their pedagogic approach cannot change because they have professional conditions and a set curriculum. However it does not necessarily follow that the pedagogies within these subjects must be content-driven. Having run courses that similarly have professional conditions, we would question this argument. Certainly, professional qualifications have a set curriculum to ensure students build up a certain knowledge base upon graduation. However, the 'banking' approach to knowledge acquisition does not have to be the default pedagogic position.

The pedagogic approach undertaken to date on Newman foundation years is underpinned by the aims outlined at the beginning of the concluding paragraphs earlier. We acknowledge that this will not necessarily mirror the educational experiences students will then get on their degree. The moot question here is whether it should. We would argue that in order to promote the institutional transformation that Thomas and May (2011) assert is needed to support student transition for students with complex lives, it is in fact the pedagogies of subject areas that need to transform and change. Indeed, as a reflection of the complexity foundation years at Newman are working with, we include commentary in the following from our last two annual reports that identifies the characteristics of our students. These include:

- Highly complex lives that need sensitive processes such as mitigating circumstances, extensions etc. that will be ongoing beyond the foundation year.
- The partial experiences of educational systems means while most students engage, this is often still fragile, fractured and needs nurturing. A lot of academic processes and conventions will not be natural to them. Many will not have the social and cultural capital of more traditional students.
- High levels of dyslexia and other learning needs, that has an impact on and is linked to their previous educational experience, often undiagnosed and unmediated.
- High levels of unresolved trauma and self-medication, that have been a part of their previous non-engagement with education. Issues this year include bereavement, domestic violence, sex trafficking, sexual abuse, sexual assault, coming to terms with sexual orientation and others' reaction to it, drug use, self-harm and suicidal ideation.
- High levels of diagnosed and undiagnosed mental health issues (around a third) as well as depression, anxiety, body dysmorphia, obsessive compulsive disorder, ADHD etc.
- Other associated issues: approximately half of our students have had practical issues with finance, accommodation and other welfare issues, as they often live independently, but precariously.

Positively, our experience of foundation year students is that they have high levels of self-awareness, resilience and ability to self-manage. The characteristics discussed earlier remain a reality and thus do not reflect the 'ideal student': the university or the sector should not expect them to be. Many of these characteristics will prevail across the students' lives while at university: such dynamics cannot be undone within one academic year nor indeed, in some instances, at all. Nonetheless, as educators and institutions, we should strive to change our practices to take account of where the people in front of us are at. Here, we can build a student's confidence in their abilities and develop their responses to the demands of university study in the hope that this simultaneously fosters a sense of agency that sets them on a road to fulfilment and human flourishing. In this, we who consider ourselves self-identified critical pedagogues (see Mike in Chapter 2 and the Conclusion) might have meaningful impact on our students through our pedagogy. Defending the rights of these students, prioritizing their needs, and forcing wider the cracks in order to allow them to 'dance' in university spaces requires a determined, educated hope (Solnit, 2016) in those of us privileged enough to work on the programme.

Response from Sarah Hale

It was Newman's foundation year, for which I acted as external validator in 2017, that first opened my eyes to their radical potential. As an autistic, working-class academic, who didn't know that I was either of those things until a few years ago, getting on in academia had always been about fitting in. It was an environment I was happy to fit into; where I felt more comfortable than almost anywhere else. But it was still always about watching, learning, assimilating – with success being judged in terms of how well I could pass myself off as an insider, someone who was there by right. Seeing the radicalism of the Newman approach, the emphasis on how the system had failed students rather than them having failed within it, started a process of questioning and exploration that has fundamentally altered how I teach, and the way I see students, the system, and myself.

Foundation year provision has expanded significantly in recent years, but very few are as explicitly radical and challenging as the one described in this chapter. Talking to foundation year practitioners about how they perceive the role and purpose of foundation years in relation to social class (Hale, 2021), three discourses emerge. There is the radical discourse outlined previously in which students are encouraged to challenge the whole system of HE and beyond, and staff do so openly. There is a second discourse where practitioners feel unable to challenge the system openly, but see the very existence of foundation years and their role in delivering them as subversive – changing the system from within by bringing working-class students into elite (and elitist) institutions. The final, and probably most common, discourse however is of assimilation; a model in which the primary function of the foundation year is to prepare and equip (i.e. alter) students to fit into an alien environment through the provision of skills – as often social as academic – and 'cultural capital'.

This last most clearly represents a deficit model in which the student is remediated to fit an institution in which change is seen as unnecessary, undesirable or impossible. In this, the student is an object to be acted upon. The discourse of subversion emerges from a more critical agenda, but casts the working-class student as a means to an end, in a process which can be damaging. Only the radical approach engendered in the discourse of challenge presents the student fully as subject – but this also brings its own problems and burdens.

Ironically, a deficit model – initially at least – provides more hope to disadvantaged students. A seductive neoliberal discourse of meritocracy tells them that individual effort will triumph over structural disadvantage, if they only work hard enough to transform themselves. The more radical model confronts students with the fact that the odds are stacked against them. How the ensuing anger and frustration is channelled into a renewed sense of agency rather than a spiral into despair is the delicate path negotiated by foundation years such as Newman's.

Part II C

Becoming the Hopeful Pedagogue

Chapter Thirteen

A Mindful Journey

Person-centred and Contemplative Critical Approaches to Higher Education

Ruth Roberts, Response from Luca Tateo

Introduction

This chapter is a personal reflection on my experiences of working as a counsellor and lecturer in higher education. As a counsellor and lecturer, my work draws on several theoretical influences and these underpin my reflections and recommendations in this chapter. Primarily, these influences come from the person-centred approach, mindfulness-based approaches and critical pedagogy. Another important influence is the concept of the therapeutic contract which has strongly influenced my thinking here. To begin with, it might be useful to provide brief definitions of concepts and theoretical strands which may be less familiar to a critical pedagogy readership:

> Mindfulness: a purposeful attentional focus on the present moment, characterized by an attitudinal stance that is non-judgemental and welcoming of experience.

> The person-centred approach: characterized by a non-judgemental, genuine and empathic stance towards the experience of others (Rogers, 1957) underpinned by a belief in the inherent tendency of all organisms to move towards growth (Rogers, 1959a).

> Therapeutic contract: a clearly explained and consensually agreed contract between counsellor and client regarding the boundaries of the therapeutic relationship; the expectations of each person in the relationship and the logistic arrangements of the agreement to work together (BACP, 2018).

Summary

The aim of this chapter is to consider concerns about student well-being and engagement in the context of the contractual relationship between universities and students.[1] I will argue that the use of the term 'potential' in higher education policy and institutional advertising contributes to drawing students into an ill-defined contractual relationship with their institution. From a therapeutic point of view, this is a poor starting point for a working relationship. This is particularly important when expectations about performance and outcome are based on tacit assumptions or ideological discourse.

I will argue that a prevailing 'ideology of success' (Ichheiser, 1943; Tateo, 2018) which draws on intangible goals such as 'reaching one's potential' supports a consumerist, marketized model of higher education (Newman and Jahdi, 2009; Saunders and Blanco Ramírez, 2017). Current higher education policy promotes a rhetoric of potential (Sellar, 2015) and an ideology of success (Ichheiser, 1943) which create the expectation that an engagement with education on a transactional basis (Newman and Jahdi, 2009) will deliver success for the individual. However, this rhetoric also dictates a prescriptive view of personal growth focused on the employability and economic productivity of the individual. In my experience of supporting students, this instrumental motivation for learning and desire to 'reach one's potential' can lead to a denial or avoidance of certain aspects of experience resulting in anxiety and dissatisfaction.

As an antidote to this, I suggest that contemplative practices such as those used in secular mindfulness-based approaches can help students develop an awareness of internal motivations for study and encourage questioning of assumptions about the purpose of being at university. Similarly, the adoption of mindful approaches to the use of language and clear contracting by universities can serve to lessen the messiness of unclear expectations and boundaries of the academic contract with students. A more mindful approach to our engagement with students can also serve to highlight investments in outcomes which undermine intrinsic and transformational aspects of learning as a process of personal growth.

---

[1] The notion of a contract for therapy is underpinned by the psychodynamic concept of the therapeutic frame which provides a safe 'container' for the therapeutic work through the use of clearly articulated boundaries (Gray, 2014). The therapeutic frame serves a developmental purpose in that the containing environment allows for frustrations and anxieties to be worked through safely until such time as the client is able to work through their concerns independently (Gray, 2014, p. 31). The clear stating of boundaries, expectations and goals at the start of therapy is now considered as standard good practice in counselling (BACP, 2018).

Comparisons might be drawn here to the notion of the 'psychological contract' used in organizational psychology to describe the mutual obligations that a person believes to exist between themselves and another party, such as an employer (Rousseau, 1989). However, the developmental nature of the academic contract would seem to lend itself well to the psychotherapeutic notion of contract and frame.

The Concept of Potential – Affective and Contractual Implications

Vignette

> The young woman sitting in front of me is distressed and miserable. She is unable to complete her assignments and has become trapped in a cycle of procrastination, anxiety and perfectionism. She says to me emphatically, 'I'm here because I'm not reaching my potential'.

As an educational counsellor at a large university from 2006 to 2015, I came across many students who uttered this line as they sat opposite me in my counselling room. Those who presented for educational counselling attended because of 'psychological difficulties pertaining to their studies'. As an educational counsellor, I was often presented with students who were academically gifted and had been labelled as 'having potential' by schools and/or parents. 'Missing one's potential' seemed to be an important factor as clients tried to work through their unexpected struggles with the academic life.

The concept of 'fulfilling one's potential' has a particular currency in education policy (Sellar, 2015). Governments use the concept of potential when introducing new educational policy frameworks (Department for Education, 2017b) and institutions use the term as part of marketing strategies designed to attract students (Newman University, 2019c). The recent 'Augar Review' (2019) defines the primary 'core purpose' of tertiary education as promoting 'citizens' ability to realise their full potential, economically and more broadly'. In addition to this, Universities UK makes the link between student mental health, the concept of potential in education and its economic promises: 'Good mental health helps students and staff to fulfil their individual potential and brings wider benefits to our society and economy' (UUK, 2019).

In common parlance, the term 'potential' has various meanings. It can be employed as a noun, to imply 'latent qualities or abilities that may be developed and lead to future success or usefulness' or as an adjective implying the quality of 'having or showing the capacity to develop into something in the future' (OED, 2019). Both usages describe something which is 'possible as opposed to actual' (OED, 2019) and its use in education usually implies a connection between the process of education and an imagined and socially desirable endpoint for the person in that process. This understanding of 'potential' often seemed to apply to my educational counselling clients. They had been identified as 'having potential' but were floundering academically in ways which seemed inexplicable to them.

Sellar (2015) argues that the use of the term 'potential' in higher education functions affectively to drive a bargain with prospective students based on the notion that success can be derived from a combination of aspiration, talent and hard work. The usage of potential in this context is defined as 'Weak potential [. . .] the set of actual capacities of a body that may be realised, whereas strong potential is the capacity for a body to become other through processes of actualisation' (Sellar, 2015, p. 206).

The differentiation between 'weak' and 'strong' usages of the term 'potential' relates to theory of actualization in the person-centred approach and other humanistic models of therapy. In a humanistic understanding of 'potential', change occurs paradoxically through a process of acceptance and openness to current experiences rather than a striving to become different in response to externally prescribed expectations. Beisser's (1970) 'Paradoxical Theory of Change' summarizes this process as follows: 'that change occurs when one becomes what he is, not when he tries to become what he is not'.

Both the person-centred approach and contemplative practices provide an alternative and paradoxical approach to the concept of individual potential. They offer the means and practice by which to explore a non-future orientated understanding of potential, that is, as relating to moment-by-moment actualization and authenticity rather than aspiration and striving.

The student in the earlier vignette exemplifies the use of the term 'potential' in the 'weak' sense. She has subscribed to what Sellar (2015, p. 206) calls the 'performative potential of "potential"' in her expectation that she *will* attain success by the application of some hitherto identified personal talents. The performative character of the term also applies to the institution to which she has now turned for help, since, in the implicit bargain struck with this student prior to entry to university, she had the expectation that the university would provide her with the conditions to 'unlock her potential'. As such, it falls to the university to attend to, and ameliorate, her distress. However, in light of her perceived academic failure, the university has now become both the source and remedy of her distress. Psychologically, such a relationship could be characterized as co-dependent (Zaidi, 2015). It is potentially abusive, especially when boundaries are blurred and responsibilities are unclear (BACP, 2018).

Expectations, Student Engagement and Hope

In 1943, psychologist Gustav Ichheiser identified the inherent impossibility of education delivering 'success' based solely on the ideas of 'competence' and 'worthiness'. Since, as he noted, success does not necessarily follow this ideologically prescribed route and the interplay of 'personal and situational' factors often mean that 'consequently, many people are successful who *should* fail; and many fail who *ought* to be successful' (Ichheiser, 1943, p. 137). As such, the 'fundamental conflict between expectations and realizations [. . .] must therefore call forth some kind of self-defensive reaction from the individual in later life' (Ichheiser, 1943, p. 138). According to Ichheiser (1943), the inherent contradiction between ideological notions of success and actuality become most apparent at times of economic crisis. Faced with the dissonance between expectations and realization, the individual reacts defensively in various ways, from neuroticism to cynicism, adaptation, denial or revolt.

It might be tempting to apply the defensive reactions identified by Ichheiser to the various expressions of distress and dissatisfaction seen in university counselling services and via the various feedback mechanisms operating in today's universities. In particular, the 'cynic' might be seen in those students who take a strongly instrumental view of learning as a largely impersonal endeavour pertaining only to the next hurdle in a series of externally prescribed steps to economic success.

From an ethical perspective however, we cannot guarantee that the student who disengages from lectures or operates in this instrumental way, has fully agreed and freely consented to the contract, as it is understood and presented by the institution; since, as has been discussed, the marketing of the contract is based on the promise of an undefinable, future outcome for which neither party has full responsibility. For example, 'We will challenge you to reach your potential'. Furthermore, the contract is agreed at a time of transition and stress for the student and the very idea of coming to university might be based on unchallenged assumptions and recommendations from schools, families and friends.

Vignette

> 'That was really interesting. I've never put myself at the centre of my experience before. There's always someone else's opinion to think about'.

These were the striking words said to me by a first-year undergraduate after I had conducted a five-minute mindfulness exercise at the beginning of a lecture. I was attempting to introduce the idea of present moment awareness to students in preparation for a reflective assignment due later that semester. I had not anticipated that such a short and seemingly simple intervention could provide the opportunity for someone to experience themselves in a wholly new way, that is, that the student had fleetingly experienced herself in the present moment and without external judgement.

This interaction exemplified for me the condition of 'being a student' for many (usually young) people in higher education in the UK today, namely, that they have rarely had the opportunity to reflect on their learning choices and experiences in a way that is unmediated by the expectations and recommendations of other people (Tucciarone, 2007).

Tateo (2018, p. 161) describes the complex negotiation between the child's 'subjective world, the window of potential future selves provided by the school, and the contextual conditions in which the experience takes place'. This complex interaction of factors applies equally to the expectation of transition to higher education. It can be seen as 'the implicit teleological presuppositions about the process of education that society attached to its system of values and tends to naturalize as the "right" trajectory of development' (Tateo, 2018, p. 162).

Universities now find themselves subject to stringent marketing regulation (CMA, 2016) yet a more prosaic and less affective approach to marketing may not appeal to prospective students and cannot account for social messages based on word-of-mouth, hearsay and outdated reputational status. From a counselling perspective, disaffection and disengagement might be seen as the inevitable consequence of a poorly agreed and ill-defined contract. This is even more important when the person presenting for counselling is not there of their own accord but on the recommendations of others. Can we honestly say that all of our students present at university because of an intrinsic motivation to be there? Can we also say that the contract has been fully explained and consensually agreed?

Faced with such a situation, an ethical counsellor who provides adequate conditions for therapy might hope for their client to experience some sense of autonomy in the relationship. In these circumstances, the decision not to comply or to leave therapy would be seen as therapeutically valid. As a parallel to this, poor attendance rates and critical feedback on teaching might then be seen as valid responses to a structurally unethical system on the part of students.

An empathic, critical and non-reactive stance to student disengagement and distress requires an ethical review of the purpose of higher education. However, such a non-defensive stance might offer opportunities for hope by cultivating understanding of difficult student experiences and the systemic mechanisms underlying distress and its expressions.

Student Well-being in Context

Recent concerns about the mental health of university students have sparked heated public debate in the UK (BBC, 2019; Wakeford, 2017). This debate comes in the light of an increase in reported mental health problems among students (IPPR, 2017) and subsequent calls on universities to address the mental health needs of their students (IPPR, 2017). While estimated figures for student suicide have shown an overall upward trend since the turn of the century (ONS, 2018), rates of student suicide continue to be lower than for those of the general population. Nevertheless, there is a strong acceptance, currently, that student mental health and well-being should be top priorities for UK universities (UUK, 2017).

As a former university counsellor, I welcome any focus on improving well-being and the educational experience of students. However, strategic objectives and financial commitments aimed at improving student well-being (UUK, 2017) are unlikely to succeed if they fail to consider a vital systemic contradiction that exists in HE today; this being that higher education does not necessarily deliver the personal experience of growth and economic success propounded by HE policymakers (Augar, 2019) and which many students might expect for themselves and of their education within an increasingly marketized model of HE provision (Carey, 2013; Lynch, 2006). As noted previously, this disappointment of expectations leads to an incongruence between the marketing and delivery of HE and a sense of dissonance (and even exhaustion) for many of the individuals within its systems. Therefore, it seems to me that if we are to do anything about student well-being, we must first reflect on the contextual factors that are influencing well-being in negative ways. These factors are as basic as our definition of the purpose of higher education, our contractual relationship with students and the language we use to promote HE as a worthwhile individual investment.

Also, my sense is that a discussion about the redefinition of the role of higher education is particularly relevant at this moment in time. This is not just because many institutions, and programmes within institutions, face an existential threat brought about the increased marketization of HE (Newman and Jahdi, 2009) (recognized by Augar (2019) as unsustainable) but because the new imperative is one of environmental sustainability (UNFCC, 2018). The concerted action, called for by the United Nations Framework Convention on Climate Change (UNFCCC, 2018), will require a different definition of success that is based less on the economic contribution of individuals to society through increased earning capacity and personal wealth, and more on the impact of our choices on the ability of others to live in ways that are sustainable for all.

Vignette (Composite Vignette)

J. attended counselling for low mood and aggressive outbursts. He considered his behaviour to be uncharacteristic and was close to failing his studies as he was unable to engage with his academic work. J. was engaging and intelligent but he came across as deeply troubled. He was aware of his strong conceptual abilities but lacked hope for the future.

J. was a first-generation university student and his home environment was characterized by high levels of unemployment, drug addiction and self-harm among his peers. J. talked about his difficulties in bridging the gap between home and university. He felt alienated from both settings and had difficulty finding any intrinsic relevance to his studies despite having been identified as 'gifted' in his subject at school. J. found his fellow students competitive and critical.

J. attended every counselling session offered. The sessions were person-centred, with no agenda or direction from me. They were highly dialogical. In addition, J. attended a weekly, taught mindfulness group. He began practising for himself and was open to exploring new ways of being. Gradually, he began to address his studies.

At the end of the year, J. graduated with a good degree and went home to look for work, confident that neither setting could now define him as a person. He found his own, authentic voice by being listened to and by learning to listen to himself as well as other people.

J. was lucky. When he attended counselling, the institution still offered open-ended sessions to students. He had time and space to understand his experience. In the end, he was able to see his studies as optional. If the route to potential seems to depend solely on academic and financial outcomes, I am reminded of Mirabai Bush's (2011, p. 196) question: 'Is it alright to give them [students] a goal of academic attainment to motivate them and trust that it will lead to an understanding that the journey is the goal, that there is no place to go other than right where you are?'

Authenticity, Awareness and Praxis

In this final section, I will set out what I see as an attitudinal stance to higher education practice. I will begin by briefly describing the relationship of the person-centred approach and contemplative attitudes to critical pedagogy. To finish, I will suggest ways in which small disruptions to everyday living and learning habits might provide opportunities for altered perspectives and greater authenticity in relationships between students and staff.

The set of conditions that lead to the development of a person's self-concept are complex and varied. As a person-centred practitioner, I advocate Rogers' view of the person as an organism inherently capable of, and continually moving towards, growth and creativity (Rogers, 1967, p. 351). Rogers used the word potential or potentialities to mean that expression of the individual's organismic experiencing which, when unmediated by external conditions of worth, allows the person to develop and grow in ways that are constructive and creative (Rogers, 1967). Furthermore, there is no prescribed or externally validated direction to this growth in person-centred theory. When external conditions dictate, or do not value, certain expressions of organismic experiencing, then the person adapts to the environmental conditions by denying aspects of themselves to awareness or by experiencing an internal dissonance which creates tension and anxiety (Rogers, 1957a).

O'Hara (1989) argues that there is much in Rogers' writing on education that aligns with that of Freire and I would argue that there are threads of commonality that make Rogers, Freire and contemplative pedagogical approaches a useful group of theoretical bedfellows as we strive to understand the possibility of critical pedagogy in HE today.

These threads of commonality can be seen in a radical commitment to non-oppressive practices, a commitment to social transformation through dialogue and to a set of value positions that support the 'conscientization' or coming to 'awareness' of persons and groups. In addition, both Rogers and Freire acknowledged the ongoing and evolutionary nature of their work and the necessity for a continual 'reinventing' (Roberts, 2010) and development of their ideas by students and associates (Roberts, 2010; Sanders, 2013).

Roberts (2010) outlines the intellectual values identified in Freire's work that support 'conscientization'. These are briefly listed as a willingness to question; a probing and inquiring stance; open-mindedness; curiosity; humility; seeking to know oneself, others and the world; an ethical and political commitment; an awareness of oneself as unfinished and living with and embracing uncertainty. Such values would also seem central to a person-centred way of being which is fundamentally characterized by a non-judgemental stance to self and other. With regard to political and liberatory commitment, O'Hara (1989, p. 17) notes that 'Person-Centered approaches have their origins in Rogers's search for strategies of liberation for people oppressed by dehumanizing ideologies, institutions, technologies, religious beliefs, personal myths and orthodoxies'.

To bring contemplative approaches into this mix, the intellectual values identified by Roberts (2010) earlier, would seem to be in keeping with the attitudinal commitments of trust, non-judging, beginner's mind and acceptance characteristic of secular mindfulness practices developed by Kabat-Zinn (1990, pp. 33–46) and which are increasingly popular as 'stress reduction' interventions in schools and universities.

The connection between internal and external experience is what links contemplative practices, the person-centred approach and critical pedagogy. Despite, or perhaps because of, a focus on interiority, contemplative practices have socially transformative possibilities (Sheldrake, 2008) in that they foster awareness of interconnectedness, authenticity and intentionality (Kaufman, 2017). Such attitudes coupled with an increased capacity for regulating emotions and attention (Comstock, 2015) promote the possibility of a responsive as opposed to a reactive form of social engagement. Kaufman (2017) describes the 'logical and maybe even necessary fit' between critical and contemplative pedagogic practices. The contemplative in society 'therefore, has a strange and paradoxical power to confront a world infected by false consciousness' (Sheldrake, 2008, p. 4).

Hyland (2017) is critical of the rapid expansion of mindfulness-based interventions in society, fearing for the separation of ethics and attitudinal foundations from techniques and strategies. I am sympathetic to this view and would argue that a critical contemplative pedagogy calls for embedded, as well as discreet, practices grounded in a critical commitment to awareness, understanding and transformation.

Bringing critical pedagogy, contemplative practices and the person-centred approach together is an ambitious idea and much more could be done to explore the theoretical alignments than there is space to do here. However, in my own work, I have found that contemplative practices can help students develop an awareness of internalized and oppressive conditions of worth and that such awareness can have a radical effect on a person's capacity for self-direction and learning.

Vignette

A group of students ask me if I will provide a weekly informal mindfulness practice. We meet one morning a week during term-time for a twenty-minute practice. Some weeks there are four students, occasionally there is only one. There are two weeks when I am unable to attend but make the space available to the students. On my return, I do not expect anyone to attend due to my previous absences. That morning, there are five students in the group.

In 'Learning in Large Groups: Their Implications for the Future' (Rogers, 1980, pp. 333–4) Rogers and colleagues noted that given the appropriate conditions,

persons began to seek within for what they were *experiencing* as valuable, instead of looking for what they were *told* was valuable. Without question, they were beginning to meet the first condition for living in the new age. They were discovering the sources of the good life within themselves, not in some outer dogma or dictum, or in some material form.

In the light of my own experiences of higher education, first as a student, then as postgraduate student, university administrator, university counsellor and now a novice academic, I have come to realize that universities offer tantalizing and exciting opportunities for personal and professional growth. They are institutions that encourage engagement with the world through a process of personal introspection and criticality within the context of a community. Increasingly, however, they are also institutions where the threat of failure and anxiety are endemic. When there is much at stake, institutions, students and staff become fearful and defensive.

Fear does not foster growth but it does foster competition and insularity. Fear operates best when information is limited and intentions are unclear. My recommendations therefore are that:

- Educational institutions and policy bodies take mindful steps in addressing the language used to describe the nature of the educational contract and in defining the expectations of those engaged by it.
- We understand our personal investment in the contract with students (Sellar, 2015) and personal meanings of education.
- We inquire mindfully into student distress (including disengagement) and notice the impact of it on ourselves.
- We are mindful of institutional reactivity to distress and take steps to address it mindfully.
- That we foster spaces in our buildings, our lectures and assessment methods, where students can be encouraged to take note of their own experience of learning and of the world around them. And that they do this without striving or in pursuit of a particular outcome or goal but with a kindly acceptance of experience as it is; of uncertainty, and challenge in the process of learning.

Response from Luca Tateo

It is without doubt that humans made a big mistake by turning education into a commodity, knowledge into a means, teaching into a service and learners into customers. Ruth Roberts gently and adamantly illuminates this mistake by providing examples taken from her own experience as university teacher and counsellor, dealing with British students' distress, uncertainty, anxiety, fear and frustration. It seems that the solution could be that of releasing students from the ambiguity of the institutional practices, the learning goals and the future expectations of the job market. In particular, Roberts addresses the issue of the language used by the institution to describe the nature of the educational contract in higher education. All the rhetoric of performance, meritocracy and competitiveness in universities is a source of disorientation and fear for students, because it shifts all the burden of the academic success onto the students themselves. 'You are responsible for your own learning' is a kind of mantra in the contemporary university, so, in case of failure, it is always on the student, not on the institution. This is not a pathology of education, rather an aspect of any educational institution, whose messages are inherently ambivalent (Tateo, 2019). Any school is filled with ambivalent messages, like 'be independent but follow the teacher', 'be creative but do as you are told', etc. The student must navigate ambivalence and negotiate between the institutional message and her own self-development. Probably, we underestimate the student's ability to deal with ambivalence, because we believe that ambivalence is a negative feature, rather than a constitutive element of any human experience. Students are surprisingly able to live the ambivalence nature of educational experiences (Hammer, Madsen and Tateo, 2019). Dealing with ambivalence – as well as dealing with hardships – could thus be an important developmental task. I am afraid that the mindfulness approach, if understood in a neoliberalist way, can end up selling the idea that we can find relief from hardship and suffering, because these are negative things and we all deserve happiness and good life. The risk is that happiness becomes a new commodity, like education. Happiness, understood as a permanent life condition, is of course a new utopia of neoliberal society. Happiness, understood as a temporary condition that in the life-course always alternates with its opposites, acquires its true meaning and its value precisely because it is ephemeral. We should neither aim to sell an education which is smooth and easy, nor sell education as something that you can buy. In many countries, higher education is still the most important means of empowerment and social mobility for a number of people in disadvantaged social groups. These people struggle every day for education as personal achievement and revolutionary act. They are aware of the difficulties and ready to overcome them. Working hard and fighting against the unfairness and discrimination within higher education is a second developmental task of students. Yet, the social role of public university as social promoter is under attack by the neoliberalist politics of the privatization of education, turning the latter into a privilege. This is the kind of reality we should become aware of, and we should mindfully preserve the value of public higher education for improving individual and collective life. This is the deep sense of mindful practices that link individual flourishing with the collective good.

Chapter Fourteen

Rethinking Critical Pedagogy in Higher Education through a Psychosocial Lens

Pete Harris, Response from Jo Trelfa

A Psychosocial Perspective

The term 'psychosocial' is generally taken to refer to an approach to understanding human subjectivity and behaviour that sees it as a product of the combined influence of psychological factors and the surrounding social environment. It is an approach used in a broad range of helping professions in health and social care settings as well as by medical and social science researchers, and is perhaps most commonly associated with Erikson's (1959) description of the stages of psychosocial development. The body of empirical and theoretical work that emerged under the auspices of psychosocial studies from the University of East London in the early 1980s draws on this broad tradition. It sees the subject as both a centre of agency and the subject of external forces, and seeks to understand research subjects as simultaneously psychic and social (Hollway and Jefferson, 2013) but is distinguishable by certain characteristics (for a summary and history of this emerging tradition see, for example, Frosh, 2003 and the Association for Psychosocial Studies website http://www.psychosocial-studies-association.org/about/). Notably the intent of this group of academics and researchers is to blend psychoanalytic with poststructuralist sociological insights into a range of cultural phenomena. While retaining an interest in themes of structure, culture, poverty, social control, politics, power and social identity in the form of class, gender, race, etc. this contemporary configuration of a psychosocial frame employs contemporary branches of psychodynamic thought (notably Kleinian object relations and relational psychoanalysis) to anticipate that individual psyches alter how these social themes impact on them individually. The modern notion of a rational, unitary subject is replaced with a non-unitary, multiple and also 'defended' subject, with unconscious motivations, and is constituted historically, culturally and relationally (Aron, 2013; Clark, Hahn and Hoggett, 2008; Mitchell and Aron, 1999). Notably, it employs the Foucauldian notion of discourse in order to capture how subjects position themselves within a number of competing social discourses *and* the psychological function this serves for them.

Whereas other disciplines have largely turned away from clinically based psychoanalysis, these psychosocial theorists argue that bringing psychoanalytic accounts of subjectivity into dialogue with sociological discourses can serve to more fully hypothesize the relation between psychic and social change by examining the dialectic between the inner worlds of subjects and their outer lives. This taking of psychoanalytic ideas seriously when seeking to understand the formation and maintenance of subjectivities allows the consideration of psychodynamic processes such as defence and identification at play in identity construction, without denying the impact of social environment.

Seeing Critical Pedagogy Through a Psychosocial Lens

Countering Resistance

I want to suggest that this specific psychosocial frame is particularly well suited to the exploration of critical pedagogic practice as explored in this volume (H. A. Giroux, 2004; Kincheloe, 2005; McLaren, 2003b). It can capture both the psychological and social dynamics of relationships between students and between students and tutors, including the complex, defended nature of their subjective selves and unconscious motivations. Incorporating psychoanalytic theory into critical pedagogy means acknowledging critiques that identify the patriarchal and anti-democratic determinism perceived to be at its root. This includes associations with undemocratic and non-dialogical modes of intervention where the therapist holds power over the client and over-values certain theoretical precepts before perhaps engaging in 'wild analysis'. Historical psychodynamic ideas such as the oedipal complex and penis envy seem to embody the very structural gendered inequalities that critical pedagogy seeks to destabilize. Then there is the epistemic bias of Freudian theory to counter; its Eurocentricity and inherent homophobia. Traditional psychodynamic terminology such as 'patient' seems at odds with critical pedagogy's distaste for deficit-based models seen as casting students as objectified subjects in need of medical intervention. Within this construct, students could become the object of off-the-shelf 'treatment', the purpose of which is solely to deconstruct their defensive structures and help them know themselves better.

I wish to suggest that any perceived incompatibility of this framework with critical pedagogy would be predicated on a characterization of psychodynamic psychology as devoid of any structural analysis or the power hierarchies in which we live. To characterize psychodynamic theory in this way would be to insufficiently acknowledge how psychodynamic theory has always recognized the impact of the social on the individual (see Freud's *Civilization and Its Discontents*, 1929) and how it has subsequently evolved and been adapted through feminist and relational critiques. The major revisions and critiques of Freudian psychoanalysis (from Klein and Lacan and critical psychology onwards) point towards more co-produced and 'relational' rather than 'top-down' practice (Ogden, 2009). For example, Melanie Klein's work (1935, 1946, 1957) and her notion of object relations are particularly helpful in explaining how childhood experiences can lead to splits between the 'me' and 'not me' – that is, identity. It posits that at the heart of children's, young people's and adult's psychic lives are both external and internal relationships. This perspective leads to a set of distinct ideas about human development, pedagogic technique, motivation and action. It helps us to explore how students and tutors at university may be busy figuring out what aspects of themselves are acceptable and rapidly disowning those that are unacceptable.

Moreover, these perspectives foreground the importance of uncovering how both students and tutors studying and working in higher education (HE) may have experienced early lives and relational matrices that include separation, trauma, dependency, conflict, physical illness and pain, sibling comparison and competition. These early relational experiences will have a considerable impact on students' and tutors' sense of self, their behaviour and pathways through their education/careers. Evidence shows that students resist and reject critical pedagogical efforts for a variety of reasons (Berlak, 2004; Boler and Zembylas, 2003; Ellsworth, 1989). As Zembylas (2013) argues, this evidence 'exposes how some assumptions that are made in critical pedagogy may overlook the complexity of students' emotional investments, in particular social positions and discourses' (p. 17). Given this is the case, critical pedagogues need a means to unpack the complex, unpredictable nature of the intersubjective dance that all professional relationships, including those in education, entail. The fusion of psychodynamics with post-structural notions of social discourses within psychosocial theory can, I believe, offer this more fully encompassing framework.

A Relational Dialogical Model

A relational, psychosocial model of subjectivity can help to avoid the reductive casting of tutors as all-knowing role models and mentors. Applying a relational psychodynamic frame (Mitchell and Aron, 1999) within the context of critical pedagogy is consistent with a democratic, dialogical and Freirean (1972b, 1976) view of relationships where students are influenc*ing* as well as influenc*eable* subjects. The pedagogical relationship can then be viewed as two idiosyncratic subjectivities interacting with each other and permeated by social discourses generated within the family, subcultures and hegemonic social structures, all of which impact on the psyche. The educative process becomes more comprehensible within dyads and groups if both parties can avoid foisting on the other a template of previous relationships imbibed in the course of development, the impact of which may be out of either party's conscious awareness. The pedagogue's role becomes not to sit neutrally outside the relational field conducting some kind of psychic surgery, but squarely within it; not as some reified objective detached observer but as someone seeking to understand and make sense of a co-created reality. This involves making him or herself available to the learner as another thinking, feeling being, within whom the student can see there is another subjectivity 'at home'. Tutors need to be willing to be affected and moved by what students say, fully aware of how it reverberates within their own lifeworld.

Adopting a psychosocial frame also opens up the possibility of employing key psychodynamic insights into intersubjectivity and relationships rooted in the notion of the unconscious mind, such as transference and countertransference. These insights enrich a model of relationships between the teacher and learner in that they acknowledge the interaction between two unconscious minds, operating within power relations that are both symmetrical and asymmetrical. What emerges is a view of relationship in which two defended subjects, both knowing and unknowing, defend against each other and the altering patterns of their interpersonal relationships. Proponents of a psychodynamic perspective on the human mind would argue an over-exclusive focusing on *conscious* thinking patterns alone might not provide the space to acknowledge these *unconscious* processes behind the stories students and tutors tell others (and themselves) about their experiences of education.

Crucially, the need to account for the unconscious, pre-reflexive nature of these internal psychic processes applies to both the tutor and student. These emotional and unconscious aspects of subjectivity will inevitably feed directly into intersubjective processes between the student and tutor. This has significant implications for the framing of professional relationships in HE, such as for example the perceived appropriateness of the use of self-disclosure on the part of the tutor. There is a further level of complexity engendered when intersecting indices of social identity such as gender, race and class are 'in the mix'.

The challenge for educators becomes whether they can form a fundamentally interdependent relationship – what Ogden (2009) calls a 'third space' – in which they and the students identify with each other, but also fully recognize each other too. Jessica Benjamin's intersubjective perspective on interaction (2004, 2007, 2013, 2017) seeks to supplement *intra*-psychic Kleinian notions of 'object relations' with *inter*-psychic notions of subject and the 'Other', what she calls 'recognition' – that is, how both parties within a relationship make known their own subjectivity and learn to perceive and appreciate that of the 'other'. Promoting critical and truly dialogical pedagogy therefore involves sustaining these psychic processes of recognition that can apprehend the separate positions of self and other, while also acknowledging interdependence.

Finding Safer Pedagogical Spaces

As Zembylas (2013) states, 'It has long been acknowledged in critical pedagogy rhetoric that the classroom is not a safe space and that some teachers and groups of students may be (unintentionally) burdened, for example, through their minority status in the classroom as representatives of their group' (p. 181). The experiences and struggles of students and tutors in higher education are both institutional and interactional; that is to say that higher education can be both a hegemonic space which subordinates and marginalizes, but also a space where identities can be negotiated, subjectively and intersubjectively. Staff, students and individual degree programmes are located differentially within this structure, some complicit within it and others set more in opposition. However, oppositional spaces can provide localized 'safer spaces' in which critical pedagogy can emerge. By using the term 'safer space' I mean a generative, situational context which acts to frame, motivate, support and sustain the actions of those located within it, owing to the relative absence of exposure to constricting factors and the presence of facilitating factors. These factors involve both pedagogical and intersubjective processes and these will be central to identity formation. Students and tutors approach or will inhabit these spaces with differing levels of biographically contingent resources and as complex, fluid, multi-layered and ultimately unique (rather than rational and unitary) subjects. This will then lead them to differentially emphasize and invest in the different social discourses which are available to them in those spaces.

Students and tutors arriving from oppositional and marginalized social contexts might be able to negotiate a distinct social space in higher education institutions in which social goals and values are shaped by the characteristics and imperatives of this safer pedagogical space that they encounter. This space can become the governing or customary social context and, in the sense of Bourdieu's habitus and associated doxa (1975, 1977a), the characteristics of the context can generate ongoing motivations and rationales. This is an aggregate phenomenon whose force derives from the dynamic interaction of the internal characteristics of students and tutors and their articulation with larger, external, socio-economic and cultural patterns.

Building Identities

This relationship between context and the construction of an identity is brought into sharp focus in a pedagogical setting, primarily because of the developmental stage students could be characterized as passing through. Some, notably those younger in age, will simultaneously be concerned with establishing an identity in the eyes of others, a task identified by Erikson (1959) as identity achievement, and further elaborated by interactionists such as Goffman as the presentation of self (1959) and performance. Forming an identity involves a dialogue between individual, particular experience and collective representations for experience and this always occurs in both private and public environments of shared meaning. Thus, identity is intersubjectively negotiated, because it is propagated among a group through the way specific behaviours are valued and represented. These representations form the basis for development of identity in that they include available representations of self from which individuals can build their self-concept, that is, processes by which individuals become new selves. Erikson called these 'resources of identity'. For Goffman this is primarily a social rather than an individual process and involves the performance of the represented self. This is an understanding of the social self that has its roots in symbolic interactionism and seeks to describe the task of managing the information about the self, or impression management, followed by validating actions. Others within the social context provide both the audience to which (and means by which) the individual can construct and perform their new identity, create narratives of their selves, conceive of alternatives and seek to gather feedback. These narratives are in part constructed form public models and discourse that exist within and across sociocultural groups, some of which will have greater resonance than others.

The distinct contribution of the psychosocial perspective is that it seeks to understand *why* certain discourses have more or less resonance for the individual, and to locate this in the personal biography. In this sense it is concerned with how subjects seek to psychically invest in available discourses in a running series of stories or staged narratives. We can use this perspective to explore why both students and tutors deploy certain discourses to draw distinctions between themselves and others. The psychoanalytic approach allows recognition that all parties in higher education may be investing in discourses with an incomplete awareness of their own subjectivity and what is driving their behaviour. Students and tutors may be more or less equipped to deal with feelings that emerge as they become more aware of what is driving their behaviour, and thereby more or less able to create and inhabit pedagogic spaces in such a way that they can freely engage in both their personal and pedagogical development. A critical pedagogic approach therefore requires an ability to swim with the emotions, tensions and anxieties engendered in this twin-tracked educational and identity formation process.

Defended Subjects

The psychosocial frame also allows a more nuanced account of identity which allows for differences to emerge within social categories and uncovers the psychological defences and vulnerabilities that lie beneath the surface of all different social identities. For the students this might mean that the indomitable face of hegemony is more insurmountable than for others. Tutors who are key to this, while also struggling with their own path through it all, need also to be viewed through this differentiating lens. Their pedagogic practices such as intensive support, student-centred teaching, a degree of self-disclosure on their part and the drawing on their own lived experiences to create dialogue, can involve troublesome tension, dissension and discomfort. As well as recognizing the intertwining effect of racism, sexism, poverty, class, etc. as factors in student and tutor behaviour, it highlights how there needs to be an acknowledgement of how lecturers' own biographies influence their interactions. A psychosocial perspective might suggest that, for example, tutor approaches to learning and teaching may be as a result of any number of social, external factors but are also likely to involve psychodynamic processes of transference, countertransference and psychological defences such as displacement, projection, splitting, etc. These could be linked to their own experiences of emotional deprivation, lack of permanence, abuse, rejection or abandonment in childhood, relationships (or not) with parents and siblings or spouses, etc. These experiences may lead to individual differences in the ability of both tutors and students to process experience and verbalize feelings, distort their images of self and others, engender feelings of inadequacy, confusion or anger and even in some cases lead to self-hatred, sabotage or drug and alcohol abuse; all of which will then of course affect the educational experience and career progression. Students and tutors may use cultural and linguistic devices as defensive operations to deal with anxiety-laden situations, or use aspects of racialized, gendered or classed experience to consolidate their sense of self and defend against deep anxieties over their personhood. For students and tutors studying and working in universities, this can be exacerbated as neither the university community nor their own community can serve as an effective means of identification. Both can begin to feel alien.

McLaren (1994) has argued for the consideration of how tutors might need to surface their own employment of defence mechanisms. Critical pedagogues, he suggests, should seek to not 'project onto the student-as-Other that part of themselves that out of fear and loathing they rejected or subtracted from their identities in their attempt to become unified subjects' (p. 216). Tutors, for example, may lack insight into how their own biographies, work settings and contexts structure their pedagogical activities and students might be misinterpreting them too. An example of this inner/outer world entanglement would be one where tutors become prone to nurturing (or avoiding) relationships with students in order to buttress their own self-esteem, gain peer recognition and acceptance or cope with their own fears of rejection. Certain aspects of the educational experience may still be triggering tutors own defences against feelings of inferiority or guilt. This might lead to a range of tutor and/or student behaviours that might affect pedagogy, such as bias, favouritism, bluntness, verbosity, patronizing or over-intellectualized forms of communication, or inappropriate curiosity in the 'otherness' of others. Learning might therefore get side-tracked, topics be avoided (foreclosed?) or the pedagogic relationship be undermined entirely and broken down. For example, a tutor may, as a result of unexpiated guilt, be reluctant to confront student's hypersensitivity or over-identification as a victim and overcompensate in any number of ways, so encouraging a dependent relationship rather than one that built on autonomy.

Recognition and Containment of the Other

Defended areas of self for students and tutors, some clearly rooted in structural oppression, others more personal and biographical, can be disentangled and lowered through evolving relationships with each other (student–student and tutor–student) in which they recognize (Benjamin, 2017) each other despite seemingly asymmetrical life trajectories. This recognition or bridging can happen within the pedagogical context, and this experience can significantly and materially alter both students' and tutors' experience of their education, their own selves and others' 'difference', and their sense of personal agency. Respective biographies may mean that developing relationships between students and between students and tutors may involve students and tutors facing up to repressed traumatic events in their childhood and gradually revising their preconceptions of embodied 'otherness'. The critical pedagogue tutor needs therefore to be able to recognize his/her own defence mechanisms and 'contain' (Bion, 1962c) the troubling tension, dissension and inner conflicts which can result from exchanges between themselves and students, and between students too. That is, the theory-informed action (or praxis) and the inner resources of the tutor and the students are all integral to the creation of the kind of pedagogical critical and safer pedagogical spaces required for transformative learning. This is not to propose the kind of therapeutic education that Ecclestone and Hayes (2008) critique which, framed as concern for students' well-being, limits the possibility that they will experience what Berlak (2004) calls the 'pedagogy of discomfort' necessary for critical inquiry. Rather it is simply to acknowledge the demands for emotional labour that such inquiry places on both student and tutor.

Some Final Remarks – A Way Forward?

Critical pedagogic practice seeks to equip teachers and students to become transformative agents who can challenge taken-for-granted conceptions of truth and inequitable social structures that perpetuate social injustice (Darder, Baltodano and Torres, 2003). I wish to suggest that to retain its radical potential we need a conceptualization of critical pedagogical practice that is (in the sense outlined earlier) fully psychosocial; that is, can encompass the psychic and social dimensions of subject positions and how these operate within intersubjective relations. As well as recognizing the intertwining effects of discrimination and disadvantage as factors in student experience in the overarching higher education space there is also a need to acknowledge how within some spaces both lecturer and student biographies inform their interaction with each other, different aspects of the institution and wider society. This suggests a need to disentangle tutor and student struggles and to maintain a focus on building the transformative critical praxis of lecturers and reflexivity within all those who teach and learn within the HE sector. As Worsham (2001) states, the affective dimensions of disempowerment and empowerment and how these are practised across differences of race, class, and gender must be placed at the heart of critical pedagogy.

Considering *unconscious* processes that arise out of student and tutor past experiences in education and relationships with friends, families and figures in authority and understanding something about lecturers' and students' individual paths into education involves acknowledging that it is at least possible that they will not understand how this is related to their experiences and practices in HE. Both the tutors' and students' practical knowledge and self-knowledge may be inferior to some aspects of theoretical knowledge; the accounts they construct and how they perceive their relationships may be flawed. Adopting a psychosocial approach when trying to understand how students and tutors are constructing their identities allows for the deploying of a vocabulary that also includes these unconscious elements and the 'defended' self. This helps illuminate how the tutors and students structure, repress and displace their feelings and respond emotionally to the troubling tension which results from the dialectical approach to identity formation in which the students are engaged. When this is operating across entrenched lines of sociological and political difference, the psychosocial disposition of tutors, carved out of their own biography and professional experience is, I argue, central to their own well-being and student trajectories within the pedagogic process. These trajectories also reflect the complex interweaving of multiple social categories of being which students and tutors simultaneously inhabit and articulate. This requires that both student and tutor experience be read more ambivalently and with a recognition of multiple relations of power that do not fall neatly into binaries.

To fully understand this complex process, we need pedagogical research that brings tutors' and students' social and psychic realities together as mutually constitutive and avoid reifying one or the other. To do otherwise risks either problematically pathologizing students' and tutors' experience or reducing them to socially reproduced figures, devoid of intention and agency. The possibility of a psychosocial critical pedagogy can be opened up by putting into words all the contradictory and mixed-up elements of experience of those involved, which can constrain, undermine or strengthen their ability to make the most of the opportunities they are presented with. One way forward would be in-depth psychosocially informed research that could provide a detailed analysis of the psycho-biographical specificity of both students and tutors, their unique journeys prior to meeting each other and then the journey they take together. Writing out these individual motivations in such research and marking points of convergence and divergence is one way of realistically beginning to make efforts to create the transformative change in higher education that proponents of critical pedagogy seek.

Response from Jo Trelfa

Pete's paper brings to mind my earlier work in the area of domestic violence. A deeply political endeavour, myself and a colleague stepped out from the typical and crucial practices of working with its victims/survivors to focus on its perpetrators instead. Our contention was that without this we would perpetually be picking up the lives of those whom they impact on – and indeed in towns and rural areas of South West England, where we were based, it could well be the same perpetrator and different victims.

However, the approach we wanted to take was critiqued in some quarters. For us the practice could not be divorced from a psychosocial base. But where did this sit within a feminist standpoint critique when applied to domestic violence? How did its assumed undemocratic and non-dialogical practices fit in a context of violence and abuse where power to define is held over another? How would its influences of psychodynamic pathologizing empower victims/survivors to see they are not responsible for the violence and abuse, despite the implicit and explicit claims to the opposite from their abuser?

As Pete describes, this is a view predicated on a characterization that the psychodynamic aspect of a psychosocial approach drains out – or is even devoid of – any structural analysis and practice.

Yet feminism itself has shaped its precepts, and critical psychology its theories and practices. For the very reasons that Pete identifies, how can a psychosocial perspective not be brought to bear to fully, deeply, richly engage in appreciation of relationships and the structural contexts in which they exist. One can understand individuals to be multi-dimensional, and hold a fundamental belief and practice in agency, in recognition of self and other and the communities and societies we operate in. It is indeed a 'third space'. As Sue Holland phrases it, it enables movement 'through psychic space into social space and so into political space' (Holland, 1995, p. 141), thus is entirely a process of conscientization.

Now in my current role as Head of Academic Professional Development, with a focus on the development and enhancement of teaching (and therefore learning) in a university, my background in working in 'third spaces' brings with it a significant contribution. Pete's paper articulates this. Indeed, might I suggest, in the way that he describes it, this third space represents a move on from important 'safe spaces' to 'brave spaces' (Arao and Clemens, 2013), where lecturers and students locate discourses in personal biography and explore the impact on others, and learn to develop their own (and empower others') informed critical voice in that process, to take the risk of understanding how they 'construct their identities' through 'complex interweaving of multiple social categories' and move to (and from and away and back to) the third brave space of engaging in learning and teaching in higher education differently.

The same critique that met myself and my colleague in our work in domestic violence in the mid-1990s can silence educators who are interested in a psychosocial lens to pedagogy. Pete's paper is a striking rallying call for it to be reconsidered.

Chapter Fifteen

It's Been Emotional

Exploring the Emotional Impact of Critical Pedagogy Practice with Non-traditional Students

Pauline Grace, Lorna Morgan and Adellah Snape, Response from Fin Cullen

Introduction

At its heart, education is perceived as a transformative process: the teacher teaches, and the learner learns. Critical pedagogy disrupts that comfortable dynamic, challenges the hegemony of 'the expert' and enables a dialectical engagement with the contradictions of the relationship between self and society. By its nature transactional, critical pedagogy demands an emotional rather than a purely cerebral engagement with the educational process within both the formal and non-formal realms. Within the academy, critical pedagogy offers the opportunity of a rejection of the overly simplistic assessment that all education establishments are wedded to a deterministic agenda designed to reproduce uncritical drones, in favour of the more risky adventure of co-creating knowledge absent the certainty of measurable outcomes. Critical pedagogy eschews the simplicity of the binary: of prevailing attitudes of right and wrong, of left and right, of black and white; to be replaced with an examination of the distinctive influences, the critical characteristics and the multi-faceted nature of our increasingly complex societies. Recognition is paid to the inevitable interplay between interests; herein lies the tangled nexus of oppression, of cross-cutting influences representing, for example, race, class, gender identity and others, in an intersectional relationship. Making sense of these tangles inevitably engages with emotion, and is often the locus of pain, of exploitation, of unresolved conflicts.

> Critical pedagogy is fundamentally concerned with the relationship between education and power in society and, thus, uncompromisingly committed to the amelioration of inequalities and social exclusions in the classroom and society at large. (Darder, Mayo and Paraskeva, 2016, p. i)

In this chapter it is necessary to acknowledge from the outset that the current trajectory of higher education policy in the UK is one of increased commodification; the academy has become a site of business rather than a seat of learning.

> Most colleges are now dominated by conservative ideologies, hooked on methods, slavishly wedded to instrumentalized accountability measures, and run by administrators who lack either a broader vision or critical understanding of education as a force for strengthening the imagination and expanding democratic public life. (Giroux, 2010, p. 715)

Within this sclerotic context, education as a praxis is under siege; neoliberalism dictates that the student is consumer, reducing the education process to a mere contract. But there is hope, for not all students see themselves as consumers; for some, the discovery of self, the acknowledgement of agency and the co-production of learning are liberatory. As co-authors, we continue to explore the tensions, dilemmas and contradictions. But it is necessary to be wary; the dominant ideology survives not only because of an uncoordinated opposition, and a prolonged exposure to sophistry, but also through deliberately benign conduct that, like an indulgent parent, recognizes the need for challenge from below and invisibly orchestrates a carefully choreographed resistance. This is classic misdirection, behaviour designed to deceive; it is illusory. McLaren considered this activity by the dominant as containment since 'by absorbing these contradictory values, they are more often than not able to domesticate the conflicting and contradictory values' (McLaren, 2003a, p. 82).

Our focus is on the experiences of teaching non-traditional students, and on their experiences of learning, on a youth-work degree within a higher education institution in England. It examines the impact that using a critical pedagogy philosophy, approach and practice, has on the students' university experience; with a focus on the emotional state that this approach inevitably brings about. In particular, it explores and shares from direct experience, from both the student and the lecturer, the nature of this emotional response. It is posited that this emotional response comprises two complimentary components: partly based on a student's recognition of inequality; but also on the use of non-formal learning methodologies within classroom.

The chapter contributes to the discussion about critical pedagogy, Giroux (2011) transformative learning and what Freire (1970) describes as 'conscientization' – the latter concerning the experiences of non-traditional students, and the role and responsibilities of the lecturer. This two-way, collaborative, responsibility for the 'education' journey is also explored. Drawing on co-operative enquiry (Heron, 1996) methodology, and narrative interviews (Clandinin and Connelly, 2000) with 'non-traditional' students, the chapter explores the contemporary nature of inequality and how the various forms of inequality intersect (Cho, Crenshaw and McCall, 2013) and overlap in higher education and society. An overtly critical feminist standpoint will be explored, as well as critiquing the notion that emotion has no place within the academic realm. Utilizing a dialogic, participatory and experiential (DPE) approach to teaching and learning (Chow et al., 2003), this chapter seeks to speak, capture and value this complex process as well as to privilege the students' narratives. Giroux synthesizes Paolo Freire's conceptualization of critical pedagogy as:

> A political and moral practice that provides the knowledge, skills, and social relations that enable students to explore the possibilities of what it means to be critical citizens while expanding and deepening their participation in the promise of a substantive democracy. Critical thinking for Freire was not an object lesson in test-taking, but a tool for self-determination and civic engagement. (Giroux, 2010, p. 716)

The understanding of power is important as is the way in which identity and power interplay. The yearning to make connection within the 'classroom' using non-formal learning methodology is risky; it has possibilities of 'eureka' moments but also of tension and challenge. These risks and tensions exist within the classroom setting but also challenge the market concept that now dominates. By its very nature, critical pedagogy is a disruptive practice.

> These concerns reflect the normative and political dimensions of intersectionality and thus embody a motivation to go beyond mere comprehension of intersectional dynamics to transform them. (Cho, Crenshaw and McCall, 2013, p. 786)

Thus, the interplay between the personal and the political is held as a collective responsibility within the educational setting, wherever that might be.

Pedagogy of Love

hooks, in *Hopeful Pedagogy* (2003), talks about love within the educational space, and Noddings' (2013) work on the ethics of care usefully amplifies the concept of emotion as legitimate educational experience. We come from a philosophical paradigm that utilizes a person-centred approach; Rogers (1961) described the process of interacting with people, which results in them being truly heard and understood. It is a paradoxical stance; as Ruth Roberts states in her chapter on mindfulness, 'Both the person-centred approach and contemplative practices provide an alternative and paradoxical approach to the concept of individual potential.' The fine balance between agency, living in the moment and worry about the future is a constant stress and challenge for students and lecturers, all, it would seem, caught in the 'imposter syndrome'. The critical pedagogy space seeks to create an authentic exchange of ideas, experiences, beliefs and attitudes.

A discursive and dialogical approach to learning and teaching is not without its challenges; and the use of the dialogic, participatory and experiential approach to teaching and learning (Chow et al., 2003) is heavily reliant upon emotional openness. This was an aspect that some of the group found difficult, especially if, as is the case for the co-authors of this chapter, some of them come from an emotionally manipulative and abusive background, where to be open about oneself and to question core aspects of identity was to be emotionally open and dangerous.

The culture of openness, from students and lecturers, has highlighted the power of vulnerability and allowed some to take a stronger position of pride and open up more about identity, its impact, especially in terms of transness, queer relationships and life generally. That vulnerability, and the anxiety that it provokes, is a powerful manifestation of personal power and it being positioned in opposition to the hegemonic powers of oppression – a manifestation of conscientization in regard to the emotional self and a pedagogic expression of love and acceptance that is beyond anything.

An intrinsic part of research for this chapter is the hegemony of emotions and gaining the power to challenge our more toxic emotional inhibitions that were placed upon us via the structural state of society through a collective enquiry. From toxic masculinity to the fetishization and erasure of gender identities beyond the binary and the invalidation of queer thought, many issues that are deemed 'taboo' can be challenged and reconsolidated into a position of understanding and acceptance. Our experiences have enabled us to fight the hegemonic structures of gender, race, identity and queer.

Vulnerability and Validation

From our discussions, the common experience of critical pedagogy within the classroom setting was one that covered aspects of vulnerability, validation and facing structurally embedded prejudices. The nature of youth work, as an emancipatory practice (Batsleer and Davies, 2010), places its student practitioners in the position of addressing their own prejudices and the structures (Thompson, 2016) and intersections (Crenshaw, 1989) of inequality with which they have been affected, in both the visible and unseen aspects of their life.

This process is one that has been described as 'turning me inside out' in many ways; for some in our group it ended up pushing them to question issues of race, gender identity, sexuality and relationship to the very concept of youth work and being a youth worker. For others in the cohort, traumas and relationships have been addressed, leading to them being placed into a state of aporia much like Jung's (1998) disintegration. This vulnerable state was then, for the cohort, held in a humanistic and empathetically constructive space of collaborative iterative emotional development similar to action research (Bradbury and Reason, 2008) in which the individual journeys of resolution added to the understanding and knowledge base of the group, in a process much like Poland's (2000) 'witnessing and mirroring', wherein our similarities were mirrored and our differences witnessed and validated by one another.

From the lived experience of one of the authors:

> This experience, seeing others going through it in tandem with me and learning about their perspectives, their revelations, has in many ways brought me back to my days in my youth club as a young person. The very process that helped me to manage the abuses of my childhood was helping me and my academic peers to unpack the damages of living in a hegemonically anti-queer society (Freire, 1970;

Thompson, 2016; Foucault, 1979 and Crenshaw, 1989) while held by an empathetic and genuinely caring but professional facilitator. That, to me at least, is the core of what all education should be and what youth work certainly is (Batsleer and Davies, 2010; Jeffs and Smith, 2010; Sapin, 2013 and K. Young, 2006). Experiencing it as an adult has crystallized the experiences that had been gestating since I first experienced youth work as a young person into a praxis that I can use to hold the vulnerable and threatened young people of the transgender community and help them to live in pride of who they are and who they can be.

For many students, and particularly those from non-traditional (in university terms) backgrounds, the idea of a university education was never within their contemplation. Lives and identities were forged in often challenging circumstances: poor inner-city neighbourhoods and inadequate quality housing; an education often characterized by fractured school attendance; home lives disrupted by parental, or care-giver, traumas; and on the receiving end of shifting governmental initiatives designed and delivered by those with little or nothing in common with the people upon whom such projects were visited. It is within this milieu that a radical, class-based youth and community work education regime finds opportunities to explore critical alternatives to society's status quo; it is here that a critical pedagogy, an exploration of self and a commitment to social change coalesce into action.

Interpreting Freire, and Giroux, the pursuit of student self-determination is to be found both within and beyond the academy: as an overt act of civic engagement with the student body, and the staff; and as a febrile conduit to the wider community without. In this quest for emancipation, this search for agency, students (and maybe teachers?) discover 'pedagogy as a practice for freedom' (Giroux, 2010, p. 715).

For one of the authors, it was the following realization:

> The introduction to Paulo Freire's (1970) *Pedagogy of the Oppressed* was liberatory through an academic lens. It confirmed for me that my thinking was abstract, radical and has the power to activate consciousness in others.

To be a consciously aware person is to be attuned to intuition and emotions, as well as rational and logical thinking. A critically pedagogical youth and community work education values and encourage emotional thinking; it is acknowledged, encouraged and nurtured within the academy, and in turn enables a raised consciousness. For non-traditional students, this radical approach can both disrupt and emancipate; it does not conform to their stereotypes of a university education since it values, validates and, indeed, reifies their own knowledge and experience; and the process requires that students find new ways of developing and interpreting knowledge through collaboration, co-operation and a collective understanding both of who they are and how they can effect change. Past experiences and conflicts around, for example, gender, sexual identity, race and ethnicity, or faith, are explored anew through a lens of radical solidarity; acknowledging diversity and difference, but celebrating new understandings of a wider, more inclusive, intersectionality.

By re-examining past wrongs, wrought perhaps by inflexible state-supported agencies, it is easy to identify the negativity, and prejudice, of many actions as defined by Lipsky's 'street-level bureaucrats' (2010), as oppressive; nowadays the emancipated youth and community worker's role is to engage with such contemporary state initiatives, and work collectively with communities not only to ameliorate the potential for negative impact but to encourage the active involvement of all social actors to co-design and co-deliver services that are of benefit to all.

Delivering a critical pedagogy of practice is hard work: an honest acknowledgement of self; a regime of reflection with integrity; and a continuous examination of praxis. To be meaningful it requires a commitment to shared values, to peer scrutiny and an acceptance of collectivity. The authors remain challenged by the co-creation of knowledge but excited by the continued influence of praxis. This collective work acknowledges the significance of informal learning and education (Smith, 2008) as being on a par with the formal educational demands; this mixed-methods approach engages and encourages students across the range of learning styles. Recognizing this, one of the authors concluded:

> I will probably struggle to write at a high academic level, but here is the thing; that's not my goal. My goal is to embody what I have learned and to give it away to others.

It is this selflessness, this self-awareness and this personal commitment to class solidarity that provides both the individual and the collective hallmarks of a critical youth and community work pedagogy: integrity of praxis.

Youth and community students, soon to be workers, emerging as activists, informal educators and democratic advocates are engaged in a performative practice: they are democratic disrupters, intersectional influencers, a cadre of Gramscian 'organic intellectuals', who act in combination with others, in community settings, to challenge the hegemonic structures and strictures that seek to control society's functions. The skill is to translate the visceral, the emotional and the desire to serve into social hallmarks through a combination of small acts of local activism, acts of care and maybe even love; of transformation through transgression.

The journey of education cannot be easily travelled when your social capital according to Bourdieu is lacking. At the start of this writing process, it was difficult to justify time spent on creating spaces for the co-authors to meet, think, laugh and question the status quo. It was difficult as we are all trying to survive within the pressure cooker environment of the academy. However, we persevered, met over lunch-times, made food for each other, and when necessary left our worries at the door and saved each other via our conversation and realization that together we were transgressing and acquiescing at the same time. The process of teaching and learning, of reflecting upon our journey, provided an opportunity to seek to understand each other's lived reality, and intersection of experiences. It would not have been possible to have spoken about trauma, and triumph, without a great deal of trust in each other. That trust has, in part, been earned by the risk-taking and rule-breaking. We hope bell hooks would be proud of us!

Response from Fin Cullen

The increasing corporatization and marketization of contemporary higher education has arguably produced 'care-less institutions' (Rogers, 2017) – favouring competition and business values over the critical, the reflective and the hopeful (Gill, 2009). This chapter provides a welcome counter-narrative and invites the reader to think and act differently.

When reading this chapter, I reflected on another everyday moment of practice in higher education. A recent tutorial with a postgraduate student was framed around discussion of youth rights. The student's initial optimism was soon tempered by a discussion of critical theorists' distrust of 'easy' answers, and the recognition that small acts of resistance, while commonplace, were most often co-opted, rarely challenging dominant discourse in a meaningful or sustained way. What then for hope? Pessimism and cynicism create unfavourable conditions for inspiring counter-hegemonic (youth-work) praxis.

Grace, Morgan and Snape's dialogue provides a welcome blend of the reflective with a critical engagement of the feminist contributions of hooks and Noddings and broader critical pedagogy. This provides an important counter-narrative and imaginary from which to carve out the emotional space to consider and sustain a different practice. This is reminiscent of the sociologist Les Back's question of how do we politically 'think and act in the service of hope?' (Back, 2015). Hope is about remaining uncertain. It is ambiguous – a process of doing and thinking differently – and in this contingency dreams up spaces of radical possibility (Back, 2018).

Finding new narratives and ways of applying these fresh understandings generates new emotional subjectivities that straddle the tensions between the theory–practice divide. These complex hybrid spaces – stretching between the lecture hall, the library, the youth centre and the street – trouble existing hierarchical ideas around legitimate knowledge production, status and authenticity. Youth work – as a practice – in common with higher education has been radically reshaped by neoliberal ideologies of austerity. Many youth-work programmes have faced closure, as budgets dwindled and youth centres closed (Bradford and Cullen, 2014). In this austere landscape, the remaining youth-work classrooms are important sites for critical reflection in order to consider the possibilities and potentialities of thinking, practising and dreaming differently. This is vital work.

Part II D

Hopeful Pedagogies in the Spaces In-between

Chapter Sixteen

Sit Down Next to Me

Reflections on Academic Advising and Pedagogical Love

Peter Sharpe, Response from Stephen Cowden

Introduction

In this chapter I discuss issues arising from reflection on twelve years of higher education (HE) academic advising and student support, including two years as an Academic Support Advisor (ASA) in Newman University. Demand for the ASA service was invariably intense and extremely pressurized. A high proportion of Newman University's students come from 'non-traditional' or 'widening participation' (WP) backgrounds, living in local communities dealing with the intersectionality of historic socio-economic decline characterized by experiences of structural injustice, inequality and oppression, social exclusion, deprivation and financial precarity. The issues that students disclosed to the ASA service might include personal and familial relationship challenges; accommodation, employment, financial, criminal or legal issues; physical and/or mental health problems; and perhaps specific issues relating to a student's gender, cultural context or ethnic background.

Students attempting to deal with personal issues while engaging in HE study do so within an HE system subject to successive waves of ideologically driven neoliberal policy initiatives. These have had major impacts on the HE regulatory, financial and operational environment. This is principally seen in the marketization of provision; the commodification of knowledge; and attempts to reframe the value of education purely in terms of its economic benefit to the student as a private good, and in its contribution to the economy via cultivation of student skills hard-linked to employability (Mahoney and Weiner, 2019; Naidoo and Williams, 2015). Within this contested HE environment I see the student advisory encounter as one important space offering opportunities to counter some of the alienation experienced by students and contribute to creating a more authentic, progressive and human pedagogy.

A vast body of metric data is now demanded by which institutions are held accountable for the 'success' outcomes and 'return on investment' of the courses they deliver. (Ball, 2012; Feldman and Sandoval, 2018). Potential risks of losing funding or market position from failing to meet external measures of 'success' are too serious for HE managers to ignore and scarce resources are allocated to mitigate this risk. Our institutions can thus become complicit partners in facilitating the neoliberal agenda. If we accept the validity of its values, we are at risk of internalizing, legitimizing and reproducing them through our pedagogy and practice. I believe it is important that we recognize and understand where and how the adoption and implementation of these values occurs and seek to resist, rather than falling into rhythm to dance uncritically to the tune being played to us.

One of the characteristics of adopting the neoliberal worldview is that it fosters the tendency to objectify and instrumentalize individuals. Metrics used to compare 'success outcomes' of higher education institutions (HEIs) are evaluated as though, in some sense, all students are homogenous and have an equal capacity to 'succeed'. A concomitant assumption is that any differences between performance measures of HEIs is attributable to relative quality (or otherwise) of their teaching and support. Creating market rankings for HEIs based on these metrics takes no account of the difference between (for example) the difference in student demographics between an elite Russell Group institution and one with a high percentage of WP students.

Where particular demographic segments of the student body are recognized to be underperforming, rather than critiquing or addressing the deeper societal issues and socio-economic factors which negatively impact them, the tendency is for government and other commentators to frame these as problems wherein the answer is that 'universities must do more'. Examples include BAME students (UUK and NUS, 2018) and students with mental health problems (Department of Education, 2018). This is not to suggest that HEIs cannot and should not 'do more' to address their practice to help specific categories of students. Rather, my point is that the neoliberal agenda, reproduced by HEI providers, creates a context which disassociates students from fully integrating the material and social conditions and experience of their lives into their HE study. It is as though their lived experience (and the reasons for it) are to be left at the university door, and it is for the individual student and the institution to overcome any deficits or obstacles without naming or addressing the oppression and injustice of the external world. (Thornton, 2016). Clearly this is ripe ground for a critical pedagogical approach across the curriculum and institution.

My experience of how this alienation impacts students is that they often have no expectation that the institution or its representatives would – or should – have any real concern about their personal issues. They believe the institution is only *really* interested in their academic performance and classroom engagement. However, students often *do* expect that if they disclose problems they will be judged as weak or failing by the institution and be at risk of being thrown off their course. I have frequently had to reassure students that university processes for mitigation and extension are there precisely to help their situation and they will not be viewed negatively for applying. Generally, much more needs to be done to effectively communicate the degree of support available for students, and that the institution is positive about providing it.

Internalizing and operationalizing neoliberal values can corrupt the motivation underlying why we do what we do as educators and further exacerbate the alienation students already experience. For example, a genuinely student-centred approach to student retention will focus on the benefit to the student in completing their studies. We would want to scaffold transition into HE; to understand and help the student overcome any obstacles or problems; to talk to them and advise them about what is best for them; to provide encouragement and motivation where this might be beneficial; and to link them to all sources of support to help them complete their studies at the highest level possible. However, a more instrumental approach might have stronger focus on retaining the student's course fees and on meeting external retention targets. Such motivation might incline someone to attempt to keep a student enrolled at all costs – even if this were to the detriment of the individual and not actually the path that was truly in their best interest. Actions taken by an advisor or tutor to try and retain the student might be the same in both scenarios but it is the *motivation* – the spirit underlying actions taken – which is different.

Similarly, is recent HE enthusiasm for promoting 'resilience' genuinely student-centred and primarily concerned with the well-being of the individual? Or is the motivation more instrumental in viewing resilience as a pragmatic tool to head off the escalating volume of student support and mental health issues? Is the true motivation to minimize drop-outs and deferrals and stay on track with the metrics? When students experience problems created by macro conditions of oppression, disadvantage, social exclusion and inequality, if our answer is merely 'become more resilient' then I would suggest we are failing in what should be our mission as partners in the personal and educational formation of our students, and in our role as critical pedagogues. We might similarly question motivation for the upsurge of interest in 'student well-being' in HE (Dhillon, 2018). Is this genuinely motivated by concern for promoting the human flourishing of our students? Or is it really just the latest addition to the neoliberal retention toolkit?

Neoliberal values in education, driven by market ideology and competition for deliberately restricted economic assets, will always tend to result in a race to the bottom. Austerity economics can lead universities to adopt 'industrial' approaches to student support structures and processes, motivated by desire to achieve economies of scale and efficiency. To be fair, industrializing support processes can also be driven by desperate attempts to manage overwhelming demand while lacking capacity to resource services properly. When a university takes a highly instrumental and managerialist approach to its teaching, student support, personal tutoring and advising, the capacity of the institution to engage deeply with students as individuals is quickly lost. Industrial systems are designed to function *efficiently*, but often at the expense of having time to really *know* students or relate on a meaningful human and personal level. Support systems tend towards being reactive and function from a deficit model, primarily seeking to 'fix' problems that might impact on retention and progress.

I would advocate for the whole educational enterprise to be conceptualized within a framework of 'pedagogical love'. I see this as a human and ethical approach that seeks alternatives to the problems caused by neoliberal colonization of our education system and society at large. Love is central to Freire's critical pedagogy, and throughout the body of his work he talks about love as the necessary foundation for both our engagement with students and with the world we cohabit:

> Because love is an act of courage, not of fear, love is commitment to others. No matter where the oppressed are found, the act of love is commitment to their cause – the cause of liberation. And this commitment, because it is loving, is dialogical. [...] Only by abolishing the situation of oppression is it possible to restore the love which that situation made impossible. If I do not love the world – if I do not love life – if I do not love people – I cannot enter into dialogue. (Freire, 1996, pp. 70–1)

The strong social justice ethic of Freire's pedagogy recognizes the role of education in cultivating critical consciousness that can lead to the creation of a world in which love is more possible, liberating both oppressed and oppressors from entrapment in anti-human and non-loving systems and ideologies. This creates the pedagogical arena within which it is possible to take account of the material conditions of our students' lives and critically engage with the reasons the reasons why these conditions are as they are. Schoder (2010) recognizes that Freire was never fully explicit about defining *exactly* what he meant by 'love' in his educational philosophy, but makes a good job of exploring this question and discusses in some depth how different attributes of love are manifested in Freire's pedagogy. In addition to Freire's work I also recommend articles by Liston (2008), who discusses the idea of 'attentive love', and Fitzsimmons and Uusiautti (2014), who discuss the connection between critical revolutionary pedagogy and pedagogical love.

What, then, does it mean to love our students? I would say that it means we need to *see* our students, to *know* them, and to *value* them. We do not truly love unless we know students as unique human beings rather than as a depersonalized and alienated consumers with whom we engage merely to fulfil a commercial contract about knowledge transfer in a 'banking' model of education.

I would say that to love our students means we have to be attentive to the reality of conditions of their inner and outer worlds and lives lived outside the classroom; and that we have to understand and reflect on how these conditions impact on their capacity to engage in the learning we seek to facilitate. The result of this attention should then intentionally shape our practice, policies and procedures to authentically place the needs of students first. Love should mean that we seek to liberate students and educators alike from oppressive aspects of our institutional systems and processes. Our objective should be to optimize conditions for learning and support and maximize their capacity to learn, grow and flourish as human beings while they study with us. For me this describes what is – or should be – the framework for being authentically 'student-centred'.

To know our students at anything other than a superficial level requires time and intentional effort. This comes at a cost in institutional terms of finance and resource; but also often commands a personal cost in terms of the emotional labour involved in attending deeply to our students. For this reason it matters hugely what types of people are appointed to roles providing or managing student support. We do not love our students if we appoint people who lack emotional intelligence and empathy and are more concerned with process and regulations rather than motivated by pedagogical love. The best advisors and tutors have capacity and willingness to give repeatedly of themselves in such emotional labour as a vocation, not because this fulfils a role function.

The 'efficiencies' of an industrial model generally constrain the amount of time an advisor can allocate to a student, especially in high-volume service contexts. The objective is to triage a student's query as quickly as possible to resolve it or direct them to other internal and external services. In my view this model falls far short of the potential power of the advisory meeting as a loving, human encounter during which the advisor gives time and attends deeply: not just identifying the information or referral needs of the student but also engaging with how that student *feels* about the situation they are in. In innumerable experiences it was relatively straightforward for me to identify why a student was asking for an extension. It would then have been simple to advise them on the evidence and application process. In an industrial model that would be 'job done', and I could have legitimately ended the meeting to move on to the next student. However, my repeated experience is that asking the student *one* more question about how they are feeling or coping – giving them time and permission to open up about the situation they are in and how they feel about it – can open the floodgates. This has led many times to the student opening up about trying to handle a catalogue of horrific issues for perhaps the next hour. Students often tell me 'I have never talked like this about my situation to anyone before' and that it has been incredibly helpful and releasing to have been able to talk about it.

I feel such instances can only occur where the advisor is able to give full and loving attention to the individual student who is with them. Students recognize and respond positively to encountering authentic care and interest in their circumstances, and express gratitude in finding someone who genuinely wants to listen to them. Sadly, it often seems something that they are not used to experiencing and certainly do not expect. I believe giving such attentive and loving focus that invites a student to talk about the deep issues and struggles of their life can in itself be a transformational pedagogical activity, and also a revolutionary activity that counters the alienating diktats of neoliberal thinking. It tells the students that their lived experience is important; that they matter as individuals beyond their academic performance; and that it is valuable, legitimate and of authentic interest to the institution to understand and provide support where possible. Giving this attention and care often has the effect of strengthening a bond between the student and the institution, or at least with the advisor as its proxy representative. Students have told me on many occasions that talking to me made the difference between them being able to continue their studies or leaving the institution.

I note with concern the potential for the introduction of more industrial systems to reduce opportunities wherein this loving, attentive encounter can occur (for example the implementation of online systems that preclude the need for students to meet in person with an advisor). This approach may appear to offer advantages of time and resource savings, perhaps by using administrative staff rather than more skilled (and expensive) advisors. However, on many occasions the primary issue presented by a student only touches the edges of a much larger set of problems they are facing but not disclosing. Without the personal interaction and skilled probing of an experienced advisor the full dynamics of a student's situation might never come to light until problems escalate further down the line to an even greater degree.

It is worth noting that institutions operating with a reactive deficit model run the risk of missing those students who might be living with very difficult problems but are still just managing to perform and engage academically to the extent that they do not show up as being 'at risk'. An unknown number of students in this category who might have benefitted from being connected with support, advice and understanding thus pass through the system 'below the radar', probably under-achieving in terms of what they may have attained had appropriate support been put in place for them. We therefore need to be able to 'know' our students in ways that are not conditional on them presenting with problems in order to provide equity of support.

To pay loving attention to the fraught complexity of many of our students' lives should mean radical reappraisal of some of the traditional HE structures and processes we have inherited from earlier, less complex and resource-constrained times. Regrettably, it seems that common framings of regulations for extensions and mitigation can exacerbate the problems students face. Our evidence-heavy systems convey to students that the institution will not believe or help you unless you can prove what you are saying with documentary evidence. In numerous circumstances furnishing documentary evidence is not possible The typical university's legalistic and adversarial approach in this regard does not foster a humane and loving approach to its students, and is increasingly out of step with the complexity of the social conditions and demands of their lives (Stowell, 2004). While I can understand the rationale for asking students to provide supporting medical evidence for health conditions this typically means students incur costs for their GP to write a letter. Many students are in difficult financial circumstances so we are adding to that problem by demanding evidence in this form. We also place a burden on overstretched GP services by expecting them to allocate limited appointment spaces to students whose issues may not at that point strictly require them to be seen for medical purposes.

Those of us who work as advisors and tutors on the front line of student support are often the first to see the negative impacts on students of having to negotiate university systems and attitudes that are out of step with the needs and realities of their lives. If others at more senior management levels in the institution lack the contact and insight to recognize these problems then we have to be the ones who seek to raise awareness and engage with internal processes to bring about meaningful changes for our students.

I note that there can be a tendency for certain sectors of a university to be very 'rules focused' and behave as though the regulations were dispensed in some sort of inviolable sacred form – rather than that they were crafted *by* the institution and can be *changed* by the institution. It is not uncommon to have to act as mediator between a student and the university where the student's situation and legitimate needs are inadequately provided for by the regulations. Once again, an industrial model will tend to default to 'the rules say' and demonstrate no inclination to flexibility or recognition that the rules are not equal to the situation. Where the rules are deemed more important than the genuine and legitimate needs of the student, I would say that the rules need to be challenged with a view to being revised.

There is a real need for enhanced flexibility of provision in course delivery and submission schedules that goes beyond the traditional full-time/part-time options – flexibility that can accommodate the complexity and constraints that students living difficult lives have to manage while studying. For example, student parents have additional burdens that HEIs seldom seem to take substantive account of (Moreau, 2016; Moreau and Kerner, 2012, 2015). Parents can be disadvantaged by when assessment submissions are set. Caring for children during school holidays means they often cannot give that time to working on assignments or attending classes and they can consequently struggle to cope with submitting work on time. There is seldom any provision within regulations to allow for extensions under such circumstances.

I believe we also have to critically question what 'success' in HE means, and who gets to define it. Attaining a qualification to a good standard is a wholly valid measure of success. However, for some students success can be marked in much more gritty terms. That they are still attempting to engage with their studies, despite living with horrific personal pressures and toxic circumstances, is a huge success. The fact that some of them are even still *alive* is a huge success. Eventually attaining a qualification after dealing with extreme circumstances resulting in multiple extensions, mitigation and deferral of studies, is a huge success. And of course there are all the intangible dimensions of positive personal formation and development that occur during the student's HE study that cannot be simply measured and are thus deemed irrelevant to the external metrics of the banking model of education. It is important that we recognize and affirm these successes with our students.

Creating the capacity for students to succeed and flourish is a whole institutional responsibility and is positively or negatively affected by the design and fitness for purpose of our practices in course design and delivery, policies and procedures, transition, skills development, and support services. We face an uphill struggle against the relentless incursions of the neoliberal agenda that seeks to instrumentalize, industrialize and redefine the meaning and value of our work as educators. Nonetheless, the authentic heart of what we do as personal and academic tutors and advisors is fundamentally human, relational and driven at its best by love. We have a responsibility to practice and cultivate these values throughout the institution. We should also be actively prepared to challenge, expose and disrupt practices and values that are contrary to them, whether we encounter them within our institutions or in the wider social and policy environments.

While we may not be able to easily effect desired changes at the macro level, either in our institutions or in wider society, what we do, and why we do it truly does matter to our students as individuals. Who knows what positive impacts upon the world may flow from the loving pedagogy we enact in our teaching and support of students?

Response from Paul Prinsloo

Reading Peter Sharpe's reflections, 'Sit Down Next to Me: Reflections on Academic Advising and Pedagogical Love', reminded me of the work by Sandy Grande (2018) – 'Refusing the university'. Like Sharpe, Grande (2018) grapples with higher education as '*an arm of the settler state* – a site where the logics of elimination, capital accumulation, and dispossession are reconstituted' (p. 47; italics in the original) and reflects on institutions of higher learning that are incapable and/or unwilling to care and love. She refers to the need for an 'undercommons', or fugitive spaces, 'where students and faculty work to cleave study and struggle, where they can be *in* but not *of* the university' (p. 49; italics in the original).

In a context where teaching is often instrumental in sustaining and perpetuating legacies of historical exclusion, misrecognition and marginalization, 'refusing the university' is not a passive act of withdrawal or retreat 'but rather understood as an active instantiation' of radically different modes-of-being and modes-of-doing (p. 58). Refusing the university is very different from resisting the university, as resisting takes the assumed authority of universities and those in power as a given. In contrast to resistance that can be negotiated or acknowledged, refusing the university questions and doubts the very foundations of neoliberal colonialism. Pedagogies and student support that support refusal 'offends institutional authorities offering "the gift" of belonging, creating conditions of precarity for the refuser' (Grande, 2018, p. 59). Those refusing the university can become demoralized, ever more precarious and disempowered, and therefore need communal safe spaces or an 'undercommons'. The latter is 'a space of possibility: a fugitive space wherein the pursuit of knowledge is not perceived as a path toward upward mobility and material wealth but rather as a means toward eradicating oppression in all of its forms' (p. 60).

A pedagogy of love, suggested by Freire and reflected on by Sharpe, is, and requires in its essence, a commitment to refusal and the creation of safe, rehumanized, fugitive spaces of recognition and disobedience where students (and staff) are not advised to become more resilient in a house that is burning, but share a commitment to build a new house, one conversation at a time. Committed to pedagogic love will require us to work 'within, against, and beyond the university-as-such' and to 'refuse the university' (Grande, 2018, p. 51). Pedagogic love as refusal requires a commitment to collectivity, reciprocity and mutuality and resembles a Zapatismo scholarship commitment to rehumanizing the university.

'If you have come to help us, you can go home. If you have come to accompany us, please come. We can talk' (Glesne, 2016, p. 169).

Chapter Seventeen

Pushing at an Open Door

Tina McLoughlin

My role is that of international co-ordinator in a small Midlands university. Through experience in my working life and my membership of the university's critical pedagogy group, I have formed a view of the work of professional staff, academics and students that will allow us to co-construct outcomes that enable us to be more student-centred. However, there are boundaries and tensions in a traditional model of working in a higher education (HE) setting that can be troublesome for some members of staff. I therefore intend to examine the roles of professional and support staff through a critical pedagogy lens in order to look at means of making the experience more democratic for all. We can see that since the massification of HE (Tight, 2017), professional and support staff are in increasingly important roles in higher education, so for them not to fulfil their potential or use their abilities seems a terrible waste, both for them and our students. At Newman the proportions are close to 50/50 professional and support and academic staff.

> Critical pedagogy seeks to give those who have been excluded from power the right and ability to have an input into civic life. (Kincheloe, 2007)

One thing I want to explain is that the usual assumption when talking of critical pedagogy is that we are taking about teaching and learning. However, I see that the underpinning ideology is of humanity, working and learning from each other, side by side. I feel that the role of professional and support staff in contributing to the quality of teaching and learning is undervalued. Celia Whitchurch has written a number of times on relationships and recognition of non-academic roles. She has referred to the role of 'third-space professionals' that has emerged as universities have grown and changed. Lewis (2014) and Miskelly and Duncan (2014) have written about professional identity in higher education and the way non-academic staff can be perceived as implementing a managerialist agenda. Dobson and Conway (2003) have concentrated on the relationship between administrators and academics in Australia, particularly about the tensions between academic and administrative roles, their nomenclature and the impact of a growing 'profession' of non-academic staff.

Professional and support staff have a vast amount of experience and expertise. They are also responsible for and committed to a wide range of work. As Graham (2012) writes, not only do staff need to rise to the challenge of an ever-changing and more complex environment, they often relish this challenge as it adds to motivation and engagement in their work. This is mirrored by findings in my own small-scale study involving professional support staff at Newman, discussed in the following. As one participant remarked, 'I have to care about my work, it is my identity' (service area manager).

The pressure on resources in the last few years has increased as tuition fees have been frozen and other costs, in particular staffing, have risen, making it logical to utilize the experience and knowledge of all staff to enhance student learning. After joining the critical pedagogy group, I began to reflect on why more professional and support staff were not engaging with this group and using their experience to critically engage with the status quo. I reflected that my own experience – eldest of a large family where being responsible and independent was expected, first in the family to attend university, a mature student, widening participation officer and manager, experience in the public and private sectors as well as a time being self-employed – gave me a form of privilege that other colleagues may not have felt. My own experience had been relatively smooth and I felt that the university was an open and nurturing place for staff as well as students. I undertook a Master's degree and a PGCert without having to pay fees and with the support of managers, academic staff and colleagues. I work with colleagues across subject areas and professional and support departments.

But with reflection came the realization that I was what Whitchurch referred to as an 'unbound professional'. Where I encounter barriers, I seek out alternative pathways, but this is not always an easy (or perceived as easy) option for other professional and support staff colleagues. I therefore decided that I needed a wider range of views. I identified eight areas in the university from which to interview colleagues about their experience. The number of areas itself was a surprise to me, making me realize how easy it is to forget the wide range of contributions that are made and that are mostly unseen.

The following is a summary of areas of advantage and disadvantage as perceived by the colleagues I interviewed.

Good Points

Everyone generally felt respected and benefitted from having a good reputation both individually and their departments.

- Staff felt they could work well, especially with academic colleagues.
- High level of professional qualification and work experience.
- The 'Newman' factor, the collegiality and community support.

Problem Areas

The main issues for participants were all based in the traditional working methods and structures. Relationships were good but progress was often stymied by old processes.

- Other service departments either not understanding their range of work or being willing to collaborate.
- Felt expertise/advice ignored by senior management.
- Being under-resourced and expected to plug gaps.
- Some departments felt shut off and their contribution invisible.
- Lack of investment in systems that improve students experience and work load but not visible so sidelined.
- No parity on pay, pensions or hours with academics.

From talking to academic colleagues, it should be pointed out that these issues are, in the main, very close to their experience.

Although the list of positives is comparatively short, their effects were felt to be powerful. Some of the problem areas may be seen as hard to change, especially when they are due to entrenched processes. However, like many things, an impact can be made one step at a time.

One important factor inhibiting this is lack of confidence among professional and support staff when facing change or challenge. I myself had experienced this when I undertook my PGCert. On the first weekend of the course, I was asked by an academic, 'Why are you here?' My interpretation of this remark was a deep moment of fight or flight. Academic qualifications are regarded as the currency of worth in HE, a view supported by Whitchurch: 'Academic credentials, particularly doctorates, were perceived by those individuals who had them as a key element in establishing their credibility with academic colleagues' (2013, p. 71). In my institution, 28.5 per cent of professional and support staff hold an HEA fellowship, and a growing number are undertaking the PGCert.

> My purpose in doing the (PGCert) course was to gain confidence and credibility when speaking to academic staff about my practice. The course gave me a broader understanding of pedagogical practice which, I trust, will enable me to speak with academics from a more informed position. I had assumed that academics would know a lot about . . . practice, from teaching in schools and that I wouldn't have anything additional to contribute. This perception proved to be very wrong, which has increased my confidence in what I have to offer as a specialist. I've also built some good relationships with academic staff, who I had little contact with before. (Support service manager)

Yet staff with higher degree qualifications also stated that they would not question an academic member of staff, even if it concerned an area in which they had expertise. Another staff member, referring to their own MA studies, talked about feeling a 'fraud' when attending an internal conference as a student. They explained that because they were a member of support staff, they felt they were not a 'real' student even though they were following the same course as everyone else.

Another underlying consideration for lack of confidence could lie in the gender nature of professional and support roles. At Newman 60 per cent are female, similar to a total UK figure of 62 per cent (HESA, 2020a). I have discussed the issue with academic and professional colleagues and would encourage us to apply Pat Thompson's view of dispensing with being the 'good girl' of production and then the rejection of doing the right thing, of being the 'good girl' (Thompson, 2018, p. 243).

The question for me, then, is how we overcome this inhibition that prevents colleagues from moving away from a traditional model of working. One of the attractions for me of Freire's writing is the levelling of power in learning when he describes student–teacher relations and, for me, this is also a way to read all staff relations with students and each other.

> Through dialogue, the teacher-of the-students and students-of-the-teacher cease to exist and a new term emerges: teacher-student with students-teachers . . . they become jointly responsible for the process in which all grow. (Freire, 1970, p. 61)

To me, the responsibility to try and achieve this is everyone's. Yes, we would like to know that the door is open but we also have to put some effort into opening it further. The physical invisibility of many staff members works against moving away from doing things as they have always been done. One participant said attending the learning and teaching conference that year was 'an eye opener'. This person realized how much more they need to communicate what the department's contribution was to student success.

It is not just lack of confidence that prevents our growth. As Freire writes, there can be another contributory factor, the fear of freedom, something I can feel now as I write this and consider the prospect of judgement. Lack of confidence and fear of freedom are scary for some because the way we work within the institution can replicate social hierarchies. It is not for nothing that we talk of the devil we know. It is that seduction of tradition, of the normal, the certainty in the familiar. I found Freire's statement useful to remember here when he writes:

> The oppressed, having internalized the image of oppressor and adopted his guidelines, are fearful of freedom. Freedom would require them to reject this image and replace it with autonomy and responsibility. (1970, p. 29)

Stepping out of one's comfort zone means being or feeling vulnerable. However, we need to be our own agents of change as we cannot always rely on others to give us permission. We need to take the lead. It is possible, and it can be difficult, but the potential rewards are enormous for us and others. It is all too easy to worry about the judgement of others and we need to accept the uncertainty and do it anyway, as the uncertainty is the result of the pull of tradition.

We need to realize we are not alone in trying to use the full gamut of our abilities. I found both resonance and encouragement in many of the respondents to Whitchurch's study, for example:

> I am a mover and a shaker and a . . . change agent, especially in those areas I feel passionate about. (Programme co-ordinator, state institution, United States)
>
> Our successes are because we're agile and . . . we're smart and . . . we invent or we do the research on our own . . . our successes are basically our own

doing. (Development manager, state institution, United States) (Whitchurch, 2013, p. 115)

As well as finding encouragement externally it is important to find it in our own institutions. In Chapter 16, my colleague Peter writes of the place for pedagogical love where 'we need to see our students, to know them, and value them'. I would go further and add that we should see our colleagues in this light too. I would ask this of all staff at every level, including management, seeing who staff are beyond their role titles and being open to what we can offer as whole people to the university endeavour. As with students, we need to allow staff to grow and teach each other and not just be trained in their roles.

As we expect our learners to be critical and questioning, as staff we need to encourage each other in ways of questioning the norms, testing traditions and looking for new ways of working to meet the complexities and challenges of higher education in the twenty-first century that require the abilities, talents and creativity of all staff to achieve. One way we have been achieving this at Newman is in what Julie, Jane and Wahida describe in Chapter 6 as 'hopeful playful spaces'.

There are concrete examples of these hopeful playful spaces. I was able to gain encouragement and support from the critical pedagogy group for an Erasmus staff and student week working with a senior academic colleague, as we discuss in Chapter 19. It wasn't just that we held the week but that it was in a new and untested form that we shared with international colleagues.

This model was taken up by others in recent learning and teaching conferences that have developed from a top-down and academic focus to an organizing group of academic, professional and support staff and students. This has not been without problems, as doing something different has been questioned. However, this democratic approach has led to it being possible to discuss sometimes sensitive issues with a wider range of stakeholders, in particular students followed by further calls to action and change.

This book itself is another example of how stepping out of our standard roles enables us to work collaboratively across the institution to learn from each other, support each other and thereby enhance students' learning. It is one of the characteristics of Newman that we are able to do this. It is easy to think that as a small university we do not have as much to offer as larger, more influential universities. But this is not the case; our community enables us to come together and be creative, to experiment and work in partnership.

A purpose of writing this chapter is to raise awareness in the hope that we have a discussion and reflect on how we can be agents of change or help those trying to do so. My recommendation for fellow professional staff from personal experience is to step up and be seen. You can initiate events and discussions and open the 'crack' or widen cracks started by others through collaborative working. 'A crack is the perfectly ordinary creation a space or moment in which we assert a different type of doing' (Holloway, 2010, p. 21). As Holloway states, it can be the ordinary action or gesture that can lead to change. The beauty of this is it means we have it within our power to be a catalyst for change, by asking a question, volunteering for a task, being in a space, being at a meeting or attending an event. Sometimes I have seen surprise in colleagues' faces when I have attended an 'academic' event. Hopefully, after their surprise they may reflect on their reaction and re-evaluate. The more we do this, the more we work to make it a norm, and so gently the ground will shift.

We all need to step out of our comfort zone but I appreciate that means being or feeling vulnerable. Another purpose is to let you all know how it can feel and how much there is to gain. We are all here to provide a better place for our students to learn, but perhaps we can all also be a bit kinder to each other, more curious, more welcoming. As I edit the final draft of this chapter I am conflicted, in tears. I tell you that not for sympathy but to be truthful about how hard it is to let the mask of confidence down. It is so hard to offer up what we write to be judged but that is what it is like to break with tradition. I have to remind myself that I have chosen to do this. Remember, everyone is worried and we need to be brave in making the first step and believe we are pushing at an open door.

Chapter Eighteen

Quality Assurance or Assured Silence?

Lorraine Loveland-Armour, Response
from Seán Bracken

My Professional Background and Approach

Although I have worked as a teaching assistant, high school English teacher, residential counsellor, advocate, diagnostician, clinic manager and a lecturer (FE and HE), it is as a specialist dyslexia support tutor that I have found my *métier*. Over the last twenty years, in my role as dyslexia support services team leader and specialist tutor, I've had the opportunity to meet hundreds of students, many of whom were identified with dyslexia after the age of sixteen. While it cannot be overstated that the individual journeys of these students are diverse and unique, throughout my years of practice some similarities regarding how students come to understand their dyslexias have emerged.

These students' stories are shared, in part, because we spend some time building a rapport and relationships both with learning and each other through dialogues, mindful of the ethics of care (Gadamer, 2013; Noddings, 2013), that stem from an in-depth induction. Within their university education, I am positioned as a stranger to them; as such, I have to fit into their otherwise clearly delineated academic landscapes whereby introductions require careful navigation. The holistic nature of my role allows space for trustworthy relationships to grow through a shared purpose to explore potentiality for learning differently together.

As a facilitator, I ask Socratic questions, fostering heuristic conversations (Moustakas, 1990) and transition into a curator holding a mirror to students so that they can see themselves reflexively. We begin our conversations alongside a review of a student's diagnostic report, which confirms dyslexia. Students will often begin this journey by saying something along the lines of 'I always knew there was something wrong with me'. The diagnostic report can present barriers and cause confusion as the report typically emphasizes the quantification of dyslexia and heavily accentuates the areas of difficulty using hierarchical language that exacerbates these feelings of 'wrongness'. Therefore, I reiterate that while the numbers and the assessment language within the report provide us with a helpful snapshot, they only act as an initial framework to inform our conversation, which focuses on improved understanding of approaches, barriers to learning and, importantly, underlying strengths. We discuss historic academic experiences, considering where strengths as well as difficulties may have been most prevalent and how the student feels about their educational experiences. From here we dive into the past, situate dyslexia into educational contexts and co-construct an initial plan of strategies and reflective activities to support the student to approach university education with their strengths in mind.

My Theoretical Stance

In my professional practice, teaching and learning with students is a reciprocal and collaborative process, which purposefully explores means to reduce power differentials and challenges the oppression that learners have historically endured in their educational engagements. This approach nurtures opportunities to co-construct new structures within university education, which not only resist the traditional hierarchical roles of educator–student, but also fosters improved dialogue that often places students directly into the role of more knowledgeable other to teach lecturers about dyslexia and about themselves as learners. Recognizing the political act of disclosure and the power of owning one's own dyslexia, my practice seeks to support students to embrace a developing hopeful andragogy.

This chapter, informed by my professional experiences, provides my interpretation of critical pedagogy in practice in a somewhat liminal space within university settings, since I am neither an academic lecturer nor solely a pastoral care professional. This is further complicated by the student being positioned as an employer, required to sign tutor timesheets. I have presented a number of pen portraits to illustrate how my interactions with students contribute to self-understanding.

Many conflicting definitions of dyslexia frame how educators understand and respond to the individual needs of university students newly identified with dyslexia. The created myths of dyslexia affect decisions about whether or not university students with dyslexia should be granted access to specialist resources or support to reduce disabling barriers to learning (Elliott and Grigorenko, 2014; Elliott and Nicholson, 2016). Consequently, many university students with dyslexia, who have successfully integrated compensatory strategies for managing information, may not anticipate that the reason they learn differently could be attributed to dyslexia. For the purposes of this chapter, dyslexia is described as a language processing difficulty that stems from inconsistencies in working memory (access to sequential and procedural aspects of organizing language), processing speed and phonological awareness (Eide and Eide, 2012). Processing speed is most observable in a student's ability to make paraphrased and succinct notes in response to spoken or visually presented information gleaned from lectures. Poor phonological awareness can result in misreading of words, multiple re-reads, misspellings and inconsistent comprehension of main concepts. A crucial element of understanding what dyslexia is, what it is not and how to observe it in university students involves direct communication with students about their educational histories, approaches to learning, barriers and identifiable strengths.

Student Journey to Identification

Contextually, at least 80 per cent of students identified with dyslexia within our institution are recognized while studying at university (see Figure 18.1). For many students, learning that dyslexia is lifelong and has not been recognized until now, often after the student has self-referred for a dyslexia assessment, can be overwhelming. Frequently, students experience a sort of grieving process whereby they feel a combination of emotions including:

- Relief: knowing there is a *reason* that some aspects of learning are challenging.
- Eagerness: a desire to learn as much as possible about dyslexia and where their experiences of dyslexia situate within what is known about it.
- Anger: wondering why no one previously recognized dyslexia as a factor along their educational journey.
- Confusion: puzzling about why, now that they finally have a name for their learning differences, they cannot immediately access support.
- Hope: believing that resources, human support and reasonable adjustments will allow them to thrive academically.

Diving into the Quagmire of Bureaucracy

The navigation of the process from screening to accessing DSA-funded specialist dyslexia support can be arduous and bewildering (see Figure 18.2). Despite the Department for Education's (2017a) stated intentions to reduce barriers to learning, the depth of bureaucratic monitoring by Student Finance England (SFE) Disabled

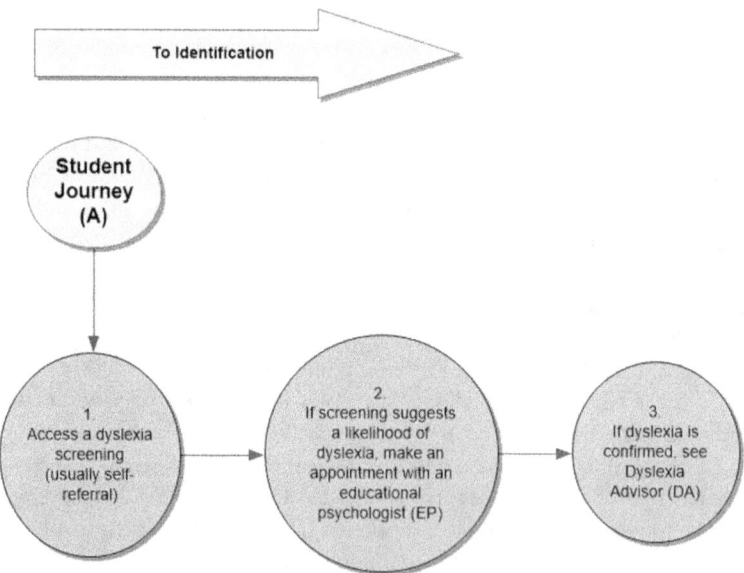

Figure 18.1 Initial stages of dyslexia identification journey for university students.

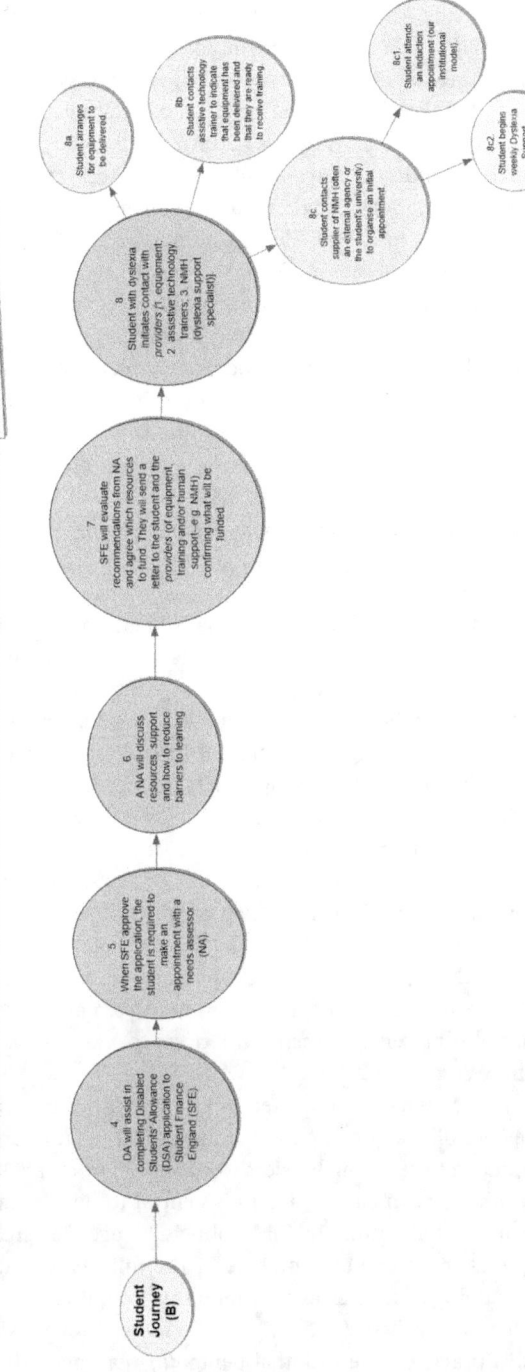

Figure 18.2 Additional access stages required for university students recently identified with dyslexia.

Students Allowance Quality Assurance Group (DSA-QAG, 2017), frequently restricts access to Disabled Students Allowance (DSA) funding for students with dyslexia at university and further contributes to delays in accessing support. In part, it could be argued that completing the DSA application itself acts as a gate-keeping exercise, presenting challenges due to the length and details required to gain access to entitled resources (Pennacchia, Jones and Aldridge, 2018). Additionally, imposing a cost for enabling resources in order to cut the public expenditure to improve access to university for students with dyslexia can delay support further. In effect, the complexity of the system and processes to access enabling resources may highlight difficulties implicit for individuals with dyslexia. Plausibly, these acts embody neoliberalist efforts to justify the free-market business of universities, moving further away from the state's responsibilities to ensure university students can access their education. To this end, neoliberalism can be understood as: 'a theory of political economic practice that proposes that human well-being can best be advanced by liberating individual entrepreneurial freedoms and skills within an institutional framework' (Harvey, 2005, p. 2), while simultaneously offering 'a market view of citizenship that is generally antithetical to rights, especially to state-guaranteed rights . . . [whereby], the individual (rather than the nation) is held responsible for her or his own well-being' (Lynch, 2006, p. 1). Consequently, the bureaucratic process of applying for and completing the next steps required to access dyslexia support, under the guise of quality assurance and student choice, can actually result in silencing the student. As Freire (1985, p. 50) explains, 'in the culture of silence the masses are mute, that is, they are prohibited from creatively taking part in the transformation of their society and therefore prohibited from being'. The student, often grappling with understanding their new identification, can struggle to explain it to multiple agencies, resulting in passive acceptance of recommendations by others. Somewhat problematically, the 'needs assessors' are largely generalists in broad areas of disability (NNAC, 2012; DSA-QAG, 2016), which may mean that dyslexia, as it affects the individual, rarely becomes more clearly defined or understood at this point. Additionally, because of repetitive checks of students' documents, which are distributed to service (support) providers, needs assessment centres, SFE and the Student Loans Company, there can be substantial delays in the journey to weekly support appointments. Arguably, annual audits, requirements to reapply for DSA funding each year and excessive scrutiny of DSA applications also present unnecessary barriers to learning within university education (Shore and Wright, 1999, 2015).

Once the student's needs are documented in a report and the student's payment of £200 clears, they are officially ready to be a dyslexic student at university (Gov. uk, 2019). This approach to reducing barriers to education by emphasizing learning differences and requiring payment for access is central to neoliberalist notions of inclusion (Cameron and Billington, 2017). Neoliberalist agendas create the veneer of individualized assessment of needs outside of the university and state welfare contexts by commodifying difference as a disability that requires products provided through independent businesses (Giroux, 2014). Thus, through what might be termed 'neoliberalist practices', the idea that being *different* means that the student with dyslexia must independently navigate a series of bureaucratic systems in order to be granted a semblance of improved access to university. Put simply, learning differently is a problem that the university student with dyslexia must correct. Therefore, the manifesto of neoliberalism that comes in the guise of quality assurance is, arguably, a form of oppression that subjugates the power of students within university contexts.

Providing students with resources, 'for a small fee' and the cost of imposing a disability identity, leaves many students feeling further conflicted about their dyslexia. Feeling lost within the assessment process, may, in part be a consequence of being required to have a second interaction with Student Finance England through the Disabled Students' Allowance application. Once students receive a letter from SFE that confirms DSA funding, they have a further requirement to attend an appointment with another unknown professional (needs assessor) who will determine which resources will be recommended so that, following a third interaction with SFE, university students with dyslexia can finally access curriculum. In a free-market context, the needs assessor's role in enacting policy can be perceived as a means of exercising control and power over the student, and of power relations, surveillance and panopticism (Foucault, 1995 [1975]; Foucault, 1998 [1976]; Morley, 2003). These experiences thus can contribute to a sense that a dyslexia identification differentiates them from their peers, creating a palpable power imbalance when, following these steps, I meet the student (Foucault, 1971). While, on one hand, the diversity of resources can appear to be a substantial *gift* to reduce barriers to learning, the added requirement to engage with multiple processes and agencies may cast doubts about who this process serves. Furthermore, it could be argued that for some students, having to accept an identity of 'disabled' stigmatizes dyslexia because it implies that they are unable to engage with their university studies without these resources. Having to learn how to use these resources and being granted a non-medical helper can also further disable students by creating a narrative of student incapability without *help*.

Personalizing Dyslexia

Once embarked on the rather tortuously bureaucratic journey towards dyslexia support, there remains the matter of learning which aspects of dyslexia actually apply to the individual's context and if/how to articulate this to others. Therefore, as part of their induction appointment, I systematically review and reflect meaning behind numbers that have imposed a dyslexic identity on students, giving space for reflection and recognition of how the student understands and articulates their learning experiences. Additionally, such induction dialogues support students to learn about their rights to reasonable adjustments covered under the *Equality Act 2010*, which correspond to the dyslexia identification. Following the induction, multiple continuous dialogues inform how dyslexia support tutors create rhizomatic crevices within the borderlands where learning differently is celebrated and nurtured in partnership with students. Subsequently, these dialogues serve to support students to understand the role that dyslexia plays in learning as well as how to enter into disclosure conversations with lecturers.

Dialogical Practice

Dialogical practice thus fosters conscientization, which supports students not only to better understand how to frame and communicate their dyslexia but also to understand that developing critical relationships with words is work that contributes to praxis. Unlike pedagogical approaches practised largely in school environments, students with dyslexia, especially within support contexts, often engage in heutagogical approaches to learning. Thus, students identify questions to inform how they want to improve their subject knowledge alongside questions about how to best articulate their knowledge to actively determine how they direct their learning. By developing a corpus of heutagogical practices that correspond directly with their individual lived experiences of education, students with dyslexia can begin to forge a reflexive relationship with learning (Hase and Kenyon, 2013, 2007). Thus, through critical dialogue, university students with dyslexia knowingly embed reflexivity in their study approaches, which fosters active changes in learning processes and their ability to communicate about these (Freire, 1985). Moreover, self-knowledge contributes to self-advocacy and acts as a means to empower university students with dyslexia to articulate their strengths and how they can utilize these to manage areas of learning they find less strong.

Pen Portraits: Heutagogy in Practice

Having established some of the issues inherent in my role as a university-based dyslexia support tutor and examined the scenario of how being identified with dyslexia at this stage in their education raises challenges, I now present pen portraits to illustrate examples of experiences in practice.

Pen Portrait 1

A female student, Sasha, aged 36, had returned to education to study on a BA Youth and Community Work course. This student had a particularly harrowing experience with dyslexia identification, having been initially segregated then subsequently reintegrated where she was tormented about the identification.

Initially, talking about her dyslexia in many ways, felt like she was being re-traumatized. However, through induction, she began to ask questions, including those about her learning as a child, and this fostered an opportunity for open dialogue.

Within this conversation, she asked, 'So, are you really telling me I'm not just thick and stupid or slow?' She indicated that she spends a lot of time puzzling over her ability to complete the work required of her since dyslexia previously meant she was incapable when in school. Throughout our induction appointment, she shared insightful moments of her past learning challenges and how these contributed to feelings of inadequacy. Nevertheless, after our two hours together, she concluded: 'I'm still not sure if I have dyslexia or not, but I do feel like I understand my way of learning much better now. I'm looking forward to support appointments each week'. This was a substantial change in attitude from when she entered the room.

From this pen portrait, arguably, trustworthiness and a willingness to focus on learning approaches rather than dyslexia identification is a critical element of hopeful pedagogy. I attempt to recognize that university students have a living history of education that needs to be acknowledged alongside the transition into university.

Teaching university students with dyslexia such as Sasha takes place within the liminal space of Dyslexia Support Services, within Student Services. Like McLaren's (1999) suggestion that learning requires a critical pedagogy of space, dyslexia support occurs in an integrated aspect of university studies in an individual teaching room, much like a tutorial space.

We can see from Sasha's portrait that the temporality of student experience is critical in developing relational learning and teaching strategies collaboratively. Consequently, andragogical practice acknowledges that students with dyslexia are 'critical citizens capable of governing rather than simply being governed' (Giroux, 1997, p. 259). Andragogical principles suggest that adults learn from broader contexts and that these emphasize processes of problem-centred thinking over the acquisition of factual knowledge content (Knowles and Associates, 1984). Freire and Macedo (1987, p. 33) explain that 'reading a text as a pure description of an object (like a syntactical rule), and undertaken to memorize the description, is neither reading nor does it result in knowledge of the object to which the text refers'. Applying andragogical principles to developing academic literacy, while simultaneously integrating individual strengths derived from dyslexia, supports a collaborative, strategy-based approach to reading that is purposeful. Hopeful andragogy that is both relational and dialogical therefore shines a much-needed light on an otherwise bleak and oppressive journey towards the contribution dyslexia has on university engagement (Knowles, Holton and Swanson, 2012; Gadamer, [1975] 2013).

Pen Portrait 2

Mandeep approached her dyslexia support sessions with some scepticism at first. She recognized that she had to make time for support within a very crowded timetable as well as family responsibilities and part-time work. She had been urged to leave her employment by lecturers; however, she required income to pay bills.

We began our goal-setting session by first creating a timetable of her work schedule, family commitments, scheduled modules and her waking and sleeping hours. In populating this, we were able to identify time that was occupied and time that appeared available. Once we were able to *see* time, we were able to begin to consider what each module required and identify how some of the available time could be protected for independent study within her daily activities. In setting goals, Mandeep recognized that she is actually much more organized than she realized. This recognition of ability helped her to then contain specific aspects of organization that required adaptations. Two goals she and I set collaboratively then included:

1. Plan time to pre-plan for assignment writing.
2. Reflect and annotate notes when reading to include feelings and observations about how reading is happening.

> Accordingly, the in-between space of dyslexia support also offered her a safe haven to discuss her dyslexia and her relationship with it. At our mid-semester review, she remarked:
> 'Pre-planning and time reviews have changed my life... over the semester, I have now learned how to break things down into smaller chunks. These chunks also have specific things I need to complete and include: how much to read; how many notes to make (and where to make them); and how it all links into my assignments. I know it's working too because I'm remembering more and I'm getting better marks.'

This reflective process, shown by Mandeep, whereby each session affords time to consider how learning has taken place throughout the previous week and how previous strategies inform developing strategies can be liberating. Marcel (2010, p. 24) suggests that taking time to understand hope as an active process can release students from the captivity that darkness, derived from feelings of helplessness, can impose.

Consequently, I would argue that hope is implicit in reflexive learning and can act as emancipation from the enslavement of an oppressive system of educational compliance, which many students assume that they will have to fit into when completing assessments as they perceive the requirements dictate. Marcel (2010, p. 25) further emphasizes that hopefulness can shine a light towards recognizing the power that stems from believing that 'the nature of that lost integrity which I now long to regain' is not only achievable but that it is led by hope. Fundamentally, by creating learning spaces that specifically embed critical dialogue and reflexive learning approaches, dyslexia support practitioners act as public intellectuals; we can translate the world of academia into personal contexts and work co-operatively with students. This creates an academic vernacular that not only legitimizes the right for university students with dyslexia to participate differently in education, but also transforms their own education and that of others, as active change agents shaping the way dyslexia is understood and the way individuals with dyslexia contribute to the dismantling of structural inequalities.

Making a decision to disclose dyslexia when newly identified can be a daunting task, particularly when historic school experiences strongly inform university students' relationships with learning and communicating with educators in positions of authority. The tensions between articulating needs, difficulties and abilities and the power that lecturers ostensibly possess over students' futures, perceptually or otherwise, can result in a desire to struggle through learning rather than communicate about difference with lecturers. On the other hand, because students are simultaneously introduced to dyslexia, disability and their corresponding rights through induction, they are positioned in a more empowered location from which to disclose dyslexia.

Pen Portrait 3

An illustrative example of the perceptions that students often consider is captured in the dialogue about disclosure that follows.

> LL-A: Do you feel like you can have conversations about your dyslexia with your lecturers now at university?
>
> SK: Yes, now I do. I didn't think that I could when I first found out though . . .
>
> LL-A: Ah, so do you feel like you can explain that to others now?
>
> SK: Yes, I mean I don't always, but there are some lecturers who really get it and I think they want to know because they want to improve their teaching in some way or something . . . so I do go to tutorials and I say stuff like, if you just make the slides available like a few days before, that makes a big difference. . . . I mean it's not really big stuff, but I do think it helps when they know that I might do things a little differently.
>
> It's like when we talk about how I learn in our sessions. I mean we have to discover it sometimes by doing something different – trying a different strategy or tweaking something that worked last time, but doesn't work so well this time when I have a different kind of assignment. It means I can see how I can – how I need to adapt.
>
> LL-A: Do you generally feel comfortable talking about your dyslexia now?
>
> SK: I would say that I do, but that is because I understand it better now . . . .
>
> LL-A: So what does it mean when you disclose or talk about your dyslexia with lecturers – I guess I'm asking why you do it – why tell lecturers?
>
> SK: Oh – well, at first it was – I – dunno, I guess it was to kinda explain or maybe make excuses for any mistakes . . . [now] I just ask to discuss it because I'm a university student – I mean we should be having these conversations, shouldn't we? So I don't feel like I have to make excuses . . . but then for those ones who seem like – it's hard to explain, but kinda like they aren't interested or they think oh here we go – the dyslexic needs help – I kinda remind them about my right to record stuff or have access to information before lectures – or that kind of thing. I mean, I'm not rude about or anything, but I do have rights and so I want to make sure that they know that I know so that I don't have to keep asking for help all the time. I know sometimes they just forget or have too much on, but in a way that isn't good enough. I mean we all have a lot on . . . I mean what use is it to teach something that people can't understand only because they can't read it during class – sending it through even the day before would mean I could participate!

A key point of interest in this conversation is that the student recognized her strengths and felt that by talking about them, she could feel that she created space for herself to be included in the class. Verbalizing her needs acted as a means of breaking silence that the hidden curriculum had previously imposed on her participation in classroom learning. The tension lay in the perception that she felt that her lecturers might not believe that she actually has dyslexia and that she would have to understand the nature of her dyslexia well enough not only to self-advocate but also to educate her lecturers on the many facets and individual nature of dyslexia. However, knowing her *rights* meant that she was able to make *reasonable* requests that improved her access to information and through this she was able to educate her lecturers about her needs as well as tactfully inform them of their legal responsibilities enshrined in UK legislation. The reference to knowing her rights is particularly interesting, and not at all uncommon in terms of how students approach their lecturers when requesting that reasonable adjustments are made. Many students, when they know that what they are asking is reasonable, tend to find that they have improved relationships with their lecturers. This perceptual shift in relationship is not necessarily because there was tension previously. Indeed, it is more likely that the student felt that she did not have the language to explain her dyslexia and felt concerned about how to communicate her needs without sounding unreasonable or making excuses. Nevertheless, transparent communication that is informed by both the language of dyslexia and the language of law provides a useful foundation for empowered disclosure.

The Self-disclosure of Dyslexia: A Political Act?

Critical shifts in dispositions emerge when we illuminate the social injustice of educational barriers that students have experienced historically in their learning journeys. By recognizing the root of these barriers as educational malpractice as a consequence of neoliberalist influences, rather than framing dyslexia as something wrong or disabled, the student begins to explore methods of accessing information using individual strengths, thus increasing engagement with the academy. This approach of illuminating cognitive strengths and navigating academic language by using these strengths improves access by disrupting the narrative that learning differently means disability. Arguably, critical andragogy is initiated in this approach because the hierarchy of the knowledge economy that is driving many aspects of UK university education begins to flatten for students with dyslexia, whose critical reasoning strengths and creative problem-solving abilities place learning processes above fact retention. A renegotiation of power begins to occur and rather than view andragogy as a formulated set of teaching techniques, there is an organic recognition of how the student has acquired *knowledge* through multiple means driven by curiosity rather than through the single institutional structures of educational systems.

A Practical Proposal

As a critical pedagogue, I would propose that, after reading the dialogical student portraits in this chapter, you consider asking yourself the following questions about students with dyslexia to help rise above the statutory and bureaucratic duties of inclusive practice.

- Do you know what dyslexia is (and what it is not)?
- What informs your understanding of dyslexia and to what extent is this driven by your tutorials with university students?
- Do you share your own approaches to learning with students to identify strategies, commonalities and differences around how they access information?

- What could you do with enhanced dialogue about learning to extend learning opportunities?
- What opportunities do you create for students with dyslexia to explore and articulate their strengths and strategies?
- To what extent do you embed critical dialogue in your practice?

Response from Seán Bracken

Beyond the Liminal: Reimaging the Inclusive University

Across Europe, resource provision for students identified as having additional learning requirements is under strain. As this chapter has identified, in a context of increased marketization of student service support, learners in higher education who have been identified as having dyslexia frequently become entangled in Kafkaesque and labyrinthine bureaucratic systems and processes. Students are posited as objectified commodities competing with needy peers to gain access to increasingly scarce external resource availability. Learners' experiences of engaging with such inhibiting processes may result in feelings of further marginalization, disempowerment and despair. However, as Freire has shared: 'it is imperative that we maintain hope even when the harshness of reality may suggest otherwise' (Freire in hooks, 2003). As identified in the pen portraits, through encouraging a conscientious reauthoring of the dyslexic self, Lorraine Loveland-Armour and her colleagues facilitate an imperative first step on the journey to agency within a wider academic community.

The chapter challenges academics, and others who constitute differing attributes of that wider university community, to consider how best the (re)imaging of self can be positively fostered beyond the 'liminal' and, to some extent, liberating space of initial encounters with student services. By suggesting that learning spaces develop communities founded on principles of andragogy that are further enriched through collegiate research and interaction, the chapter provides a hopeful vision. This vision is premised on principles of interagency and underpinned by democratic practices of learner, teacher and facilitator (read services) dialogic collaborative construction. Taking the lead from this chapter then, it is quite possible to reimagine the nature of a university, not as it encounters the 'difference of dyslexia' but also as it systemically self-reflects and grows in awareness regarding the nature of diversity as an existential facet of university values, ethic and identity.

To some extent this model for institutional transformation illustrates how Courtney Cazdan's three 'r's framework for social justice in education (2012) might be realized in university practice. It does so by positing the *recognition* of all learners at the hub of dialogic interactions among constituent agents responsible for fashioning a meaningful learning experience. These agentive teams may be comprised of colleagues from library and information services, student services, technology support, estates, the academy and students' unions. A community emerges with the expressed aim of 'overcoming the subordination of identities and addressing in particular moment-to-moment teacher-student interactions' (Hanesworth, Bracken and Elkington, 2019). Further, through meaningful learner *representation* there is scope for developing a partnership approach that maps out how inclusive learning spaces can be jointly brought into being. Ultimately, the shared objective for espousers of hopeful pedagogy is to address systemic inequities in learning outcomes. There is further scope to redress some of the inequities experienced by students with dyslexia, as well as other marginalized learners, by drawing on the potential of asset-based conceptual frameworks such as universal design for learning and culturally sustaining pedagogies as they offer iterative pathways for bringing about more systemic changes. Taken together such frameworks will enable a cultural and resource-based *redistribution* so the educational terrain becomes more familiar, meaningful, navigable and purposeful for all learners in higher, further and employment-based domains.

Drawing on her strengths of interpersonal empowerment and her values-based approaches honed through experience, Lorraine Loveland-Armour enables learners with dyslexia to reauthor their higher education experiences. By doing so, she also encourages educators to envision how wider university policies and practices might become ever more inclusive.

Part II E

Hopeful Pedagogies beyond the Institution

Chapter Nineteen

University as Community

Breaking the Circle of Certainty

Tina McLoughlin, Lea Randolf and Mike Seal, Response from Simone Helleren

Introduction

In November 2018 Newman hosted an Erasmus staff week. The genesis of the week was easy as it grew naturally from a discussion with colleagues in our critical pedagogy group. It was something Tina had been planning to do for several years but she knew she wanted to organize it differently from the formal and sometimes over-organized events she had attended. She wanted something where everyone who attended had the chance to grow, challenge and be challenged. The staff week was entitled 'University as community: Breaking the circle of certainty – students and staff working together'. We had thirty participants from European countries including Hungary, Germany, Portugal, Spain, UK, Poland, Italy, as well as staff and students from Newman University. The event was held over four, intense days. After discussions with Mike we decided to use Open Space Technology (OST) as the framework for the event.

This chapter is written by Tina, international co-ordinator and event creator; Mike, academic and experienced OST practitioner; and a second-year German, Erasmus social work student. It also draws upon comments from various participants, some during the event, some at the end evaluation and in subsequent correspondence. We reflect on the week and draw out any new learning for others intending to run such an event. We aim to extend some of the organizing principles of Open Space Technology.

Open Space Technology

The approach taken was Open Space Technology, as developed by Harrison Owen (2008). Owen, an American educator and writer on organizations and management, believed that most of the effective learning in conferences happened in the informal spaces outside of, and around, the formal session. Consequently, the organizing principles for such learning events should be based on what happens in these spaces rather than the formal ones. Owen (2008) developed techniques for running events on this basis. First, the agendas of conferences are not decided until people arrive. There may be a general theme, and people are sent papers to stimulate thinking beforehand, but the actual sessions are planned on the day. The idea is that you cannot really know what is going to be the most effective discussion until you know who is in the room. The start time is dedicated to setting an agenda which is not done beforehand. Ideas are generated from discussions and then people identify specific session topics, with an individual taking responsibility for naming and explaining the workshop themes to others and starting off the workshop. In this way, if you have an idea, you have to take responsibility for starting up the debate. There are also facilitators; their responsibility is for holding the space and attending to process according to the principles and rules (see the following). We have ideas about an expanded role for facilitators.

There are four principles to the sessions. Two of them are about the content and approach. 'Whoever comes are the right people' is intended to stop people saying there is no point to this session unless x is here – you work with what you have got, which is those people in the room. The second, 'Whatever happens is the only thing that could have', is actually about making sure that those in the room take responsibility for what happens in the room. The other two principles are related to the timing of the sessions. The attendees organize each session as they go, which may finish earlier or later than the allotted time: principle three, 'Whenever it starts is the right time'. Finally, principle four stops people feeling obliged to carry on when a session has naturally finished (the principle is 'When it's over, it's over') or stop before that point has been reached.

There is also one rule: 'The rule of two feet'. It means participants are free to decide which session they want to attend and may switch to another one at any time. Owen talks about his frustration at going to a session at a conference only to quickly find it's not what you thought it would be but you feel obliged to stay. This might mean a session may have no one in it. This can be good for testing out when a person claims that everyone agrees their issues are important. There are also certain characters that are named to enable movement. People can be 'bumblebees', who fly from group to group, cross-pollinating the discussions, or 'butterflies' sitting around looking relaxed –interesting discussions emerge around them as people find them and pause to chat. This means that people can leave and come together in more informal spaces and set up their own session. Open spaces are created where people can come together and do something different, as long as they take responsibility for feeding back what they discuss and agree. Networking can occur before, during, after and in-between the actual face-to-face meetings, so discussions can continue seamlessly.

Arising Themes

We detected a number of themes arising out of the running of the week, which we hope will expand and deepen Owen's vision for Open Space Technology. These were:

- Fear, certainty and trust.
- Hierarchies, power and liminal space.
- Physical and planned space.

Fear, Certainty and Trust

Fear was certainly both a driving force and an ever-present reality for both Mike and Tina. As Tina reflects:

> The easy part is to be creative, to have ideas. It is exciting, especially when you have others to bounce ideas off, but the feeling of elation dwindles when I am alone. The doubts move in as everything thing approaches. Reality kicks in! It is difficult enough to put yourself purposely in a liminal space, even harder to lead others in as you deal with your own doubts while appearing steady and confident. You are living on hope! Is it not disingenuous? Something inside you tells you it is right, it will work. It is an intense, tiny dense seed, hope, doubt and fear are huge but not as strong as they first appear. I drew the strength from the faith of friends and colleagues.

Tina describes the fear she had building up to the day because it was not planned, the difficulty of letting go of certainty, even when this is what we want to do rather than continually work to reproduce the norms we know, particularly in education (Bourdieu, 1977b). Similarly, Mike, even though he had run a number of these events before and was confident, was nervous in his first presentation to the group. This uncertainty, or its more positive expression, freedom, was something we tried to instil in the group from the outset. We created a physical, intellectual and mental space and said, 'You are free' – not so straightforward.

A significant issue for participants can be deciding to even attend an event they don't recognize. On subsequent events we have collected comments from attending students and staff and many said they struggled with imaging how an event with no 'plan' could work, although they were intrigued. However, having attended, they were energized, inspired, had learnt news things, met new people and had conversations they could not have anticipated. If we were to describe the conference in sound it would be the sound of a busy, happy hive of bees. Our challenge, then, is to encourage participants to enter into this space, without making it too safe.

Participants were asked to introduce themselves with a one-minute video they sent before the event. This kept the introductions tight and allowed for creativity and it really helped to break the mould from the start. It gave us all an unexpected and personal view of each other. We saw character, humour, interests. Unlike a 'normal' and formal introduction, you wanted to meet these people afterwards, you had a way in to them and their lives. You wanted to know more about them, where they had filmed, the decisions they had made, why they had a life-sized Queen Elizabeth in their Hungarian living room. Asking people to be authentically present is very important, a space where everyone can be with you (Owen, 1998, p. 22).

That people felt ownership was important and we tried to get this across as soon as we could, although this is again not simple. Getting people to believe they had any ownership was difficult at first. This is where we saw their 'fear'. Participants were resistant to begin with, checking and double checking they were not misunderstanding the freedom they had. There was the feeling for some participants that they had come in spite of themselves, intrigued but hardly believing. The emotion and discomfort created here were important to move into a different phase, something we will expand upon later; we were trying to achieve a more balanced practice. As Freire says, this entails a shift in how we view knowledge creation and who is leading.

> Through dialogue, the teacher-of-the-students and the students-of-the-teacher cease to exist and a new term emerges: teacher-student with student-teachers. The teacher is no longer merely the one-who-teaches, but one who is himself taught in dialogue with the students, who in turn while being taught also teach. (Freire, p. 61)

However, it is not to say this was a perfect world. The uncertainty and people feeling their way in a new space meant there were moments of tension. One was where the normal hierarchies were brought into a session, probably unconsciously as we cannot leave behind our habituated self so easily – we will come back to this. It was not uncovered until a post-event discussion. Another occasion involved participants using the law of two feet. Although they knew this to be the right thing they were still uncomfortable with it until in dialogue with a facilitator. We realized we did not have all the answers straightaway. A short event such as ours only gives us the opportunity to trial a new way of being. It needs much more practice to overthrow our deeply engrained behaviour.

These examples remind us how hard we have to consciously work in order to break the circle of certainty as we take so many actions without thinking. Our support in facing the fear of acting and being different is trust in our own actions and in the response of others. We also asked people to have some faith in the process, and there was certainly suspicion to begin with, but people were prepared to give it a go and this seems important – without it we would have found it hard to progress. This faith-giving had other impacts, as Tina reflects: 'That trust in the process gave us a palpable sense of energy all week, in workshops, presentations or a shared meal.' Once people got rewards they started to question the process less and embrace it. Tina described how this physically manifested with one participant:

> One, participant came from a very traditional and hierarchical Catholic university. He began the week physically buttoned-up in that he always had his jacket on and buttoned. He kept on the periphery of discussions, both verbally and in the space he took up. The breaking point came after two days when he broke into a discussion about questioning authority. 'You can't ask me to do that, I can't question professors!'. Our response was why not? Although shocked, he considered this and by the next day he had unbuttoned his jacket and on the final day asked us all who would like to be involved in writing a paper about change.

We are as a young child again learning how to walk, talk and act, all the time believing we can do it. We experiment and observe what happens in response to our actions. We are not fully formed and knowledgeable; we are the child that at every turn asks, why? In our child form we are natural problematizes; how can we regain this as adults?

(Bruner, 1966). This resonates with the discussions on hopeful playful spaces in Jane and Debbie's chapter.

Hierarchies, Power and Space

Enable students to become witnesses to the material and cultural relations of power that often prevent them and others from speaking and acting in particular ways.
(Giroux describing Miklitsch, p. 80)

As Miklitsch indicates, power is important, and enabling participants to be aware of and navigate power is a crucial role of a critical pedagogue. Other big themes in the week were hierarchies, power and space. As themes they were linked to the role of the facilitator, and the group, in how they might highlight and manage them. Lea notes that people reproduced hierarchies and oppression through their behaviour without even noticing – citing how she was interrupted and dismissed by a participant in a higher position to her. As she says, it's internalized, unconscious. She goes on to say that hierarchies can be understood as a 'space-taking' thing – people in a higher position take other people's space to grow, they 'occupy' the space or set barriers (not necessarily on purpose or consciously).

She goes on to note that if people don't challenge or respond to it, we normalize it and thereby maintain the system (we don't break the circle of certainty). This was an individual example of hierarchy at work. Another, more public, example, is when the thanks came at the end of the conference. An assumption was made by the senior manager/director that Mike, the academic, had taken the lead and was thanked for his leadership, whereas Tina had created and led the week. Mike colluded with the situation by not challenging this assumption in the moment. There was also a gender issue at play. Neither were intentional, nevertheless they had an impact, which illustrates the importance of challenging power dynamics in the moment.

It therefore seems important that the operation of hierarchies and power is something that is named, and while it is the duty of all to name it, it is perhaps that facilitators role to name it if others do not. To help people be more comfortable power and hierarchies need to be highlighted during the introduction to the event. Owen also talks about the role of a facilitator is to 'create space/time and to hold space/time' (Owen, 1998, p. 20). He elaborates, saying that we should 'be present authentically', in that our attention is on what is happening in the room at that moment, rather than 'being' somewhere else. He also suggests that we be honest, be critical, share openly and let go, that is, to let go of our own sense of time and space and concentrate on what time and space is meaningful for the group at any given moment. Naming power as it operates seems to be a part of this holding.

Of particular importance seemed to be the breaking down of power barriers between academic and support staff and students. A conscious decision was not to have roles on name badges so people were not defined by them and any preconceptions could be challenged. A first-year student led one of the first sessions. A member of support staff took up roles, such as facilitating a drama workshop, that other staff had not seen them in before, and this positively challenged their perceptions as they did not know of the member of support staff's theatre expertise.

> This has definitely changed the way I see colleagues and students, particularly academic colleagues, we are all trying to work for the same thing, although it often does not feel like this. I normally feel isolated and marginalized – but not this week, which shows it does not have to be like this. (Staff participant)

However, it is not a simple dynamic. Mike asked this colleague whether others seeing her in a different role would affect how they would see her subsequently. She said that they probably would not make the connection, as she was 'invisible' – they would only see her role, which was one many were oppositional to – they would not see beyond this to the person behind. This greatly affected Mike emotionally, and has haunted him since, but positively has become a reminder of how deep prevailing hegemonies can penetrate. He could not imagine such a naturally vibrant person feeling invisible; nevertheless this was her reality. In their chapter Mike and Leoarna talk about hooks's (2004) view of the 'engaged pedagogue' – who needs to feel haunted – for it is the ghosts that stop the institution becoming the machine. Even when we cannot impact on such structural constructions of each other, we act as though we can, not in a naive way, but so that such moments become nourishing and sustaining and symbols of hope rather than ones of despair. We dance in the cracks to sustain ourselves and in the hope that in time, and in the right conditions, they can be enlarged.

Taking risks and allowing oneself to be vulnerable seemed to be a catalyst in the breaking down of barriers.

> Thinking, working and playing together. I've never seen lecturers share their vulnerabilities, but I admire them more for it, it shows that we all have them and admitting them means we build strength, not weakness. (Student participant)

Authors such as McLeod (2011), talk about the importance of vulnerability as a component of trust-building. As Tina reflects on how she presented herself to colleagues in the week:

> They knew me as strong, but I also showed my fear and they responded. You have to be vulnerable to gather the support you sometimes need. It also becomes clear that fear is not unique to oneself.

It therefore seems important to expand on what is meant by the holding of these 'spaces' – what the characteristics of these spaces are. Owen (1997) and others (Baber and Murray, 2001; Mansfield, 2015) often call on these spaces to be 'safe'. The aforementioned 'vulnerability' is not always associated with feeling safe (McLeod, 2011, Seal, 2014). Also, as Lea says, acting upon and naming power and the operation of hierarchies can be uncomfortable/emotional as it might concern the structures that give a powerful person confidence/a feeling of security. At the same time challenge should not be left to the person with least power. The powerful need to constantly check their privilege.

As Allen (2015) says, true pedagogy should embrace a lack of 'safety' as pedagogically productive, dislodging it from its negative connotations for learning (Allen, 2015, p. 767). These pedagogic spaces need to 'de-construct and reconstruct pedagogical power and knowledge, in line with critical pedagogy's ambitions. Breaking the circle might therefore be emotionally destabilising', and so has to be managed carefully, acknowledged from the outset and part of the facilitator's role. Hierarchies are something that people feel not just an abstract structure – so it should be tackled on an emotional/internal level as well as on a structural level.

Cousins (2006) talks about liminal spaces which are 'holding environments for the toleration of confusion'. Participants need to be able to 'contain' (Bion, 1961) the pain and emotionality which can result from the disruption of worldviews and the deeply held values and positions. All participants need to commit to a raw honesty, but also challenging each other, again from the outset. It needs to be acknowledged that participants will be exploring views and personal identities, with a commitment to working through previously hidden emotions and projections that need to be absorbed, detoxified and re-articulated. Initially there was a view that this containment lies within the facilitator, but this seems to perpetuate inequality and a dependency relationship. It should certainly be present within the facilitator, but not in them alone. We struggled with what term to use in describing these spaces– They are not safe, but should not be unsafe, they are liminal, but also pedagogic and are there to be re-shaped and transformed. Other key words included vulnerability as something to be embraced and that the spaces would be unpredictable, shifting, open, risky and ambiguous. Lea talked about the 'ambiguity of closeness and distance' in these spaces. In that the facilitator is both present in the group and outside of it. This is similar to Owen's description of the facilitator 'as fully present and totally invisible' (Owen 2008, p. 8). However, this responsibility is not the facilitator's alone. We all need to attend to the visceral nature of encounters, but concurrently encourage each other to abstract from the particular, and make wider links. Lea says, 'We are there to support you to find your unique way of doing things and understanding the world, I'm here for your support and assisting you in overcoming barriers and withstand ambiguity'.

Physical and Planned Space

One of the hardest sells was that there was no planned programme. It was hard to deal with for the organizers, so even harder for delegates. Even though this was clearly articulated in all promotion, it was still regarded with suspicion and there was even the expectation we would produce one on the day, to the extent that one of the delegates held up a 'programme' at the first session after Mike's introduction and said, 'You really mean it!'. The 'programme' she referred to was one we had 'fashioned' to look like one, to assuage the doubts of managers agreeing attendance and delegates themselves (see the following).

At first glance it looks like a standard week of events. However, if you look for the detail, there is none. We added an inaugural lecture and a dinner but everything else was to be decided by the delegates at the event.

The delegates were also free to reorganize time slots, lunch was whenever groups wanted it to be and sessions were not restricted to the rooms booked, as other more informal spaces were available and used during the week. An important aspect was the time taken on the first day explaining the open nature of the week and time spent together getting to know one another. This was through the short video introductions from each delegate which allowed people to be creative and concise. The first meal and social event gave us time to get to know one another and have fun building up trust and openness for the next day.

As Tina reflects:

> One of the enabling elements of our week was the spaces we were in. The simple proximity of our four rooms and the common foyer space outside them allowed us to be flexible, for people to ebb and flow, congregate and disperse at will.
>
> One of the beauties of having external visitors to work with is they highlight what you have missed. As one participant remarked, 'you have flexible furniture . . . meeting places in hallways'.

The other important element was that the group had space to reflect together, and this again had close and distant elements. Owen calls these communal times 'morning announcements' and 'evening news' and portrays them as organizing spaces, which hopefully the group takes over in time. However, our spaces seemed to take on a different characteristic. First, we also built in reflective spaces at lunchtime. Initially this was an organizational thing, in recognition that a negotiation was needed if session/groups needed time. However, it was also used as an emotional check-in, where people did share how they were feeling, their frustrations and joys.

It was at this point that several participants shared how they had found the spaces at times challenging, but that it was a challenge they were prepared to hold, linking to the importance of faith in the process, something Tina talked about earlier. Informal and evening spaces were also used in a deliberative way. The sharing of food was powerful in that discussion of the day carried on, but in an informal way, and people recognized this as part of the process. A colleague also did their professorial inaugural lecture, normally a very formal event, in a different way that challenged convention, in that it was participatory/interactive and ended with a whole audience kazoo singalong and this also became a point of discussion and reflection on how the traditional can be done differently, breaking the circle, dancing in the cracks.

Conclusion: Where is the Hope?

Impact

We observed change in participants during the week and afterwards many participants told us of the impact experiencing a different way of working has had on them. As one colleague from Germany said, 'I am a lot more relaxed about not having everything planned.' More widely, there was also a significant impact institutionally.

By concentrating on what was possible in the final session we were able to focus the participants on something achievable. Some ideas were small and easily achieved afterwards, some were major ideas that would require co-ordination and work over a longer period. But the thing was that we were clear and there was excitement that they felt they could engineer change. It was decided to change the format of the annual teaching and learning conference. This engaged a wider range of staff and students. This has then led to more engagement in the critical pedagogy group, in particular from students and in the nascent Romero Freire Centre. Beyond Newman many of the participants have engaged at home with the new experience they had during the week.

Rehearsal Space

What was particularly useful was the opportunity to rehearse working in a different way. It can be a big leap of faith to ask participants and organizers to hold such an open event. But the value is that each participant can practice using their voice, challenging power, being listened to and holding their power, listening and letting others lead. As we can see, stepping outside our comfort zone or questioning those we perceive to have more power than us can be difficult. As we experienced, there can be a lot of emotion involved in stepping into the unknown, so an opportunity for a trial performance can tell us a lot about ourselves and others. As Giroux writes, 'Critical pedagogy opens up a space where students should be able to come to terms with their own power as critically engaged citizens' (Giroux, 2011, p. 157). People wanted to know what they would get out of it and this can never be clear in advance, which makes it difficult for participants to know if it is worth committing the time. Perhaps in a way, principle one, 'Whoever comes are the right people', is true. If they have enough belief to take the chance then they are the right people because they can cope with working with the unknown. Having said that, we would try to give enough information to allow the widest range of people to feel secure enough to attend.

The Enhanced Role of the Facilitator

As well as how we set up expectations for the events we think that there are additional roles needed for the facilitator and skills needed to fulfil that role.

To Assure All That Fear Is Normal, Productive and a Sign of the Breaking down of Barriers and Conventions

This is going back to the old adage of 'feel the fear and do it anyway'. Fear is a sign that we are outside of our comfort zone, but also that we are breaking through the dominant hegemony of which we are a part. We need to support each other in this as it is an emotive process and the facilitator needs to remind people of the importance and necessity of this.

Asking for Some Faith in the Process and an Embracing of Uncertainty

People, including the facilitator, will need to have faith in the process as constant questioning of the approach can mean that you never get started. To a degree you just have to do it to see that it will work. However, this is conditional rather than unconditional faith and if, after extending faith for a time and things do not start working, the group, perhaps prompted by the facilitator, might need to ask questions about what is going on.

Holding the Space and Encouraging Others to Co-contain It

As we have said, spaces can be emotional, visceral and liminal. People might need reminding at the start of the event that this is ok, and discussions might be held about how to make it productive without trying to close it down.

Naming Power and Hierarchy as It Operates

As stated already, this is not necessarily the role of the facilitator to name, but if no one else does then perhaps they should, and then go on to ask the group why no one else named it. Hierarchy, power and privilege will operate and people need to be mindful of it and attend to it.

In terms of skills, the main one is for the facilitator to be able to see what is going on in the room in the moment, name it and work with it. Baizerman names it well, as well as outlining what it can achieve:

> facilitating the process by which an individual penetrates his taken-for-granted reality and, by so doing, comes to understand how reality for him is constructed. Thus are extended the possibilities of finding moments of/for choice, and, in this, for extending and living his freedom. (Baizerman, 1998, p. 1)

Response from Simone Helleren

I really enjoyed this reflection on the experience of Open Space Technology. The lively description of the type of terror inherent when inviting people into an experiment one is not certain will work particularly resonated with me. This is how I felt when I facilitated my first OST event for Housing Justice[1] in 2013 when working with the homelessness charity Groundswell.[2] The one-day event was called 'Hand up or hand out?' and was peopled by individuals connected in some way with faith-based homelessness projects in London. Despite having attended a training session, participated in an OST event and read and re-read Harrison Owen's (1997) brilliant

---

[1] http://housingjustice.org.uk/
[2] https://groundswell.org.uk/

book, I was a bag of nerves. OST is an invitation to take a leap into something different – different, and bereft of the traditions of conferences. As a facilitator, the only planning is deciding to use the OST format. Without a plan I personally feel vulnerable. Shifting the responsibility for solutions/outcomes onto participants can seem reckless – lazy – bonkers. But as the authors here point out – how can we avoid reproducing norms (here in education) if we perpetuate the traditions that have shaped them? It offers the alluring hope of seeing old issues anew by way of a different approach to knowledge production.

An innovation from this OST event that intrigued me was the use of video to introduce the participants. I like that it enables the shaking of foundations that occurs in OST to begin well before the event. I imagine that it alerted participants to two of the fundamental principles of OST: as the participant you are first signed up to the event because it is a topic that you *care* about; second, you will have the *responsibility* for doing something about it. Owen writes of an exercise that he uses in the early stages of the introduction to an event where he describes the care and responsibility that propel an OST event and then 'walks the circle' (1997, p. 83). Walking very slowly in silence around the inside of the circle he asks the group to follow (with their eyes) just behind him and take in each caring and willing-to-act individual. In the circle you have the eyes of all 20–100 others on you; even for a brief moment this is powerful. One also really takes account of all these individuals, not knowing anything about them – just acknowledging them minus the traditions of greeting. As a facilitator, I find this exercise excruciatingly uncomfortable but see it as my duty to go first – come into the centre of the group and be seen as the one who had this crazy plan to begin with – hopefully making it more comfortable for the first folk who will boldly come into the centre and shout out their title for the session they will facilitate. By doing this I am making myself vulnerable and showing that I did not die as a result, in the hope that this will increase the trust in the group (an essential ingredient, as the authors note) and hence increase their willingness to take risks. I am not always certain that this exercise has this effect but think that the innovation of inviting introductory interviews might be an alternative way to achieve some of the expectations of 'walking the circle' without the personal discomfort. Appealing! I wonder too if something is lost. The authors here recall Owen's concern that individuals are authentically present – this is a tall order. It requires vulnerability that is essentially uncomfortable, which 'walking the circle' delivers in truckloads.

The resistance to abandoning tradition in an OST event manifests in different ways, as the authors here illustrate. The description of folks acting out about the one law (of two feet) resonates with me; in all my experience of facilitating and participating in OST, people drag their feet when it comes to it. It tends to come down to participants not wanting to be rude to whoever is leading the discussion or fearing others second-guessing what it was that made them stand up when they did. At Groundswell we invented some ways to encourage movement between groups, including sounding a horn every ten minutes (suggesting people who wanted to move could use that moment) and giving people laminated cards with butterflies on one side and bees on the other so they could indicate to a group that they were leaving and to do what. Neither of these made much difference to the problem. As the authors point out here, it is uncomfortable. Letting go of traditions and norms is uncomfortable. The explication of an OST journey in this chapter usefully highlights some of the real challenges and the real promises of this way of working together to unseat some of the intractable issues in education specifically, and across the social world in general. 'Be prepared to be surprised' (Owen, 1998, p. 73) and be prepared to get uncomfortable.

Chapter Twenty

College-Based Higher Education

A New Hope

John Keenan and Karima Kadi-Hanifi, Response from Paula McElearney

Introduction

Having managed a higher education (HE) course based in further education (FE) settings and both worked as teachers in the sector we came to realize the strengths that the sector has: student-centred with an action-meaning and action-taking pedagogy. The FE sector (and by this term we mean the tertiary sector – all providers of education in the UK between school and university level) has provided HE-level study since the 1950s (Parry and Thompson, 2001) through universities or other validating bodies. There was no identifiable term for HE-level study in FE and it was known (and still is sometimes) by the rather cumbersome 'Higher Education in Further Education (HEinFE)', until the Association of Colleges and Association for Research in Post-compulsory Education introduced the terms 'College Higher Education (CHE)' and/or 'College-Based Higher Education (CBHE)' respectively. This lack of an established title is part of the 'terminological confusion' (Lea and Simmons, 2012) reflective of the lack of a central identity. CBHE expanded after the *Further and Higher Education Act* of 1992 which was part of a desire to increase student numbers to 50 per cent of the school-leavers in ten years (DES, 1991; Labour Manifesto, 2001), meaning universities could not meet the needs and the sector was called in to support. Today, there is a fast-growing number of institutions alongside the mainstay of the tertiary sector, FE colleges, who are able to apply for government funding to offer HE courses to students (Lea, 2016) and to award degrees though only a few have actually been granted such powers by the Privy Council (see FE Week, 2017). CBHE delivers a higher proportion of the following subjects than universities (ETF, 2016): business, administration and law; education and training; arts, media and publishing; manufacturing technology/construction. Indeed, CBHE accounts for around 10 per cent of the total HE provision in England and has done so for many years (DfES, 2003; Avis and Orr, 2016). It has 187,000 students with 240 FE colleges providing HE-level courses (UCAS, 2019). This chapter examines some of the challenges affecting the sector and why it may provide a new hope for HE. As a result of the sector's relatively lowly status in the academic hierarchy, CBHE may not be considered to constitute a worthwhile model for the development of academic as well as agentic adults. FE's history as a second-chance (and for some policymakers, second-rate) sector have given it a sense that it is a Cinderella sector, underfunded, under-appreciated – particularly as FE has been 'marginal' to government concerns (Parry, 2009; Scott, 2009). We believe, however, that CBHE is ripe for growth and it is a good time to review the way the ideas of Freire (1996), Goodson (2008) and others who herald a pedagogy of and for 'the oppressed' can be realized. Here, we are not denying that FE has adapted to the needs of a marketized, outcomes-based education but that there is 'refraction' (see Goodson and Lindblad, 2010) by lecturers who have strong beliefs in inclusive pedagogy, learner-centred teaching and local provision with diverse profiles and experiences which affect the way students are treated and taught.

What Are the Challenges Facing CBHE?

As Karl Marx and Frederick Engels predicted, capitalism must 'nestle everywhere, settle everywhere' (1848). Having in the past been funded by the state and underwritten by Local Education Authorities (LEAs), FE colleges, in 1992, in England and Wales 'became businesses, academic principals became chief executives and . . . college governors were made responsible for financial management, strategic direction and getting their institutions 'competition-ready' (AoC, 2015). Despite the initial enthusiasm with which some leaders of FE greeted the 1992 *Further and Higher Education Act* the new 'freedoms' brought new controls, which is a typical contradiction in neoliberalism (see Harvey, 2005). FE is prone to the same neoliberal trends in society, including a focus on individualism, private enterprise and accountability. While the 1992 Act was heralded as 'a defining moment of liberation' (Foster, 2005) there was external control from those funding courses including the Funding Council and Training and Enterprise Councils (in various guises over the decades). These placed the sector in 'quasi-market relations' (Avis and Orr, 2016) with government-funded bodies who wanted data justification for their money. In this battle to justify funding, 'datafication' (focusing on numbers as evidence of success – see Kitchin, 2014) and 'dataveillance' (using these numbers to monitor performance – see Mattern, 2013) are the main systems which control FE. Inevitably, this led to 'performativity', 'efficiency' and a fierce 'audit culture', or, as is critically analysed by Trotman (2018, p. 73): 'A corollary of the performative drive for efficiency is the assumption that it is possible to precisely gauge and make transparent the performance of so called core activities of organisations through the use of audit technologies'. This is no surprise given the instruction by the Committee for Public Accounts (2018) for setting up the new HE overseeing body, the Office for Students, for 'data to support robust oversight' (p. 11). To survive (and many have not) these half-private, half publicly accountable organizations 'game' the system with a focus on end-data and the new 3 'r's of recruitment, retention and results. While universities become 'tribes and territories' (Becher and Trowler, 2001) – constituted by Royal Charter (see Privy Council, 2019) with internal systems of quality assurance and external advisory monitoring by the Office for Students (OfS) and the Quality Assurance Agency (QAA) – CBHE, in addition to its own internal checks and those of the OfS and QAA, also has external scrutiny by the link universities that validate their higher education provision, as they usually do not hold degree-awarding powers as FE institutions. Such external scrutiny leads to 'managerialist' (see Randle and Brady, 1997) approaches, obsessed with business concerns (see Robson, 1998), with a focus on benchmarks and 'best business practice' and with a commitment to the brand values or 'mission statements' of the organization (Mulcahy, 2004; Simkins, 2000). CBHE lecturers, therefore, are essentially judged on how they meet targets (Simmons and Lea, 2013; see also Brown et al., 1996). As Lea and Simmons (2012, p. 4) state: 'It is our contention that these dimensions have so permeated the typical FEC, that it has had the effect of constituting a serious barrier to their ability to produce a culture of HEness.'

Those cynical of the neoliberal agenda to equalize society may believe: 'Meritocracy does not aim to create a classless society, but it legitimizes the given hierarchical structure and empowers people to be socially re-classified' (Liu, 2011, p. 391). CBHE, while reaching out to those from poorer backgrounds, may therefore be HE for 'other people's children' (Richardson, 2007) while justifying and maintaining the position of higher income groups – another 'opiate of the masses'. The Sutton Trust (2010) found that less than 2 per cent of those on free school meals (FSM) – the indicator that the UK government use to label those from low-income families – went to Russell Group universities as opposed to 26 per cent of its population from the independent school sector. In 2016 (Sutton Trust, 2016) only 50 FSM pupils went to the 'top two' universities of Oxford and Cambridge. According to Participation of Local Area figures, 60 per cent of young people in the highest fifth of the country's income groups went to university in comparison with 20 per cent in the least privileged fifth. Those in this lowest fifth are twice as likely to be in CBHE (see Harrison and McCaig, 2014) than in the university sector and, as the status of CBHE is below that of many other HE providers, it can be seen as a reproduction of social and economic differences (see Teichler, 2008). Writing more than forty years ago, Bourdieu and Passeron's (1990) study of the segmented and elitist French education system can be seen through the eyes of today's UK one, where there is a clear hierarchy of educational institutions (see also Hayward and Hoelscher, 2011). The idea that CBHE improves the lives of the poorest may be confusing us into thinking that there is genuine widening participation with the aim of erasing social inequality in society (Avis and Orr, 2016). Indeed, when we look closer, students in CBHE have very different destination profiles to those who attend universities (see Zipin et al., 2015). The proportion of graduates from FE colleges in 2010–11 employed full-time in professional occupations was 8 per cent, compared to the 23 per cent in universities (HEFCE, 2013). The average starting salaries for CBHE graduates was 16 per cent lower than those from universities (HEFCE, 2013) and in the long term CBHE graduates earn less than university graduates (see DfE, 2011). As Gale (2012, p. 138) puts it: 'While university student recruitment departments focus on "bums on seats", equity advocates draw attention to which bums, in what proportions and, more to the point, which seats, where. But if the counting of "bums" is crude, so is the differentiation of seats'.

CBHE providers hold a lowly position in the hierarchy of HE institutions. Universities position themselves in the market with budgets with which CBHE cannot compete (see Molesworth, Scullion and Nixon, 2011; Hanna-Mari, Tienari and Waeraas, 2015). In so doing, they work on the 'cultural capital' (see Bourdieu and Passeron, 1990) the university brand gives to the student (Warwick University even used the tagline 'The Cultural Capital' in 2008). Some universities gain much of their funding through government awards for research so strive to maintain their research status (Marginson, 2008). These awards and the funding give them status, ability to build statement architecture and gain privilege – such as by the way the self-nominated twenty-four-member Russell Group calls itself 'leading' (Russell Group, 2018). This battle for hierarchical position and growing global competition is revealed in HE league tables in which CBHE is not even included, making it, to use football parlance, non-league. If CBHE is recognized in government reports, it is downgraded in terms of importance and charged with connecting to the particular needs of local economies (Slane, 2015). The FE system hardly features in green and white papers except as an occasional mention that it is part of the market (this word is used fifty times in the 2016 White Paper on HE (DfE, 2016)) as an 'alternative' one, a term which the Higher Education Statistics Agency uses for some providers of CBHE (HESA, 2020b). Furthermore, FE is bundled in with other responsibilities for the Minister for Apprenticeship and Skills (see FE Week, 2017) in England and Wales, which shows that it is expected to continue to fulfil the traditional role as a provider of vocational qualifications and Higher National Certificates or Diplomas (HNCs/HNDs) and therefore be subject to the 'social and cultural prejudice against vocational education' (DfES, 2003).

Another barrier to CBHE's success is that, unlike in universities, there is comparatively little published research among CBHE lecturers compared to their counterparts in universities (Elliott 1996; Jameson and Hillier, 2003). One reason may be that CBHE is in a 'double-edged context' (Lea, 2016) where there seems to be a peculiar English malaise, set in opposition between the academic end and the vocational one; FE is suspicious of 'ivory tower' scholarship while HE is suspicious of CBHE's right to publish. This may be because CBHE departments are much smaller than university ones, so this engenders a belief that there is little discipline specialism, even within the FE institutions where HE courses exist. It could also be due to how CBHE lecturers often see themselves more as 'practitioners than as researchers or scholars' (Feather, 2011). It may also be because CBHE lecturers have a roughly 800-hour teaching contract (ATL, 2016) and so, little time for research (see Feather, 2011).

Solutions for CBHE: A New Hope

So far, with these issues in place there does not seem to be 'a new hope'. To extend the phrase's origins, it seems more like the dark forces are winning, but, just as with *Star Wars*, the 'resistance' is forever growing and the light forces of the joy of education, equality and a humanist focus are gaining power. One way this is happening at the moment is if we considered this through the conceptual lens of 'refraction'. Goodson, indeed, offers hope in the way individuals change or refract the power hierarchy through pedagogical practice which becomes resistant to waves of intermittent policies (see Goodson and Lindblad, 2010).

From our research of CBHE lecturers (see Kadi-Hanifi and Keenan, 2015, 2016) we learned how CBHE lecturers refract the concerns of management by their core belief systems including: the importance of working-class values; the storying of family history; and negative experiences at school. The CBHE lecturers we studied seemed to realize most clearly how the FE sector was a place for second chances as they had achieved success from being located within it. Coming from this centred position, CBHE provides a highly committed workforce, 'more likely to be around for most of the day and ready to offer that support, in contrast to a typical HE environment, where an academic (often for good reason) may not be so readily available' (Lea and Simmons, 2012, p. 187). This is what Tummons called FE lecturers' ethic of care (see also Noddings, 1995) which drives them towards an ethos of 'emotional labour', a form of 'supererogatory professionalism', whereby 'they attend to the bureaucratic, managerial demands of their workplaces, sometimes more-or-less willingly, invariably strategically, whilst simultaneously ring-fencing their pedagogic practice as a locus for autonomy' (Tummons, 2019, p. 11). It is not surprising, therefore, that those who teach in the CBHE sector have been distinctly recognized and targeted by SEDA (Staff and Educational Development Association) who now offer a postgraduate Award for Teaching and Learning in CBHE (SEDA, 2019) leading to recognition and eventual fellowship of the Higher Education Academy. While the widely used measures of ranking and metrics such as the TEF (Teaching Excellence Framework) are disputed (see French and O'Leary, 2017), for not only reinforcing performativity, marketization and competitiveness (not to mention the contested methodologies for judging the quality of the educational experience) out of the seventy-six institutions awarded Gold status, seventeen were CBHE providers (OfS, 2019).

Refraction can come from a celebration of the mission CBHE has to improve the lives of those from lower-income families. From the tertiary sector's creation, in Mechanics' Institutes in the late eighteenth, early nineteenth centuries (see Barton, 1993, p. 47) FE has had 'strong bonds with disadvantaged groups and communities' (Duckworth, 2014, p. 6). FE students tend to be working class (Thompson, 2009). CBHE continues this role, as HE students in colleges are more likely to be older, study part-time and come from less advantaged backgrounds than those in universities (Avis and Orr, 2016). CBHE, as a relatively new sector of HE, further widens access in a sector with substantial historical pedigree, which, since the ninth century's University of Karaouine in Morocco (UNESCO, n.d) and, in the UK, at Oxford University from the eleventh century onwards (Oxford University, n.d.), has been for adults with social and economic status. One reason for the greater affordability is that, while many universities in the UK would traditionally involve a 'rite of passage' of the student moving away from home, CBHE is community-based. CBHE contributes to what Hodgson and Spours (2013) have called 'local learning ecologies' which reflect the communities they serve with a diverse heterogeneity in both their staff and student bodies. CBHE courses are often specifically designed to provide vertical progression from their own BTEC National and A-level courses. This may be because many CBHE students have an inability or unwillingness to travel, as well as fears about the costs associated with high fees and student living. Also, if we can apply the results of McTaggart's (2016) Irish CBHE research, CBHE students may not have the appropriate capital – economic and social – to take part in university education. They also have a diverse (some might argue even 'divergent') social and cultural capital, maturity in age and outlook, family and parenting ties (including caring responsibilities) and the need to work full- or part-time (Bathmaker, 2016), all of which are among the reasons they choose to remain local. CBHE provides flexible attendance requirements, and supports learning opportunities in environments adapted to suit student needs, characteristics and capabilities (Elliott, 1999).

Refraction can come from changing perceptions about the perceived benefits of the traditional rite of passage of leaving home for HE study to allow greater consideration of the financial, familial, environmental and community benefits of studying close to home. Locality, therefore, might be the new 'pulling power' of CBHE which is positioned within a geographical community. FE has a 'vital role in vocational and community education' (Duckworth, 2014, p. 3), in meeting the needs of local communities (O'Leary and Rami, 2017) and of fostering local and regional level partnerships with employers (Hodgson and Spours, 2017). As far back as the 1956 White Paper, 'Technical education' (see National Archives Cabinet Papers, n.d.), 'meeting local needs' was a central role, while the funding council in the 1990s, the Further Education Funding Council, defined FE education as 'within reasonable daily travelling distance from (students') . . . homes' (Further and Higher Education Act, 1992). This is still the case with the March 2016 report by the Education and Training Foundation, for example, which considered CBHE's impact on 'local priorities as set by the relevant Local Enterprise Partnership (LEP) and local community' (ETF, 2017, p. 3).

For research, refraction can come from a grassroots, meaningful engagement with theory. There are powerful pedagogies of transformation that are enacted within CBHE. Kendall et al. (2016) explored how CBHE research can be shaped by both tutors and students on an equal footing, removing the conventional, hierarchical and deterministic ontology of HE-ness and giving it a new grassroots dimension which leads to successful studentship. Ingleby and Gibby (2016) also reported on the student-led positives enacted on a paralegal course in CBHE at foundation degree level. Unlike universities stuck in 'custom and practice' or as Hargreaves (1995) puts it, 'the way we do things around here', there is a more creative approach to curriculum (Ainley and Bailey, 1997; BIS, 2012). CBHE could be a push-back from the research farms universities have created in order to gain not knowledge or a contribution to humanity but the funding to build ever-larger campuses.

Conclusions

One way of refracting the current situation is to see CBHE as a settled part of the HE landscape, with each provider bringing its unique contribution to the student and the area. The alternative – setting itself up as a new force – would see CBHE as what it is not (university), which, if the rules of structural binary opposition still apply, 'university' and 'CBHE' would be considered to be opposite concepts. This would mean that, whatever HE is (elite, intelligentsia, successful, rich), it will impact on FE which will gain the opposite connotations or characteristics (commoners, mentally slow, strugglers, poor) and, 'Such a binary plays down institutional differentiation both within and between FE and HE' (Bathmaker, 2009; see Parry et al., 2012). So, we should perhaps be more aware of the uniqueness of the providers of CBHE and the way they connect with their localities, seeing beyond the binary to complexity where 'material form assumed by . . . social activity' would need to evolve over time (Richardson, 2001). Here, culture is situated in language in its wider sense of discourse (see Foucault, 1980, 1991) and is 'discernible in how lives are lived through actions and social relationships' (Geertz, 1993). It is worth considering, at a time of 'liquid modernity' (see Bauman, 2005) in a late modern or postmodern period, the amount of flexibility given to social interpretation and the liquid foundations on which the current HE hierarchy sits and, just as the 'polys' or polytechnics of thirty years ago first gained reputations for quality courses, then became universities of high standing, so might be the trajectory of CBHE.

We believe in CBHE and that through refraction there is a way of positioning it as a powerful new hope for the future of HE. The Augur Review of 2019 (see May, 2019) has further demonstrated that the trajectory of HE education could be moving towards more balance between CBHE and universities. and so we conclude that CBHE, which has come out of a social-reform past, has a thriving and a purposeful present and a bright future. We also think that there should be a fair degree of suspicion towards a governmental rhetoric of fairness and that justifying the expansion of HE through CBHE may be no more than 'hope-goading gloss' (Zipin et al., 2015) for those from lower-income families because it has not meant genuine social mobility (see Avis and Orr, 2016; Brown, Lauder and Ashton, 2008). Therefore, more needs to be done for the sector of CBHE from concerned scholars and researchers. It would help if there were collaborative research in which partners of HE and FE are treated equally and learning from each other is to be encouraged. This could lead to improvement in wider policy and practice, as CBHE is still caught out in an unequal system of higher education, fast-changing policies and lack of funding. As a result, it is sometimes unable to do what it has always done very well, which is to provide a flexible, student-centred, multi-faceted, modern, diverse and empowering education to the communities that have had (and still do have) faith in its ability to meet their needs, including those of its lecturers.

In CBHE, we need to be minded of what Le Grange has stated in her evaluation of the 'Hope' project at university level in South Africa (2011, p. 184), that: 'Performing work after Freire (in imitation of) can't mean offering hope to communities (in all scalar contexts), as if it is something that we possess and that we can give/offer. Rather hope is what emerges through serious and critical engagement in authentic partnerships with real life challenges faced by contemporary society at local, regional and global scales.' This is essential if we wanted to really liberate ourselves too, not just our students, and it is befitting at this juncture to end with what Le Grange concludes in her article, that (2011, p. 188) 'If "a pedagogy of hope" is to become useful, then it needs to be grounded in the lived experiences and interactions of people on the ground and not remain ensconced in policies or academe, nor form part of a corporate agenda.'

To end the chapter, we join with Stevenson (2019): 'in a world of privatisation of education and divisions, there is now an urgent need in the fractured English education system to build broad alliances around an alternative prospectus for education'. The kind of culture in CBHE we are advocating was summed up by James and Biesta (2007) as 'both structured and structuring', organization run in a 'dialectical process' where 'individuals can form and evolve through interaction'. CBHE is a relatively new sector and one which is being encouraged by current policy. There is the opportunity for it to realize UNESCO's recommendation of *'éducation permanente'*: lifelong, purposeful, humanistic, emancipatory and 'aimed at bringing out the full potential of human beings and enabling them to shape their societies' (Effert, 2018, p. 1). The UK should, in our view, remove from the sector those aspects which include dataveillance, market-focus, subject and institution elitism and focus on the promotion of education that brings a holistic sense of the self.

Response from Paula McElearney

This chapter provides a coherent account of CBHE, which will be an extremely useful resource for students of post-compulsory education and lifelong learning, and education studies. It moves onto a proposal for hope, within a sector which has become mired in the policy effects of neoliberal, marketized, performative and managerial cultures. CBHE has the two-fold constraint of being located in this sector, yet also being accountable to its higher education hosts. However, unlike much further education provision, CBHE may be less constricted by an instrumental, pre-packaged qualification system. This gives CBHE the potential to combine the creative intellectualism of higher education in terms of curriculum design and development, with the advantages of 'local learning ecologies' (Hodgson and Spours, 2013). This makes way for the possibility of pedagogies of hope. The authors highlight the vertical progression possibilities inherent in some further education programmes, arguably a key ingredient in widening participation. Sadly, this has been compromised in many further education colleges due to the demise of community education, adult education, and A-levels, which for some students, formed their progression route into CBHE.

The authors cite Goodson and Lindland's (2010) concept of refraction as a way for CBHE lecturers to resist current educational agendas, and provide evidence that this is indeed happening (Kadi-Hanifi and Keenan, 2015, 2016). The challenge now may be to provide opportunities for CBHE lecturers to come together in communities of practice, to support and encourage this refraction. Work is taking place in the further education sector to do this (Daley, Orr and Petrie, 2015), and it may well be that CBHE is even better placed to do this due to its greater freedoms in curriculum design and approaches to teaching. CBHE could potentially be a forerunner of pedagogies of hope in further education, lighting the way for the rest of the sector.

Conclusion

Hopeful Pedagogies Are Possible in Higher Education

Overall, we have a simple conclusion: critical hopeful pedagogies are possible in higher education, but there are permanent tensions to be ameliorated in trying to enact them. Some of the respondees in this book would question this conclusion, and call for creating other critical pedagogic space outside of the institution – we welcome this, and the debate, and it is for this reason that we invited such responses. In taking this stance we are not social liberals. We want to frame our critique as Freirean – an attack on the capitalist system through educational practices that still operate, for now, within that system. We agree that ultimately the contradictions of the neoliberal capitalist university cannot be resolved. We are not naive about the possibilities and politics – it is a question of where we start. Fighting outside of the system can be liberating, but while that freedom can be seductive it should not be conflated with effectiveness. The dull grind of working within the modern university is far less appealing and often less rewarding but it does allow the possibility of direct influence in the here and now. Yet we should not succumb to constructing it as an either/or – we have to work in tandem. The cracks that emerge from the irresolvable contradictions within the capitalist university need to be created and opened from both inside and the outside the university for maximum purchase. Working to create critical pedagogy within the university is hard and the odds are against us. We will make compromises which we will be uneasy with, and constantly need to question whether it is a compromise too far, yet, as Alinsky says, 'everyone else who wants to be effective in politics has to learn to be "unprincipled" enough to compromise in order to see their principles succeed' (Alinsky, 1989, p. 12). Moments of success are often fleeting before they are almost inevitably colonized and compromised. Yet we hope they act as beacons of hope for others and ourselves, glimpses of what *could* be to sustain us in the periods of not *yet*.

In some ways, as is discussed in Chapter 3, higher education is one of the least logical sites in which to enact critical pedagogy. What was less emphasized in that chapter was the potential for critical pedagogy in higher education. Unlike in schools, in higher education staff develop the curriculum, devise the teaching and learning strategy, quality assure and assess courses. This is also done relatively close to the ground, at lecturing team and programme manager level. I will not re-rehearse how this autonomy is being eroded, but the organizing structures remain. We may be judged on our teaching in a very reductive market-orientated way – but does this not just become another thing to subvert with our close allies, the students? The sector still talks about the concept of 'academic freedom', and, again, the degree to which this has any meaning left in it is debatable. Yet until it disappears completely it is still symbolically important, a reference point, leverage, something to signify hope.

There are a number of themes in the book that have emerged, and criss-cross across the chapters, and it has been a pleasure to bring these together collectively. We have constructed them as action points, in the spirit of critical pedagogy. Also, in keeping with its sprit, we would not expect the reader to follow them as a blueprint. They are provocations, food for thought, discussion points and perhaps occasionally solace when, as a self-identifying critical pedagogue, you find the road occasionally lonely or you feel marginalized or vulnerable. Remember this vulnerability is also a source of strength.

Self-identifying Critical Pedagogues (SICPs) Need to Cultivate Hope and Articulate Its Importance

Throughout the book every author has placed emphasis on the importance of the cultivation and maintenance of hope. However, we need to make a case for it, be clear about what kind of hope we are endorsing, and what its function is. Perhaps an examination of its opposite – hopelessness – is useful. Even Marcuse, in *One Dimensional Man*, recognized that his overwhelmingly bleak vison of capitalism's encirclement of both the material and the conceptual realms left little way out, and was not necessarily useful. Lorraine talks about this in her chapter, saying hopeful andragogy that is both relational and dialogical shines a much-needed light on an otherwise bleak and oppressive journey.

Alinsky (1989) was less forgiving, seeing in a left-doomed worldview, a glorification of failure. It is an elevation of principle over practice, where as long as values and the right analysis are maintained, failure, or worse, inaction, is preferable to compromise. Alinsky (1989) calls them rhetorical radicals 'who sacrifice the mass good for his personal conscience has a peculiar conception of "personal salvation"'; he doesn't care enough for people to 'be corrupted' for them. (Alinsky, 1989, p. 25). As Sarah and Leoarna say earlier, 'hopeful critical pedagogy is not so lofty that it cannot squeeze good work out of the pragmatism of circumstance'. Lorraine adds to this, recognizing that there is a link to autonomy and regaining a sense of self, saying that hope encapsulates 'the nature of that lost integrity which I now long to regain', which is not only achievable but is led by hope.

Alternatively, we are left with a very structural analysis, which leaves little space for individual or collective autonomy. This is where we perhaps need to look to post-critical pedagogy's contribution which, as Leoarna and Mike say, is arguing for us to act, consciously, in ways that do not (just) sustain the negative critique of the world as it is, but instead create hope through the doing of work that is performed with good intent. Similarly, Sarah says that 'hope is only a beginning; it's not a substitute for action, only a basis for it.' As Leoarna says, hope locates itself in the premise that we don't know what will happen, and that in the spaciousness of uncertainty there is room to act.

Having established the necessity for hope, what is the nature of the hope we endorse? In an earlier chapter, Mike S talked about the dangers of instilling a 'knowing hopelessness' in people. Perhaps what we are aiming for is the opposite. It is a 'knowing' hopefulness, not naive about the structural conditions we operate in, or of the chances critical pedagogues have of making a material difference. Both Mike S and Leoarna talk about a selfish radicalism that says that unless change happens in our situation and lifetime, it is a failure. Radical change is unlikely to happen, and it is selfish and consumerist to expect it to – we are a part of a greater movement, and it is others who may bear the fruit of our endeavours. At the same time, hope and utopianism are not enough in and of themselves. They have a function: to sustain us and give us a vision to carry us when prevailing hegemonies pervade our thinking, However, change is not inevitable; it will not happen just because it is right or moral, and we should never descend into letting hope become an escape. Our early years colleagues talk about hope being 'playful', and this seems attractive as a counter to misery and despondency. It also gives an image that, whatever is done to us, we will remain joyful, dance in their contradictions and play with whatever structures we are subject to. In this sense, hope can be symbolic, symbolic of what could be, and that cracks can be opened, even if they close again, many times before opening fully.

SICPs Need to Loosen, and Be Sure of, Our Boundaries, and Develop Explicit Contracts with Students Including Expectations of Each Other

Ruth successfully critiques the current 'rhetoric of potential' whereby we have an implicit contract with student that they will be materially and psychologically 'successful' after their degree. Ruth suggests that embedded contemplative practices and dialogic encounter with students can help develop an awareness of internal motivations for study and encourage questioning of assumptions about the purpose of being at university – an explicit contract should encapsulate this. Both Pete H and Mike S also talk about how the critical educational experience can be challenging, as they explore in more depth later, and we should not shy away from this in any contract.

Perhaps this redrawing of a contract can include principles of boundary crossing and border pedagogy (Freire, 1996) where we question who the expert, the educator, the knowledge giver and the knowledge creator are. This means the relatively privileged academic will need to recognize their privilege as both oppressive and constricting on them and commit to countering it at every opportunity. Our starting point should not be what students need to know, but what they already know, and furthermore what they have to teach us. It is also being honest about the limitations and boundaries that we operate within, but always trying to push them. Helen and Mike G give a visceral example of this when they were initially put into the position of the oppressor in the boundaries they put on the critical pedagogy module, until the group recognized where the true power lay. Embracing action as part of being a critical pedagogue means putting ourselves on the line. It can mean challenging our own, and more senior, managers, knowing that this might come back on us. This is something that we often expect students, with often less power and more consequences, to do every day. Challenging expected role boundaries requires a willingness to take risks and to tolerate ambiguity. It requires us to recognize the emotional and psychological investment in expected trajectories and outcomes of learning. Ruth argues for institutions to model responsiveness and curiosity when ambiguity and unexpected outcomes trigger distress in both students and staff.

SICPs Should Have a Collective Approach and Need the Right Practice Architectures to Be Effective

To put ourselves on the line means first having a group behind us to back us up and nurture us. Most authors talked about different ways that they found collective experiences powerful as 'sources of solidarity, inspiration, information, and as sites of critical exchanges and stirring each other into critical language'. They are part of what Debbie and Jane call a relational pedagogy Brownlee and Berthlesen (2005). Mike S explores this more in his second chapter, seeing that the danger of the lone SICP is that they become a tolerated maverick at best and are waiting to be picked off at worst. Identifying as a lone SICP is in danger of being indulgent – there is a martyrdom in being the only radical in the village. It is rarely true; it means we have to define ourselves against a negative other; the group can achieve more together and we need others to hold each other to account for when hegemony and our privilege bites, which it will always do. While there is some symbolic power in the martyr, they are utopian symbols and idealistic rather than pragmatic. Alinsky calls them suicidal radicals who 'take took the grand cop-out, suicide. To these I have nothing to say or give but pity – and in some cases contempt, for such as those who leave their dead comrades and take off for other points' (Alinsky, 1989, p. xvii). A self-identified radical professor, who doesn't acknowledge the enormous privilege they have, is rarely something to be admired.

However, a group is not enough; structural conditions, contextual practices and individual actors interrelate and constrain us in complex ways. We need the right practice architectures (Kemmis et al., 2012, 2014). These can be cultural-discursive (university mission; discourses regarding pedagogy); material-economic (allocation of staff to subjects; employment of casual vs continuing staff; workshops spaces; staff meeting spaces; workload allocation; staff–student ratios; study leave); and social-political (decision-making; surveillance measures; power attached to particular positions). Mahon (2014) found other enablers to include student engagement, student feedback and positive student–teacher relationships. All the chapters give examples of ways that individuals and teams are trying to do this with students.

The theme of Leoarna and John's chapters are staff–student partnerships, which are both symbolic and catalysts for a questioning of staff–student relationships and seem to have made for a cultural change in relationships in some quarters of Newman. Mahon (2014) also calls for having opportunities to influence curriculum with 'opportunities for critical dialogue, building relationships, challenging assumptions, and drawing critical resources into the pedagogical encounters' (Mahon, 2014, p. 76). Again, several chapters show how, even with some strong managerial resistance, teams are managing to do this, and that higher education mechanisms can be imaginatively worked with.

It is only through such a collective, and the critical pedagogy group, and now the Romero Freire Institute that we can begin to counter the disablers that Mahon (2014) catalogues, such as the intensification of academic work, the lack of (or diminishing) teacher–student contact time, over-regulation and standardization of practice, promotion of technical, virtual, neoliberal constructions of pedagogical practice, and a shift from a critical and collegial culture to one of compliance and competition. Examples of these battles for integrity and meaning can be found throughout this book.

Critical Pedagogical Spaces Should Be Authentic, Visceral, Pedagogic and in the Moment, but Not Necessarily Safe

Tina and Mike S, Helen, Jane, Pete H, Pete S and Leoarna all talk about the nature of critical pedagogic spaces. Safety seems to make sense in a therapeutic context, but may hold less in a pedagogical one. The breaking down of perceptual barriers, even if they oppress you, is not an easy emotional process. As Pauline describes, a lot of emotions need to be held, worked with, and as she, Pete H and Mike S go on to say, be deconstructed, detoxified and re-articulated. This takes particular skills. Lecturers in tutor groups, used by the foundation year and youth and community work, need the confidence not to lead, and not to privilege their interpretations, but to let others develop their ideas, sometimes stumbling, sometimes in a flurry of articulation. These spaces will be visceral, emotionally charged and not always rational and linear (at least not in a traditional, covertly masculine sense), but liminal and horizontal.

Most importantly, in terms of our own skills as pedagogues, we need to be able to work in the moment. Critical reflective practice (Finlay, 2008) has this tradition but the skills of reflective in action are under-theorized (Trelfa, 2016). Ruth argues that a critical contemplative pedagogy also encourages a paradoxical approach to change whereby intentionality and authenticity arise from moment-by-moment awareness of experience. Working viscerally in the moment also dovetails with our desire to develop agency, for it is in these moments that we are existentially free, and we should cherish them as they may give us the fortitude to carry on when putting these ideas into practice. As Baizerman emphasizes (1989), experience of critical reflective spaces should be

> a facilitating process in which an individual penetrates her taken-for-granted reality and, by so doing, comes to understand how reality for her is constructed. Thus are extended the possibilities of finding moments of (for) choice and, in this, for extending and living her freedom. Critical Pedagogy is a process of creating the opportunities for a person to choose more often about more things in her everyday life and in this way more thoroughly construct herself.

Crucially, the desire for safety is often a call from the privileged (Seal, 2018, 2019c). The oppressed are quite used to functioning in unsafe, unstructured, emotionally driven and fractious circumstances. The question must be asked: who is this place of safety for? This is not to deny that they should be unsafe, fearful of damaging spaces, but interpretations of what constitutes these terms need to be deconstructed and negotiated.

SICPs Should Not Forget Our Indigenous Knowledges Once We Enter HE

One phenomenon to come out of the critical pedagogy group, and it is present in this volume in contributions from early years and, to a degree, youth and community work colleagues, is the collective amnesia people experience regarding their indigenous knowledge of what is good educational practice once they enter academia. Both traditions, although sometimes drawing on different authors, emphasize non-traditional learning, experimentation, use of self, play, non-linear and scaffolded approaches etc. Yet somehow when we come into academia, we feel we have to adhere to a conventional lecture, then seminar, structure. Within the context of research Smith (1999) talks about how indigenous ways of knowing are colonized, and people are asked to operate a double consciousness towards what they know they know, and supress and undermine its validity. I think this extends to pedagogy within higher education.

I remember vividly at a session I ran for the foundation year network throwing out the challenge that we should stop doing lectures as we know they rarely work and, in times of virtual learning environments, are moribund as a means of information transmission, let alone learning. The collective intake of breath and then defensive reactions afterwards were telling. I remember one colleague talking to me afterwards and saying that he constantly did not feel, and was challenged as not being, a 'proper' lecturer, so if I took lectures away from him, what did he have left. This is where we do need to resist the neoliberal constructions of pedagogy that favour the content transmission of knowledge because it can be 'measured' and supports an economic imperative for lecture halls with hundreds of people in them

SICPs Have More in Common than We Do Difference, Across Subjects and Staff Divides – Our Differences Enrich Us

Reading the chapters in this book and sitting in our editorial meetings foregrounded that most of the authors, despite coming from a variety of academic and practice backgrounds, were coming from a similar place theoretically and pedagogically without realizing it. A common author was Freire, but there was a plethora of different subject specific authors that were enriching, and thus the cannon expands. As Pete argues, 'disciplinary splits can hinder processes of inquiry into the contemporary social relations in which both students and tutors in higher education are enmeshed'. Another division between academics are the multiple inherent hierarchies. We had associate lecturers on exploitative part-time and temporary contracts, senior lecturers, readers, and professors writing. A friend of Mike S pointed out the contradiction of being a reader (denoting distinguished research and scholarly record in the subject, an international expert) in critical pedagogy (which rejects hierarchies of knowledge worth and supports the democratization of its creation). We lived such contradictions and tried and use their tensions productively. We commented on each other's work critically and without regard to rank. This was not always easy, as we often slipped back into hegemonic roles but learnt to hold each other to account when we did this.

As Tina discusses in her chapter, perhaps the biggest division that needed, and needs, to be overcome is between academic and professional and support staff. As she notes, differences between staff can at times feel like apartheid both with differences of conditions and of focus. However, borrowing the somewhat colonized term, we are all meant to be working towards enhancing the same student experience. A crucial distinction here is that knowledge creation is traditionally seen as the preserve of academics, something we have tried to dispel in this book. Of particular interest in this regard are third-space professionals such as Sarah, Leoarna, Tina, Peter S and Lorraine, who write about the phenomena as well as about their own pedagogical practice. They seem to occupy spaces of support and transition, with unifying features of empowering students to transcend their experiences, recognize their own worth and develop the resilience necessary to traverse the sometimes-disabling landscapes of higher education. Third-space professionals are seen as both the future and an example of the dissolving of academic/professional/support staff divisions (Whitchurch, 2008).

However, the division remains that academics are, at least in theory, given research time while professional and support staff members of staff are not. In the critical pedagogy group, we heard multiple tales of colleagues and managers being suspicious of their attending the critical pedagogy group (what has it to do with their job?), let alone engaging with research and knowledge creation. More insidiously, some colleagues censored themselves in that they did not ask managers if they could have time for the group, believing that the answer they would get would be 'no'. Others did not see research as their role. We need to articulate the value and necessity of engaging all staff in pedagogic research, including their managers – their contracts need to reflect this so that they and managers have the leverage to achieve this.

Students are Pedagogues, Producers and Partners, not Consumers and Customers

Equally important, hence warranting its own section, but indivisible from the previous point, is that we need to articulate and enact a new relationship with our students. Leoarna and John's principles for partnership are a great starting point. However, we have to acknowledge the tensions trying to change our relationship with students brings. Many students are used to consumer and customer models. They, as us, have to learn that their knowledge and ways of knowing have legitimacy. Many, as described in Tina and Mike S's, John and Leoarna's, and other chapters, embrace the visceral excitement of becoming a partner, producer and pedagogue. However, this reaction is not universal. Many of our students come to us with their prime motivation being a better paying job at the end of the degree, and they pay a lot of fees for their degree. The consumer and customer model is seductive in its promise of putting the student at the centre of the educational experience and the undoing of this deception can lead to anger and disillusionment.

Finding out that degrees are not all equal, even if they are equally hard, can be difficult. A degree from a Russell Group university is different from a degree at Newman, particularly how it is received in the marketplace (Belfield et al., 2018). Even harder is the realization that more important than the degree and where it is from, are the contacts you make on your degree (Granovetter, 2018), and they are likely to be more wide-ranging at Oxford than at Newman. Harder still is knowing that even more important than the contacts you make is the contacts your parents have (Macmillan, Tyler and Vignoles, 2015). These factors are difficult not to get disillusioned about, particularly for widening participation students. The potential is for learned hopelessness to comes back and bite us all; as a student said in the foundation year chapter, 'I knew I was oppressed from when we looked at it in the first semester and now it's just making me feel hopeless'. We therefore also have to maintain and cultivate the hope that we mentioned earlier. Staff need to realize their relative privilege and use what power they have to undo and deconstruct this privilege.

However, there are mechanisms that, while often intended to reinscribe existing economic arrangements, can work to our advantage. Impact is something we can still demonstrate more easily than others and while purists would argue that we are in danger of reinscribing its legitimacy, any act in higher education is in danger of this. We need to be mindful of the dangers and use it to our advantage. Particularly under-used is the idea of public engagement and the legitimation of impact on pedagogic practice within higher education – we can demonstrate this in our partnerships with students and should take advantage of it.

Being Student- and Staff-centred Have Been Colonized Terms. Do Not Invest in Internal Conflicts and Let Them Become Part of Your Identity Terms – We Need to Move Towards Being Human

Many of the authors in this volume have talked about the penetration of the thinking of neoliberalism, neo-conservatism and new managerialism into higher education, and this is no better exemplified than the term 'student-centred' and 'staff-centred'. Perhaps more insidious are accusations, and counter-accusations, of being neoliberal between staff. Constructions from management of staff being obstinate, lazy, unrealistic, selfish and the cause of inertia do not help. Similarly, sweeping accusations of management being neoliberal, vindictive, biased, bullying and managerialist are unhelpful. This is not to say that there are many legitimate examples of both, and they should be dealt with appropriately, but when whole groups of colleagues are constructed in this way there is no room to move.

Familiar cries of 'that is above my pay grade', or 'that is management's responsibility' – or, conversely, management platitudes of 'we are all in this together', when we patently aren't, doing consultations that aren't acted on or pretending decisions are democratic, when they are not – re-enforce institutional divides. Perhaps worse is where management has abdicated the management function itself, often concurring with staff feeling that the resolution of conflicts is all management's responsibility. Institutions need to look at their wider cultures as there are often ingrained conflicts which both sides have invested in and have come to define their subjectivities and identifies. This results in cultures where positivity is squashed, innovation seen as something to be exploited, and awkwardness and negativity rewarded on all sides.

In the development of the last strategic plan at Newman the term 'human' seemed to have resonance. It started from the fact that we are small, so, surely, we can treat each other humanely. It also started from a debate among professors and readers of what they wanted from the plan and from the new vice chancellor who was being recruited. There was a divide between those who wanted the vice chancellor to be an academic (ill-defined but seen as the opposite to being a manager, favourable to research and scholarship, or certainly academics) or a manager (to manage those individuals that need managing, though, obviously, not them). Human is a term that Freire used frequently, and as a counter to the dehumanizing effects of oppression on those subject to it. It has interestingly not been colonized by neoliberalism, probably because of its collective connotations. Being human seemed a way that we could break how we were constructing each other and allow for movement, even if it was still within the cracks.

It is, like many terms, contested. It is also in danger of being essentialist. However, this is not the way that Freire used it – he did not think there was a *fixed* human nature but saw it as an evolving, shifting thing. Freire was materialist in that there is an objective world, and that there are real causal mechanisms in that world, physical and social, independent of human perception, but as our perception of them is partial at best, our account of them is equally partial and contingent. However, he was also not a relativist; he did not see value in human nature being viewed as entirely social constructed. To do so falls into the aforementioned neo-Marxist trap of seeing capitalism as a monolithic hegemonic machine that constructs an understanding of being human that we cannot escape. Human agency disappears, as does hope.

For Freire, human nature is transfactual (Martinez, Martin and Marlow, 2014) and gives a person room to feel outside our received hegemony and therefore have the potential to challenge the social constructions we are subject to. Otherwise, neoliberalism would be an unbreakable hegemony, an inescapable part of the ideological state apparatus; yet even within the most oppressive regimes people's impulses come through such conditioning. There is therefore potential to rescue the idea of agency. It is an impulse, logical or not, and while we may not be able to escape our language to articulate it, we are nevertheless aware of it, and it disrupts us. This disruption allows us to break, albeit temporarily, our social conditioning. For Freire, being human means we will revolt and resist.

We Can Work Within Higher Educations' Structures, but Continually Need to Push Them and Highlight Their Absurdity

A central tenant of this book is that it is possible to work meaningfully and enact hopeful critical pedagogies within the structures of higher education. We are not saying that it is always possible, or that meaningful critical pedagogy cannot happen outside of, and adjunct to, higher education. We can joke that the Teaching Excellence Framework is not about teaching or excellence, and is not a framework, or that the Office for Students is neither an office, or for students. However, these mechanisms and evaluative frameworks are here, and look like they are here to stay for the foreseeable future.

However cynically we view it, the Conservatives have made manifesto commitments to strengthen academic freedom and free speech in higher education, to strengthen universities' and colleges' civic role and require the Office for Students to look at universities' success in increasing access across all ages, not just young people entering full-time undergraduate degrees. Inevitably, given their ideologies, this will be constructed through a market lens, but we can engage with these processes, try and make them work for us, and, where they do not, highlight their absurdity.

As stated before, we can engage with quality systems and make them work for us, with chapter examples of negotiated and evolutionary learning outcomes and curriculum, negotiated assessments, students assessing their own work and creative placements. Colleagues' cries of 'I would love to do that but our structures do not allow it' often do not bear out. Karima and John's chapter also illustrates that exciting work can be carried out in our partnership with FE, who may actually have longer traditions of working with marginalized groups, or dedication to a critical pedagogy and of finding spaces to enact it. Mike Neary has been developing co-operative universities alongside traditional higher education and appreciating the cross-fertilization that is possible.

Perhaps most interesting is the co-operative college's bid to become a university. While the *Higher Education and Research Act 2017* has been robustly criticized for encouraging and allowing private providers into the higher education sector, it simultaneously removed some of the barriers for alternative providers and the co-operative college subsequently committed to seeking university status. The college is characterized by 'deeply democratic structures, based on full student and member participation, equality and decent work'. They intend that the Co-operative University will be governed by a democratically elected board with staff and student representation. All staff and students will be members of the university with full voting rights at the AGM.

Planned degrees include a BA in International Development and Co-operation: theory, practice and possibilities; BA – Social Movements and Parallel Histories: organizing, shaping and learning; BA – Co-operative Leadership, Culture and Management; PG Certificate – Co-operative Education and Practice. Future degree offer will include subjects such as democratic practice, social and community organizing, community history and culture, human ecology, art and community, alternative forms of social and economic organization and the nature and future of work.

The first common module is perhaps an indicator of exciting things to come. It is called 'Co-operative learning, research and practice'. It aims to prepare all students to become skilled and confident co-operators and motivated and critical learners. Students are introduced to new ways of thinking about alternative models of social and economic organization and will learn to: work both as an individual and as a collective, supporting each other's academic development; apply a range of exciting and creative research, study and communication skills; reflect on, critically review and comment on our work; engage in structured group work; and be an active co-operator

SICPs Need to Help Rearticulate What a University Is and Could Be

In Chapter 3 Mike S explored in part what modern universities are and could be. Mahon (2014) defined their aspects as knowledge and cultural production, civic responsibility and economic development. The recent Pearson debates posed whether they are about the preservation of knowledge and inquiry regardless of society's civic needs or are an instrument for social mobility. Inevitably, a university is a mix of Mahon's (2014) functions, and the Pearson debates set up an artificial binary that is not helpful.

The last thirty years have seen the growth of higher education with a concurrent eroding of further education, adult education and meaningful apprenticeships. Higher education has taken advantage of this erosion. Our partnership and forays into these areas have often been motivated by expanding student numbers, rather than any desire for genuine partnership or to widen participation. A chance was missed with the abolition of polytechnics in 1992 to honour the difference between polytechnics and universities and define the 'new' university. Former polytechnics, even more so colleges of higher education, firmly became second- and third-class distinctions. Rather than trying to articulate and cement their different approach, 'new' universities accepted their status and tried to game going up the league tables designed to place them low, to escape the stigma. Yet the divides remain.

Prestige funding has been ever more concentrated in the Russell Group in recent years (Millionplus, 2016). Old universities have an apprenticeship for lecturers/researchers whereby they build up their Arts and Humanities Research Council and Economic and Social Research Council profiles in ways that 'new' universities have never been in a position to do. Pedagogy and education have been marginalized as subjects and teaching relegated to something we do until we have got enough funding to get our PhD student to do it, so we can get on with the 'real' job of research. In many institutions the return to concern about student numbers and experience is largely driven by a reduction in research funding. 'New' universities buy in professors in the hope that they will bring in funding and kudos only to find that most of both stays with the prestige institution they came from. New universities also tolerate professors and readers who, even when they produce the outputs, rarely cover their wages in the income they bring in and their contributions to REF returns similarly do not bring in substantive income. Research is subsidized by teaching, and the promise of research-informed teaching rarely seems value for money. 'New' universities cling to their 'researchers' and a dwindling pool of similarly unprofitable doctoral students in the hope of developing a 'research culture', as otherwise, what is it to be a 'university'?

Commitment to social mobility in the guise of widening participation is espoused by most universities and governments, though increasingly not in the form of giving resources. Yet widening participation as a term misses the point. It is premised on persuading and 'supporting' marginalized groups to achieve a 'standard' that was purpose-built to keep them out and engage with a higher education system that was never designed with them in mind, and in some ways was designed to exclude them. The Office for Students is committed to eliminating the recruitment, continuation and attainment gap in higher education with no regard for the structural issues at play. When this fails, as it inevitably will, we need to be there with arguments about why this has happened, and, more importantly, for how a university could reorientate itself to come close to achieving these things.

To do this we need to change our whole pedagogic approach and notion of what constitutes legitimate knowledge creation and dissemination. We need to change our internal and external partnerships and relationships with each other in order to do this. Research and teaching are not only not in opposition, they are indistinguishable, a part of the same process. Research and pedagogy should not need to 'demonstrate' impact, for without impact, neither is true research or pedagogy. We have a civic responsibility, because engagement with the community is also a necessary part of effective research and pedagogy. However, it is going to be far more political than we imagined. A recent report showing that Muslims are retreating from civil society and engagement (Commission for Islam and Public Life, 2017) reveals the political nature of the project ahead.

Market mechanisms will not provide what we need to stimulate the economy or address the climate crisis (Klein, 2014). We need critical innovative thinkers and neoliberal and new-public-management approaches to higher education have been shown to fail to provide such graduates. Social mobility is more than a moral imperative for a modern university, it is what is needed for our economy and planet to thrive. We need people to realize and develop their potential for economic, ecological as well as social justice reasons. When the seemingly all-pervasive market and neoliberal approaches collapse under the weight of their own irrationality, critical pedagogues need to be waiting in the wings with new answers and visions. This collapse also needs to be managed and facilitated, as it is not inevitable, and neoliberalism will go a lot further and deeper before it happens. There is also a danger that if it penetrates too far there will be little to build from, if all hope has been extinguished. As Freire says:

Without a minimum of hope, we cannot so much as start the struggle. (Freire, 2014, p. 3)

References

AbuHilal, F. and Abu-Shomar, A. (2014), 'On pedagogy and resistance: Unravelling the post-colonial politics in the literature classroom', *Realis*, 4 (2): 176–92.

Ainley, P. and Bailey, B. (1997), *The Business of Learning: Staff and Student Experiences of Further Education in the 1990s*, London: Cassell.

Akinbosede, D. (2019), 'The BAME attainment gap is not the fault of BAME students', *THE*, 5 December 2019.

Aliakbari, M. and Faraji, E. (2011), 'Basic principles of critical pedagogy', *Paper Presented at 2nd International Conference on Humanities, Historical and Social Sciences* [IPEDR] Vol. 17.

Alinsky, S. (1971), *Rules for Radicals*, Chicago: Random House.

Alinsky, S. D. (1989), *Rules for Radicals: A Practical Primer for Realistic Radicals*, New York: Vintage.

Allen, L. (2015), 'Queer pedagogy and the limits of thought: Teaching sexualities at university', *Higher Education Research & Development*, 34 (4): 763–75.

Altbach, P. G. (2004), 'Globalisation and the university: Myths and realities in an unequal world', *Tertiary Education & Management*, 10 (1): 3–25.

Altbach, P. G., Reisberg, L. and Rumbley, L. E. (2009), 'Trends in global higher education: Tracking an academic revolution' (A report prepared for the UNESCO 2009 World Conference on Higher Education). Available at: http://atepie.cep.edu.rs/public/Altbach,_Reisberg,_Rumbley_Tracking_an_Academic_Revolution,_UNESCO_2009.pdf.

Amos, V. and Doku, A. (2019), *Black, Asian and Minority Ethnic Student Attainment at UK Universities: #Closingthegap*, London: Universities UK and NUS.

Amsler, S. (2013), 'Criticality, pedagogy and the promises of radical democratic education', in S. Cowden and G. Singh (eds), *Acts of Knowing: Critical Pedagogy In, Against and Beyond the University*, 61–84, London: Bloomsbury.

Amsler, S. (2015), *The Education of Radical Democracy*, London: Routledge.

Andreotti, V. (2011), *Actionable Postcolonial Theory in Education*, New York: Palgrave MacMillan.

Andrews, K. (2016), 'Changing the nature, not just the face, of the academy', in K. Andrews and L. A. Palmer (eds), *Blackness in Britain*, 203–14, Abingdon: Routledge.

Andrews, K. and Palmer, L. A., eds (2016), *Blackness in Britain*, Abingdon: Routledge.

Antonucci, L. (2016), *Student Lives in Crisis*, Bristol: Policy Press.

AoC (2015), Available at: https://www.aocjobs.com/article/history-of-further-education-1945-1992/.

AoC (2018a), Available at: https://www.aoc.co.uk/sites/default/files/AoC%20College%20Key%20Facts%20201718%20%28web%29.pdf.

AoC (2018b), Available from: https://www.aoc.co.uk/about-colleges/college-mergers.

Arao, B. and Clemens, K. (2013), 'From safe spaces to brave spaces. The art of effective facilitation: Reflections from social justice educators', 135–50.

Arendt, H. (1961), 'The crisis in education', in H. Ardent (ed.), *Between Past and Future: Eight Exercises in Political Thought*, New York: The Viking Press.

Arendt, H. (1968), 'Education, markets and audit culture', *Critical Quarterly*, 47 (1–2): 11–29.

Aristotle (1976), *The Nicomachean Ethics*, London: Penguin.

Aron, L. (2013), *A Meeting of Minds: Mutuality in Psychoanalysis*, London: Routledge.

Aronowitz, S. and Giroux, H. (1985), 'Radical education and transformative intellectuals', *CTheory*, 9 (3): 48–63.

AtL (2016), Available from: https://www.atl.org.uk/advice-and-resources/rights-and-conditions/lecturers-employment-rights-summary-further-education-0.

Augar, P. Chair (2019), 'Independent panel report to the review of post 18 education and funding'. Available at: https://assets.publishing.service.gov.uk/government/uploads/system/uploads/attachment_data/file/805127/Review:of_post_18_education_and_funding.pdf (accessed 20 June 2019).

Ausabel, D. (1968), *Educational Psychology: A Cognitive View*, New York: Holt, Rinehart and Winston.

Avis, J. and Orr, K. (2016), 'HE in FE: Vocationalism, class and social justice', *Research in Post-Compulsory Education*, 21 (1–2): 49–65.

Baber, K. M. and Murray, C. I. (2001), 'A postmodern feminist approach to teaching human sexuality', *Family Relations*, 50 (1): 23–33.

Back, L. (2015), 'Blind pessimism and the sociology of hope', *Discover Society*, Issue 27. Available at: http://discoversociety.org/2015/12/01/blind-pessimism-and-the-sociology-of-hope/ (accessed 14 July 20).

Back, L. (2018), 'Taking and giving hope: A response to Ros Gill's "What Would Les Back Do? If Generosity Could Save Us… a Review of Les Back's Academic Diary: Or Why Higher Education Still Matters (2016: Goldsmiths Press, 272 pp)"', *International Journal of Politics, Culture, and Society*, 31 (1): 111–25.

BACP (2018), *Ethical Framework for the Counselling Professions*, Lutterworth: BACP. Available at: https://www.bacp.co.uk/events-and-resources/ethics-and-standards/ethical-framework-for-the-counselling-professions/ (accessed 20 June 2019).

Bae, B. (2009), 'Children's right to participate – Challenges in everyday interactions', *European Early Childhood Education Research Journal*, 17 (3): 391–406.

Baizerman, M. (1989), 'Why train youth workers', *The Child Care Worker*, 7 (1): 1–8.

Baizerman, M. (1998, December), 'Rites of passage: From here to there, from now to then, along these roads and paths', *Child and Youth Care Forum*, 27 (6): 441–5.

Ball, J. and Pence, A. (2001), 'A generative curriculum model for supporting child care and development programs in the first nation communities', *Journal of Speech-Language Pathology and Audiology*, 25 (20): 114–24.

Ball, J. and Pence, A. R. (1999), 'Beyond developmentally appropriate practice: Developing community and culturally appropriate practice', *Young Children*, 54 (2): 46–50.

Ball, S. (2007), 'Intellectuals or technicians? The urgent role of theory in educational studies', in M. Hammersley (ed.), *Educational Research and Evidence-Based Practice*, 106–20, London: Open University Press/Sage.

Ball, S. (2013), *Foucault, Power, and Education*, Abingdon, Oxon: Routledge.

Ball, S. (2017), *The Education Debate*, 3rd edn, Bristol: The Policy Press.

Ball, S. J. (2004), *Education for Sale! The Commodification of Everything? King's Annual Education Lecture*, London: University of London.

Ball, S. J. (2012), 'Performativity, commodification and commitment: An I-Spy guide to the Neoliberal University', *British Journal of Educational Studies*, 60 (1): 17–28. doi: 10.1080/00071005.2011.650940.

Barad, K. (2007), *Meeting the Universe Halfway*, Durham: Duke University Press.

Bari, M. (2014), 'Who does not agree with British values that are universal?' Available at: https://tinyurl.com/vo6hwxw (accessed 29 January 2020).

Barnett, R. (2000), 'University knowledge in an age of supercomplexity', *Higher Education*, 40: 409–22. https://doi.org/10.1023/A:1004159513741.

Barnett, R. (2007), *A Will to Learn: Being a Student in an Age of Uncertainty*, London: Open University Press.

Barnett, R. (2008), 'Critical professionalism in an age of super complexity', in B. Cunningham (ed.), *Exploring Professionalism*, London: Bedford Way Papers.

Barton, S. (1993), 'The mechanics institutes: Pioneers of leisure and excursion travel'. Available at: https://www.le.ac.uk/lahs/downloads/1993/1993%20(67)%2047-58%20Barton.pdf.

Bathmaker, A. (2009), 'Further higher project working paper 5 fieldwork studies: The making and shaping of student transitions in "Dual Sector" institutions'. Available at: http://www.shef.ac.uk/furtherhigher/.

Bathmaker, A. M. (2016), 'Higher education in further education: the challenges of providing a distinctive contribution that contributes to widening participation', *Research in Post-Compulsory Education*, 21 (1–2): 20–32.

Batsleer, J. (2012), *What Is Youth Work*, London: Learning Matters.

Batsleer, J. and Davies, B. (2010), *What Is Youth Work?*, Exeter: Learning Matters.

Bauman, Z. (2000), *Liquid Modernity*, Cambridge: Polity Press.

Bauman, Z. (2005), *Liquid Life*, Cambridge: Polity Press.

Bauman, Z. (2007), *Consuming Life*, Cambridge: Polity Press

Baxter-Magolda, M. (2012), 'Building learning partnerships', *Change*, 1: 32–8.

Bay, D. and Daniel, H. (2001), 'The student is not the customer—An alternative perspective', *Journal of Marketing for Higher Education*, 11 (1): 1–19.

BBC (2019), 'Dying for a Degree (2019)', *BBC One Television*, 30 May. Available at: https://www.bbc.co.uk/programmes/m0005jsb (accessed 16 June 2019).

Becher, T. and Trowler, P. (2001), *Academic Tribes and Territories: Intellectual Enquiry and the Cultures of Disciplines*, Buckingham: Open University Press.

Beckman, A. and Cooper, C. (2013), 'Neoliberal globalisation, managerialism and higher education in England: Challenging the imposed "order of things"', *Educational Policy Analysis and Strategic Research*, 8 (1): 5–24.

Beckmann, E. A. (2018), 'Professional staff, professional recognition: Bringing learner support staff into the fellowship of university educators', in C. Bossu and N. Brown (eds), *Professional and Support Staff in Higher Education. University Development and Administration*, Singapore: Springer.

Beisser, A. (1970), 'The paradoxical theory of change', in J. Fagan and I. L. Shepherd (eds), *Gestalt Therapy Now*, 77–80, Gouldsboro: Gestalt Therapy Press. Available at: http://www.gestalttherapy.org/wp-content/uploads/2014/09/paradoxical_theoryofchange.pdf (accessed 20 June 2019).

Belfield, C., Britton, J., Buscha, F., Dearden, L, Dickson, M., van der Erve, L. Sibieta, L., Vignoles, A. Walker, I. and Zhu, Y. (2018), *The Relative Labour Market Returns to Different Degrees*, London: Institute for Fiscal Studies.

Bell, L. (2012), 'Teaching in public: Participation and access in twentieth century education', in H. Stevenson, L. Bell and M. Neary (eds), *Towards Teaching in Public: Reshaping the Modern University*, London: Continuum.

Belton, B., ed. (2014), *'Cadjan–Kiduhu': Global Perspectives on Youth Work*, New York: Springer.

Beniston, J. and Harris, D. (2017), 'To engage or not to engage? That is the question, students' perceptions of engagement at a West Midlands University', *The Journal of Educational Innovation, Partnership and Change*, 3: 135–46.

Benjamin, J. (2004), 'Beyond doer and done to: An intersubjective view of thirdness', *Psychoanalytic Quarterly*, 1: 5–46.
Benjamin, J. (2007), 'Intersubjectivity, thirdness and mutual recognition', in *Institute for Contemporary Psychoanalysis, Los Angeles, CA, 2007*.
Benjamin, J. (2013), *Shadow of the Other: Intersubjectivity and Gender in Psychoanalysis*, London: Routledge.
Benjamin, J. (2017), *Beyond Doer and Done To: Recognition Theory, Intersubjectivity and the Third*, London: Routledge.
Bentham, J. (1789), *A Introduction to the Principles of Moral and Legislation*, Oxford: Clarendon Press.
Berlak, A. (2004), 'Confrontation and pedagogy: Cultural secrets and emotion in anti-oppressive pedagogies', in M. Boler (ed.), *Democratic Dialogue in Education: Troubling Speech, Disturbing Silence*, 123–44, New York: Peter Lang.
Bhopal, K. (2018), *White Privilege: The Myth of a Post-Racial Society*, Bristol: Policy Press.
Bion, W. R. (1959), 'Attacks on linking', *International Journal of Psychoanalysis*, 40: 308–15.
Bion, W. R. (1961), *Experiences in Groups and Other Papers*, London: Tavistock Publications.
Bion, W. R. (1962a), 'A theory of thinking', *International Journal of Psychoanalysis*, 43: 306–10.
Bion, W. R. (1962b [1984]), *Learning from Experience*, London: Karnac.
Bion, W. R. (1962c), 'The psychoanalytic study of thinking', *International Journal of Psycho-Analysis*, 43: 306–10.
Bion, W. R. (1963), *Elements of Psychoanalysis*, London: Heinemann.
BIS (2012), 'Understanding Higher Education in Further Education colleges'. Available from https://assets.publishing.service.gov.uk/government/uploads/system/uploads/attachment_data/file/32425/12-905-understanding-higher-education-in-further-education-colleges.pdf.
Black, P. (1998), *Testing: Friend or Foe? Theory and Practice of Assessment and Testing*, London: Routledge Falmer.
Bleiklie, I. (1998), 'Justifying the evaluative state: New pubic management ideals in higher education', *European Journal of Education*, 33 (2): 299–316.
Boler, M. and Zembylas, M. (2003), 'Discomforting truths: The emotional terrain of understanding differences', in P. Tryfonas (ed.), *Pedagogies of Difference: Rethinking Education for Social Justice*, 110–36, New York: Routledge.
Bolton, G. (2010), *Reflective Practice, Writing and Professional Development*, 3rd edn, Thousand Oaks: SAGE Publications.
Borg, C., Buttigieg, J. and Mayo, P., eds (2002), *Gramsci and Education*, Lanham: Rowman and Littlefield Publishers.
Bossu, C. and Brown, N., eds (2018), *Professional and Support Staff in Higher Education, University Development and Administration*, Singapore: Springer.
Bourdieu, P. (1975), 'The specificity of the scientific field and the social conditions of the progress of reason', *Social Science Information*, 14 (6): 19–47.
Bourdieu, P. (1977a), *Outline of a Theory of Practice*, Cambridge: Cambridge University Press.
Bourdieu, P. (1977b), *Reproduction in Education, Society and Culture*, trans. R. Nice, London: Sage.
Bourdieu, P. (1998), 'The essence of neoliberalism, Le Monde Diplomatique'. Available at: https://mondediplo.com/1998/12/08bourdieu.
Bourdieu, P. (2010), *Distinction*, London: Routledge.

Bourdieu, P. and Passeron, J. (1990), *Reproduction in Education, Society and Culture*, London: Sage.

Bovill, C. and Felten, P. (2016), 'Special issue: Engaging students as partners in learning and teaching: Implications for academic development', *International Journal for Academic Development*, 21 (1): 1–3.

Braa, D. and Callero, P. (2006), 'Critical pedagogy and classroom praxis', *Teaching Sociology*, 34 (4): 357–69.

Bradbury, H. and Reason, P. (2008), *The Sage Handbook of Action Research: Participative Inquiry and Practice*, London: SAGE.

Bradford, S. and Cullen, F. (2014), 'Positive for youth work? Contested terrains of professional youth work in austerity England', *International Journal of Adolescence and Youth*, 19 (suppl. 1): 93–106.

Brady, J. (1994), 'Critical literacy, feminism, and a politics of representation', *Politics of liberation: Paths from Freire*, 2: 142–53.

Braidotti, R. (2012), 'Nomadic ethics', in D. Smith and H. Somers-Hall (eds), *The Cambridge Companion to Deleuze*, 170–97, Cambridge: Cambridge University Press.

Braidotti, R. (2013), *The PostHuman*, Cambridge: Polity Press.

Breunig, M. (2005), 'Turning experiential education and critical pedagogy theory into praxis', *The Journal of Experiential Education*, 28 (2): 106–23.

Brito, I., Lima, A. and Auerbach, E. (2004), 'The logic of nonstandard taching: A course in Cape Verdean language, culture, and history', in B. Norton and K. Toohey (eds), *Critical Pedagogies and Language Learning*, 181–200, Cambridge: Cambridge University Press.

Brookfield, S. D. (2005), *The Power of Critical Theory for Adult Learning and Teaching*, Maidenhead: Open University Press.

Brown, L., Seddon, T., Angus, L. and Rushworth, P. (1996), 'Professional practice in education in an era of contractualism: Possibilities, problems and paradoxes', *Australian Journal of Education*, 40 (3): 311–27.

Brown, P., Lauder, H. and Ashton, D. (2008), 'Education, globalisation and the future of the knowledge economy', *European Educational Research Journal*, 7 (2): 131–56.

Brownlee, J. (2004), 'Teacher education students' epistemological beliefs: Developing a relational model of teaching research', *Education Journal*, 72 (1): 1–17.

Brownlee, J. and Berthelsen, D. (2005), 'Personal epistemology and relational pedagogy in early childhood teacher education programmes', *Early Years: An International Journal of Research*, 26 (1): 17–29.

Bruner, J. (1966), *Towards a Theory of Instruction*, Cambridge, MA: Belknap Press.

Buckley, W. (1998), *Society – A Complex Adaptive System: Essays in Social Theory*, Luxembourg: Gordon and Breach Publishers.

Budd, Y., Kell, M. and Humphry, N. (2015), 'Graduate outcomes: A generative curriculum model for international students', *Research and Development in Higher Education: Learning for Life and Work in a Complex World*, 38: 21–30.

Bullen, E., Kenway, J. and Fahey, J. (2010), 'The knowledge economy and research governance: How we got to where we are', in J. Blackmore, M. Brennan and L. Zipin (eds), *Re-positioning University Governance and Academic Work*, 53–66, Rotterdam: Sense.

Burke, C. and Grosvenor, I. (2013), 'The Steward Street School experiment: A critical case study of possibilities', *British Educational Research Journal*, 39 (1): 148–65.

Burke, P. and Hayton, A. (2011), 'Is widening participation still ethical?' *Widening Participation and Lifelong Learning*, 13 (1): 8–26.

Burrawoy, M. (2005), '2004 American Sociological Association presidential address: For public sociology', *The British Journal of Sociology*, 56 (2). doi: 10.1111/j.1468-4446.2005.00059.x.

Bush, M. (2011), 'Mindfulness in higher education', *Contemporary Buddhism*, 12 (1): 183–97. doi: 10.1080/14639947.2011.564838.

Butler, J. (1990), *Gender Trouble*, New York: Routledge.

Butler, J. (2011), *Gender Trouble: Feminism and the Subversion of Identity*, London and New York: Routledge.

Cabinet Office (2011), *Opening Doors, Breaking Barriers: A Strategy for Social Mobility*, London: Cabinet Office.

Cagliari, P., Castagnetti, M., Giudici, M., Rinaldi, C., Vecchi, V. and Moss, P. (2016), *Loris Malaguzzi and the Schools of Reggio Emilia: A Selection of his Writings and Speeches, 1945-1993*, London: Routledge.

Calhoun, C. (2006), 'The university and the public good', *Thesis Eleven*, 84 (1): 7–43.

Callinicos, A. (1999), 'Social theory put to the test of politics: Pierre Bourdieu and Anthony Giddens', *New Left Review*, 236: 77–102.

Cameron, H. and Billington, T. (2017), '"Just deal with it": Neoliberalism in dyslexic students' talk about dyslexia and learning at university', *Studies in Higher Education*, 42 (8): 1358–72.

Carey, P. (2013), 'Student as co-producer in a marketised higher education system: A case study of students' experiences of participation in curriculum design'. *Innovations in Education and Teaching International*, 50 (3): 250–60.

Carr, M. (2001), *Assessment in Early Childhood Settings: Learning Stories*, London: Paul Chapman.

Carr, W. and Kemmis, S. (1989), *Becoming Critical: Education, Knowledge and Action Research*, Lewes: Falmer.

Carruthers Thomas, K. (2019), *Rethinking Student Belonging in Higher Education: From Bordieu to Borderlands*, London: Routledge.

Cates, R., Madigan, M. and Reitenauer, V. (2018), '"Locations of possibility": Critical perspectives on partnership', *International Journal of Students as Partners*, 2 (1): 33–46.

Cazden, C. (2012), 'A framework for social justice in education', *International Journal of Educational Psychology*, 1 (3): 178–98.

Chappell, D. (2004), 'Buddhist social principles', in K. Dockett, R. Dudley-Grant and C. Bankart (eds), *Psychology and Buddhism: From Individual to Global Community*, 259–74, New York: Kluwer.

Cho, S. (2010), 'Politics of critical pedagogy and new social movements', *Educational Philosophy and Theory*, 42 (3): 310–25.

Cho, S., Crenshaw, K. and McCall, L. (2013), 'Toward a field of intersectionality studies: Theory, applications, and praxis', *Signs*, 38 (4): 785–810.

Chow, E., Fleck, C., Fan, G.-H., Joseph, J. and Lyter, D. (2003), 'Exploring critical feminist pedagogy: Infusing dialogue, participation, and experience in teaching and learning', *Teaching Sociology*, 31 (3): 259–75.

Clandinin, D. J. and Connelly, F. M. (2000), *Narrative Inquiry: Experience and Story in Qualitative Research*, San Francisco: Wiley.

Clandinin, D. J. and Connelly, F. M. (2004), 'Knowledge, narrative and self-study', in J. J. Loughran, M. L. Hamilton, V. K. LaBoskey and T. L. Russell, *International Handbook of Self-Study of Teaching and Teacher Education Practices*, 575–600, Dordrecht: Springer.

Clark, L. (2018), 'Critical pedagogy in the university: Can a lecture be critical pedagogy?', *Policy Futures in Education*, 16 (8): 985–99.

Clark, S., Hahn, H. and Hoggett, P. (2008), *Object Relations and Social Relations: The Implications of the Relational Turn in Psychoanalysis*, London: Karnac.

Cleary, J. and Hogan, P. (2001), 'The reciprocal character of self-education: Introductory comments on Hans-Georg Gadamer's address "education is self-education"', *Journal of Philosophy of Education*, 35 (4): 519–27.

Coffield, F. (2008), 'Just suppose teaching and learning became the first priority...', *Learning Skills Network*. Available at: https://weaeducation.typepad.co.uk/wea_education_blog/files/frank_coffield_on_teach_and_learning.pdf (accessed 06 October 2019).

Cohen, L., Manion, I. and Morrison, L. (2007), *Research Methods in Education*, 6th edn, London: Routledge.

Coleman, R. and Ringrose, J., eds (2013), *Deleuze and Research Methodologies*, 1st edn, Edinburgh: Edinburgh University Press Ltd.

Collini, S. (2012), *What are Universities For?* London: Penguin.

Committee for Public Accounts (2018), Available from: https://publications.parliament.uk/pa/cm201719/cmselect/cmpubacc/736/736.pdf.

Competition and Markets Authority (2016), 'Letter from the CMA to Higher Education providers'. Available at: https://www.gov.uk/government/publications/letter-from-the-cma-to-higher-education-providers-on-its-compliance-review (accessed 20 June 2019).

Comstock, P. W. (2015), 'The politics of mindfulness', *Democracy and Education*, 23 (2): 1–4.

Connell, R. (2013), 'The neoliberal cascade and education: An essay on the market agenda and its consequences', *Critical Studies in Education*, 54 (2): 99–112.

Connell, R. W., Ashenden, P. J., Kessler, S. and Dowsett, G. W. (1982), *Making the Difference*, Sydney: George Allen and Unwin.

Conway, M. and Dobson, I. (2003), 'Fear and loathing in university staffing: The case of Australian academic and general staff', *Higher Education Management and Policy*, 15 (3): 123–33.

Cook-Sather, A., Bovill, C. and Felten, P. (2014), *Engaging Students as Partners in Learning and Teaching: A Guide for Faculty*, San Fansisco: Jossey Bass.

Cook-Sather, A. and Felten, P. (2017), 'Ethics of academic leadership: Guiding learning and teaching', in F. Su and M. Wood (eds), *Cosmopolitan Perspectives on Academic Leadership in Higher Education*, London: Bloomsbury.

Cooper, C. (2015), 'Critical pedagogy in higher education', in C. Cooper, S. Gormally and G. Hughes (eds), *Socially Just, Radical Alternatives for Education and Youth Work Practice*, 39–64, London: Palgrave Macmillan.

Cousin, G. (2006), 'An introduction to threshold concepts', *Planet*, 17: 4–5.

Cowden, S. and Singh, G. (2013), *Acts of Knowing: Critical Pedagogy in, Against and Beyond the University*, 240 pp, London: Bloomsbury Publishing.

Crenshaw, K. (1989), 'Demarginalizing the intersection of race and sex: A black feminist critique of antidiscrimination doctrine, feminist theory and antiracist politics', *The University of Chicago Legal Forum*, 140: 139–67.

Crick, B. (2004), 'The novel as a Satire', in H. Bloom (ed.), *Bloom's Guides – George Orwell's 1984*, New York: Chelsea House.

Crotty, M. (1998), *The Foundations of Social Research*, London: Sage.

Cuthbert, R. (2010), 'Students as customers?', *Higher Education Review*, 42 (3): 3–25.

Dahlberg, G. and Moss, P. (2005), *Ethics and Politics in Early Childhood Education*, London: Routledge.

Dahlberg, G., Moss, P. and Pence, A. (2013), *Beyond Quality in Early Childhood Education and Care: Languages of Evaluation*, 3rd edn, London: Routledge.

Dale-Rivas, H., ed. (2019), *The White Elephant in the Room: Ideas for Reducing Racial Inequalities in Higher Education*, London: HEPI.
Daley, M., Orr, K. and Petrie, J., eds (2015), *Further Education and the Twelve Dancing Princesses*, London: IOE Press.
Darder, A., Baltodano, M. and Torres, R. D. (2003), *The Critical Pedagogy Reader*, New York: Routledge.
Darder, A., Mayo, P. and Paraskeva, J., eds (2016), *The International Critical Pedagogy Reader*, Abingdon: Routledge.
Darder, A., Torres, R. and Baltodeano, M., eds (2017), *The Critical Pedagogy Reader*, 3rd edn, Abingdon: Routledge.
Davies, B. (2018), 'Ethics and the new materialism: A brief genealogy of the 'post'philosophies in the social sciences', *Discourse: Studies in the Cultural Politics of Education*, 39 (1): 113–27.
Davies, B. and Bansel, P. (2005), 'The time of their lives? Academic workers in neoliberal time(s)', *Health Sociology Review*, 14 (1): 47–58.
Davies, B. and Bansel, P. (2007), 'Neoliberalism and education', *International Journal of Qualitative Studies in Education*, 20 (3): 247–59.
Davies, M. and Barnett, R. (2016), *The Palgrave Handbook of Critical Thinking in Higher Education*, 648 pp, London: Springer.
Davies, R. (2012), 'Youth work, "Protest" and a common language: Towards a framework for reasoned debate', *Paper Delivered at the Annual Conference of the Association of Lecturers in Youth and Community Work 2012, Lake District*.
Davis, A. (2014), *Lecture*, Carbondale: Southern Illinois University.
DBIS (Department for Business, Innovation and Skills) (2016), *Higher Education: Success as a Knowledge Economy - White Paper*, London: HMSO. Available at: https://www.gov.uk/government/publications/higher-education-success-as-a-knowledge-economy-white-paper.
De Houwer, J., Barnes-Holmes, D. and Moors, A. (2013), 'What is learning? On the nature and merits of a functional definition of learning', *Psychonomic Bulleting and Review*, 20: 631–42.
De St Croix, T. (2018), 'Youth work, performativity and the new youth impact agenda: Getting paid for numbers?' *Journal of Education Policy*, 33 (3): 414–38. doi: 10.1080/02680939.2017.1372637.
Dearing Report (1997), *Higher Education in the Learning Society*, London: HMSO.
DeCharms, R. C. (1968), *Personal Causation: The Internal Affective Determinants of Behaviour*, New York: Academic Press.
Deci, E. L. (1971), 'Effects of externally mediated rewards on intrinsic motivation', *Journal of Personality and Social Psychology*, 18 (1): 105–15.
Deem, R. and Brehony, K. (2005), 'Management as ideology: The case of "new managerialism" in higher education', *Oxford Review of Education*, 31 (2): 217–35.
Degener, S. (2001), 'Making sense of critical pedagogy in adult literacy education', *Review of Adult Learning and Literacy*, 2 (2): 23–45.
Dei, G. J. S., ed. (2010), *Fanon and the Counterinsurgency of Education*, Rotterdam: Sense.
Dei, G. J. S. and Simmons, M., eds (2010), *Fanon and Education: Thinking Through Pedagogical Possibilities*, 2nd edn, New York: Peter Lang.
Deleuxe, G. and Guattari, F. (2000), *A Thousand Plateaus: Capitalism and Schozophrenia*, London: Continuum.
Deleuze, G. and Guattari, F. (1994), *What Is Philosophy?* New York: Columbia University Press.

Delucchi, M. and Korgen, K. (2002), '"We're the customer – we pay the tuition": Student consumerism among undergraduate sociology majors', *Teaching Sociology*, 30: 100–7.

Department for Business, Innovation and Skills – DBIS (2010), 'Securing a sustainable future for higher education: An independent review of higher education funding and student finance'. Available at: https://www.gov.uk/government/publications/the-browne-report-higher-education-funding-and-student-finance (accessed 20 March 2018).

Department for Business Innovation and Skills – DBIS (2011), 'Higher education: Students at the heart of the system'. Available at: https://www.gov.uk/government/uploads/system/uploads/attachment_data/file/31384/11-944-higher-education-students-at-heart-of-system.pdf (accessed 01 May 2012).

Department for Business, Innovation and Skills – DBIS (2016), 'Higher education: Teaching excellence, social mobility and student choice'. Published 16 May 2016

Department for Education – DFE (2017a), 'Inclusive teaching and learning in higher education as a route to excellence'. Available at: https://assets.publishing.service.gov.uk/government/uploads/system/uploads/attachment_data/file/587221/Inclusive_Teaching_and_Learning_in_Higher_Education_as_a_route_to-excellence.pdf (accessed 25 November 2019).

Department for Education (2017b), 'Unlocking talent, fulfilling potential, a plan for improving social mobility through education'. Available at: https://assets.publishing.service.gov.uk/government/uploads/system/uploads/attachment_data/file/667690/Social_Mobility_Action_Plan_-_for_printing.pdf (accessed 20 June 2019).

Department of Education (2018), 'New package of measures announced on student mental health'. Available at: https://www.gov.uk/government/news/new-package-of-measures-announced-on-student-mental-health.

Department of Education (2019), 'Post-18 review of education and funding: Independent panel report: A report from the independent panel to the review of post-18 education and funding'. Available at: https://www.gov.uk/government/publications/post-18-review-of-education-and-funding-independent-panel-report.

DES (1991), *White Paper: Higher Education: A New Framework*, London: HMSO.

DfE (Department for Education) (2010), 'The importance of teaching'. Available at: https://www.gov.uk/government/uploads/system/uploads/attachment_data/file/175429/CM-7980.pdf.

DfE (Department for Education) (2011), 'Youth cohort study & longitudinal study of young people in England (2010), The Activities and Experiences of 18 Year Olds: England 2009–2010'. Available at: https://www.gov.uk/government/statistics/youth-cohort-study-and-longitudinal-study-of-young-people-in-england-the-activities-and-experiences-of-19-year-olds-2010.

DfE (2016), 'Educational excellence everywhere'. Available from https://www.kelsi.org.uk/__data/assets/pdf_file/0005/55841/Summary-DfE-White-Paper-Educational-Excellence-Everywhere.pdf.

DfES (Department for Education and Skills) (2003), *The Future of Higher Education*, London: HMSO.

Dhillon, S. (2018), 'Whose wellbeing is it anyway?', *Journal of Learning Development in Higher, Special Edition: 2018 ALDinHE Conference*. Available at: http://journal.aldinhe.ac.uk/index.php/jldhe/article/view/460.

Disabled Students Allowance Quality Assurance Group – DSA-QAG (2016), 'Updates'. Available at: https://www.dsa-qag.org.uk/application/files/7214/8705/6024/DSA_Guidance_NEW_DSA_Students_in_AY_2016-17_0916.pdf (accessed 01 July 2019).

Disabled Students Allowance Quality Assurance Group – DSA-QAG (2017), 'Non-medical helper providers: Quality assurance framework'. Available at: https://dsa-qag.org.uk/application/files/7215/1213/6252/NMH_Quality_Assurance_Framework_V2.0.pdf (accessed 06 June 2018).

Doku, A. (2018), 'OfS board appointments and the death of irony', *WonkHE*. Available at: http://wonkhe.com/blogs/the-death-of-irony/ (accessed 08 March 2018).

Donnelly, M. and Gamsu, S. (2018), *Home and Away: Social, Ethnic and Spatial Inequalities in Student Mobility*. Project Report, London: The Sutton Trust.

Downs, Y. (2017), 'Neoliberalism and the value of higher education', in T. Rudd and I. Goodson (eds), *Negotiating Neoliberalism: Developing Alternative Educational Visions*, 59–71, Rotterdam: Sense.

Driscoll, M. (2000), *Psychology of Learning for Instruction*, Needham Heights: Allyn and Bacon.

Duckworth, V. (2014), *How to be a Brilliant FE Teacher*, London: Routledge. Available at: https://www.ucl.ac.uk/ioe/departments-centres/centres/centre-for-post14-education-and-work/projects/fe-skills-four-countries-uk/pdf/FE_and_Skills_-_the_case_of_England_Final.pdf.

Duckworth, V. and Tummons, J. (2010), *Contemporary Issues in Lifelong Learning*, Maidenhead: McGraw Hill.

Dweck, C. (2014), 'The power of believing that you can improve', *TED Talks*. Available at: https://www.ted.com/talks/carol_dweck_the_power_of_believing_that_you_can_improve (accessed 20 June 2018).

Ecclestone, K. and Hayes, D. (2008), *The Dangerous Rise of Therapeutic Education*, London: Routledge.

Ecclestone, K., Hayes, D. and Furedi, F. (2005), '"Knowing me, knowing you": The rise of therapeutic professionalism in the education of adults', *Studies in the Education of Adults*, 37 (2): 182–200.

Edwards, C. (1983), 'Student-centred learning and trade union education: A preliminary examination', *The Industrial Tutor*, 3 (8): 45–54.

Effert, M. (2018), *UNESCO's Utopia of Lifelong Learning: An Intellectual History*, Abingdon: Routledge.

Egan, K. (1988), *Teaching as Storytelling*, London: Routledge.

Eide, B. L. and Eide, F. F. (2012), *The Dyslexic Advantage: Unlocking the Hidden Advantage of the Dyslexic Brain*, New York: Plume.

Elias, J. L. and Merriam, S. (1980), *Philosophical Foundations of Adult Education*, Huntington: Robert E. Krieger Publishing Co.

Elliott, G. (1996), 'Why is research invisible in further education?', *British Educational Research Journal*, 22 (1): 101–11.

Elliott, G. (1999), *Lifelong Learning: The Politics of the New Learning Environment*, London: Jessica Kingsley.

Elliott, J. and Nicholson, R. (2016), *Dyslexia Developing the Debate*, London: Bloomsbury Academic.

Elliott, J. G. and Grigorenko, E. L. (2014), *The Dyslexia Debate*, New York: Cambridge University Press.

Ellsworth, E. (1989), 'Why doesn't this feel empowering? Working through the repressive myths of critical pedagogy', *Harvard Educational Review*, 59: 297–324.

Enright, E., Coll, L., Chroinin, D. N. and Fitzpatrick, M. (2017), 'Student voice as risky praxis democratising physical education teacher education', *Physical Education and Sports Pedagogy*, 22 (5): 459–73.

Erikson, E. H. (1959), 'Identity and the life cycle: Selected papers', *Psychological Issues*, 1: 5–173.
ETF (2016), 'The local impact of college based higher education'. Available at: https://www.et-foundation.co.uk/wp-content/uploads/2016/04/CHELIS-report-final.pdf.
ETF (2017), Education and Training Foundation. June 2017.
Fanon, F. (1952 [1986]), *Black Skin White Masks*, London: Pluto Press.
FE Week (2017), Available at: https://feweek.co.uk/2017/11/30/miltons-mission-an-interview-with-the-apprenticeships-skills-minister/.
Feather, D. (2011), 'Culture of HE in FE – Exclave or enclave?', *Research in Post-Compulsory Education*, 16 (1): 15–30.
Feather, D. (2016), 'Organisational culture of further education colleges delivering higher education business programmes: Developing a culture of "Heness" – What next?', *Research in Post-Compulsory Education*, 21 (1–2): 98–115.
Feldman, Z. and Sandoval, M. (2018), 'Metric power and the academic self: Neoliberalism, knowledge and resistance in the British University', *Triple C: Communication, Capitalism and Critque: Journal for a Global, Sustainable Information Society*, 16 (1): 214–33.
Felten, P., Abbot, S., Kirkwood, J., Long, A., Lubicz-Nawrocka, T., Mercer-Mapstone, L. and Verwood, R. (2019), 'Reimagining the place of students in academic development', *International Journal of Academic Development*, 24 (2): 192–203.
Felten, P. and Lambert, L. (2020), *Relationship-rich Education: How Human Connections Drive College Success*, Baltimore: John Hopkins University Press.
Fielding, M. (1999), 'Radical collegiality: Affirming teaching as an inclusive professional practice', *Australian Educational Researcher*, 26 (2): 1–34.
Finlay, L. (2008), *Reflecting on 'Reflective Practice*, Milton Keynes: Open University.
Finnis, J. (2011), *Intention and Identity: Collected Essays II*, Oxford: Oxford University Press.
Fisher, B. and Cordeiro, P. (1994), 'Generating curriculum: Building a shared curriculum', *Primary Voices K–6*, 2 (3): 2–7.
Fisher, M. (2009), *Capitalist Realism: Is there no Alternative?*, London: John Hunt Publishing.
FitzSimmons, R. and Uusiautti, S. (2014), 'Critical revolutionary pedagogy spiced by pedagogical love', *Journal for Critical Education Policy Studies*, 11 (3): 1–11. Available at: http://www.jceps.com/archives/444.
Foley, P. (2007), 'A case for and of critical pedagogy: Meeting the challenge of library education at Gallaudet University', *Paper Presented at the American Communication Association's Annual Conference, Taos, New Mexico*.
Foster, A. (2005), *Realising the Potential: A Review of the Future Role of FE Colleges*, Nottingham: DfES. Available at: http://dera.ioe.ac.uk/5535/.
Foucault, M. (1971), 'Orders of discourse', *Social Science Information*, 10 (2): 7–30.
Foucault, M. (1979), *Discipline and Punish: the Birth of the Prison*, London: Penguin.
Foucault, M. (1980), *Power/Knowledge: Selected Interviews and Other Writings 1972–1977*, Brighton: Harvester Wheatsheaf.
Foucault, M. (1990), *The History of Sexuality: An Introduction*, London: Penguin Books.
Foucault, M. (1991), *Discipline and Punish: The Birth of the Prison*, London: Penguin
Foucault, M. (1995 [1975]), *Discipline & Punish: The Birth of the Prison*, trans. Alan Sheridan, New York: Vintage Books.
Foucault, M. (1998 [1976]), *The Will to Knowledge the History of Sexuality Volume 1*, trans. Robert Hurley, London: Penguin Books.
Francis, B. and Skelton, C. (2005), *Reassessing Gender and Achievement*, London: Routledge.

Freire, A. (2007), 'Introduction', in P. Freire (ed.), *Daring to Dream: Toward a Pedagogy of the Unfinished*, London: Paradigm.
Freire, P. (1970), *The Pedagogy of the Oppressed*, London: Penguin Books.
Freire, P. (1972a), *Cultural Action for Freedom*, London: Penguin Books.
Freire, P. (1972b), *Pedagogy of the Oppressed*, Harmondsworth: Penguin Books.
Freire, P. (1976), *Education: The Practice of Freedom*, London: Writers and Readers Publishing Cooperative.
Freire, P. (1985), *The Politics of Education: Culture, Power and Liberation*, trans. Donaldo Macedo, Westport: Bergin & Garvey Publishers, Inc.
Freire, P. (1990), 'Educational practice', in M. Horton and P. Freire (eds), *We Make the Road by Walking: Conversations on Education and Social Change*, 145–90, Philadelphia: Temple University Press.
Freire, P. (1993), *Pedagogy of the Oppressed*, New York: Continuum Books.
Freire, P. (1995), *Pedagogy of Hope: Reliving Pedagogy of the Oppressed*, New York: Continuum.
Freire, P. (1996), *Pedagogy of the Oppressed*, London: Penguin Books.
Freire, P. (1997), *Pedagogy of the Heart*, New York: Continuum.
Freire, P. (2000), *Pedagogy of Freedom: Ethics, Democracy, and Civic Courage*, Lanham and Oxford: Rowman & Littlefield Publishers.
Freire, P. (2004a), *EPZ Pedagogy of Hope: Reliving Pedagogy of the Oppressed*, London: A&C Black.
Freire, P. (2004b), *Pedagogy of Hope*, London: Continuum.
Freire, P. (2004c), *Pedagogy of Indignation*, Boulder: Paradigm.
Freire, P. (2006), *Pedagogy of the Oppressed*, 30th edn, London: Continuum.
Freire, P. (2007), *Daring to Dream: Toward a Pedagogy of the Unfinished*, London: Paradigm.
Freire, P. (2016 [1974]), *Education for Critical Consciousness*, trans. Myra Bergman Ramos, London: Bloomsbury Academic.
Freire, P. (2017), *Pedagogy of the Oppressed*, Middlesex: Penguin Books.
Freire, P. and Macedo, D. (1987), *Literacy Reading the Word and the World*, South Hayley: Bergin & Garvey Publishers, Inc.
French, A. and O'Leary, M., eds (2017), *Teaching Excellence in Higher Education: Challenges, Changes and the Teaching Excellence Framework*, Bingley: Emerald Publishing Ltd.
Freud, S. (1929 [2002]), *Civilization and Its Discontents*, London: Penguin.
Fromm, E. (1977), *To Have or to Be?* New York: Harper and Row.
Frosh, S. (2003), 'Psychosocial studies and psychology: Is a critical approach emerging', *Human Relations*, 56 (12): 1545–67.
Further and Higher Education Act (1992). Available from https://www.legislation.gov.uk/ukpga/1992/13/contents.
Gadamer, H.-G. (2013 [1975]), *Truth and Method*, trans. Joel Weinsheimer and Donald G. Marshall, London: Bloomsbury Academic.
Gale, K. (2018), *Madness as Methodology: Bringing Concepts to Life in Contemporary Theorising and Inquiry*, Abingdon: Routledge.
Gale, T. (2012), 'Towards a southern theory of student equity in Australian higher education: Enlarging the rationale for expansion', *International Journal of Sociology of Education*, 1 (3): 238–62.
Gale, T. and Parker, S. (2014), 'Navigating change: A typology of student transition in higher education', *Studies in Higher Education*, 39 (5): 734–53.

Geertz, C. (1993), *The Interpretation of Cultures*, London: Fontana.
Gewirtz, S., Ball, S. J. and Bowe, R. (1995), *Markets, Choice and Equity in Education*, Buckingham: Open University Press.
Gewirtz, S. and Cribb, A. (2009), *Understanding Education: A Sociological Perspective*, Cambridge: Polity Press.
Giannakaki, M. S., McMillan, I. D. and Karamichas, J. (2018), 'Problematising the use of education to address social inequity: Could participatory action research be a step forwards?', *British Educational Research Journal*, 44 (2): 191–211.
Gibbs, G. (2010), *Dimensions of Quality*, York: HEA.
Gibbs, P., Angelides, P. and Michaelides, P. (2004), 'Preliminary thoughts on a praxis of higher education teaching', *Teaching in Higher Education*, 9 (2): 183–94.
Giddens, A. (1976), *New Rules of Sociological Method: A Positive Critique of Interpretative Sociologies*, London: Hutchinson.
Gill, R. (2009), 'Breaking the silence: The hidden injuries of neo-liberal academia', in R. Flood and R. Gill (eds), *Secrecy and Silence in the Research Process: Feminist Reflections*, 228–84, London: Routledge.
Gillard, D. (2018), 'Education in England: A history (online only)'. Available at: www.educationengland.org.uk/history (accessed 17 June 2018).
Gilroy, P. (1987 [2002]), *There Ain't No Black in the Union Jack: The Cultural Politics of Race and Nation*, Abingdon: Routledge Classics.
Gimyah, S. (2018), 'Delivering value for money in the age of the student', *HEPI Annual Conference*. Available at: https://www.gov.uk/government/speeches/delivering-value-for-money-in-the-age-of-the-student (accessed 15 June 2018).
Giroux, H. (1992), *Border Crossings: Cultural Workers and the Politics of Education*, New York: Routledge.
Giroux, H. (2004), 'Cultural studies, public pedagogy and the responsibility of intallectuals', *Communication and Critical/Cultural Studies*, 1 (1): 59–79.
Giroux, H. (2006), 'The promise of democracy and Edward Said's politics of worldliness', in C. Robbins (ed.), *The Giroux Reader*, 297–313, Boulder: Paradigm.
Giroux, H. (2010), 'Rethinking education as the practice of freedom: Paulo Freire and the promise of critical pedagogy', *Policy Futures in Education*, 8 (6): 715–21.
Giroux, H. (2019), 'Pedagogical terrorism and hope in the age of fascist politics', *Counterpunch*. Available at: https://www.counterpunch.org/2019/05/10/pedagogical-terrorism-and-hope-in-the-age-of-fascist-politics/.
Giroux, H. and Giroux, S. (2006), 'Challenging neoliberalism's new world order: The promise of critical pedagogy', *Cultural Studies, Critical Methodologies*, 6 (1): 21–32.
Giroux, H. A. (1997), *Pedagogy and the Politics of Hope Theory, Culture and Schooling*, Boulder: Westview Press.
Giroux, H. A. (2001), *Theory and Resistance in Education: Towards a Pedagogy for the Opposition*, Westport: Bergin & Garvey.
Giroux, H. A. (2004), 'Critical pedagogy and the postmodern/modern divide: Towards pedagogy of democratization', *Teacher Education Quarterly*, 31 (1): 132–53.
Giroux, H. A. (2010), 'Bare pedagogy and the scourge of neoliberalism: Rethinking higher education as a democratic public sphere', *Educational Forum*, 74 (3): 184–96.
Giroux, H. A. (2011), *On Critical Pedagogy*, London: Continuum.
Giroux, H. A. (2014), *Neoliberalism's War on Higher Education*, Chicago: Haymarket Books.
Giroux, H. A. (2017 [2011]), *On Critical Pedagogy*, New York: Bloomsbury Academic.
Giroux, H. A. (2018), *Terror of Neoliberalism: Authoritarianism and the Eclipse of Democracy*, London: Routledge.

Giroux, H. A. (2020), *On Critical Pedagogy*, London: Bloomsbury Publishing.
Glass, R. D. (2001), 'On Paulo Freire's philosophy of praxis and the foundations of liberation education', *Educational Researcher*, 30 (2): 15–25.
Glesne, C. (2016), 'Research as solidarity', in T. Kukutai and J. Taylor (eds), *Indigenous Data Sovereignty: Toward an Agenda*, 169–78, Canberra: Australian National University Press. Available at: https://press.anu.edu.au/publications/series/centre-abo riginal-economic-policy-research-caepr/indigenous-data-sovereignty.
Goffman, E. (1959), *The Presentation of Self in Everyday Life*, New York: The Overlook Press.
Goodson, I. (1992), *Studying Teachers' Lives*, London: Routledge.
Goodson, I. (1997), '"Trendy theory" and teacher professionalism', *Cambridge Journal of Education*, 27 (1): 7–22.
Goodson, I. (1999), 'The educational researcher as a public intellectual', *British Educational Research Journal*, 25 (3): 277–97.
Goodson, I. (2008), *Investigating the Teacher's Life and Work*, Rotterdam: Sense Publishers.
Goodson, I. (2013), *School Subjects and Curriculum Change*, London: The Falmer Press.
Goodson, I. and Lindblad, S., eds (2010), *Professional Knowledge and Educational Restructuring in Europe (Studies in Professional Life and Work)*, Rotterdam: Sense Publishers.
Gorard, S. (2010), 'Education can compensate for society – A bit', *British Journal of Educational Studies*, 58 (1): 47–65.
Gov UK (2014), 'Birmingham schools: Secretary of State for Education's statement', Available at: www.gov.uk/government/speeches/birmingham-schools-secretary-of-st ate-for-educations-statement (accessed 19 January 2021).
Gov UK (2019), 'Help if you're a student with a learning difficulty, health problem or disability'. Available at: https://www.gov.uk/disabled-students-allowances-dsas (accessed 30 June 2019).
Gove, M. (2011), Available at: https://www.gov.uk/government/speeches/michael-gove-to-cambridge-university.
Graham, C. (2012), 'Transforming spaces and identities: The contribution of professional staff to learning spaced in higher education', *Journal of Higher Education Policy and Management*, 34 (4): 437–52.
Graham, C. (2016), 'Exploring the contribution of professional staff to student outcomes: A comparative study of Australian and UK case studies', *Journal of Higher Education Policy and Management*, 38 (6): 595–609.
Gramsci, A. (1971), *Selections From the Prison Notebooks of Antonio Gramsci*, trans. and ed. Q. Hoare and G. Norwell-Smith, London: Lawrence & Wishart.
Grande, S. (2018), 'Refusing the university', in E. Tuck and K. W. Yang (eds), *Toward What Justice? Describing Diverse Dreams of Justice in Education*, 47–65, London: Routledge Books.
Granovetter, M. (2018), *Getting a Job: A Study of Contacts and Careers*, Chicago: University of Chicago Press.
Gray, A. (2014), *An Introduction to the Therapeutic Frame*, Hove: Routledge.
Gray, B. (2009), 'The emotional labour of nursing 1: exploring the concept', *Nursing Times*, 105 (8): 26–9.
Green, B. (2012), 'Addressing the curriculum problem in doctoral education', *Australian Universities' Review*, 54 (1): 10–18.
Green, J. (2011), *Education, Professionalism and the Quest for Accountability: Hitting the Target but Missing the Point*, London: Routledge.

Greenbank, P. (2007), 'From foundation to honours degree: The student experience', *Education and Training*, 49 (2): 91–102.

Griffiths, M. (1998), *Educational Research for Social Justice: Getting off the Fence (Doing Qualitative Research in Educational Settings)*, Buckingham: Open University Press.

Groenke, S. L. and Hatch, J. A., eds (2009), *Critical Pedagogy and Teacher Education in the Neoliberal Era: Small Openings*, 272 pp, London: Springer.

Grossberg, L. (1996), 'Identity and cultural studies: Is that all there is?', in S. Hall and P. du Gray (eds), *Questions of Cultural Identity*, 87–107, London: Sage.

Guba, E. G. and Lincoln, Y. S. (1994), 'Competing paradigms in qualitative research', in N. K. Denzin and Y. S. Lincoln (eds), *Handbook of Qualitative Research*, Beverley Hills: Sage Publications.

Guha, R., ed. (1982), *Subaltern Studies 1: Writings on South Asian History and Society*, 7 Vols, New Dehli: Oxford University Press.

GuildHE (2015), *Making Student Engagement a Reality: Turning Theory Into Practice*, London: GuildHE.

Habermas (1989), *The New Conservatism: Cultural Criticism and the Historians' Debate*, Cambridge, MA: MIT Press.

Hale, S. (2021), 'The class politics of foundation years', *Journal of the Foundation Year Network*, 3 (December 2020 forthcoming).

Halstead, J. and Taylor, M., eds (1996), *Values in Education and Education in Values*, London: Falmer Press.

Hammer, P., Madsen, T. and Tateo, L. (2019), '"I See Stress in Many Places Around Me, but as Such, I'm Over it": Understanding Psycho-Cultural Dimensions of University Students' Experiences', in L. Tateo (ed.), *Educational Dilemmas: A Cultural Psychological Perspective*, 146–70. Abingdon, Oxon: Routledge.

Hammond, C. (2017), *About Hope, Utopia and Creativity in Higher Education*, London: Bloomsbury, 224 pp.

Hanesworth, P., Bracken, S. and Elkington, S. (2019), 'A typology for a social justice approach to assessment: Learning from universal design and culturally sustaining pedagogy', *Teaching in Higher Education*, 24 (1): 98–114.

Hanna-Mari, A., Tienari, J. and Waeraas, A. (2015), 'The university branding game players, interests, politics', *International Studies of Management & Organization*, 45 (2): 114–20.

Hardy, I. (2010), 'Teacher talk: Flexible delivery and academics' praxis in an Australian university', *International Journal for Academic Development*, 15 (2): 131–42.

Hargreaves, D. (1995), 'School culture, School effectiveness and school improvement', *School Effectiveness and School Improvement*, 6 (1): 23–46.

Harney, S. and Moten, F. (2013), *The Undercommons: Fugitive Planning and Black Study*, New York: Minor Compositions.

Harris, P., Haywood, C. and Mac an Ghaill, M. (2017), 'Higher education, de-centred subjectivities and the emergence of a pedagogical self among black and Muslim students', *Race Ethnicity and Education*, 20 (3): 358–71.

Harrison, N., and McCaig, C. (2014), 'An ecological fallacy in higher education', *Journal of Further and Higher Education*, 39 (6): 793–817.

Hartman, Y. and Darab, S. (2012), 'A call for slow scholarship: A case study on the intensification of academic life and its implications for pedagogy', *Review of Education, Pedagogy, and Cultural Studies*, 34 (1–2): 49–60.

Harvey, D. (2005), *A Brief History of Neo-Liberalism*, Oxford: Oxford University Press.

Hase, S. and Kenyon, C. (2007), 'Heutagogy: A child of complexity theory', *Complicity: An International Journal of Complexity and Education*, 4 (1): 111–19.

Hase, S. and Kenyon, C. (2013), *Self-Determined Learning Heutagogy in Action*, London: Bloomsbury Academic.

Hatherley, O. (2017), *The Ministry of Nostalgia: Consuming Austerity*, London: Verson.

Hayward, G. and Hoelscher, M. (2011), 'The use of large-scale administrative data sets to monitor progression from vocational education and training into higher education in the UK: Possibilities and methodological challenges', *Research in Comparative and International Education*, 6 (3): 316–29.

Healey, M. (2019), 'Students as partners and change agents: A selected bibliography'. Available at: www.mickhealey.co.uk/resources.

Healey, M., Flint, A. and Harrington, K. (2014), *Developing Students as Partners in Learning and Teaching in Higher Education*, Manchester: Higher Education Academy.

Hedges, H. and Cooper, M. (2018), 'Relational play-based pedagogy: Theorising a core practice in early childhood education', *Teachers and Teaching: Theory and Practice*, 24 (4): 369–83.

HEFCE (2001), *Supporting Higher Education in Further Education Colleges: Review of Colleges' Strategy Statements and Support Needs: A Report to the HEFCE by the Further Education Development Agency*, Bristol: HEFCE.

HEFCE (2003), *Supporting Higher Education in Further Education Colleges: Good Practice. A Guide for Tutors and Lecturers*, Bristol: HEFCE.

HEFCE (2006), *Higher Education in Further Education Colleges: Consultation on HEFCE Policy*, Bristol: HEFCE.

HEFCE (2013), *Destinations of Leavers from Higher Education in Further Education Colleges: Key Findings: Leavers up to Academic Year 2010–11*, Bristol: HEFCE.

HEFCE (2014), *Further Information on POLAR3: An Analysis of Geography, Disadvantage and Entrants to Higher Education*, Bristol: HEFCE.

Heleta, S. (2016), 'Decolonisation of higher education: Dismantling epistemic violence and Eurocentrism in South Africa', *Transformation in Higher Education*, 1 (1): 1–8. Available at: https://tinyurl.com/yxyva97j (accessed 29 January 2020).

Her Majesty's Government (1991), 'White paper: Higher education: A new framework'. Available at: http://www.educationengland.org.uk/documents/wp1991b/index.html (accessed 10 June 2018).

Her Majesty's Government (1997a), 'The dearing report: Higher education in the learning society'. Available at: http://www.educationengland.org.uk/documents/dearing1997/dearing1997.html (accessed 09 June 2018).

Her Majesty's Government (1997b), 'Kennedy report: Learning works widening participation in further education'. Available at: http://www.educationengland.org.uk/documents/kennedy1997/kennedy-report.html (accessed 06 September 2018).

Her Majesty's Government (1998), 'Teaching and higher education act'. Available at: http://www.legislation.gov.uk/ukpga/1998/30/pdfs/ukpga_19980030_en.pdf (accessed 20 February 2018).

Her Majesty's Government (2017), 'Higher education and research act'. Available at: http://www.legislation.gov.uk/ukpga/2017/29/contents/enacted (accessed 03 January 2018).

Heron, J. (1996), *Cooperative Inquiry: Research into the Human Condition*, London: Sage.

HESA (2016), 'Higher education statistics for the UK 2015/16'. Available at: https://www.hesa.ac.uk/data-and-analysis/publications/higher-education-2015-16/introduction.

HESA (2017), Available from: https://www.hesa.ac.uk/data-and-analysis/publications/higher-education-2015-16/introduction.

HESA (2019a), 'HE staff data: What are their employment conditions'. Available at: https://www.hesa.ac.uk/data-and-analysis/staff/employment-conditions (19 June 2019).

HESA (2020a), Higher Education Staff Statistics: UK, 2018/19.
HESA (2020b), Higher Education Student Statistics: UK, 2018/19 – Student numbers and characteristics. Available from https://www.hesa.ac.uk/news/16-01-2020/sb255-higher-education-student-statistics/numbers.
Higher Education Academy (2016), *Framework for Student Engagement Through Partnership*, York: HEA. Available at: https://www.heacademy.ac.uk/system/files/downloads/student-enagagement- through-partnership.pdf.
Higher Education Statistics Agency – HESA (2015), 'Figure 4 - HE student enrolments by personal characteristics 2013/14 to 2017/18'. Available at: https://www.hesa.ac.uk/data-and-analysis/sb252/figure-4?fbclid=IwAR13JPd0HIwr4ru3yx9_Z4innfUwJqwKI5mMug0AWGe4rTNWkTDlzhuKnqc (accessed 28 November 2019).
Hill, C. and Fraser, S. (2017), 'More-than-reflective practice: Becoming a diffractive practitioner', *Teacher Learning and Professional Development*, 2 (1): 1–17.
His Majesty's Government (1945), 'The percy report: Higher technological education, education in England: The history of our schools'. Available at: http://educationengland.org.uk/documents/percy1945/percy1945.html (accessed 3 March 2018).
His Majesty's Government (1946), 'The Barlow report, scientific man-power', *Education in England: The History of Our Schools*. Available at: http://www.educationengland.org.uk/documents/barlow1946/ (accessed 3 March 2018).
HM Government (2011), *Prevent Strategy*, London: TSO.
Hodgson, A. and Spours, K. (2003), *Beyond A-levels: Curriculum 2000 and the Reform of 14–19 Qualifications: Reforming the Curriculum and Qualifications System from Post 14+*, London: Kogan Page.
Hodgson, A. and Spours, K. (2013), What is happening with 17+ participation, attainment and progression in London? Paper 3. Colleges in London (Report to London Councils Centre for Post-14 Education and Work) UCL Institute of Education.
Hodgson, A. and Spours, K. (2017), 'Policy and policy learning across the four countries of the UK: The case of further education and skills. An initial scoping paper May 2017'. UCL Institute of Education. Available at: https://www.ucl.ac.uk/ioe/sites/ioe/files/fe-skills-across-uk-scoping-paper.pdf.
Hodgson, N., Vlieghe, J. and Zamojski, P. (2017), *Manifesto for a Post-Critical Pedagogy*, Santa Barbara: Punctum Books.
Hodgson, N., Vlieghe, J. and Zamojski, P. (2018), 'Education and the love for the world: Articulating a post-critical educational philosophy', *Foro de Educacion*, 16 (24): 7–20. doi: 10.14516/fde.576 (accessed 31 October 2019).
Hoerder, D. (2014), 'Education for a transcultural life-world or for a hegemonic nation? Schooling in the British empire, in France, and in Canada, 1830s-2000s', *Studia Migracyjne - Przeglad Polonijny*, 40 (3): 17–32.
Holland, J., Blair, M. and Sheldon, S., eds (1995), *Debates and Issues in Feminist Research and Pedagogy: A Reader*. Multilingual Matters.
Holloway, J. (2010), *Crack Capitalism*, London: Pluto Press.
Hollway, W. and Jefferson, T. (2013), *Doing Qualitative Research Differently: A Psychosocial Approach*, 2nd edn, London: Sage.
Holmwood, J. and O'Toole, T. (2018), *Countering Extremism in the British Cchools: The Truth About the Birmingham Trojan Horse Affair*, Bristol: Policy Press.
Holt, J. (1964), *How Children Fail*, New York: Dell Publishing.
hooks, b. (1994), *Teaching to Transgress: Education as the Practice of Freedom*, London: Routledge.
hooks, b. (2003), *Teaching Community: A Pedagogy of Hope*, New York: Routledge.

hooks, b. (2004), *We Real Cool: Black Men and Masculinity*, New York: Routledge.
hooks, b. (2015), *Yearning: Race, Gender, and Cultural Politics*, New York: Routledge.
House of Commons Education Committee (2015), *Extremism in Schools: The Trojan Horse Affair*, London: The Stationery Office.
House of Lords Economics Affairs Committee (2018), 'Treating students fairly: The economics of post-school education, 2nd Report of Session 2017–19'. Available at: https://publications.parliament.uk/pa/ld201719/ldselect/ldeconaf/139/139.pdf (accessed 20 July 2019).
Hughes, G. (2006), *An Encyclopedia of Swearing*, Armonk: M. E. Sharpe.
Humboldt, W. (1810), 'On the internal and external organization of the higher scientific institutions in Berlin', *German History in Documents and Images*, 1: 1648–815.
Hursh, D. and Hall, D. (2008), 'Re-politicizing higher education and research within neoliberal globalization', *Policy Futures in Education*, 9 (5): 1–31. doi: 10.2304/pfie.2011.9.5.560.
Hyland, T. (2017), 'McDonaldizing spirituality: Mindfulness, education, and consumerism', *Journal of Transformative Education*, 15 (4): 334–56. doi: 10.1177/1541344617696972.
Ichheiser, G. (1943), 'Ideology of success and the dilemma of education', *Ethics*, 53 (2): 137–41. doi: 10.1086/290338.
Illich, I. (1971), *Deschooling Society*, New York: Harper and Row.
Illich, I. (1978), 'Disabling professions', *India International Centre Quarterly*, 5 (1): 23–32.
Ingleby, E. and Gibby, C. (2016), 'Law and ethics: Problematising the role of the foundation degree and paralegal education in english post-compulsory education', *Research in Post-compulsory Education*, 21 (1–2): 151–62.
Institute for Public Policy Research (2017), 'Not by degrees: Improving student mental health in the UK's universities'. Available at: https://www.ippr.org/research/publications/not-by-degrees (accessed 20 June 2019).
Jacobs, H. L. M. (2008), 'Perspectives on information literacy and reflective pedagogical praxis', *The Journal of Academic Librarianship*, 34 (3): 256–62.
Jacoby, B. (1989), *The Student-as-Consumer: Developing a Comprehensive Institutional Response*. ASHE_ERIC Higher Education Report 7.
Jahi, J. (2014), 'Why isn't my professor Black?' Available at: https://tinyurl.com/uozr88r (accessed 29 January 2020).
James, D. and Biesta, G., eds (2007), *Improving Learning Cultures in Further Education*, Oxford: Routledge.
Jameson, J. and Hillier, Y. (2003), *Researching Post-Compulsory Education*, London: Continuum.
Jeffs, T. and Smith, M. (2010), *Youth Work Practice*, London: Red Globe Press.
Jivraj, S. and Simpson, L. (2015), *Ethnic Identity and Inequalities in Britain*, Bristol: Policy Press.
Joldersma, C. (1999), 'The tension between justice and freedom in Paulo Freire's epistemology', *Journal of Educational Thought*, 35 (2): 129–48.
Jones, I. (2018), '"A commitment to a form of togetherness?" How students and lecturers worked together to develop a curriculum within a subject in a university in England', *ESREA Conference*, Turin, March 2018.
Jones, R. (2008), 'Student retention and success: A synthesis of research' [online], *Higher Education Academy*. Available at: https://www.heacademy.ac.uk/system/files/wp_retention_synthesis_for_pdf_updated_090310_0.pdf (accessed 08 November 2017).

Jones, R. and Thomas, L. (2005), 'The 2003 UK government higher education white paper: A critical assessment of its implications for the access and widening participation agenda', *Journal of Education Policy*, 20 (5): 615–30.

Jung, C. (1998), *The Essential Jung*, London: Fontana Press.

Kabat-Zinn, J. (1990), *Full Catastrophe Living, How to Cope with Stress, Pain and Illness using Mindfulness Meditation*, London: Piatkus.

Kadi-Hanifi, K., Dagman, O., Peters, J., Snell, E., Tutton, C. and Wright, T. (2014), 'Engaging students and staff with educational development through appreciative inquiry', *Innovations in Education and Teaching International*, 51 (6): 584–94.

Kadi-Hanifi, K. and Keenan, J. (2015), 'Singing better songs? A life history study of Higher Education teacher educators working in the English Further Education sector', *Power and Education*, 7 (3): 338–54.

Kadi-Hanifi, K. and Keenan, J. (2016), 'Finding the "a-ha" moment: An exploration in HE in FE teacher self-concept', *Research in Post-compulsory Education*, 21 (1–2): 73–86.

Kaufman, P. (2017), 'Contemplative critical pedagogy', *Radical Pedagogy*, 14 (1): 1524–45. Available at: http://radicalpedagogy.org/kaufman.html 05/06/2018.

Kaye, T. (2006), 'Criticizing the image of the student as consumer: Examining legal trends and administrative responses in the US and UK', *Education and the Law*, 18: 85–129.

Kemmis, S. and Carr, W. (1986), *Becoming Critical: Education Knowledge and Action Research*, London: Routledge.

Kemmis, S., Edwards-Groves, C., Wilkinson, J. and Hardy, I. (2012), 'Ecologies of Practices', in P. Hager, A. Lee and A. Reich (eds), *Practice, Learning and Change: Practice-Theory Perspectives on Professional Learning*, 33–49, Dordrecht: Springer.

Kemmis, S. and Grootenboer, P. (2008), 'Situating Praxis in practice: Practice architectures and the cultural, social and material conditions for practice', in S. Kemmis and T. Smith (eds), *Enabling Praxis: Challenges for Education*, 37–62, Rotterdam: Sense.

Kemmis, S., Wilkinson, J., Edwards-Groves, C., Hardy, I., Grootenboer, P. and Bristol, L. (2014), *Changing Practices, Changing Education*, Singapore: Springer.

Kendall, A., Gibson, M., Himsworth, C., Palmer, K. and Perkins, H. (2016), 'Listening to old wives tales: Small stories and the (re)making and (re)telling of research in HE/FE practitioner education', *Research in Post-compulsory Education*, 21 (1–2): 116–36.

Kennedy, M. (2017), 'Cambridge academics seek to "decolonise" English, Available at: syllabus', *The Guardian*, 25 October 2017. Available at: https://tinyurl.com/s62ht3p (accessed 29 January 2020).

Kernohan, D. (2018), 'Major reviews of higher education through history', *WonkHE*. Available at: https://wonkhe.com/blogs/major-reviews-in-history/ (accessed 6 November 2019).

Kessing-Styles, L. (2003), 'The relationship between critical pedagogy and assessment in teacher education', *Radical Pedagogy* 5 (1): 11–20.

Khan, A. and Gabriel, J. (2009), 'Resisting the binary divide in higher education: The role of critical pedagogy', in R. Wilkinson and K. Pickett (eds), *The Spirit Level: Why More Equal Societies Almost Always Do Better*, 30–58, London: Allen Lane.

Khan, A. and Gabriel, J. (2018), 'Resisting the binary divide in higher education: The role of critical pedagogy', *Journal for Critical Education Policy Studies*, 16 (1): 30–58.

Kift, S., Nelson, K. and Clarke, J. (2010), 'Transition pedagogy: A third generation approach to FYE: A case study of policy and practice for the higher education sector', *The International Journal of the First Year in Higher Education*, 1 (1): 1–20.

Kincheloe, J. L. (2005), *Critical Pedagogy Primer*, New York: Peter Lang Publishing.

Kincheloe, J. L. (2007), *Teaching City Kids: Understanding and Appreciating Them*, New York: Peter Lang Publishing.
Kincheloe, J. L. (2012), 'Critical pedagogy in the twenty-first century: Evolution for survival', *Counterpoints*, 422: 147–83.
Kitchin, R. (2014), *Big Data, New Epistemologies and Paradigm Shifts*, Big Data Society.
Klein, M. (1935), 'A contribution to the psychogenesis of manic-depressive states', *International Journal of Psychoanalysis*, 16: 145–74.
Klein, M. (1946), 'Notes on some schizoid mechanisms', *International Journal of Psychoanalysis*, 27: 99–110.
Klein, M. (1957), *Envy and Gratitude and Other Works 1946–1963*, London: Virago.
Klein, N. (2014), *This Changes Everything: Capitalism vs the Climate*, New York: Simon Shuster Paperbacks.
Knowles, M. and Associates (1984), *Andragogy in Action*, Houston: Gulf Publishing.
Knowles, M. S., Holton, E. F. and Swanson, R. A. (2012), *The Adult Learner the Definitive Classic in Adult Education and Human Resource Development*, 7th edn, Abingdon, Oxon: Routledge.
Kopelson, K. (2003), 'Rhetoric on the edge of cunning; or, the performance of neutrality (re)considered as a composition pedagogy for student resistance', *College Composition and Communication*, 55 (1): 115–46.
Kreisberg, S. (1992), *Transforming Power: Domination, Empowerment and Education*, Albany: State University of New York Press.
Kuh, G. (2001), 'Assessing what really matters to student learning: Inside the national survey of student engagement', *Change*, 33: 10–17.
Kumashiro, K. (2002), *Troubling Education: Queer Activism and Anti-Oppressive Pedagogy*, New York: Routledge Falmer.
Labour Manifesto (2001), Available at: http://labourmanifesto.com/2001/2001-labour-manifesto.shtml.
Lather, P. (1986), 'Issues of validity in openly ideological research: Between a rock and a soft place', *Interchange*, 17 (4): 63–84.
Le Grange, L. (2011), 'A pedagogy of hope after Paolo Freire'. Research Gate (accessed 24 April 2019).
Le Grange, L. (2016), 'Decolonising the university curriculum', *South African Journal of Higher Education*, 30 (2): 1–12.
Lea, J. (2015), 'The landscape of higher education', in J. Lea (ed.), *Enhancing Learning and Teaching in Higher Education*, 173–97, Berkshire: Open University Press.
Lea, J. (2016), 'Enhancing learning and teaching in HE: Engaging with the dimensions of practice', *Educational Developments*, 17 (1): 9–13.
Lea, J. and Simmons, J. (2012), 'Higher education in further education: Capturing and Promoting HEness', *Research in Post-Compulsory Education*, 17 (2): 179–93.
Leach, L. (2013), 'Enagaging ethnically diverse first year students: A practice report', *The International Journal of the First Year in Higher Education*, 4 (2): 117–24.
Ledwith, M. (2011), *Community Development: A Critical Approach*, 2nd edn, Bristol: Policy Press.
Lee, A. and Dunston, R. (2011), 'Practice, learning and change: Towards a re-theorisation of professional education', *Teaching in Higher Education*, 16 (5): 483–94.
Lepper, M. R. and Green, D., eds (1978), *The Hidden Costs of Reward: New Perspectives on the Psychology of Human Motivation*, Hillsdale: Lawrence Eribaum.
Levinas, E. (1987), *Time and the Other*, Pittsburgh: Duquesne University Press.

Levitas, R. (2013), *Utopia as Method: The Imaginary Reconstitution of Society*, London: Springer.
Levy, P., Little, S. and Whelan, N. (2011), 'Perspectives on staff-student partnership in learning, research and educational enhancement', in S. Little (ed.), *Staff-Student Partnerships in Higher Education*, 1–15, London: Continuum.
Lewis, G. E. (2014), 'Collaborative improvisation as critical pedagogy', *Journal of Contemporary African Art*, 2014 (34): 40–7.
Lilley, S. and Papadopoulos, D. (2014), 'Material returns: Cultures of valuation, biofinancialisation and the autonomy of politics', *Sociology*, 48 (5): 972–88. doi: 10.1177/0038038514539206.
Lipman, M. (2003), *Thinking in Education*, 2nd edn, Cambridge: Cambridge University Press.
Lipsky, M. (2010), *Street-Level Bureaucracy: Dilemmas of the Individual in Public Services*, New York: Russell Sage Foundation.
Liston, D. P. (2008), 'Critical pedagogy and attentive Love', *Studies in Philosophy and Education. An International Journal*, 27 (5): 387–92. doi: 10.1007/s11217-007-9082-y.
Liu, A. (2011), 'Unravelling the myth of meritocracy within the context of US Higher education', *Higher Education*, 62: 383–97.
Loomba, A. (2015), *Colonialism/Postcolonialism*, 3rd edn, London: Routledge.
Loveland-Armour, L. A. (2018), 'Recently identified university students navigate dyslexia', *Journal of Applied Research in Higher Education*, 10 (2): 170–81. doi: 10.1108/JARHE-04-2017-0033.
Lucas, N. (2004), *Teaching in Further Education*, London: Institute of Education.
Lucey, H., Melody, J. and Walkerdine, V. (2003), 'Uneasy hybrids: Psychosocial aspects of becoming educationally successful for working-class young women', *Gender and Education Online*, 15 (3): 285–99. doi: 10.1080/09540250303865.
Luo, B., Matthews, K. E. and Chunduri, P. (2019), 'Commitment to Collaboration: What students have to say about the values underpinning partnership practices', *International Journal for Students as Partners*, 3 (1): 123–39.
Lynch, K. (2006), 'Neo-liberalism and marketisation: The implications for higher education', *European Educational Research Journal*, 5 (1): 1–17. doi: 10.2304/eerj.2006.5.1.1.
Lyotard, J.-F. (1984), *The Postmodern Condition*, Minnesota: University of Minnesota Press.
Mac an Ghaill, M. (1988), *Young, Gifted and Black: Student-Teacher Relations in the Schooling of Black Youth*, Milton Keynes: Open University Press.
Macartney, B. C. (2012), 'Teaching through an ethics of belonging, care and obligation as a critical approach to transforming education', *International Journal of Inclusive Education*, 16 (2): 171–83.
MacFarlane, B. (2017), *Freedom to Learn: The Threat to Student Academic Freedom and Why it Needs to be Reclaimed*, Society for Research into Higher Education, Oxon: Routledge.
MacLure, M. (2013), 'Researching without representation? Language and materiality in post-qualitative methodology', *International Journal of Qualitative Studies in Education*, 26 (6): 658–67.
Macmillan, L., Tyler, C. and Vignoles, A. (2015), 'Who gets the top jobs? The role of family background and networks in recent graduates' access to high-status professions', *Journal of Social Policy*, 44 (3): 487–515.
MacNaughton, G. (2005), *Doing Foucault in Early Childhood Studies: Applying Poststructural Ideas*, London: Routledge.

Maguire, D. and Morris, D. (2018), 'Homeward Bound: Defining, understanding and aiding "commuter students"', *Higher Education Policy Institute Report 114.*

Mahmoudi, A., Khoshnood, A. and Babaei, A. (2014), 'Paulo Freire critical pedagogy and its implications in curriculum planning', *Journal of Education and Practice*, 5 (4): 86–93.

Mahon, K. (2014), *Critical Pedagogical Praxis in Higher Education*, Unpublished PHD thesis.

Mahoney, P. and Weiner, G. (2019), 'Neo-liberalism and the state of higher education in the UK', *Journal of Further and Higher Education*, 43 (4): 560–72. doi: 10.1080/0309877X.2017.1378314.

Mallman, M. (2016), 'The perceived inherent vice of working-class university students', *The Sociological Review*, 65 (2): 235–50.

Mannheim, K. (1943), *Diagnosis of Our Time: Wartime Essays of a Sociologist*, London: Routledge.

Mansfield, K. C. (2015), 'The importance of safe space and student voice in schools that serve minoritized learners', *Journal of Educational Leadership, Policy and Practice*, 30 (1): 25.

Marcel, G. (2010), *Homo Viator Introduction to the Metaphysic of Hope*, trans. Emma Craufurd and Paul Seaton, South Bend: St. Augustine's Press.

Marcuse, H. (1964), *One Dimentional Man*, Boston: Beacon.

Marginson, S. (2008), 'Global field and global imagining: Bourdieu and worldwide higher education', *British Journal of Sociology of Education*, 29 (3): 303–15.

Martinez A., Martin, L. and Marlow, S. (2014), 'Developing a critical realist positional approach to intersectionality', *Journal of Critical Realism*, 13 (5): 447–66.

Marx, K. and Engels, F. (1848),' Manifesto of the communist party'. Available at: https://www.marxists.org/archive/marx/works/download/pdf/Manifesto.pdf (accessed 04 May 2019).

Massey, D. (2008), *For Space*, London: Sage.

Matheson, D. and Wells, P. (1999), 'What is education?' in D. Matheson and I. Grosvenor (eds), *An Introduction to the Study of Education*, 12–24, London: David Fulton.

Mathias, L. and Peters, J. (2018), 'Student-staff partnership in educational development: A source of hope in dark times', *Educational Developments*, 19 (4): 4–7.

Mattern S. (2013), 'Methodolatry and the art of measure: The new wave of urban data science'. Design Observer: Places, 5 November 2013.

Matthews, K. E., Cook-Sather, A., Acai, A., Dvorakova, S.L., Felten, P., Marquis, E. and Mercer-Mapstone, L. (2019), 'Towards Theories of Partnership praxis: An analysis of interpretive framing in literature on students as partners in teaching and learning', *Higher Education Research and Development*, 38 (2): 280–94.

Matthews, K. E., Dwyer, E., Russell, A. and Enright, E. (2018), 'It is a complicated thing: Leaders' conceptions of students as partners in the neoliberal university', *Studies in Higher Education*, 44 (12): 2196–208.

Matusov, E. (2011), 'Irreconcilable differences in Vygotsky's and Bakhtin's approaches to the social and the individual: An educational perspective', *Culture and Psychology*, 17 (1): 99–119.

May (2017), Theresa May Conservative conference speech, 4 October 2017.

May (2019), 'Speech on the Augur review'. Available at: https://www.gov.uk/government/speeches/pm-speech-at-augar-review-launch-30-may-2019.

Mayo, P. (2004), *Liberating Praxos: Paulo Freire's Legacy for Radical Education and Politics*, London: Praeger.

McCarthy, C., Pitton, V., Soochul, K. and Monje, D. (2009), 'Re-ordering the organization of knowledge in schooling and the university in a time of globalisation and neoliberalism', in J. Satterwaite, H. Piper and P. Sikes (eds), *Power in the Academy*, 35–60, Trent on Stoke: Trentham Books.

McCulloch, A. (2009), 'The student as co-producer: Learning from the public administration about the student-university relationship', *Studies in Higher Education*, 34 (2): 171–83.

McLaren, P. (1994), 'Multiculturalism and the postmodern critique: Towards a pedagogy of resistance and transformation', in H. Giroux and P. McLaren (eds), *Between Borders: Pedagogy and the Politics of Cultural Studies*, 192–222, New York: Routledge.

McLaren, P. (1999), 'Revolutionary pedagogy in post-revolutionary times: Rethinking the political economy of critical education', *Educational Theory*, 48: 432–62.

McLaren, P. (2003a), 'Critical pedagogy: A look at the major concepts', in A. Darder, M. Baltodano and R. Torres (eds), *The Critical Pedagogy Reader*, 151–84, New York: RoutledgeFalmer.

McLaren, P. (2003b), *Life in Schools: An Introduction to Critical Pedagogy in the Foundations of Education*, 4th edn, Boston: Allyn and Bacon.

McLean, M. (2006), *Pedagogy and the University: Critical Theory and Practice*, London: Continuum.

McLeod, J. (2011), *Qualitative Research in Counselling and Psychotherapy*, London: Sage.

McManus Holroyd, A. E. (2007), 'Interpretive hermeneutic phenomenology: Clarifying understanding', *The Indo-Pacific Journal of Phenomenology*, 7 (2): 1–12.

McTaggart, B. (2016), 'Modern higher education students within a non-traditional higher education space: Not fitting in, often falling out', *Research in Post-Compulsory Education*, 21 (1–2): 86–97.

Mellow, G. (2017), 'The biggest misconception about today's college students: On campus', *New York Times*, 28 August 2017.

Mercer-Mapstone, L., Dvorakova, S. L., Matthews, K., Abbot, S., Cheng, B., Felten, P., Knorr, K., Marquis, E., Shammas, R. and Swaim, K. (2017), 'A systematic literature review of students as partners in higher education', *International Journal for Students as Partners*, 1 (1): 1–23.

Meyer, J. and Land, R. (2005), 'Threshold concepts and troublesome knowledge: Epistemological considerations and a conceptual framework for teaching and learning', *Higher Education*, 49: 373–88.

Mignolo, W. D. (2009), 'Epistemic disobedience, independent thought and decolonial freedom', *Theory, Culture & Society*, 26 (7–8): 159–81.

Millionplus (2016), *Is Science and Research Funding in Higher Education Meeting the Challenges of the 21st Century?*, London: Million Plus.

Mills, C. W. (2000), *The Sociological Imagination*, Harmondsworth: Penguin.

Milojevic, I., (1998), 'Women's higher education in the 21st century', *Futures*, 30 (7): 693–704.

Minnich, E. (2003), 'Teaching thinking', *Change*, 35 (5): 18–24.

Miskelly, P. and Duncan, L. (2014), '"I'm actually being the grown-up now": leadership, maturity and professional identity development', *Journal of nursing management*, 22 (1): 38–48.

Mitchell, S. A. and Aron, L. (1999), *Relational Psychoanalysis: The Emergence of a Tradition*, Hillsdale: The Analytic Press.

Molesworth, M., Nixon, E. and Scullion, R. (2009), 'Having, being and higher education: The marketisation of the university and the transformation of the student into consumer', *Teaching in Higher Education*, 14 (3): 277–87.

Molesworth, M., Nixon, E. and Scullion, R., ed. (2011), *The Marketization of Higher Education and the Student as Consumer*, London: Routledge.

Molesworth, M., Scullion, R. and Nixon, E. (2011), *The Marketization of Higher Education and the Student as Consumer*, Oxon: Routledge.

Moreau, M. P. (2016), 'Regulating the student body/ies: University policies and student parents', *British Educational Research Journal*, 42 (5): 906–25 doi: 10.1002/berj.3234.

Moreau, M. P. and Kerner, C. (2012), *Supporting Student Parents in Higher Education: A Policy Analysis*. Final Report, Nuffield Foundation. Available at: https://www.nuffieldfoundation.org/supporting-student-parents-he.

Moreau, M. P. and Kerner, C. (2015), 'Care in academia: An exploration of student parents' experiences', *British Journal of Sociology of Education*, 36 (2): 215–33. doi: 10.1080/01425692.2013.814533.

Morgan, J. (2000), 'Critical pedagogy: The spaces that make the difference', *Pedagogy, Culture and Society*, 8 (3): 273–89.

Morley, L. (2003), *Quality and Power in Higher Education*, Berkshire: Open University Press.

Mortimore, P. (2013), *Education Under Siege: Why There is a Better Alternative*, Bristol: Policy Press.

Moss, P. (2007), 'Bringing politics into the nursery: Early childhood education as a democratic practice', *European Early Childhood Education Research Journal*, 15 (1): 5–20.

Moss, P. (2017), 'Power and Resistance in early childhood education: From dominant discourse to democratic experimentalism', *Journal of Pedagogy*, 8 (1): 11–32.

Moss, P. (2019), *Alternative Narratives in Early Childhood*, Oxon: Routledge.

Moss, P. and Petrie, P. (2002), *From Children's Services to Children's Spaces: Public Policy, Children and Childhood*, London: Routledge.

Motta, S. C. (2013), 'Pedagogies of possibility: In, against, and beyond imperial patriarchal subjectivities of higher education', in S. Cowden and G. Singh (eds), *Acts of Knowing: Critical Pedagogy in, Against and Beyond the University*, 85–124, London: Bloomsbury.

Mountford-Zimdars, A., Sabri, D., Moore, J., Sanders, J., Jones, S. and Higham, L., eds (2015), *Causes of Differences in Student Outcomes*, Report by KCL, ARC Network and the University of Manchester, London: HEFCE.

Moustakas, C. (1990), *Heuristic Research Design, Methodology and Applications*, Newbury Park: Sage Publications, Inc.

Mulcahy, D. (2004), 'Making managers within post-compulsory education: Policy, performativity and practice', *Research in Post-Compulsory Education*, 9 (2): 183–202.

Naidoo, R. and Williams, J. (2015), 'The neoliberal regime in English higher education: Charters, consumers and the erosion of the public good', *Critical Studies in Education*, 56 (2): 208–23. doi: 10.1080/17508487.2014.939098.

National Archives Cabinet Papers (2018), Available at: http://www.nationalarchives.gov.uk/help-with-your-research/research-guides/technical-colleges-further-education/.

National Archives Cabinet Papers (n.d.), Available at: http://www.nationalarchives.gov.uk/cabinetpapers/themes/colleges-polytechnics.htm.

National Audit Office – NAO (2007), 'Staying the course: The retention of students in higher education' [online]. Available at: http://www.nao.org.uk/publications/0607/student_retention_in_higher_ed.aspx (accessed 02 June 2009).

Neary, M. (2012), 'Beyond teaching in public: The university as a form of social knowing', in M. Neary, H. Stevenson and L. Bell (eds), *Towards Teaching in Public*, 149–64, London: Bloomsbury Academic.

Neary, M. (2015), 'Student as producer: Authority and authorship in authoritarian times', in J. Lea (ed.), *Enhancing Learning and Teaching in Higher Education*, Maidenhead: Open University Press.

Neary, M. and Saunders, G. (2011), 'Leadership and learning landscapes: The struggle for the idea of the university', *Higher Education Quarterly*, 65 (4): 333–52.

Neary, M. and Saunders, G. (2016), 'Student as producer and the politics of abolition: making a new form of dissident institution', *Critical Education*, 7 (5): 2–23.

Newman, J. H. (1852), *Discourses on the Scope and Nature of University Education: Addressed to the Catholics of Dublin*, Wm. C. Brown Reprint Library.

Newman, J. H. (1875), *The Idea of a University*. Oxford: Oxford University Press.

Newman, J. H. (2001 [1907]), 'Discourse 7. Knowledge viewed in relation to professional skill', *The Idea of a University*. The National Institute for Newman Studies. Available at: http://www.newmanreader.org/works/idea/discourse7.html (accessed 11 December 2019).

Newman, S. and Jahdi, K. (2009), 'Marketisation of education: Marketing, rhetoric and reality', *Journal of Further and Higher Education*, 33 (1): 1–11. doi: 10.1080/03098770802638226.

Newman University (2014), 'Strategic plan 2014–2010'. Available at: https://www.newman.ac.uk/knowledge-base/strategic-plan-2020-2025/ (accessed 12 December 2017).

Newman University (2019a), 'TEF year two provider submission'. Available at: https://apps.officeforstudents.org.uk/tefoutcomes2019/docs/submissions/Submission_10007832.pdf (accessed 06 May 2019).

Newman University (2019b), 'Access and participation plan 2020-21 to 2024–25'. Available at: https://www.newman.ac.uk/knowledge-base/access-and-participation-plan/ (accessed 11 December 2019).

Newman University (2019c), 'Your University'. Available at: https://www.newman.ac.uk/ (accessed 20 June 2019).

Newman University (2019d), 'Access and participation plan'. Available at: https://apis.officeforstudents.org.uk/accessplansdownloads/2024/NewmanUniversity_APP_2020-21_V1_10007832.pdf.

NICHE (1997), *Higher Education in the Learning Society*. Main report, London: HMSO.

Nixon, J. (2011), *Higher Education and the Public Good: Imagining the University*, London: Continuum.

NNAC (National Network of Assessment Centres) (2012), 'The constitution of the national network of assessment centres'. Available at: https://www.nnac.org/members/constitution.php (accessed 28 June 2019).

Noddings, N. (1995), *Philosophy of Education*. Dimensions of Philosophy Series, Boulder: Westview Press.

Noddings, N. (2013), *Caring: A Feminine Approach to Ethics and Moral Education*, 2nd edn, Berkeley: University of California Press.

NUS (2012), 'A manifesto for partnership'. Available at: https://www.nus.org.uk/PageFiles/12238/A%20Manifesto%20for%20Partnership.pdf.

Office for National Statistics (2018), 'Estimating suicide among higher education students in England and Wales, experimental statistics'. Available at: https://www.ons.gov.uk/peoplepopulationandcommunity/birthsdeathsandmarriages/deaths/articles/estimatingsuicideamonghighereducationstudentsenglandandwalesexperimentalstatistics/2018-06-25 (accessed 20 June 2019).

Office for Standards in Education (Ofsted) (n.d.), Available at: https://www.gov.uk/government/organisations/ofsted.

OfS (2019), 'Odffice for students teaching excellence framework'. Available at: https://www.officeforstudents.org.uk/advice-and-guidance/teaching/tef-outcomes/#/tefoutcomes/.
OfS (2020), 'Continuation and attainment gaps'. Available at: https://tinyurl.com/vh5k5lb (accessed 29 January 2020).
Ogden, T. (2009), *Rediscovering Psychoanalysis: Thinking, Dreaming, Learning and Forgetting*, London: Routledge.
O'Hara, M. (1989), 'Person-centered approach as conscientizacao: The works of Carl Rogers and Paulo Freire', *Journal of Humanistic Psychology*, 29 (1): 11–35.
Ohara, M., Saft, S. and Crookes, G. (2000), 'Teacher exploration of feminist critical pedagogy in beginning Japanese as a foreign language class', *Paper Presented at the University of Hawai'i, Manoa*.
O'Leary, M. and Rami, J. (2017), 'The impact of austerity in Further Education: Crosscultural perspectives from England and Ireland', in B. Bartram (ed.), *International and Comparative Education*, 74–86, Abingdon: Routledge.
Olssen, M. and Peters, M. (2005), 'Neoliberalism, higher education and the knowledge economy: From the free market to knowledge capitalism', *Journal of Education Policy*, 20 (3): 313–45.
O'Neill, M. and Roberts, B. (2020), *Walking Methods: Research on the Move*, Abingdon: Routledge.
Ord, J. (2000), *Youth Work Curriculum*, Lyme Regis: Russell House.
Organisation for Economic Co-operation and Development (OECD) (1996), 'The Knowledge-based economy'. Available at: https://www.oecd.org/sti/sci-tech/1913021.pdf (accessed 13 May 2017).
Organisation of Economic Co-operation and Development (OECD) (2001), *The Well-being of Nations: The Role of Human and Social Capital*, Paris: OECD Publications.
Otto, D. (1999), 'Everything is dangerous: Some poststructural tools for human rights law', *Australian Journal of Human Rights*, 5 (1): 17–47.
Owen, H. (2008), *Open Space Technology: A Users Guide*, San Francisco: Berrett-Koehler Publishers.
Owen, H. H. (1997), *Expanding Our Now: The Story of Open Space Technology*, San Francisco: Berrett-Koehler Publishers.
Owen, H. H. (1998), *Expanding Our Now: The Story of Open Space Technology*, San Francisco: Berrett-Koehler Publishers.
Oxford English Dictionary (Online Version) (2019), Available at: https://www.oed.com/view/Entry/148805?redirectedFrom=potential#eid (accessed 20 June 2019).
Oxford University (n.d.), Available at: https://www.ox.ac.uk/about/organisation/history?wssl=1.
Page, M. (1997), 'Forbidden knowledge: The research process in a further education setting', *Research in Post-Compulsory Education*, 2 (1): 83–8.
Pajaczkowska, C. and Young, L. (1992), 'Racism, representation, psychoanalysis', in J. Donald and A. Rattansi (eds), *Race, Culture and Difference*, 198–219, London: Sage.
Papatheodorou, T. and Moyles, J. (2008), *Learning Together in the Early Years: Exploring Relational Pedagogy*, Abingdon: Routledge.
Peters, J. (2016), 'The pedagogy of partnership: Six principles for action', *Educational Developments*, 17 (4): 8–9 [December].
Peters, J. and Mathias, L. (2018), 'Enacting student partnership as though we really mean it: Some Freirean principles for a pedagogy of partnership', *International Journal for Students as Partners*, 2 (2): 53–70.

Parkes, S. (2014), 'Fostering a sense of belonging: Supporting the early formation of student identity as successful learners in Higher Education', *Journal of Learning Development in Higher Education* (7).

Parkes, S. (2018), 'A learner developer perspective: Critiquing dominant practices and cultures within university spaces', *Journal of Learning Development in Higher Education*, Special Edition: 2018 ALDinHE Conference, October 2018. Available at: http://journal.aldinhe.ac.uk/index.php/jldhe/article/view/464/pdf.

Parkes, S., Benkwitz, A., Bardy, H., Myler, K. and Peters, J. (2020), 'Being more human: Rooting learning analytics through resistance and reconnection with the values of Higher Education', *Higher Education Research & Development Special Issue*, 39: 113–26. doi: 10.1080/07294360.2019.1677569.

Parkes, S., Blackwell-Young, J., Cleaver, E. and Archibald, K. (2014), 'Academic and professional services in partnership: Literature review and overview of results', *Higher Education Academy and Leadership Foundation for Higher Education*. Available at: https://www.heacademy.ac.uk/sites/default/files/resources/prof_service_partnerships_toolkit_final_201214_updated.pdf (accessed 01 December 17).

Parkes, S., Cousins, H. and Blackwell-Young, J. (2013), 'Senior academic support tutors: Fostering student engagement through supporting academic development', in R. Clark and J. Andrews (eds), *Compendium of Effective Practice in Higher Education*, Vol. 2, York: Higher Education Academy. Available at: https://s3.eu-west-2.amazonaws.com/assets.creode.advancehe-document-manager/documents/hea/private/resources/compendium_of_effective_practice_volume_2_1568036670.pdf.

Parkes, S., Cousins, H., Brotherton, G., Thomas, L., Hill, M., Yorke, M. and O' Mahony, J. (2017), 'Newman University Final Report', What Works? Student Retention and Success Phase Two, Paul Hamlyn Foundation, Higher Education Academy and Action on Access. https://www.phf.org.uk/wp-content/uploads/2017/04/Full-report-Final.pdf.

Parkes, S., Mathias, L. and Seal, M. (2018), 'Becoming a Newman foundation year student: Conscientization to promote democratic engagement, meaningful dialogue and co-operative working', *Journal of the Foundation Year Network*, 1: 71–86.

Parry, G. (2009), 'Higher education, further education and the English experiment', *Higher Education Quarterly*, 63 (4): 322–42.

Parry, G., Callender, C., Scott, P. and Temple, P. (2012), *Understanding Higher Education in Further Education Colleges. Research Paper Number 69*, London: DBIS.

Parry, G. and Thompson, A. (2001), 'Higher education in FE colleges'. Available at: http://dera.ioe.ac.uk/9962/1/Higher_education_in_FE_colleges.pdf.

Parry, G. and Thompson, A. (2002), 'Closer by degrees – The past, present and future of higher education in further education colleges', *LSDA*.

Pence, A. R. and McCallum, M. (1994), 'Developing cross-cultural partnerships: Implications for child care quality research and practice', in P. Moss and A. Pence (eds), *Valuing Quality*, 108–22, London: Paul Chapman.

Pennacchia, J., Jones, E. and Aldridge, F. (2018), *Barriers to Learning for Disadvantaged Groups: Report of Qualitative Findings*, London: Department for Education.

Peters, J. (2014), 'The pedagogies of partnership: From Blair to Freire', *UCL an International Paulo Freire Conference*, Preston, UK.

Peters, J. (2018), 'The "Pedagogies of Partnership" in UK higher education: From Blair to Freire?', in *Paulo Freire and Transformative Education*, 175–89, London: Palgrave Macmillan.

Peters, J. and Mathias, L. (2018), 'Enacting student partnership as though we really mean it: Some Freirean principles for a pedagogy of partnership', *International Journal for Students As Partners*, 2 (2): 53–70.

Peters, M. A. (2015), 'Why is my curriculum white?', *Educational Philosophy and Theory*, 47 (7): 641–6.

Pinar, W. F. (2015), *Educational Experience as Lived: Knowledge, History and Alterity*, New York: Routledge.

Poland, W. (2000), 'The analyst's witnessing and otherness', *Journal of the American Psychoanalytic Association*, 48 (1): 80–93.

Postma, D. (2016), 'The ethics of becoming in a pedagogy for social justice: A posthumanist perspective', *South African Journal of Higher Education*, 30 (3): 310–28.

Pring, R. (2000), 'Editorial conclusion: A philosophical perspective', *Oxford Review of Education*, 26 (3–4): 495–501.

Privy Council (2019), Available at: https://privycouncil.independent.gov.uk/royal-charters/chartered-bodies/.

Prochaska, J. O. and DiClemente, C. C. (1984), *The Transtheoretical Approach: Towards a Systematic Eclectic Framework*, Homewood: Dow Jones Irwin.

Prosser, M. (2011), 'Student "satisfaction" or student "experience": Interpreting and acting on evaluation results', in P. Trowler and V. Bamber (eds), *Reconceptualising Evaluation in Higher Education*, Berkshire: Open University Press.

Quinn, J. (2004), 'Understanding working-class "drop-out" from higher education through a sociocultural lens: Cultural narratives and local contexts', *International Studies in Sociology of Education*, 14 (1): 57–74. doi: 10.1080/09620210400200119?needAccess=true.

Quinn, J. (2010), *Learning Communities and Imagined Social Capital*, London: Continuum Studies in Educational Research.

Rancière, J. (1992), *The Ignorant Schoolmaster: Five Lessons in Intellectual Emancipation*, Stanford: Stanford University Press.

Randle, K. and Brady, N. (1997), 'Further education and the new managerialism', *Journal of Further and Higher Education*, 21 (2): 229–39.

Readings, B. (2012), 'Dwelling in the ruins', *Oxford Literary Review*, 17 (1): 15–28.

Reay, D. (2017), *Miseducation: Inequality, Education and the Working Classes*, Bristol: Policy Press.

Research Briefings (2018), Available at: http://researchbriefings.parliament.uk/ResearchBriefing/Summary/SN00917.

Richardson, L. D. (2001), *Principles and Practice of Informal Education: Learning Through Life*, Abingdon, Oxon: Routledge.

Richardson, W. (2007), 'In search of the further education of young people in post-war England', *Journal of Vocational Education and Training*, 59 (3): 385–418.

Rinaldi, C. (2006), 'The child is the first citizen', in E. Junior (ed.), *Crossing Boundaries, Ideas and Experiences in Dialogue for a New Culture of Education for Children and Adults*, 101–6, London: Sightlines.

Rizvi, F., Lingard, B. and Lavia, J. (2006), 'Post colonialism and education: Negotiating a contested terrain', *Pedagogy, Culture & Society*, 14 (3): 249–62.

RMFOxford (2015), 'Rhodes must fall in Oxford'. Available at: https://rmfoxford.wordpress.com (accessed 29 January 2020).

Robbine, M. (1963), *Higher Education: Report of the Committee Appointed by the Prime Minister under the Chairmanship of Lord Robbins 1961–63 [Robbins report]*, Great Britain: Committee on Higher Education

Roberts, P. (2010), *Paulo Freire in the 21st Century, Education, Dialogical Transformation*, Boulder: Paradigm Publishers.

Robertson, D. and Schuller, T. (1982), *Stewards, Members and Trade Union Training*, Glasgow: University of Glasgow Press.

Robson, J. (1998), 'A profession in crisis: Status, culture and identity in the further education college', *Journal of Vocational Education and Training*, 50 (4): 585–607.

Rodger, J., Wilson, P., Roberts, H., Roulstone, A. and Campbell, T. (2015), 'Support for higher education students with specific learning difficulties report to HEFCE by York Consulting and University of Leeds'. Available at: https://dera.ioe.ac.uk/23654/1/HEFCE2015_spld.pdf (accessed 28 November 2019).

Rogers, C. (2017), '"I'm Complicit and I'm Ambivalent and that's Crazy": Care-less Spaces for Women in the Academy', *Women's Studies International Forum*, 61: 115–22.

Rogers, C. R. (1957a), 'The necessary and sufficient conditions of therapeutic personality change', *Psychotherapy: Theory, Research, Practice, Training* [serial online], 44 (3): 240–8.

Rogers, C. R. (1957b), 'Personal thoughts on teaching and learning', in H. Kirschenbaum and V. Henderson (eds), *The Carl Rogers Reader*, London: Constable.

Rogers, C. R. (1959), 'A theory of therapy, personality, and interpersonal relationships, as developed in the client-centered framework', in S. Koch (ed.), *Psychology: A Study of a Science, Study 1, Volume 3: Formulations of the Person and the Social Context*, New York: McGraw Hill. Available at: https://archive.org/details/psychologyastudy017916mbp/page/n197 (accessed 24 September 2019).

Rogers, C. R. (1961 [1967]), *On Becoming a Person, a Therapist's View of Psychotherapy*, Boston: Houghton Mifflin.

Rogers, C. R. (1980), *A Way of Being*, Boston: Houghton Mifflin.

Rogoff, B. (2003), *The Cultural Nature of Human Development*, Oxford: Oxford University Press.

Rousseau, D. M. (1989), 'Psychological and implied contracts in organizations', *Employee Responsibilities and Rights Journal*, 2: 121–39. doi: 10.1007/BF01384942.

Rousseau, J. J. (1762 [1991]), *Emile or on Education*, London: Penguin Classics.

Rudd, T. and Goodson, I. (2017), 'Negotiating Neoliberal Education', in T. Rudd and I. Goodson (eds), *Negotiating Neoliberalism: Developing Alternative Educational Visions*, 1–12, Rotterdam: Sense.

Russell Group (2018), Available at: http://www.russellgroup.ac.uk.

Sanders, P. (2013), '*The "family" of person-centred and experiential* therapies', in M. Cooper, M. O'Hara, P. F. Schmid and A. C. Bohart (eds), *The Handbook of Person-Centred Psychotherapy and Counselling*, 2nd edn, 107–22. Basingstoke: Palgrave Macmillan.

Sapin, K. (2013), *Essential Skills for Youth Work Practice*, London: Sage.

Saunders, D. (2014), 'Exploring a customer orientation: Free-market logic and college students', *The Review of Higher Education*, 37: 197–219.

Saunders, D. B. and Blanco Ramírez, G. (2017), 'Against "teaching excellence": Ideology, commodification, and enabling the neoliberalization of postsecondary education', *Teaching in Higher Education*, 22 (4): 396–407.

Schoder, E. (2010), *Paulo Freire's Pedagogy of Love*. Ed.D. Thesis. RUcore: Rutgers University Community Repository. Available at: https://rucore.libraries.rutgers.edu/rutgers-lib/27183/.

Schwimmer, M. (2019), 'Rorty, post-critical pedagogy and hope: A response', *Ethics and Education*, 14 (4): 497–504.

Scoles, J., Huxham, M., Sinclair, K., Lewis, C., Jung, J. and Dougall, E. (2019), 'The other side of the magic mirror: Exploring collegiality in student and staff partnership work', *Teaching in Higher Education: Critical Perspectives*, 24: 1–16.

Scott, P. (2009), 'On the margins or moving into the mainstream? Higher education in further education in England', *Higher Education Quarterly*, 63 (4): 402–18.

Scullion, R. (2011), 'Why we should resist the idea of student as consumer'. Available at: opendemocarcy.net. https://www.opendemocracy.net/en/opendemocracyuk/why-we-should-resist-idea-of-student-as-consumer/ (accessed 12 March 2018).

Seal, M. (2014), 'I like to think other people can trust me', in M. Seal and S. Frost (eds), *Philosophy in Youth and Community Work*, 121–34, Lyme Regis: Russell House.

Seal, M., ed. (2017), *Trade Union Education: Transforming the World*, Oxford: New Internationalist.

Seal, M. (2018), *Participatory Pedagogic Impact Research: Community Involvement in Action*, London and New York: Routledge.

Seal, M. (2019a), 'Threshold praxes in youth and community work: Mapping our pedagogical terrain', in M. Seal (ed.), *Teaching Youth Work in Higher Education: Tensions, Connections, Continuities and Contradictions*, 263–71, Tartu: University of Tartu.

Seal, M. (2019b), *Interrupting Heteronormativity in Higher Education: Critical Queer Pedagogies*, London: Palgrave Macmillan.

Seal, M. (2019c), 'From critical reflective practice to the pedagogical practitioner: Becoming a youth worker in late modernity', *International Journal of Open Youth Work*, 3 (1): 93–110.

Seal, M., ed. (2019d), *Teaching Youth Work in Higher Education: Tensions, Connections, Continuities and Contradictions*, Viljandi: University of Tartu, Newman University, Humak University of Applied Sciences, Estonian Association of Youth Workers.

Seal, M. and Frost, S. (2014), *Philosophy and Youth and Community Work*, Lyme Regis: Russell House.

Seal, M. and Harris, P. (2014), 'I just talk to people', in M. Seal and S. Frost (eds), *Philosophy and Youth and Community Work*, 145–56, Lyme Regis: Russell House.

Seal, M. and Harris, P. (2016), *Responding to Youth Violence through Youth Work*, Bristol: Policy Press.

SEDA (2019), 'College-based Higher Education'. Available from https://www.seda.ac.uk/college-based-higher-education.

Sellar, S. (2015), '"Unleashing aspiration": The concept of potential in education policy', *The Australian Educational Researcher*, 42 (2): 201–15.

Serrano, M., O'Brien, M., Roberts, K. and Whyte, D. (2018), 'Critical pedagogy and assessment in higher education: The ideal of "authenticity" in learning', *Active Learning in Higher Education*, 19 (1): 9–21.

Shattock, M. (2006), *Managing Good Governance in Higher Education*, Maidenhead: Open University Press.

Shattock, M. (2008), 'The change from private to public governance of British Higher Education: Its consequences for higher education policy making 1980–2006', *Higher Education Quarterly*, 62 (3): 181–203. doi: 10.1111/j.1468-2273.2008.00392.x.

Sheeran, Y., Brown, B. J. and Baker, S. (2007), 'Conflicting philosophies of inclusion: The contestation of knowledge in widening participation', *London Review of Education*, 5 (3): 249–63.

Sheldon, J. (2017), 'The pedagogy of the student', *Journal of Curriculum Theorizing*, 32 (1): 91–103.

Sheldrake, P. (2008), 'Contemplation and social transformation: The example of Thomas Merton', *Acta Theologica*, 28: 181–97.

Shor, I. (1987), *Freire for the Classroom: A Sourcebook for Liberatory Teaching*, Portsmouth: Heinemann Educational Books, Inc.

Shor, I. (1996), *When Students have Power: Negotiating Authority in a Critical Pedagogy*, Chicago: University of Chicago Press.

Shor, I. (2012), *Empowering Education: Critical Teaching for Social Change*, Chicago: University of Chicago Press.

Shor, I. and Freire, P. (1987), *A Pedagogy for Liberation: Dialogues on Transforming Education*, Westport: Greenwood Publishing Group.

Shore, C. (2010), 'Beyond the multiversity: Neoliberalism and the rise of the schizophrenic university', *Social Anthropology*, 18 (1): 15–29.

Shore, C. and Wright, S. (1999), 'Audit culture and anthropology: Neo-liberalism in British higher education', *The Journal of the Royal Anthropological Institute*, 5 (4): 557–75.

Shore, C. and Wright, S. (2004), 'Whose accountability? Governmentality and the auditing of universities', *Parallax*, 10 (2): 100–16.

Shore, C. and Wright, S. (2015), 'Governing by numbers: Audit culture, rankings and the new world order', *Social Anthropology*, 23 (1): 22–8.

Simkins, T. (2000), 'Education reform and managerialism: Comparing the experience of schools and colleges', *Journal of Education Policy*, 15 (3): 317–32.

Simmons, J. and Lea, J. (2013), *Capturing an HE Ethos in College Higher Education Practice. QAA 576 12/13*. Gloucester: Quality Assurance Agency for Higher Education. Available at: http://www.qaa.ac.uk/Publications/InformationAndGuidance/Pages/HE-ethos-Lea-Simmons.aspxAs.

Skeggs, B. (2004), *Class, Self, Culture*. Oxon: Routledge.

Slane, R. (2015), 'Report by the 157 Group and EMSI (Economic Modelling Specialists International): The economic impact of further education colleges'. Available at: https://www.economicmodelling.co.uk/wp-content/uploads/The-Economic-Impact-of-Further-Education-Colleges.pdf.

Smith, A. (1776 [2014]), *The Wealth of Nations*, London: Shine Classics.

Smith, D. and Bocock, J. (1999), 'Participation and progression in mass higher education: Policy and the FHE interface', *Journal of Educational Policy*, 14 (3): 283–99.

Smith, L. T. (1999), *Decolonizing Methodologies: Research and Indigenous Peoples*, London: Zed Books.

Smith, M. K. (1994), *Local Education*, Buckingham: Open University Press.

Smith, M. K. (1999 [2008]), 'Informal learning', *The Encyclopaedia of Informal Education*. Available at: http://infed.org/mobi/informal-learning-theory-practice-and-experience/ (accessed 27 January 2020).

Smith, T., Salo, P. and Grootenboer, P. (2010), 'Staying alive in academia: Collectice praxis at work', *Pedagogy, Culture & Society*, 18 (1): 55–66.

Solnit, R. (2016), *Hope in the Dark: Untold Histories, Wild Possibilities*, Edinburgh: Canongate Books.

Sparkes, A. (1992), *Research in Physical Education and Sport: Exploring Alternative Visions*, London: Falmer Press.

Spivak, G. C. (1985), 'Can the subaltern speak? Speculations on widow sacrifice', *Wedge*, 7 (8): 120–30.

St. Pierre, E. A. (2012), 'Another postmodern report on knowledge: Positivism and its others', *International Journal of Leadership in Education*, 15 (4): 483–503.

Stengers, I. (2002), 'A "Cosmo-politics": Risk, hope, change', in M. Zournazi (ed.), *Hope: New Philosophies for Change*, 244–74, Annandale: Pluto Press.

Stevenson, H. (2019), 'Organising (in) education unions today: How can Antonio Gramsci help?', *Education for Tomorrow* (1). https://educationfortomorrow.org.uk/organising-in-education-unions-today-how-can-antonio-gramsci-help/.

Stevenson, S., Clegg, S. and Lefever, R. (2010), 'The discourse of widening participation and its critics: An institutional case study', *London Review of Education*, 8 (2): 105–15.

Stewart, W. A. C. and McCann, W. P. (1967), *The Educational Innovators Volume 1 1750–1880*, London: Macmillan.

Stowell, M. (2004), 'Equity, justice and standards: Assessment decision making in higher education', *Assessment and Evaluation in Higher Education*, 29 (4): 495–510. doi: 10.1080/02602930310001689055.

Sullivan, A (2002), 'Bourdieu and education: How useful is Bourdieu's Theory for researchers?' *Netherlands' Journal of Social Sciences*, 38 (2): 144–66.

Sutton, P. (2015), 'A paradoxical academic identity; Fate, utopia and critical hope', *Teaching in Higher Education*, 20 (1): 37–47.

Sutton Trust (2010), *Responding to the New Landscape for University Access*, London: Sutton Trust. Available at: http://www.suttontrust.com/researcharchive/responding-new-landscape-university-access.

Sutton Trust (2016), Available at: https://www.slideshare.net/SirPeterLampl/the-sutton-trusts-oxbridge-admissions-research-feb-2016.

Taggart, G. (2016), 'Compassionate pedagogy: The ethics of care in early childhood professionalism', *European Early Childhood Education Research Journal*, 24 (2): 173–85.

Tateo, L. (2018), 'Ideology of success and the dilemma of education today', in A. Joerchel and G. Benetka (eds), *Memories of Gustav Ichheiser. Theory and History in the Human and Social Sciences*. doi: 10/1007/978-3-319-72508-6_9.

Tateo, L. (2019), 'Introduction: The inherent ambivalence of educational trajectories and the zone of proximal development with reduced potential', in L. Tateo (ed.), *Educational Dilemmas: A Cultural Psychological Perspective*, 1–21. Abingdon, Oxon: Routledge.

Teichler, U. (2008), 'Diversification? Trends and explanations of the shape and size of higher education', *Higher Education*, 56 (3): 349–79.

The Daily Telegraph (2014), Available at: http://www.telegraph.co.uk/education/universityeducation/student-finance/10987092/More-universities-to-charge-maximum-tuition-fees-of-9000.html.

Thomas, L. (2002), 'Student retention in higher education: The role of institutional habitus', *Journal of Educational Policy*, 17 (4): 423–32.

Thomas, L. (2012), *Building Student Engagement and Belonging in Higher Education at a Time of Change: A Summary of Findings and Recommendations from the What Works? Student Retention & Success Programme*, London: Paul Hamlyn Foundation. Available at: https://www.heacademy.ac.uk/system/files/what_works_final_report_0.pdf.

Thomas, L., Hill, M., O' Mahony, J. and Yorke, M. (2017), *Supporting Student Success: Strategies for Institutional Change*, Paul Hamlyn Foundation, Action on Access, Higher Education Academy. Available at: http://www.phf.org.uk/wp-content/uploads/2017/04/Full-report-Final.pdf (accessed 11 September 2017).

Thomas, L. and Jones, R. (2017), *Student Engagement in the Context of Commuter Students*, London: The Student Engagement Partnership (TSEP). Available online at: http://www. lizthomasassociates. co. uk/projects/2018/Commuter student engagement. pdf.

Thomas, L. and May, H. (2011), 'Student engagement to improve retention and success model', in L. Thomas and C. Jamieson- Ball (eds), *Engaging Students to Improve Student Retention and Success in Higher Education in Wales*, London: Higher Education Academy. Available at: https://www.heacademy.ac.uk/system/files/engagingstudentstoimproveretention_final_english.pdf.

Thompson, N. (2016), *Anti-Discriminatory Practice*, 6th edn, London: Palgrave MacMillan.

Thompson, P. (2018), 'A long goodbye to the "Good Girl": An auto-ethnographical account', in Y. Taylor and K. Lahad (eds), *Feeling Academic in the Neoliberal University: Feminist Flights, Fights and Failures*, London: Springer.

Thompson, R. (2009), 'Social class and participation in further education: Evidence from the Youth Cohort Study of England and Wales', *British Journal of Sociology of Education*, 30 (1): 29–42.

Thomson, R., Henderson, S. and Holland, J. (2003), 'Making the most of what you've got? Resources, values and inequalities in young women's transitions to adulthood', *Educational Review*, 55 (1): 33–46.

Thornton, M. (2016), 'Law student wellbeing: A neoliberal conundrum', *Australian Universities' Review*, 58 (2): 42–50. doi: 10.2139/ssrn.2887812.

Tierney, W. G. (2000), 'Undaunted courage: Life history and the postmodern challenge', *Handbook of Qualitative Research*, 2: 537–53.

Tight, M. (2017), 'Mass higher education and massification', *Higher Education Policy*, 32: 93–108. doi: 10.1057/s41307-017-0075-3.

Tinto, V. (2006), 'Research and practice of student retention: What next?', *Journal of College Student Retention*, 8 (1): 1–19.

Trelfa, J. (2016), 'What is reflective practice?', *Journal of Research Institute*, 53: 1–21.

Tronto, J. (1993), *Moral Boundaries: A Political Argument for the Ethics of Care*, London: Routledge.

Trotman, D. (2018), 'Performativity', in D. Trotman, H. Lees and R. Willoughby (eds), *Education Studies: The Key Concepts*, 73–6, London: Routledge.

Trowler, V. (2010), *Student Engagement Literature Review*, New York: Higher Education Academy.

Tucciarone, K. (2007), 'Vying for attention how does advertising affect search and college choice?', *College & University*, 83 (1): 26–35.

Tummons, J., ed. (2019), *PCET – Learning and Teaching in the Post-compulsory Sector*, London: Sage.

Tymms, M., Peters, J. and Scott, I. (2013), 'Personal development planning: Pedagogy and the politicisation of the personal', *Research in Post-Compulsory Education*, 18 (3): 257–68.

UCAS (2019), Available at: https://www.ucas.com/undergraduate/what-and-where-study/studying-uk-college.

UCAS (Universities and Colleges Admissions Service) (n.d.), Available at: http://www.ucas.com.

UCL (2014), *Why Isn't My Professor Black?* Available at: youtu.be/mBqgLK9dTk4 (accessed 29 January 2020).

UNESCO (1996), Available at: http://unesdoc.unesco.org/images/0010/001095/109590eo.pdf.

UNESCO (n.d.), Available at: https://whc.unesco.org/en/list/170.

UNFCC (2018), 'UN climate change annual report 2017'. Available at: https://unfccc.int/sites/default/files/resource/UNClimateChange_annualreport2017_final.pdf (accessed 18 June 2019).

Universities UK (2017), 'Stepchange, mental health in higher education'. Available at: https ://www.universitiesuk.ac.uk/stepchange (accessed 15 June 2019).
Universities UK (2019), 'Student and staff health and wellbeing'. Available at: https://un iversitiesuk.ac.uk/policy-and-analysis/Pages/Student-and-staff-health-and-wellbeing.a spx (accessed 20 June 2019).
UUK (Universities UK) (2016), 'Higher education in England: Provisions, skills and graduates'. Available at: http://www.universitiesuk.ac.uk/policy-and-analysis/reports/ Documents/2016/higher-education-in-england-provision-skills-and-graduates.pdf.
UUK and NUS (2018), *Black, Asian and minority ethnic student attainment at UK Universities: #ClosingtheGap*. Available at: https://www.universitiesuk.ac.uk/policy-and -analysis/reports/Documents/2019/bame-student-attainment-uk-universities-closing -the-gap.pdf.
Van Heertum, R. (2006), 'Marcuse, Bloch and Freire: Reinvigorating a pedagogy of hope', *Policy Futures in Education*, 4 (1): 45–51.
Viswanathan, G. (1992), 'The beginnings of English literary study in British India', in J. Donald and A. Rattansi (eds), *Race, Culture and Difference*, 149–65, London: Sage.
Vlieghe, J. (2016), 'Rethinking emancipation with Freire and Rancière: A plea for a thing-centred pedagogy', *Educational, Philosophy and Theory*, 2–11. doi: 10.1080/00131857.2016.1200002.
Von Humboldt, A. (2012), Essai sur la géographie des plantes: accompagné d'un tableau physique des régions équinoxiales, fondé sur des mesures exécutées, depuis le dixième degré de latitude boréale jusqu'au dixième degré de latitude australe, pendant les années 1799, 1800, 1801, 1802 et 1803. Editorial MAXTOR.
Vygotsky, L. S. (1978), *Mind and Society: The Development of Higher Mental Processes*, Cambridge, MA: Harvard University Press.
Vygotsky, L. S. (1986), *Thought and Language*, Cambridge, MA: MIT Press.
Wacquant, L. J. D. (2002), 'Scrutinizing the street: Poverty, morality, and the pitfalls of urban ethnography', *American Journal of Sociology*, 107 (6): 1468–532.
Wakeford, J. (2017), 'It's time for universities to put student mental health first', *The Guardian*, 7 September 2017. Available at: https://www.theguardian.com/education/se ries/mental-health-a-university-crisis (accessed 20 June 2019).
Walker, A. J. (2004), 'Methods, theory, and the practice of feminist research: A response to Janet Chafetz', *Journal of Family Issues*, 25 (7): 980–4.
Walker, M. (2002), 'Pedagogy and the politics and purposes of higher education', *Arts and Humanities in Higher Education*, 1 (1): 43–58.
Watts, M. and Bentley, D. (1987), 'Constructivism in the classroom: Enabling conceptual change by words and deeds', *British Educational Research Journal*, 13 (2): 121–35.
Webb, D. (2010), 'Paulo Freire and "the need for a kind of education in hope"', *Cambridge Journal of Education*, 40 (4): 327–39.
Whitchurch, C. (2008), 'Shifting identities and blurring boundaries: The emergence of third space professionals in UK higher education', *Higher Education Quarterly*, 62 (4): 377–96.
Whitchurch, C. (2013), *Reconstructing Identities in Higher Education: The Rise of Third Space Professionals*, London: Routledge.
White, M. (2018), 'Student partnership, trust and authority in universities', *Educational Philosophy and Theory*, 50 (2): 163–73.
Willets, D. (2017), *A University Education*, Oxford: Oxford University Press.
Williams, J. (2006), 'The pedagogy of debt', *College Literature*, 33 (4): 155–69.

Williams, J. (2009), '"Pedagogy of debt" in The edu-factory collective', *Towards a Global Autonomous University*, 89–96. Available at: https://libcom.org/files/The%20Edu-facto ry%20Collection%20-%20Toward%20a%20Global%20Autonomous%20University%20 -%20Cognitive%20Labor,%20The%20Production%20of%20Knowledge,%20and%20Ex odus%20from%20the%20Education%20Factory.pdf (accessed 17 November 2017).

Williams, R. (1984), *The Long Revolution*, London: Pelican.

Winn, J. (2015), 'Reimagining the University PhD Thesis'. Available at: https://research.lin coln.ac.uk/repository/.

Wokler, R. (1996), *Rousseau*, Oxford: Oxford University Press.

Worsham, L. (2001), 'Going postal: Pedagogic violence and the schooling of emotion', in H. Giroux and K. Myrisides (eds), *Beyond the Corporate University*, 229–65, New York: Rowman.

Yorke, M. and Longden, B. (2008), *The First-Year Experience of Higher Education in the UK: Final Report*, London: The Higher Education Academy.

Young, K. (2006), *The Art of Youth Work*, Lyme Regis: Russell House Publishing.

Young, M. (2006), 'Further and higher education: A seamless on differentiated future?', *Journal of Further and Higher Education*, 30 (1): 1–10.

Zachariah, M. (1986). *Revolution through Reform*, New York: Praeger.

Zaffwan, I. and Whitfield, T. (2014), 'Swayed by the logo and name: Does university branding work?', *Journal of Marketing for Higher Education*, 24 (1): 41–58.

Zaidi, U. (2015), 'Co-dependency and relationship satisfaction among spouses of alcohol abusers', *IOSR Journal of Humanities and Social Science*, 20 (1), Ver. II: 86–91. doi: 10.9790/0837-20128691.

Zamojski, P. (2015), 'Philosophy for education - An attempt at exersise in thought', *Kwartalnik Pedagogiczny*, 1 (235): 127–51.

Zembylas, M. (2013), 'Critical pedagogy and emotion: Working through 'troubled knowledge' in posttraumatic contexts', *Critical Studies in Education*, 54 (2): 176–89. doi: 10.1080/17508487.2012.743468.

Zipin, L. and Brennan, M. (2003), 'The suppression of ethical dispositions through managerial governmentality: A habitus crisis in Australian higher education', *International Journal of Leadership in Education*, 6 (4): 351–70.

Zipin, L., Sellar, S., Brennan, M. and Gale, T. (2015), 'Educating for futures in marginalized regions: A sociological framework for rethinking and researching aspirations', *Educational Philosophy and Theory*, 47 (3): 227–46.

Index

academic achievement 126
academic contract 8–9
Academic Practice Unit 59
academics, multiple inherent hierarchies 234
Academic Support Advisor (ASA) 180
accommodating intellectuals 40
accountability 82, 92
Active Culture Transformation Collaborative Development Programme 86
activity spaces 94
  and collective change 56
Alinsky, S. D. 228–9, 231
Allen, L. 214
al-Qaeda campaigns 109
Altbach, P. G. 39
alternative work model 5, 59, 60, 72
ambivalent messages, in schools 159–60
Amsler, S. 32, 70
andragogical practice/principles 201, 205
andragogic model, and issues 80–1
Apple, M. 4, 18
Arendt, H. 32
Aristotle 19
Aronowitz, S. 40
assessment 92, 103, 114–15
Assi, P. 6, 115–16
Association of Colleges and Association for Research 220
attentive love 183
attentiveness, to dissonances/discomfort 42
audit culture 11, 221
Augar Review (2019) 152, 226
Australasia 2
authentic self 122–3
axiology 82

Babaei, A. 87
Back, L. 177

Baizerman, M. 42, 217, 232
Ball, J. 93–4
Ball, S. 4, 6, 49, 55
Ball, S. J. 53
banking model, to education 33, 130, 143, 183, 186
Bardy, H. 6, 41, 100, 103, 230
Barnes-Holmes, D. 105
Barnett, R. 2, 48
Bauman, Z. 82
behaviour-modification model 104
being and having, notion of 53
being human, approach 235–6
Beisser, A. 153
Beniston, J. 4, 5, 80, 120, 192, 212, 231
Benjamin, J. 164
Bentham, J. 49
Bentley, D. 90
Berlak, A. 167
Berthelsen, D. 90
Biesta, G. 227
bilingualism 115
biofinancialization process 4
Black and Ethnic Minority (BME) 110
Bleiklie, I. 39
Boardman, J. 5, 80, 192
Bordesley Green, Birmingham 114
boundary crossers 79–80
Bourdieu, P. 23, 58, 111, 176, 222
Bowe, R. 53
Bracken, S. 205
brave spaces 169–70
Brexit 112
British Office for Students 110
British-Pakistani students 110
British values 109, 111
Brookfield, S. D. 97
Browne Review 52
Brownlee, J. 89, 90
BTEC National and A-level courses 225
Budd, Y. 93

Buddhism 31, 124
Bush, M. 156

Calhoun, C. 39
capital, and labour 72–3
capitalism 22, 29, 221
Capitalist Realism (Fisher) 46
capitalist societies 46
care, as an ethic 81
care-less institutions 177
Carr, M. 81
Cates, R. 68
Cazdan, C. 205
change, notion of 105
childhood experiences, and identity 162–3
Cho, S. 20
choice, notion of 102
Cinderella sector (FE). *See* further education (FE) sector
circle of certainty 208, 211
Clark, L. 40
Clarke, J. 121
The Coalition's 'Students at the heart of the system' paper 52
co-construction of learning 6, 68, 81, 86, 90, 92, 95–6
cognitive behavioural therapy 32
collaboration 94, 120–1, 131
collaborative pedagogies 8
  collaborative work, benefits of 10
  togetherness, and dissonance 111
collective community 56
collective praxis, notion 108–9, 112, 115
collective responsibility 11
College-Based Higher Education (CBHE) 12, 227
  committed workforce 224
  community-based, reasons 224–5
  concept of refraction 221, 224–7
  external advisory monitoring, OfS/QAA 222
  internal systems of quality assurance 221–2
  lecturers 223
  local learning ecologies and 225–7
  lowly position, in hierarchy 223
  pedagogies of transformation enacted in 225
  possibility of, pedagogies of hope 226–7
  providers uniqueness 226
  scrutiny, and managerialist approaches 222
  solutions, hope for HE 220, 223–5
  subjects offered, and students 220
  teaching and learning, recognition, and awards 224
College Higher Education (CHE) 220
Collini, S. 119
colonialism 112
Committee for Public Accounts (2018) 221
commodification of knowledge 38, 172, 180
common sense 20, 67
community-of-practice model 54
community worker's, role 176
compassionate pedagogy 83
Competition and Marketing Authority, UK 60
conscientization idea (*conscientização*) 3–4, 8, 9, 22–3, 138, 157, 169, 172, 174, 200
consciousness
  critical 22–3, 183
  emergence of 68, 89
  false 52, 58, 158
  levels of 22–3
  -raising 22–3, 63, 134, 135, 175, 183
consumer/customer model, students 13, 235
consumerist model, HE 60–1, 151
container-contained relationship 108–9
containment 108–9, 115
contemplative practices/approaches 8, 151, 153, 157, 158, 173, 230
Contemporary issues in early childhood, module 87–8
contract for therapy, notion of 151 n.1
contract marketing 154
contractual relationship, between universities/students 8, 151, 154–5, 159
Conway, M. 188
co-operative college 237
Co-operative learning, research and practice, module 238

Cordeiro, P. 94
countertransference 163, 166
Cowden, S. 2, 37, 46
Crack Capitalism (Holloway) 70
Crenshaw, K. 111
Cribb, A. 53
critical andragogy 204
critical curiosity 67-8
critical intellectuals 40
critical learning 22
critical pedagogy 1-4, 22, 188-9
 assessment 103
 attentiveness, to dissonances 42
 authentic materials using 24
 background on 18
 challenges, hegemony of 'the expert' 171
 characteristics of 5, 24-5, 37
 consciousness raising 22-4
 continued influence of praxis 176
 critique of, post-critical, written conversation
  Gilsenan, M. 29-30, 32-3
  Leoarna, M. 28-9, 31-2, 34-5
 cultural norms in 20
 deconstructing education 144
 disablers, catalogued 45, 232
 disruptive practice 171, 173
 in early year's settings 77-8 (*see also* Early Childhood Education and Care (ECEC) degree programme)
 education preconceptions and 18-19
 emotional impact (*see* non-traditional students, emotional impact on)
 enablers for 44, 231
 enacting, as lone SICP 43
 flexible curriculum, students participation in 24
 focuses on students' discovery and transformation 127
 Freire's approach, ideas of 12, 18, 98, 182 (*see also* Freire, P.)
 fundamental techniques in 24
 generative themes 25
 hopeful enactment, individual reflective accounts 125-6
 hopeful pedagogies possible, in HE 228, 237-8
 improvisation, in very moment 25
 institutions criteria for, supporting 45
 intersubjective experience, in classroom 42
 knowledge and education 18-19, 27
 knowledge creation and 20
 in 'lay' terms, idea 17
 lived experiences (*see* students' perspective)
 making critical thinkers, educators role 21-2
 module, fully handled by students 98-9
 Newman University need for 55-7 (*see also* Newman University, Birmingham UK)
 open spaces of resistance, outside classrooms 47
 paradox in, struggles with process 100
 pedagogic approaches comparison 37
 possibility within HE, perspectives on 37-8, 41-3, 46-7, 228, 232, 237
 practice delivering, hard work 176
 as praxis 19
 process of 99-101, 104
 psychoanalytic theory into 162
 psychosocial frame of (*see* psychosocial critical pedagogy)
 recognizes, interplay between interests 171
 recognizing issue, and adjustment 25
 space, authentic exchange of ideas 173
 through psychosocial lens 162-7
 transformative action 92
 transition activities 125-6
critical reflective spaces, experience of 232
critical thinkers, developing 21-2, 80
Cullen, F. 177
cultural capital 98, 147
cultural criticism 105
cultural-discursive, dimensions 43-4, 46, 231
cultural heritage 20

curriculum. *See also* pedagogy of
    partnership; student partnership
  development   109–10, 231
    assessment design   114–15
    International Education
      module   110–11
    recognition of socio-political
      context   110–12
    situated learning in
      Birmingham   112–13
  ethnic representativeness of   108
  opportunities to influence   44
  planning, people-orientated
    process   87
  tutors/students role   24

Dahlberg, G.   80
dataveillance   82
Davies, M.   2
Davis, A.   32
Debbie, H.   212, 232
deconstruction of education   144
deep learning, concept of   54
defensive reactions   153
deficit model, of student
    development   137, 147–8, 162
De Houwer, J.   105
Deleuze, G.   106
democratic engagement   5, 8, 57, 59, 115,
    138
democratic spaces   7, 118
Department of Scientific and Industrial
    Research   50
Destination of Leavers from HE
    survey   57
dialogical education   91–2, 96, 98, 116
dialogic learning process
  dialogical approaches   87, 91, 98,
    106, 116, 173
  interpersonal and intra-psychic
    108–9
dialogic, participatory and experiential
    (DPE) approach   172
dialogue
  purposeful conversation   91
  teacher-student with student-
    teachers   56, 66–7, 191, 211
DiClemente, C. C.   104
diffraction, concept of   106–7

Disabled Students Allowance (DSA)   10,
    198
Disabled Students Allowance Quality
    Assurance Group (DSA-QAG,
    2017)   198
disablers   45, 232
discrimination   112
dissonance   111
  attentiveness to   42
  defensive reactions and   153–4
  disappointment of expectations   153,
    155
Dobson, I.   188
Donnelly, M.   55
dreams   65–6
Duncan, L.   188
dyslexia
  decision to disclose   202
  defined   195
  into educational contexts   194–5, 201
  heutagogical approaches, for
    students   200
  hopeful andragogy in   201
  identification journey, for students
    additional access stages, recently
      identified   197
    DSA funding, and delays in
      accessing support   198–9
    initial stages of   196
  induction dialogues, support   199
  institutional transformation,
    model   205–6
  neoliberalist practices impact   198–9,
    204
  pen portraits, students   200–3
  phonological awareness   195
  quantification of   194
  rights to reasonable adjustments   196,
    199, 204
  self-disclosure of   204
  students with   10–11
  support services   194, 199–206
  support tutors   199–200
  working memory   195

Early Childhood Education and Care
    (ECEC) degree programme   6,
    77–8, 87
  assessment challenges   92

autobiographical narrative 78–9
contemporary issues modules 87–8
in context of HE 80–1
critical reflections on 92–3
crossing borders, for education 79
egalitarian model 89
Levels 5 and 6, student-led modules at 6, 86–7, 92
personal narrative, and life history 78–9
planning of curriculum 87–8
relationships between children and teachers 88–90
settings and universities 80–1
use of dialogue with students 91–2
Ecclestone, K. 167
economic promises 152
educated hope, form 70
educational counselling, students vignette 152, 154, 156, 158
educational institutions, hierarchy UK 222
educational relationships 104–6
educational settings, function in 85
educational spaces 10, 42, 44, 46
educational success 79. *See also* learning outcomes
educational travelogue 98
education, and knowledge 82
    answers of 67
    application, morals behind 19
    Augar Review (2019), and tertiary 152
    banking approach to 3, 17
    as business, idea of 46
    colonial legacies and 112
    commodification 38, 54, 113, 114, 172, 180
    conceptions about 18–20
    constructions of democracy in 21
    diminished view of 65
    essentials of 22
    expectations, reforming of 17–18
    Freire's views 62–3
    as hopeful enterprise 36
    instrumentalization of 38
    Mandela, Nelson about 65
    neoliberal construction, as 'form of capital' 37
    ongoing, unfinished process 63, 68
    perceived as, transformative process 171
    as political practice 85
    as positive conversation 36
    as praxis, under siege 172
    purpose of, to 'be more' 63–4
    reproduction of society, implicated in 111
    Rogers' writing on, and commonality 157
    as self-education 30
    social justice in, three 'r's framework 205–6
    state-controlled 49
    success, expectations and realization 153
    types of 19
    value, in terms of economic benefit 180
    as way, society transmit knowledge, skills, attitudes 110
Education and Training Foundation report, 2016 225
Education in Birmingham, module 110, 112–13
éducation permanente, UNESCO's recommendation 227
educators 35–6. *See also* hope
    powers of 20
    role of 23–4, 66, 88–9
Egan, K. 78
Emile (Rousseau) 49
Emilia, R. 81
emotional engagement of students 90–1
emotional impact, on non-traditional students (*see* non-traditional students, emotional impact on)
emotional inhibitions, power to challenge 174
emotional labour 183–4, 224
emotional response, components 9, 172
emotional thinking 175
emotions, hegemony of 174
empathy practice 41–2
Empowering Education: Critical Teaching for Social Change (Shor) 38
engaged pedagogue 213
Engels, F. 221

English education system 111
enlightenment 100
enquiry-based learning 68
entrepreneurialism, idea of 46
episteme 19
epistemic justice 83
epistemological disobedience 42
epistemology 82, 85
Equality Act 2010 199
equality, in education 61
Erasmus staff week, November 2018 208
Erikson, E. 161, 165
ethics of care 173
ethnic backgrounds, and resonances 109–10
ethnic diversity, markers of 113
ethnographic walk
   discussion of material and experience 113–14
   students' documentation, of localities 114, 116
   understanding of sites of contest 113–14, 116
Europe, critical pedagogy in 2
experiential learning 98
   group interviews, findings (*see* students's perspective)
   interviews, and reflective discussions 97–8
experimental approach, dangers 103
external critical pedagogues 40

facilitator, enhanced role in OST events 216–17
fairness criteria 45
faith, act of 34
Felten, P. 68
financial crisis, of 2007/8 51–2, 57
First World War in 1918 50
Fisher, B. 94
Fisher, M. 46
FitzSimmons, R. 183
Foley, P. 20
Foucauldian notion of discourse 161
Foucault, M. 26, 123
foundation year programme 137–8, 146–8. *See also* Newman University, Birmingham UK continuation and progression rates 145
   new aims, to be included 143
   student vignettes 138–43
freedom notion, ambiguity 101–2
freedom of choice 102
free school meals (FSM) 222
Freirean partnership working 7–8
Freire for the Classroom: A Sourcebook for Liberatory Teaching (Shor and Freire) 38
Freire, P. 1, 6, 26–7, 32, 67, 70–2, 78, 130, 133–4
   about human nature 236
   andragogical principles 201
   approaches to, youth and community work 98–9
   banking approach, to education 3, 17, 33, 36, 67, 130, 143
   conceptualization of critical pedagogy 18, 173
   conscientization 4, 8, 9, 22, 138, 157, 172
   critical thinking for 173
   culture of silence 198
   dialogic practice 64, 91, 163
   generative themes 9, 11
   hope need for 25–6, 64, 132, 205, 239
   human, term usage 236
   learning meaningful 89
   non-conformity before injustice 58
   notions of generative themes 92
   Partnership Project programme, on Freirean model 7–8
   pedagogy of desire 66
   Pedagogy of Hope 65
   pedagogy of love 83, 98, 182–3, 187
   pedagogy of oppressed 12, 67, 139, 175, 221
   pedagogy of partnership, principles of 59, 63–4
   planning of a curriculum 86–7, 104
   'problem posing' education 33, 67
   respectful dialogue 56, 66–7, 191, 211
   revisions and critiques, of psychoanalysis 162
   role of power in learning 11, 191, 198
   student partnership 130, 135

student-tutor relationship   89
teacher as student and student as
    teacher   33, 56, 191
threads of commonality, with Rogers'
    writing   157
French education system study   222
Fromm, E.   53
Funding Council and Training and
    Enterprise Councils   221
Further and Higher Education Act
    (1992)   220, 221
Further Education Funding Council   225
further education (FE) sector   11–12
    an 'alternative' system, neglected   223
    audit culture in   221
    CBHE sector (*see* College-Based
        Higher Education (CBHE))
    datafication and dataveillance   221
    defined by funding council   226
    disadvantaged groups and
        communities, strong bonds
        with   224
    FE colleges   12
    lecturers' ethic of care   224
    as second-chance sector   221, 224
    strengths   220
    vocational and community education,
        vital role in   223, 225

Gabriel, J.   93
Gadamer, H.-G.   30, 33
Gale, T.   222
Gamsu, S.   55
generative curriculum model   6, 56, 87,
    93–4
generative themes, concept of   9, 11
    characteristics   25
generosity attitude   36, 41, 132
George Williams College   30
Gewirtz, S.   53
Gibbs, G.   54
Gibby, C.   225
gift of education, Arendt's
    expression   32–3
Gilbert, G.   135
Gilsenan, M.   4, 28–9, 32–6, 103, 106,
    120, 124
Giroux, H.   1, 4, 6, 9, 11, 86, 89, 92
    about critical pedagogy   18, 216
    curriculum, students participation
        24
    higher education, as public good   58
    intellectuals, types of   40
    marketization, impacts   46
    student self-determination   175
    synthesizes, conceptualization of
        critical pedagogy (Freire)   173
    transformative learning   172
    university, civic purpose   39
Giroux, S.   89, 92
globalization   37
Goffman, E.   165
Goodson, I.   12, 52, 221, 224, 227
good work, in classroom   29, 32
Grace, P.   9, 42, 232
Graham, C.   188
Gramsci, A.   22, 49
Grande, S.   186
Gray, B.   82
Groenke, S. L.   2
Grootenboer, P.   109, 115
Guattari, F.   106

Haldone Report, first (1905)   50
Hale, S.   147
Hammond, C.   3
Hand up or hand out? event   217–18
happiness   160
Hargreaves, D.   225
Harrington, K.   62
Harris, P.   9, 169, 230, 232–4
Hatch, J. A.   2
hate crimes   109
'having', concept of   53
Hayes, D.   167
Healey, M.   62
hegemonic hierarchical structuring, in
    Britain   111, 114–15
hegemony   98, 106
Heron, J.   9
hierarchies, and power   212–14
higher education (HE)   2, 77–8. *See also*
    critical pedagogy
    attaining a qualification   186
    attitudinal stance to   156–7
    capitalist thinking in   37
    CBHE as new hope, through
        refraction   224–6

children/students understanding, priority to 83
condition of 'being a student' in UK 154
consumerist/marketized model of 60–1, 151
contemplative practices 8
critical hopeful pedagogies, possible in 12–13, 150, 156–8, 228–9, 237–8
disappointment of expectations 151, 153–5
domination of 'market logic' 37
early year's settings in 5–6
enacting critical pedagogy in 37–8, 40
epistemic authority, teacher as 83
expectations and realizations, conflict 153–5
funding regimes, power dynamics in 27
hegemony of neoliberalism/neo-conservatism 5, 38
hope of resistance in 58
ideology of success 151
institutional advertising 8
learning environment 83–4
learning process, and outcomes 8
link between early years and 84
managerialism within 1, 5, 37–8, 235
market impact on the learning process in 31
marketized model, provision 10–11, 155–6
means of empowerment, and social mobility 160
nature of educational contract, language used 151, 154, 159
neoliberal programme in 58
partnership working in 72
pedagogic approaches comparison 37
pedagogies, openings and spaces in 1–2
policies, hegemonic 5, 58
policy, 'potential' term in 8, 151
policy in UK, increased commodification 172
potential for critical pedagogy in 228–9

power operation within 42
professional and support staff 188
as public good, educators role 58
public, value of 160
redefinition, role of 155–6
Reggio Emilia pedagogy in 81, 83
rhetoric of potential 8, 151, 230
sector, individual reflections on 118–26, 229
settings and universities 80–1
shared hopes, dreams and visions 65
spaces supporting students in 5–6
strong learning community, role in 43
students, as consumers 84
systemic contradiction existing 155
tensions enacting, critical pedagogy within 37
transition of students to 79–80
value and worth of 4
values-based model for, with partnership principles 64–8, 72
Higher Education Academic Department's (HEAD) suite of programmes 119
Higher Education Academy 224
Higher Education and Research Act (2017) 52, 237
Higher Education in Further Education (HEinFE) 220
higher education institutions (HEIs) 181, 186
  criteria for supporting, critical pedagogy 45
  student retention, effort to 182
higher education (HE) policy, in England 4, 48
  2007/8 financial crisis 51
  context, and history 48–50
  critical pedagogic approaches, to be accepted 57
  journey from old to new neoliberal/managerial world 50–1
  neoliberalism 52, 53, 57
  Newman, John Henry (1852) role in 50
  publicly funded Higher Education Funding Councils, established 50

Rousseau, philosophical work of   49
state support for tuition, removal   51, 53
student-as-consumer, ideology of   52
student-as-consumer, problematic nature   51–5
Teaching Excellence Framework (TEF) in   51, 53
tuition fees, introduction   51–3
university-level education, for wider section   50–1
value for money, HE system   52
wealthy elite, and university participation   49
Higher Education Statistics Agency (HESA)   50, 55, 57, 223
Higher National Certificates or Diplomas (HNCs/HNDs)   223
historical materialism (Marx's)   72–3
Hodgson, A.   224
Hodgson, N.   29, 32, 33
Holland, S.   169
Holloway, J.   29, 31, 70–2, 192
Holroyd, M.   32
Homo economicus   80, 84
hooks, b.   42, 65, 176, 213
hope
  ambiguous nature   177
  creation, by doing work   229–30
  as educational attitude   36
  faith and   34–5
  Freire's views   26, 64, 226
  implicit in reflexive learning   202
  living, as moment-to-moment practice   71
  as 'method for living'   34, 229
  need of   25–6
  probability and *possibility*, difference   36
  reasons, translated into action   70–2
  symbolic, of what could be   230
hopeful andragogy   201, 229
hopeful critical pedagogue   71
hopeful pedagogic spaces, concept of   5–6
Hopeful Pedagogy (hooks)   173
Hope in the Dark (Solnit)   31
hopelessness   25, 32, 35, 40–1, 134, 229, 230, 235

Hope' project, in South Africa   2, 226
horizontal model, of pedagogical practice   89
House of Lords Economics Affairs Committee Report   52
Housing Justice, OST event for   217–18
'How we teach', document   3, 17, 21–3
human capital   47
human doing   71
humanistic theory of actualization   153
Humboldt, W.   32, 38
Humphry, N.   93
hybridity   79
Hyland, T.   158

Ichheiser, G.   153
The Idea of a University (1852)   73
identity formation   165–6
identity, process of   42
ideology critique   97
imposter syndrome   29, 68, 173
individualized learning approach   102
individual potential, concept   173
industrial approaches to student   182, 184–6
industrial systems, in education
  impact on retention and progress   182
  industrial model, failings   184–5
  provision of flexibility   185–6
  rules focused   185
industrial trainers   49
inequality, recognition of   172
inescapable selves   122–3
informal, and evening spaces   215
informal learning, and education, significance of   176
informed sense of powerlessness   40–1
Ingleby, E.   225
intellectuals, types   40
intellectual values   157
interacting with people, process of   173
International Education module   110, 111, 113, 115
  ethnographic walk, discussion of material and experiences   113–14
  Global diversity and educational inequality   111
  model practice 'inauthenticity'   115

International Freire Conference in Cyprus 2
internationalism 115
internationalization concept 37
International Journal for Students as Partners 62
intersectionality 98, 106, 173, 175, 180
interstitial spaces 31
intersubjectivity/relationships, psychodynamic insights into 163
intra-action, concept of 106
intransitive consciousness 22–3
Irish CBHE research 225
Islamic State or Da'ish 109–11
Islamophobia 109
Israeli-Palestinian conflict 109

James, D. 227
John 5, 7, 11
Joldersma, C. 20
Jung, C. 174
Jung's disintegration 174

Kabat-Zinn, J. 15
Karima 11
Kaufman, P. 158
Kell, M. 93
Kemmis, S. 43
Khan, A. 93
Khoshnood, A. 87
Kift, S. 121
Kincheloe, J. L. 4, 18
Klein, M. 162
knowledge, as interactive process 89. *See also* education, and knowledge
knowledge creation 22, 41, 211, 234
knowledge economy 4, 48, 51, 65, 204
Knowles, M. 80
Kopelson, K. 21

la facultad, defined 41
Land, R. 98
language school advertisement 113
Lea, J. 222
learned hopelessness, sense of 25, 40–1, 235
learner-centred teaching 12
learners, and learning
 decision-makers 80–1
 defined 19, 54
 discursive/dialogical approach, challenges 173
 environment 83–4, 96
 as passive receivers 20
 as personal growth process 151
 resistance and 21
 through pictures 116
 traits cultivated 18
 transformational 12
Learning in Large Groups: Their Implications for the Future (Rogers, 1980) 158
learning outcomes 17, 44, 97, 100, 104–5, 206, 237
Learning to Labour (Willis) 112
lecturer-led assessment requirements 92
Ledwith, M. 88, 89
Le Grange, L. 226
Levinas, E. 57, 81
Levy, P. 62
Lewis, G. E. 188
liberal theory 72
Lilley, S. 53
liminal spaces 1, 68, 85, 195, 201, 209, 210, 214
Lipman, M. 83
Lipsky, M. 124, 176
Liston, D. P. 183
Little, S. 62
Local Education Authorities (LEAs) 221
Local Enterprise Partnership (LEP) 225
local learning ecologies, and CBHE 225–6
logic 22, 23
Longitudinal Educational Outcomes data (LEO) 54
Loveland-Armour, L. 10–11, 205–6
love our students 10, 183
Lucey, H. 79

Macartney, B. C. 81
Macedo, D. 201
McElearney, P. 227
Maclaren (McLaren), P. 4, 18, 166, 172, 201
McLeod, J. 213

McLoughlin, T. 10–11, 41, 44, 208, 210–13, 215, 232, 234, 235
McTaggart, B. 225
Madigan, M. 68
Mahmoudi, A. 87
Mahon, K. 5, 39, 43–5, 231, 232, 238
Malaguzzi, L. 81
Mandela, N. 65
Manifesto for a Post-Critical Pedagogy (Hodgson, Vlieghe and Zamojski) 36
Marcel, G. 202
market-driven approaches, and university sector 48
marketization, in higher education (HE) 46–7, 58
Marx, K. 70, 72–3, 221
Massey, D. 56, 87, 94
material-economic dimensions 43–4, 46, 231
material engagement 107
Matheson, D. 49
Mathias, L. 4, 5, 7, 28, 29, 31–6, 44, 72–3, 119, 121, 122–6, 136, 213, 229–32, 234, 235
May, H. 146
Mayo, P. 91
Mead, M. 71
meaning-making process 114
  containment process 109
  identity and 42
Melody, J. 79
mental health problems 155, 180–1
meritocracy 222
Meyer, J. 98
Mills, C. W. 113
Milojevic, I. 51
mindfulness-based approaches 150–1, 157, 158, 160
Minister for Apprenticeship and Skills, in England and Wales 223
Miskelly, P. 188
mixed-methods approach 176
modern universities 38, 228, 238–9
modesty of impact 31
Moors, A. 105
moral practice 79
Moss, P. 80, 85

Motta, S. C. 5, 41–2
multiversity 119

National Student Survey (NSS) 45, 53, 54, 57
National Union of Students (NUS), UK 5, 54
  Manifesto for Partnership (2012) 60, 69
  resetting relationship between teachers/the taught 69–70
  responsible student partners 62
  student partnership, as 'alternative work model' 59–62, 72
  Wenstone, Rachel VP (HE) 60, 69
Neary, M. 38, 70, 72, 125, 237
Nelson, K. 121
neoliberalism, and neo-conservatism 1, 4, 5, 29, 31, 37–8, 48, 52–3, 57, 59, 64, 69, 82, 84, 172, 198–9, 221, 235, 236, 239
neoliberal policy, impacts 10, 180
neoliberal values, in education 181–2
New Labour Government (1997–2010) in UK 118
new managerialism 1, 5, 37–8, 235
Newman, John Henry 11, 38, 50, 73, 119
Newman University, Birmingham UK 5, 8, 48, 133–4, 137–8, 146–8, 188–90
  approach to policy, and problems 55–6
  ASA service 180
  characteristics of students at 146
  complexity, of students 56
  courses in, education and multi-professional practice at 115
  critical pedagogy group in 43–5, 231–2
  development projects at, co-investigation 68
  ECEC programme in 87–8
  Erasmus staff week, open event 208, 214–16
  ethics of care, key component 57
  ethnically diverse, students body 110
  faith in 'hopeful pedagogies' at 104, 146

Freirean principles, student partnership at 64–8
'How we teach', document 3, 17, 21–3
individual reflections on working 120–5
induction, transition and retention programmes 7
need for critical pedagogy 55–7
opportunity for discussions 131
pedagogy of partnership, principles 50, 59, 72 (see also pedagogy of partnership)
professional and support roles 190–1
self-transformation 9
situated learning, in Birmingham 112–13
small university, relatively 2, 5, 59, 80, 120, 135, 192
strategic plan at, human approach 236
structural features of 143–5
student-led modules in 86–7
student partnership model 128–31, 135 (see also student partnership)
student partnership projects in 71
students, disadvantaged/backgrounds of 55–6, 86, 135, 180
student-staff partnership, enacting 59, 64, 231
student transition 121–7, 146
transformative pedagogy 56
transition pedagogy in 118–21
values-based higher education 5, 59
vision of public good of degree study 119
wider student engagement, barriers to 86 (see also widening participation (WP))
'new' universities 238–9
Noddings, N. 57, 81, 173
non-academic roles. See also professional and support staff
non-academic roles 188
non-formal learning methodology 172–3
non-traditional students, emotional impact on 9, 171

aspects of vulnerability/validation 174–6
critical pedagogical, approach/practice 172, 174–6
disruptive practice 171, 173
pedagogy of love 173–4
teaching/learning experiences, emotional response, components 172, 175

object relations 162, 164
Office for Students (OfS) 51, 55, 120–2, 237, 239
Ogden, T. 164
O'Hara, M. 157
Olssen, M. 53
One Dimensional Man (Marcuse) 229
open event 216
Open Space Technology (OST) 208–9
developed by Owen, Harrison 208
facilitator's role, to create and hold space/time 209, 212, 214
fear, certainty and trust 210–11
hierarchies, power and space 212–14
OST event, resistance to abandoning tradition in 218–19
physical and planned space 214–15
principles to sessions 209
rule of two feet 209, 211
walking the circle, introduction 218
Other/otherness 81, 164, 167
outcome-focused discourse 99–100. See also learning outcomes
outcomes-based education 8, 10, 12, 221
Owen, H. 208, 209, 212–15, 217, 218

Papadopoulos, D. 53
paradigm, positivist 82
Paradoxical Theory of Change (Bessier's) 153
Parkes, S. 4, 7, 8, 118–23, 125, 126, 229, 234
participatory pedagogy 78, 82, 84, 86
partnership projects, with students 7–8, 71, 128, 235. See also pedagogy of partnership
shared responsibility 61–2
Passeron, J. 111, 222
Pauline 9

Pearson debates, on modern
         university   38, 238
pedagogical love   34, 83, 180–7, 192
   framework, educational enterprise
         of   10, 182–2
pedagogical self, ideas of   9
pedagogic practice, pointers and
         principles for   41
pedagogic spaces   12, 214
   authentic and visceral   232–3
A Pedagogy for Liberation (Shor/
         Freire)   38
pedagogy of debt   52, 131
Pedagogy of Debt (Williams)   31, 131
pedagogy of desire   66
pedagogy of discomfort   167
The Pedagogy of Hope (Freire)   65
pedagogy of love   173–4
pedagogy of partnership   5, 7, 59, 63
   an education of answers   67
   based on Freirean principles   64
   co-construction, of solutions   68
   co-investigation   67–8
   co-operation defines success   63
   diversity, as strength   67
   fundamental risk to, working   69
   HE practice, allows authentic
         hope   70–1
   hope, reasons for   70–2
   human relationships, at core   63–4
   NUS, *Manifesto for Partnership*   60–2
   as ongoing, transformative
         process   68–9
   practice of democracy   64
   principles of   59
   radical collegiality, possibility of
         achieving   71
   respectful dialogue   66–7
   shared hope principle   64–6
   shared vision, importance on   66
   student engagement in   70
   student-staff partnership   62–3
   students/teachers, dialogue   64
   subjects, treatment   64
   as transformative and collaborative
         process   68–9
pedagogy of questioning   67
pedagogy of space
   learning requires   201

'mutual caring'   90
   space for teaching and learning   90
Pence, A.   93–4
performative potential   153
performativity culture   38
personal salvation, conception   229
person-centred approach   150, 153,
         156–8
Peters, J.   72
Peters, M.   53
phronesis   19
play, ideas/possibilities   78, 83–4
Poland, W.   174
policy sociology (Ball's)   4, 48, 55
polytechnics abolition, in 1992   238
positivism   82
positivist paradigm   82
post-compulsory education   220, 227
post-critical, critiques of critical
         pedagogy   4, 28–9, 35, 71
   faith, importance   34
   impacts and, written conversation
      Gilsenan, M.   29–30, 32–3
      Mathias, L.   28–9, 31–2, 34–5
   pedagogies   1, 32, 34, 229
      post-critical thinkers   29
   take on education, hope   35
potential, concept in HE. *See also* higher
         education (HE)
   awareness of interconnectedness
         158
   competence and worthiness,
         ideas   153
   contemplative practices   151, 153,
         157–8
   contractual implications and   152–3
   expectations and realization, defensive
         reactions to   153–4, 159
   fulfilling one's potential   152
   fundamental conflict, between
         expectations/realizations   153
   meanings   152
   person-centred approaches   150, 153,
         156, 157, 173
   and psychological difficulties   151,
         152
   strong/weak   152–3
   student well-being issue   151, 155–6
   therapeutic contract, concept of   150

power dynamics, and hierarchies 212–13
practice architecture, framework 43
practice for freedom, pedagogy as 175
present moment awareness, idea of 154
principle over practice, elevation of 229
principles of action 79
Pring, R. 79
Prinsloo, P. 186
problem-based learning 68
problem-centred thinking 201
Prochaska, J. O. 104
professional and support staff 188–90
  advantages, areas of 189
  to be agents of change 192
  comfort zone, stepping out of 191–3
  divides, to be overcome 234
  fear of freedom 191
  gender nature of 190–1
  lack of confidence 190–1
  qualifications 190
  understanding staff, beyond role titles 192
professional doctorate (EdD) 77–8
progressive educators, and gaps 32
project-based learning 68
Prosser, M. 54
proxy pedagogues 40–1
pseudo authenticity 30
psychoanalysis 161–2
psychodynamic psychology/theory 162–3
psychological contract, notion of 151 n.1
psychosocial critical pedagogy 161, 168–9
  'defended' self, tutors and students 166, 168
  identity, construction of 165–6
  psychological defences 166–7
  recognition of the otherness 167
  safer space, in situational context 164–5
  transference, and countertransference processes 163, 166
  tutors, biographies and work settings impact 166–9
psychosocial development 161
public educators 49

Quality Assurance Agency (QAA) 222
quality education 96
Quinn, J. 123

Rancière, J. 4, 23, 36
Randolf, L. 212–14, 222
Realising Engagement through Active Culture Transformation Collaborative Development Programme 56, 86
reflexive learning approaches 202
refraction concept 224–7
Reggio Emilia approach (pedagogy) 6, 81, 83
Reisberg, L. 39
Reitenauer, V. 68
relationally centred approach 90
relational pedagogy 6, 231. See also critical pedagogy
  connected teaching 90
  early experiences, sense of self impact 163
  focus on parameters 89–90
  psychosocial model of subjectivity 163–4
  and tutor's role 88–90, 122
relationship-centred pedagogy 33
relationship with learners 81
relativistic epistemology beliefs 89
Research Excellence Framework (REF) 54
Research in Critical Education Studies group, at Lincoln University 38
respectful dialogue 66–7
retention, defined 120
rhizomic working 125
Rhodes must fall in Oxford' campaign (RMFOxford) 109
right-wing populist parties, and leaders 46
Rinaldi, C. 81
Roberts, P. 157
Roberts, R. 8, 56, 159, 173, 230–2
Rogers, C. R. 31, 83, 157, 173
Rogoff, B. 81
Rohingya peoples 109
Romero Freire Institute 43–4, 216, 232
Rousseau, J. J. 49

Royal Commission review of university (1850) 50
Rudd, T. 52
Rumbley, L. E. 39
Russell Group
  institutions 122, 181
  universities 222–3, 235

safer pedagogical spaces 164–5
Salo, P. 109, 115
Schoder, E. 183
Schwimmer, M. 34
scrutiny, of institutions 54, 57
Scullion, R. 54
Seal, M. 3, 5, 6, 8, 11, 46, 71, 98, 208, 210–14, 229–35
self-authorship 96
self-awareness 124, 176
self-concept 157, 165
self-identifying critical pedagogues (SICPs) 5, 12–13, 71
  articulating, hope importance 229–30
  boundary crossing, and border pedagogy 230
  categories of 40
  challenging expected role boundaries 231
  contract with students, and expectations 230
  help to rearticulate university 238–9
  hope cultivation/maintenance of 229
  indigenous knowledges use, in HE 13, 233
  lone SICP, danger of being indulgent 43, 231
selflessness 176
Sellar, S. 152, 153
semi-transitive consciousness 22–3
sense of belonging 90, 116, 119, 134, 144
Serrano, M. 89
service learning 68, 129
shared hope, principle 64–6
shared learning spaces 83
shared visions, collective hopes/dreams 66
Sharpe, P. 186, 187
Shor, I. 4, 18, 38
Simmons, J. 222

Singh, G. 2, 37
Smith, A. 26–7, 48
Smith, C. 106
Smith, M. 30
Smith, M. K. 233
Smith, T. 109, 115
social capital 25, 54, 98, 106, 135, 176
social class distinctions 111, 115
social constructivism 88, 96
social mobility 38, 51, 79, 160, 238–9
social objects 82
social policy academics, critique 34–5
social-political dimensions 43–4, 46, 231
Solnit, R. 31, 35
spaces of engagement 47
Spours, K. 224
Staff and Educational Development Association (SEDA) 224
staff-student partnerships 62–3, 231
Star Wars 223
Steinberg, S. R. 4, 18
Stengers, I. 35
stepping/standing back (pedagogical stance) 80
Stevenson, H. 227
street-level bureaucrats 176
stress reduction interventions, in schools/universities 157
structural resistance, in world 41
student activity-based education 96
student-as-consumer, concept/model 48, 51–3, 234–5
  lecturer, as service provider 54
  satisfaction, and employability 46, 47, 54
  short-term reproduction learning 54
student partnership, responding 72
student-centred perspective 10
Student Finance England (SFE) 11, 199
student partnership 234. *See also* pedagogy of partnership
  co-constructed solutions 133
  co-investigatory process of 132–3
  dialogic practice, respectful 131–2
  idea of 62–3
  in Newman university 128–9
  payment and recognition 130–1, 136
  projects, critiques 134
  shared dreams and hopes 129–31

student-staff partnership 129–30, 135–6
 transformation through, continuing 133–4
 ways of engaging with students 130
students and tutors, impact of power relationships 89
Students as partners' research project 116, 234
student self-determination, pursuit of 175
students' perspective
 on freedom 101–2
 on power 103–4
 on process of critical pedagogy 99–101
student-staff partnership 2, 59
student suicide, figures for 155
student-teacher relations 88–91, 106, 129–30, 135–6, 191
student-teacher relationships, enablers 44
student transition 121–7
student voices
 emotional engagement 90–1
 generative curriculum model 93–4
 module co-lead, with lecturer support 90
 module, responses to 92–5
 planning of a curriculum 88
 positive impacts 94–5
 provided academic sources/study materials 88
 support importance of 90–1
 transformative pedagogy 94–5
 use of dialogue with students 91–2
subjectivities sharing 41
success, in education
 circumstances role 186
 competence and worthiness, ideas of 153
 defensive reactions, by students 153–4
 educational success 79 (*see also* learning outcomes)
 ideological notions of and actuality, contradiction between 153
 ideology of 151
 interplay of 'personal and situational' factors 153
 UNFCCC definition of 156
support processes, industrializing 182, 184–5
Sutton, P. 32
Sutton Trust (2010)
 free school meals (FSM) 222
Swedish Folk High School Grundtvig model of education 144–5
symbolic resistance 26

Tarragó, M. T. 115
Tateo, L. 154
Tavistock experiential group work 145
teacher-dominated education 17
teacher education 2, 96
teachers, accepted roles 21
teacher-student power imbalance 6
teacher-student with students-teachers 56, 91
Teaching and Higher Education Act (1998) 51
Teaching Excellence and Student Outcomes Framework 45
Teaching Excellence Framework (TEF) 51, 53–5, 57, 224
teaching processes 99
Teaching to Transgress (hooks) 65–5
Teaching Youth Work in Higher Education (Seal) 30
techne 19
Te Whariki curriculum 81
therapeutic frame 151 n.1
thing-centred pedagogy 30, 33
thinking, model of (Lipman's) 83
third-space professionals 10, 188, 234
third spaces 2, 169
Thomas, L. 126, 146
Thompson, P. 191
three 'r's framework, in university practice 205–6
threshold concepts 98, 105
Thunberg, G. 71
Tierney, W. G. 79
togetherness, multiple dilemmas of 6–7
transference 163, 166
transformation
 ongoing process of 68–9

of participation 81
Rancièrian form of 30
transformative intellectuals 40
transformative pedagogy 6, 56, 94–5, 119, 121, 125
The Transformative Power of Hope in Education 3
transition, complexities of 119
transition-as-becoming 56, 120–1, 123, 126
Trelfa, J. 169
Trojan Horse affair 109, 111–12
Tronto, J. 57, 81
Trotman, D. 221
trust 210, 211, 213, 215
trust-building
    components 41
    and vulnerability 213

UK Labour Government (1997–2010) 50–1
UK's higher education sector, individual reflections on 118–26, 229
unbound professional 10, 189
uncertainty 210, 211, 217
unconditional positive regard, term 83
unconscious processes 42, 164, 168
United Nations Framework Convention on Climate Change (UNFCCC, 2018) 156
university education. See also higher education (HE)
    approach to marketing, and regulations 154
    assessed, teaching excellence 53–4, 57
    as autonomous spaces 35
    biofinancialisation of 53
    budgets, as compared with CBHE 223
    and CBHE, opposite concepts 226
    civic responsibility 39, 72
    critical pedagogy group, influence 40
    as culprit, in market economy 53
    cultural role in society 39, 51, 72
    democratic practice in 59, 61
    economic benefits, to societies 39, 180

    education, sense of 'common good' 51
    emotional practices, disrupt norms of 42
    government awards, funding through 223
    Humboldt's characterization 32, 38
    importance of hope in 35
    mindful approaches, adoption 151
    mission statements, and objectives 38–9
    performance indicators 54
    policy, and policy devices for 53
    practices 59, 68, 72
    purpose of, and debates 38
    reimaging, inclusive as 205–6
    SICPs role 40
    stress reduction interventions in 157
    students, mental health issues 155
    threat of failure, and anxiety 159
un-self, idea 123
US higher education, issues 52
utopianism 4, 6, 26, 28, 33, 230
Uusiautti, S. 183

validation, aspects of 174–5
value for money, higher education 51–3
values and attitudes 123–6
Varga, L. 95
virtual learning environment (VLE) 94, 97, 101–3, 105
Vlieghe, J. 29, 30, 32, 33, 35
vulnerability
    as component of trust-building 213–14
    culture of openness, and power of 174, 229
    defence mechanisms against 166–7
    mutual sharing of 41
    validation and 174–6
Vygotsky, L. S. 88

Walker, M. 39
Walkerdine, V. 79
war memorial 114
Watts, M. 90
Webb, D. 26
well-being of students 155–6
    student vignette 156

Wells, P.   49
Wenstone, R.   60, 69
'what-if' choice makers   80
Whelan, N.   62
Whitchurch, C.   10, 188–91
White Paper, 'Technical education', 1956   226
widening participation (WP). *See also* participatory pedagogy
  CBHE and   222
  female Muslim students   6
  Foundation Years aimed at   137, 143
  Labour Government committed to   50–1, 118
  Newman University, agenda   8, 10, 55, 79–80, 126, 131, 137, 180
  notion of   50–1
  social mobility, in guise of   239
  vertical progression possibilities and   227

Williams, J.   31, 52, 131
Williams, R.   49
Willis, P.   112
Willoughby, R.   6, 31, 83, 115–16, 157–8, 173
working class   4, 23
Worsham, L.   168

Yousafzai, M.   71
youth and community undergraduate degree
  critical pedagogy module   97–8
  interviews and reflective discussions   97–104
youth work, as practice   172, 174–7

Zachariah, M.   4, 23
Zamojski, P.   29, 32, 33
Zapatismo scholarship commitment   187
Zembylas, M.   163, 164

www.ingramcontent.com/pod-product-compliance
Lightning Source LLC
Chambersburg PA
CBHW070751020526
44115CB00032B/1615